Handwritten notes:

232

VOLUME 14 #1
SIGNS & WONDERS

BETANIA VENEZUELA
↳ EUCHRIST THAT BIED

MIRICAL VIDEO
EUCHRISTIC MINISTE MIRACLE
TYPE AB DANIEL SANFORD
RARE   329 CYPRESS AVE
ANCIENT
BLOODLINE WOODIYNNE NJ
STATUE ETC   08107
        DONATION - 10⁰⁰
SEARCH: EUCHARISTIC MIRACLES

TRUE LIFE IN GOD

Vassula: **Conversations with Jesus**

Published and Distributed by:

J.M.J. Publications
P.O. Box 385
Belfast BT9 6RQ
Northern Ireland
Fax: (0232) 331433

His Holiness Pope Paul VI has confirmed on October 14, 1966, the decree of the Sacred Congregation for the propagation of the Faith, under number 58/16 (A.A.S.), permitting the publication of writings about supernatural apparitions, even if they do not have a "nihil obstat" from ecclesiastical authorities.

ISBN 0- 9519973-0-0

United Kingdom, First Printing (English Edition) November 1991 - 10,000 copies
Canada, First Printing (English Edition) July 1992 - 20,000 copies

See back page for the addresses of distributors

"Set Our Two Hearts like a seal on your heart"

Jesus, August 2nd, 1991

"You have industrialized My House, this House which should have been a House of prayer!"

Jesus, February 7th, 1991

"I shall pour out My Spirit on this evil generation to entice hearts and lead everyone back to the complete Truth, to live a Perfect Life in Me your God."

Jesus, September 19th, 1991

"I am shouting and I am trying to break through your deafness to save you, and if I reproach you it is because of the Greatness of the Love I have for you."

Jesus, October 14th, 1991

J ♥ M

"Go out to the nations and teach them to
pray to the father this prayer:

Father all Merciful,
let those who hear and hear again
yet never understand,
hear your Voice this time
and understand that it is You
the Holy of Holies;
open the eyes of those who see and see,
yet never perceive,
to see with their eyes this time
Your Holy Face and Your Glory.
Place Your Finger on their heart
so that their heart may open
and understand Your Faithfulness,
I pray and ask You all these things,
Righteous Father,
so that all the nations
be converted and be healed
through the Wounds of your Beloved Son,
Jesus Christ; Amen"

Prayer given by Jesus through Vassula

TABLE OF CONTENTS
BOOK III

vi

INTRODUCTION I

Michael O'Carroll, CSSp

More has been written on Jesus Christ in the last fifty years than in all the previous Christian centuries. This immense volume of writing, with its echo in the spoken word, in pulpit and lecture room, constitutes undeniable testimony to His might; His uniqueness within human experience and the flow of history is manifest. A very different kind of testimony with a tragic overtone is the fact that, at the present time, more than twenty thousand churches, communities sects, groups and splinter groups claim Him as their nominal central figure or their founder. Within a cosmic or worldwide setting it is noteworthy that though He was a Jew, a Semite and an Asiatic, his following is minimal among His own people and race, and in His continent. The temptation is to settle for this in a fatalistic spirit; to do so deliberately would be to surrender belief in his universal mission and message.

Will the immense intellectual ferment, the labours of scholars, effect the change so desirable, not only among those who do not explicitly accept Jesus as their Saviour, but among those who do but pay little heed to his teaching? We have had so many Christologies; so much has been written on the "Jesus of history" and the "Christ of faith"; every possible detail and aspect of the Bible has been scrutinized; marginal disciplines like archaeology, the Qumran fields, inter-testamental and Jewish-Christian texts have been studied; we have recently had a whole new literature on the most obvious thing about Jesus, his Jewishness.

Having had to go through some of this literary forest[1] I am convinced that all who search for Jesus Christ, who wish to share in his healing, transforming self-disclosure must seriously heed the claim of the mystics. I submit that to ignore their testimony is to miss a powerful, enlightening dimension of Jesus Christ. It is also to close his mystery to the sincere votaries of the great world religions, which we are invited to view with sympathy and understanding. They are open at times strikingly to the appeal of mysticism, have not allowed perversion of its meaning. On the level of history great mystics have profoundly influenced their times. Jesus Christ, by his action on them, discloses a psychic potential, deep, subtle, rich on which he alone can directly act. What history and psychology indicate, theology clarifies and confirms.

---

[1] For a theological encyclopedia, <u>Verbum Caro</u>, on Jesus the Christ, due to appear in the United States.

I

It is in such a deep perspective that I would wish to present this volume of Vassula Ryden's writings. I would ask to be taken as speaking a strictly theological language, valid and accurate, when I describe her work as a valuable record of mystical experience. Irrespective of terminology the value is beyond question. Others like Maria Concepcion de Armida and Adrienne von Speyr have taken dictation directly from the Lord, or given it to another under his inspiration. Vassula's case is singular in that the handwriting is directly controlled. We have the transcription of an intensely personal experience of Jesus Christ with the assurance that he was involved down to the physical element of putting the words on paper.

Readers who have not seen the scientific evidence for this phenomenon, in so far as there can be evidence, may be reassured. An expert graphologist, attached to the Paris Court of Appeals, J A Munier, examined the writing with no knowledge of the author's identity and found it astonishing in many particulars; to the ordinary observer it is in marked contrast with Vassula's normal handwriting.

To those who accept the message of Jesus in Vassula's testimony, the contents of her books are thought-provoking, at times disturbing, overall elevating and powerfully encouraging. It is easy to see why her books have caused so many striking conversions. The leit-motiv throughout is the love of Jesus, expressed in the sponsal terms characteristic of mysticism, but manifested as an effulgence, an outpouring of the Sacred Heart of Jesus.

I consider this revelation one of the most helpful, promising of all that have been recorded in recent times. It is so, for the Lord's messenger is of the Orthodox Church, and we have never heard the language of the Sacred Heart from this communion. Historically unique for this reason, it is the long-awaited revival for Catholics of an ideal, an intuition of Jesus, which for centuries, especially since the age of St Margaret Mary, made countless saints and apostles. After Vatican II what really was an outlook, a total vision of the Saviour was dismissed by many as mere "devotion". Those who hoped for better days scarcely expected the dawn to appear in the East.

The message is thus an augury for the Christian unity which is a cherished theme and a promise in Vassula's pages. Where could Christians meet more securely than in the Heart of Christ? He has made it clear that the miracle of unity will be seen as his work.

It is not the first benefit that we have received from the Orthodox. During the Second Vatican Council it was the Orthodox, notably one Greek theologian, Nikos Nissiotis, who kept pressing for a theology of the Holy Spirit, without this the Council Documents would have little impact in their world. Much has been done since then to make good any possible loss. It is noteworthy that Jesus instructs Vassula on the Holy Spirit, speaks to her of Him frequently.

II

The language which He speaks to her is that of love. But He does not dispense with the Commandments; the reader is urged to contrast the clarity of His utterance with so much that is hazy and vague in some popular presentations of the faith. Ecumenists would also read with profit the warnings against dilution of doctrine; as preachers should take to heart the advice not to give priority to social concern over the divine claim to adoration - they must not cut themselves off from God the source of life, nor minimize the divinity of Jesus Christ, nor the mysteries of his life, death and resurrection.

There are searing pages in Vassula's communications on the present state of the Church. How are we to react to the application of Apocalypse XIII to our time? I would say with great humility, attentive to its realism, concerned to reap the reward of fidelity. There is much to console in the whole corpus. We have a word of reassurance on the many apparitions and visions which in our day the Spirit is bestowing on the faithful. We are reminded that the Spirit is the Spirit of Jesus. Jesus cares for His Church with all the love of His Heart, realizes its dreadful need and intends to renew it.

At this stage I am reminded of another work which has some similarity with that of Vassula, Confidences de Jesus given to an Italian priest, Mgr Ottavio Michellini of the diocese of Carpi. He was given a very clear idea of the evils within the Church, but also a firm hope that through the intercession of Mary, through her triumph over the forces of evil, the reign of Jesus would be established. Pius XII, in a broadcast message to the International Marian Congress at Lourdes on 17th September 1958, three weeks before his death, spoke these words: 'I wish to affirm my unshakeable confidence that the reign of Jesus will come through the reign of Mary.'

True to the great Orthodox tradition, Vassula believes in the power of Mary. How many people forgot this rich, living legacy when they spoke of Mary as an obstacle to Christian unity ! If Christian unity is to be complete it must include the Orthodox, who would never compromise on Marian theology or devotion. This was made crystal clear in the early days of Faith and Order by one of its most committed members, the giant of modern Russian Orthodox Marian theology, Sergey Bulgakov.

In Marian devotion Vassula is responsive to a particularly Catholic form of piety, the Immaculate Heart of Mary. The Heart of Mary united to the Heart of Jesus is a theme to inspire and encourage. Pope John Paul II speaking of it used the phrase 'Alliance of the Two Hearts.' This was chosen as the title of an international symposium sponsored in Fatima from 14th to 19th September, 1986 by Cardinal Sin. The symposium enjoyed formal approval in a special message received from the Pope, who later received the participants in Rome and was given the complete proceedings. In these papers speciality theologians had supported with impeccable research the continuity of the theme through the centuries, noting obviously the high points; the great saints of Helfta in medieval times, the saints and teachers of seventeenth century France, notably St John Eudes, the awakening of the nineteenth century and then the culmination in our time, with the formal teaching of the Popes since Pius XII, the promise of Fatima that with the triumph of the Immaculate Heart over Russia, Jesus wishes it to be glorified along with his own Sacred Heart - and so many other private revelations at the present time.

I am convinced that we may expect an enriched theology of the heart within the Church from a close, profound fusion of the eastern and western traditions. It is well known that the idea of divinization, of man made in the image of God, is basic to the thinking of the Greek Fathers, especially those of the school of Alexandria. In the theological renewal which will precede the Christian unity which we long for, there must be serious reflection on the Heart of Jesus, God-man, as the means and model of divinization.

An immense perspective opens before us in Christian theology. John Paul II has shown how his philosophy of the human person, influenced to some extent by his studies in phenomenology, may be integrated in the theology of the heart. At the symposium of Fatima the theologians agreed that it is with the idea of the Holy Spirit that the fruitful synthesis will be achieved. There is here a sense of profound spiritual harmony. But the field is still open for theological research and reflection.

It is, meanwhile, a matter for deep satisfaction that Vassula Ryden, guided word by word by Jesus, joins the company of theologians and spiritual writers vowed to the regeneration and divinization of mankind through the mediation of the two Hearts. It is an honour to commend and by so doing to support the ideal which she proposes with such clear intuition and courageous candour, with the eloquence of simplicity, at times poignant: the Ideal who is Christ himself, the "Mediator and the fullness of all revelation" as Vatican II calls him, the One who is the Centre of all life and of all creation, for He is the Origin, the Alpha and the Omega. In Him are hidden all the treasures of wisdom and understanding (Colossians 2:3); He is the first-born of all creation... in whom all things subsist (Colossians 1:15,17). To Him with the Father and the Holy Spirit be glory from all creatures evermore, through the mediation of Blessed Maria Theotokos.

19th May, 1991 - Pentecost Sunday

INTRODUCTION II

Abbé René Laurentin

For those who do not have at hand the first volume of these messages: who is Vassula?

Vassula was born in Egypt on January 18th, 1942 of Greek parents. She married a civil servant who worked for FAO. Her husband's career brought her from one country to another: sixteen years in Africa (Sierra Leone, Ethiopia, Sudan, Mozambique, Lesotho) and then for a few years in Asian Bangladesh. Today, Vassula has two teenaged sons.[1]

Born as an Orthodox, she had experienced in her childhood a dream that has a prophetic value for her today: the Virgin Mary prepared her for a marriage with Christ. However, she had rather forgotten this. Vassula was an accomplished woman in the higher spheres of society: an inspired painter, fulfilled in social relations and success, a tennis champion and fashion model in the capital city of Bangladesh. Today all these things are part of her former life, ever since the day in November of 1985, when her angel came to her in Bangladesh and prepared her for her mission through messages. To write them, her hand was moved by an irresistible force.

Then it was Christ himself who continued to guide her hand and whose Voice she learned to hear. Now she lives for Him alone and prays for six hours a day. It is at this time, during their dialogue, that she receives her messages.

Her blonde silhouette breathes an air of harmonious equilibrium, the result of a profound peace. Her perfect sense of measure, her discretion and her modesty are accompanied by great interior assurance.

Vassula never had a religious education. The messages she writes go beyond her. They are a passive grace that she receives with a hidden strength. During a period of thirty years (1955-1985), though she is from an Orthodox family, she had never put her foot in a church except for social obligations such as burials or weddings. These private revelations resulted in her total conversion. She seeks nothing more than to be re-united with Jesus in the eternal life which is already her life.

---

[1]For a further note on Vassula's family situation, see below under September 24th, 1988.

She is aware of her limitations, the limitations which are characteristic of any private revelations, influenced as they are by the personality of each seer: it is the influence of the instrument. She does not possess the authority of the magisterium, nor any official authority: what she has is simply the inherent light of these messages. These messages are destined for some more than others, submitted to their discernment in absolute freedom. She is open to criticism and presents it all to Him who guides her: Christ, as well as to her spiritual director who here presents this second volume.[1]

I, the Lord, love all of you, and it is for the sake of those who seek The Truth that I come to show them again what The Truth really is and what It means since they have forgotten it.

I Am The Truth and the Truth is Love, Fathomless love, Sublime Love, Eternal Love. My Book is a Book of Love.

Jesus on April 9th, 1988

> Father of Mercy
> In adoration, I am at Your Feet,
> In You I Hope and Believe,
> I love You boundlessly.
> Amen.

A prayer given to us by Our Holy Mother on June 7th, 1988

---

[1]For more information, see the introduction of volume one.

INTRODUCTION III

Father James Fannan, PIME

This second volume of messages of the Sacred Heart, <u>True Life in God</u>, covers the period from March 6th, 1989 to March 30th, 1992.

The first volume was an introduction to the spiritual life that is reminiscent of the Canticle of Canticles. It radiates a unity of spirit, of action, and of heart, with a God who is Love Himself.

This second volume is apocalyptic, not because it announces the end of the world, but because it speaks of a New Pentecost. It speaks prophetically for our time of the necessity of personal conversion, the state of the Church, and the future that God is preparing for us. It speaks of our God who never abandons His people, and who, in every crisis, raises up men and women to strengthen those who are faltering.

Through Vassula, God is begging us to live the New Pentecost announced by the scriptures (Joel 3 and Acts 2), and for which Pope John XXIII had so much prayed. Like the first Christians who gathered in prayer and penance to await the Holy Spirit, we too are called together for the "Great Return" of Love Himself.

In this second volume, Jesus asks more specifically that His message of hope be diffused throughout the world. He urges us to respond to this appeal. This message converges with that of other apparitions and recalls the tragic consequences of ignoring them in the past. Two key themes are emphasized: the unity of the Church and the conversion of Russia.

There is a striking message on January 4th, 1988, where Russia appears as a dead woman who is raised by Christ. She will enter into an alliance of love and peace with God, and Jesus will bring about His promise of unity for the Church and for the whole human race: "I come to unite you all."

Together with Vassula and St Paul we learn to say: "I live now not I, but Christ lives in Me" (Galatians 2:20) and we are invited to become altars for "spiritual sacrifices" offered to God our Father (1 Peter 2:5, Romans 12:1). Sharing the redemptive cross of Christ is both a burden and the glory of the Christian life: "My Father is glorified in your bearing much fruit." (John 15:8)

Throughout these messages, the Virgin Mary appears as the "Handmaid of the Lord." She joins her motherly counsels to those of Her Son. She describes herself as the

"Woman clothed in the sun" (Apocalypse 12), who will conquer Satan in his war against us and herself.

This book is a serious warning to those who fail to recognize the power of the Holy Spirit, miracles, and the word of God. This lack of faith and these negative criticisms scatter the lambs and block the path of God. Such attitudes promote atheism.

These private revelations abound in allusions to the Scriptures, revealing a profound fidelity to the meaning of the Scriptures in accordance with the Tradition of the Church. They reveal a hidden richness of the word of God, in particular as regards the priesthood.

In fact, the first priests of which the Bible speaks are Cain and Abel. The sacrifice of Abel was pleasing to God; that of his brother Cain was not. But rather than repenting, Cain, in his jealousy, slew his brother. This first tragedy foreshadowed many others, especially the Passion of Christ Himself.

All of us are sinners, whether priests or laymen; we must face up to this to truly discern the difference between good and evil and the choice this requires.

These, briefly are some of the main themes of this volume. I hope that each reader will discover others and at the same time note the progressive and harmonious development of thought in this second volume. Anyone who visits Vassula grows in an awareness each time of this message for our time that is discreet, intimate and powerful.

May he who has ears, understand.

BOOK III

NEVER CEASE PRAYING

March 6th, 1989

Peace, I am your angel Daniel. I am with you, guiding you; I am doing the Lord's Will; I am praying for you without ceasing. ♥ *Desire the Lord; accept all that He gives you, beware of evil.*

Chase away evil when it's near me please!

I do. Pray, My Vassula, with fervour for this is the way the Lord likes it. Never cease praying. Come, be in Peace. ♥

READ JONAH

March 8th, 1989

Lord?

♥ *I Am. I have guided you to read Jonah because I want you and My children to understand that I can always relent the Punishment I have in store for your evil generation. I do not wish My Cup of Justice to brim over as It does now and so I tell you: repent, fast and be holy!*

Lord.

I Am.

Lord, some are fasting, repenting and trying; is it enough? Are we not on the right road?

I had the impression that we are slightly better these few years and on the right road.

My Vassula, many are on the road to perdition because of the evil that has accumulated in them, they are like night in their insides, so how can you say that this generation is on the right road ?

What can we do to let <u>everyone</u> know that we are at the brim of a disaster? Some have no idea!

♥ *So long as My Spirit is crushed, and so long as My Own muffle My Warnings, suppressing My Spirit, treating the prophecies with contempt and taking almost a delight to announce that the apparitions of Our Presence are untrue, I will not bear it any longer, My Justice will prevail. Today still, I am coming to you as a most Merciful Friend but tomorrow I shall descend to you as a severe Judge. My Spirit they suppress, they ridicule My Blessings, these are the Cains of today. I love you all to folly. Remember always this, I will relent My Justice only when tremendous reparations will be done.* ♥ *IXθYΣ* ⊂✕ *Love loves you.*

Here is Saint Michael:

Child of God, nothing is impossible to God. Tremendous reparations are to be done. If your generation converts, the Holy of Holies will relent His Punishment. Let those who have ears hear, for His Mercy reaches from age to age for those who fear Him. Be alert. Never cease amending. Those that mock you now, will grind their teeth later on. I, Saint Michael, pray without cease for this evil generation. Pray child, and obey the Lord, praise the Lord for the outpouring of His Spirit among you all;

Saint Michael, thank you.

Peace to you. ♥ ♥ ♥

Vassula.

Yes Lord?

Add this; how could My Own pray with peace the apostles Creed and say: "I believe in the Holy Spirit", when most of them reject the works of My Spirit, deny It and crush It? I tell you truly, I find no holiness in them. When in this darkness they spot from far a little flame, they come upon it like a gale, to blow it away so that they continue their evil works in darkness and thus not be exposed to light. No Vassula, they do not seem to want to live in the Light.

I adore You Lord, my Light, Light of the world.[1]

---

[1] While I was writing "Light of this world" I hesitated, rubbed out "this" and replaced it by "the", thinking that this actual world of ours reigns in obscurity. I made Jesus smile.

Come, you rejoice Me. One day, My child, you will only see but Light, just Light!
Never be discouraged, for I am with you till the end. ♥ ⊂✕ *IXθYΣ*

Thank you Lord Jesus. Be blessed. Praised be the Lord.

LET ME PERFECT YOU

March 20th, 1989 - Lourdes, France

Vassula, it is I, Jesus. Do not allow the deceiver to deceive you, all that I have
given you is Mine. Why do you listen to him? I have trained your ear, have I
not? I have opened your eyes to see Me, so why do you doubt? Many servants of
Mine have been given the same gift as yours so why do you doubt? Vassula, My
lamb, I am your Good Shepherd who leads you in green pastures to rest. I shelter
you in My Arms; I feed you My Virtues; I let you repose in My Heart. My Eyes
are upon you always, so why do you doubt of My Works?

Because, I myself am no good.

I know, but let Me perfect you. ♥ *See?[1] I am love. Together now, I and you,*
your hand in My Hand. I shall not leave your hand so that you remember My
Presence. Come, we, us?

Yes Lord.

Let Me hear it then. ♥ ⊂✕ *IXθYΣ*

Later on at Lourdes:

We went to visit the grotto where Our Lady appeared to Saint Bernadette. We
visited the crypt which was the first church built after the apparitions. In there I had
a locution from Our Holy Mother, she said:

"In the end, Our Hearts will prevail."

---

[1] I felt a warm shower of God's love covering me. It was wonderful.

ON THE WAY TO GARABANDAL

March 23rd, 1989
Holy Thursday

We left Biarritz. Our Lady found us a "guide" volunteering to come with us, who knew Spanish, and also the area. While driving up on the mountains, after a few hours, I was wondering whether our "guide" really knew where he was taking us. It seemed endless. It was after sunset and slowly getting dark. We were now and then in fog and rain. I was wondering why would I be going there, I had really no idea, maybe to pray and bless Garabandal, as the Lord had asked me more than a year back, but then the Lord had specifically told me that all this He Himself will do it, my mission is to love Him, console Him, and allow Him to write, so I was wondering, feeling insecure. Suddenly I saw the sky, it was beautiful with orange clouds, and I felt God's Presence surrounding us. No. He will not abandon us now. I had only to abandon myself completely to Him and trust Him fully; I felt all over again this intimacy He taught me and shares with me, I called Him, Abba. yes Abba is taking care of me with great love.

Finally we arrived and found our way to the Church. Mass was still on. We entered. Facing me was a statue of the Sacred Heart of Jesus, and to His right, our Blessed Mother with open arms. I heard her say: "Thank you for coming to Me." Delighted, I answered, "Thank you for bringing me here, to you."

After Mass, our "guide" asked the priest if he knew where we could lodge. He was very nice and told us to follow him. He took us to an inn and asked the lady[1] of the inn. In spite of her work (she was serving people dinner) she led us to her house. There was one room and a hall. In the hall were two camping beds and I would share the room with Beatrice.

Before leaving from Biarritz, I had hesitated whether to take the Fatima statue of Our Lady who accompanies me in all my meetings, or not, I decided to leave her behind, until our return to Biarritz, for fear she would break.

But what do we see on the mantle? The same statue of Our Lady of Fatima, same size too. She never left me... There she was, from Fatima, in Garabandal. She carried no rosary in her hands. But I had one extra one in my handbag. It was a rosary from Medjugorje. So I placed Medjugorje's rosary in the hands of Our Lady of Fatima, at Garabandal. The three got linked, now.

---

[1] We found out later on that this lady is the sister-in-law of one of the seers.

We had no alarm to wake us up, but in our room was a big beautiful statue of Saint Therese of Lisieux. I asked Saint Therese to wake us up, at a reasonable time, not too early. We slept, then in the morning Beatrice and I were woken up by three knocks on the door. I turned on the lights to see the time and it was sharp 8.00. I said 'Oui', thinking someone is outside the door waking us. I opened the door and no one was there... So Saint Therese did not forget us...

After breakfast, I met one of the seers' brothers, then, I went up at every place Our Lady appeared, blessing it.

OUR HEARTS WILL PREVAIL IN THE END

March 24th, 1989 - Garabandal

Vassula, I have indeed brought you here. I am the Lord. ♥ *Have My Peace. Let these words be known from both My Mother and I, "In spite of the thorns covering Our Hearts by Our enemies, <u>Our Hearts will prevail in the end</u>."* ♥

Jesus and I are with you My child. We bless all of you. Come. ♥

I AM YOUR LIFE
REMAIN MY VICTIM

March 26th, 1989 - Switzerland

My rose, behold how I guide you, have you not noticed how I laid smooth your path? I have carried you to Garabandal to fulfil My desire; I had asked you to sanctify Garabandal[1]; I have lifted you there and now you have done it. ♥ *Remember, My Ways are not your ways. I have taught you to abandon yourself entirely to Me, to leave space for My Spirit to breathe in you, see? I will never forsake you ever.* ♥ *I mean to use you till the end, accomplishing your mission. Allow My Finger to rest on you, thus letting your God's desires be engraved on you.* ♥ *My rose, I love you.* ♥ *By coming to Me in this way, you are keeping My precepts, you are offering Me your will. Have Me as first, never counting the*

---

[1] In books.

time you spend with Me. Desire always to be in constant link with Me - I am your Life. Being attached to Me, favours you. I will draw you deeper into My Sacred Heart and lead your soul into perfection. ♥ *So please Me in this way by abandoning yourself into My Hands; be confident. Come, delight Me and praise Me. My Mother who is your Mother too is shielding you, guiding you, helping you. Daughter, bless her. Never cease praying.* ♥

I adore You my God.

Adore Me always. ♥

Later on today, I felt exhausted, I felt that this task God has given me is crushing me. Will all these sacrifices come to something? or will they all go in vain? Will I have still this strength to keep going as though I can never stop? or will I one day find it overwhelming and give up?

Have My Peace, hear Me: Wisdom has instructed you, do not fear. Be happy that I have chosen you to share My sufferings. My Cross, ever so precious, rests on you, I need to rest. All that you give Me, will not go in vain... nothing is going in vain, I am being Glorified. Remain My victim. ♥ *Beloved victim whom My Father favoured to share with Me My Cross of Peace and Love. Your tribulations as a victim will not be light in this world. Realize that you do not belong in this world anymore and this is why the world will reproach you for not being like them; forgetting how their bodies will turn to ashes, they will ridicule you. Beware then of complaining about nothing (Wisdom 1:11). All I ask from you is sharing, sharing out of love with Love. Love's Cup tastes bitter, very bitter - could you not share It with Me? Do not resist Me! Have I ever resisted you on hearing your plea from earth? I assure you, nothing will go in vain.* ♥ *From all eternity, I have known you to be fragile. Just as a rose which needs special care, you are being taken care of by Me. I prune your branches when I must. My Eyes are constantly on you, guarding you jealously lest a stranger plucks you. I let no one touch you, lest their fingers will crumple up your petals. I watch over you day and night. I am your Guardian, so be confident I will allow no one to harm you.* ♥

That same evening, exhausted, because of our long journey (12 hours by car) of the day before, I went to pray the rosary, my eyes posed on Fatima's statue, I was on the fourth mystery when suddenly St Mary's cape and dress started to become a bright silver, so intense was this silver light that it seemed to come <u>out</u> from <u>within</u> the statue. She seemed to come to life. This must have lasted not more than five seconds. It was beautiful because it encouraged me to pray better and made me so very happy!

The next day, when I was praying the rosary again and looking at St Mary's statue of Fatima, I was looking at Her Eyes, I suddenly noticed that the defect (which bothered me) on one of her eyes was not there anymore, both eyes were now perfect. It was a small defect; it must have been paint missing on one of the eyelids, and often I was thinking that I should paint this white line brown and paint the eyelashes which are missing because of this white line. Now it's not there, and both eyes are perfect.

AS YOU WALK, I LEVEN YOUR PATH
WISDOM IS GIVEN TO THE LOWLY AND SIMPLE

March 27th, 1989

Jesus?

♥ *I Am, beloved. My Kingdom shall come. Allow Me to use you for My Glory; I shall not forsake you, even though your spirit sometimes seems so far away from Me your God. Trust Me; rely on Me dearest child; allow My Spirit to breathe fully in you and freely; compensate Me now My child by being obedient and looking only after My interests. I am always before you, so do not fear crossing this valley, without shelter, without pastures, barren and dry, I know its gloom is terrifying your soul but I am known that those I have led through deserts never went thirsty. I am before you to shelter you from the dry winds with My Love. I feed you with My Word. As you walk, I leaven your path; I remove all the stones and rocks so that you may not stumble, I remove them to open your way. My Holy Presence chases My enemies, who are your enemies, far away. When briars and thorns come, they are quickly cut away and burnt by My angels who surround you. I, your Redeemer, do not allow any of these thorns to tear upon you My child. Dearest being, rely on Me. Almighty I Am - the Highest I Am. All I want from you is love, ♥ love, love, so come and share with Me, let Me be your Joy. Ah Vassula, love Me and console Me with your childish heart. Come and rest My Head, be My resthead, be My footstool, be My Heaven. Allow Me to lead you through this valley of death. Soon I shall take you from this desolation into My Home, which is your Home too My child. Be one with Me, O dearest child. Will you console Me your Saviour?*

Blessed be our Lord who performs marvels of love for me! Lord, how great Your goodness reserved for those who fear You, bestowed on those who take shelter in You, for all mankind to see!

Rejoice in our Lord and Saviour, exult you virtuous, shout for joy all upright hearts!

I shall unmask all My enemies and with My Breath I shall sweep away all those who block the Way to Me. I shall reveal My Holy Face once again and I shall cover this Wilderness with Purity, Holiness and Integrity. ♥ *Love and Peace will be with you and dwell among you, see? Have I not said that I shall dwell among you and that you will be My very own?* ♥ *My child, remind them how My Spirit resents boastful people and that Wisdom is given to the lowly and simple.* ♥ *Come.*

MY CHILDREN HAVE TURNED THEIR BACKS TO ME
DO NO EVIL AND NO EVIL WILL BEFALL YOU

March 29th, 1989

Messages given for the meeting at Courtetelle (North of Switzerland):

Peace be with you. ♥ *I am the Lord, feel My Presence, discern My Presence. Today I come to you, speaking through My servant. <u>I am always with you, in every moment of your life</u>.* ♥ *My Sacred Heart rejoices to feel your love to Me. My lambs, how I always wanted to gather you all in My Arms and hide you from the evil one! I love you.* ♥ *I love you with an everlasting love, a jealous love you would understand only when you will be in Heaven, yet, in spite of My Fathomless Love, most of My children have turned their backs to Me... they have forgotten My Passion and with evolution My Name is meaningless to them now. Give them idols and they will be first to adore them, but give them what is Holy and they will mock upon It.* ♥ *I, your Holy One, suffers and My Body is mutilated by disobedience, impurity and the iniquity of this dark world! Ah creation! My Cry of suffering shakes the entire Heaven, leaving My angels trembling and prostrated - have you not heard Me yet, daughters and sons of Mine? My Cries from above leave even the demons in stupor from your deafness... Tears of Blood flood My Eyes, night and day, hour after hour. Unceasingly I am in wait for you; have you rejected My Spirit forever? My Voice echoes in this devastating wilderness, without a single pasture to rest, not one spring to run and refreshen you. I descend from My Throne above into My Pastures of old to find them neglected and barren. My flowers which I planted with so much love and by My Own Hand are perishing one after the other; My flower-beds have been neglected and are dry; My wells are now only an empty, dusty, dark hole, nestling vipers.* ♥ *Where have My keepers gone? Why have they neglected My garden? On My return, will I still find one single flower? My Spirit is crushed from lack of love, lack of faith, lack of peace.*

Children of My Sacred Heart, hear My Cry in this wilderness; recognize My Voice at least recognize the Times! Come all those who have not reconciled with Me, come now and reconcile. Your iniquities have pierced all eternity, withdrawing you from Me. Do no evil and evil will not befall you. Be good to each other; love one another; forgive your enemies. I am repeating My Words which you all know, but how many of you put them into practice? Pray with you heart, I need love. Come and adorn Me with prayers that come from your heart; come and draw from My Heart which is an Abyss of Love and fill up yours.

I tell you most solemnly, the hours are fleeing dearest souls, come back to Me. Peace! Peace! Peace! Cry out to the nations for peace. Peace to unite! Peace to love! Peace to glorify Me! The day is coming that every vision My seers have seen will come true, since what I pronounce I always fulfil. Pray My beloved for My Peter; pray for the Patriarch; pray for all My priests.[1] Pray that My Fold be one, as I and the Father are One and the same; pray that My lambs return into one single Fold under the leadership of Peter until My Return. O, if you would only listen and obey!

Will you now pray the Our Father? I am listening, (we prayed) *and I promise you that My Kingdom shall come and My Will shall be done on earth as it is in Heaven.* ♥ *Children, bear fruit in Peace. I, the Lord, love and bless you all.* ♥

Message from Our Holy Mother for the same reunion:

Beloved, console Jesus... console Jesus. Be in peace with each other and love one another. ♥ Be faithful to God and abandon yourselves entirely to Him, you are only abandoning yourselves to Love and thus allowing Him to nourish you with His Love and Peace. ♥ The Lord and I bless you all. I love you. The Lord and I bless all the religious objects that are in this room. ♥

Daughter, have my peace, just abandon yourselves into Love's Hands and Love will lead you always. I love you, have my blessings. ♥

---

[1]In saying "priests", Jesus' Sacred Heart swell with a special love for them, but at the same time a pain pierced His sensitive Holy Heart, piercing mine as well when I felt His sorrow. My eyes filled.

DESIRE THE FATHER

April 1st, 1989

Jesus?

I Am. Let Love guide you. Do not listen to the wise, they are like the scribes in My time. Evangelize with love for Love, let them feel My Infinite Love. ♥

I long for You Lord!

Little one, My Heart rejoices to feel you and hear you say: "I long for you Lord...", this is the fruit of devotion. Be My reflection, a copy of Me. Desire the Father. I longed for the Father while I was on earth. I prayed without ceasing; I longed to be in constant link with My Father, in union of Love ♥

Pupil, I am your Teacher who raised you up with Wisdom, so fill Me with joy and be in constant link with Me. Place Me as first and desire Me always. Rejoice when meeting Me in this way I have given you. Stay close to Me, all I ask from you is Love. ♥

Lord, I pity the souls that go to hell, after all they were like us, one of us on earth. If there was somehow one way to bring them out of hell and change them...

I had given them the freedom to choose good from evil, but they preferred evil in spite of My supplications and calls of Love.

But Lord why couldn't there still be a chance...

Child, you do not understand their total rejection of Me, I have loved them to their last. Led by Satan they preferred to follow him. Even after their death I have been before them, yet they willingly followed Satan without the slightest hesitation. It is entirely their choice, they chose hell for always.

O Lord, let me always do Your Will.

Vassula, never leave My Hand. ♥ *We, us, for all eternity. Every drop of love is used. I need love to save souls on their way to perdition.* ♥ *Come.*

MY PROPHETS ARE PART OF MY BODY TOO

April 2nd, 1989

Lord?

I Am. Look at Me with a child-like faith and embellish My Church.

Lord, why is it that it is so very hard for some to accept this era's prophets and the Word said from You?

I tell you most solemnly that My sheep recognize My Voice.

But Lord, even when one can prove to the sceptics that there are conversions and healings from great sinners, still, with these fruits, they are not convinced.

♥ *My Vassula, even if someone should rise from the dead before their very eyes they would not be convinced. To these, Isaiah's prophecy still stands[1] "you will listen and listen again, but not understand, see and see again, but not perceive, for the heart of this nation has grown coarse, their ears are dull of hearing and they have shut their eyes, for fear they should see with their eyes, hear with their ears, understand with their heart and be converted and be healed by Me."* ♥ *Many forget that My prophets are part of My Body too. I have indeed allotted to each one of you a grace so that all of you make a unity. Dearest child, I have formed some to be apostles, some to be priests, teachers, and some to be prophets in times of rebellion, so why are so many of you surprised and reject My prophets? How can My Body function with one of it's members being cut off? I am weary, My Body is constantly mutilated and torn. Flower, accept with love your persecutors, do not judge them. My prophets will always be persecuted, judged, scourged, suppressed, hunted from town to town, looked upon with contempt and crucified and so you will keep drawing down on yourselves the blood of every holy man that has been shed on earth. Scripture never lies, I am the Word.* ♥ *Come my child, I have formed you to amend for souls in purgatory. Pray flower, little do you know what effect prayers have on souls in purgatory; extinguish their fire with prayers;* ♥ *amend for them.* ♥ *Come.*

---

[1] Isaiah 6:9-10.

LET MY WORD BE YOUR LAMP

April 5th, 1989

My Jesus?

I Am. Ah! how I delight in these moments when you come to Me, offering Me your will! Stay with Me and I will write to My children. ♥

(Jesus will write the message for the reunion which will be for April 21st, 1989[1].)

Peace be with you. ♥ *I am the Lord, I am the Word and I am among you, feel My Presence My little children.* ♥ *My Sacred Heart delights to see you all assembled all in one[2]. I mean to progress you in the Way of Holiness. Those who still have not penetrated in My Path, I shall not leave behind, I will go back and look for them. I will fetch each one of you and show you My Path of Righteousness and Holiness; I will lift you and carry you. Like a tender father I shall raise you up and teach you My precepts, I will enrich you with My Spirit of Love. I, who am Master of Love, will teach you to love Me fully and love one another as I love you, this will be your first step towards Me. I look upon you all as My little children, hardly knowing how to walk alone.* ♥ *I shall offer you both My Hands and you will place your little hands into Mine, and together, together you and I will make a few steps forward... Do you know how I delight already?[3] I will progress you and I will embellish your soul, leading it into perfection if you are willing to open yourselves entirely to Me. Allow Me to teach you My statutes and I shall explain to you how to keep My precepts.* ♥ *I shall open the Gates of Virtues to all who wish to learn. Yes, I shall, Myself, with My Own Hand, place into your mouth My Fruits. Cling to Me and I shall rescue you in these difficult times where Fury has been let loose; these times when many fall into confusion, not knowing their left hand from their right hand.* ♥ *Today, more than ever, the evil one and the demons are roaming in every corner of this earth, seeking to deceive you all, setting traps for you to fall; this is the reason why I am asking you to pray without ceasing. Do not let My adversary find you asleep; be on your guard these days. Do not let him find an empty corner in you either, fill yourselves with My Word, with My Love, with My Peace, with My Virtues. Come often and receive Me in the little white Host, in purity* ♥ *so that you do not yield into temptation. Pray without ceasing. I know your needs even more than you do and even before you ask Me, I know your heart. In every possible occasion face Me*

---

[1] Jesus asked me to read them from Scriptures, Ephesians 4:17-32 and 5:1-20.
[2] Here Jesus means all Christians, from Roman Catholic, to Protestants and Orthodox.
[3] Jesus appeared so very happy.

and pray; pray to amend and make up for the lack of prayers of this earth. ♥ *Let your prayers be your armour, shielding you from all evil that is roaming around you, disarm the demon with love, let love be your weapon, let peace be written on your foreheads, so that everyone may see it. You should make every part of your body into a weapon fighting on My side and then sin will no longer dominate your life[1]. Let My Word be your Lamp. Spread My Message of Love and Peace in every corner of the globe to attain hearts and convert them. Let those who do not know Me yet, come and see what a Furnace of Love My Sacred Heart is; come and feel My Sacred Heart in Flames of Love and when you do, even if your heart is petrified and arid from lack of love, I will with My Flame of Love entice your heart into a living torch.*

Beloved and blessed of My Soul, how My Heart pains when I see some of you still resisting Me... Behold, was I ever known to be unfaithful? I am The All-Faithful One, who never denies you or abandons you in times of distress, ♥ I have not forsaken you ever. I will pursue you, like a young man who pursues his maiden, because I am your Faithful God who looks on you from above with great love. ♥ Come to Me and offer Me your sufferings with love. I and you, you and I will share those sufferings. Daughters and sons of Mine, shall you and I pray together the Our Father? Before you do, recollect yourselves and pray slowly from your heart, let this prayer reach the Father. Meditate on what you are saying. Pray, I am listening... and My Kingdom will come and My Will, will be done on earth as it is in Heaven. ♥ I shall substitute the present darkness for light; I shall substitute wickedness for love and this lethargy into a vivid brightness to guide your step, I shall not fail you. I shall heal your sores and clean your blemishes with My Tenderness, so come to Me and love Me. Let your love extinguish My Flare of Justice; let your prayers from your heart soothe My Wounds; let your prayers rise in Heaven like incense, glorifying Me and praising Me.

Amend the faults of others who come by night, to destroy My Vineyard from yielding Its grapes. Do good and cease to do evil. Whatever you do, do it for My Glory. Come beloved souls and share My Cross with Me. My Cross cries out for Love, Peace and Unity, together we shall carry It, you and I, I and you, united in Love. I, your Lord Jesus Christ, give you all My blessings. ♥ Be One. ♥

Later on:

Flower, I give you My Peace; upon you is My Spirit. Renew My Church, like in the beginning, in the times of old, with Love among you, till My Return. ♥ Rise the dead with love and peace, let this land of ghosts give birth to a new life. ♥ Ah beloved! How I long for this Glorious Day of Mine!

---

[1] Romans 6:13-14.

Later on, Our Holy Mother gives her message for the reunion:

Praise the Lord My child for giving you Wisdom.

Praised be the Lord for His Mercy, for His Love and for sharing His Works with me.

TAKE SHELTER IN OUR HEARTS

Here is My Message for My little souls:

Peace be with you children. ♥ Beloved ones approach God in simplicity - be like children, since the Lord is to be found by those who do not put Him to the test. He shows Himself to the humble and to those who do not distrust Him. ♥ You see My children, Omnipotence put to the test confounds the foolish. No, Wisdom will never make its way into a crafty soul. ♥ So, open your hearts to the Lord and receive Him in simplicity of heart. Allow yourselves to lean on Him for you will be leaning on Wisdom. Augment your faith in the Lord by praying, to have faith is also a grace given from the Lord.

My beloved ones come into My Immaculate Heart and I will rest you ♥ all, you who suffer, all you who are in pain, come to Me and I, who am your Mother, will console you. As any mother consoles her child in distress, I too will do even more, I shall intercede for you to the Father and I will never fail you. Come and take shelter in Our Hearts, let this wreath of thorns that now chokes Our Hearts, loose its thorns and put forth young shoots which will bloom into flowers. Have faith in God, trust Him. I bless you all in the Name of the Father and of the Son and of the Holy Spirit. ♥ Amen.

Here is Saint Michael.

Children of God, <u>do not listen nor conversate with Satan</u>. To lie is to conversate with the demon. To accumulate anger in you is to give the devil a foothold. Do not let your tongue be the cause of your falls. Pray to Me and I shall intercede for you. Have confidence in God ♥ and in His Infinite Mercy. I bless you all. ♥ ♥ ♥

BLESS YOUR PERSECUTORS

April 11th, 1989

Today the real persecution starts. Jesus made me understand that this Greek Orthodox Easter I shall feel His Passion. We are close to our Easter. Lord, many accuse me of being a false prophet. They are seeking for an evidence against me, however false, on which they might say that the message is not divine. There are already several lying witnesses. I am accused of being the weapon of the demon to destroy another movement of another charismatic.

Hold on to Me. Peace My child. Refuse Me nothing. We[1] are both with you. Remember it is Satan's smoke and believe Me, smoke never lasts, it evaporates and vanishes. ♥ Vassula, I, your God love you with a love you will only understand in Heaven. Be blessed My child for all the calumnies said about you and for all the false statements they accuse you of. ♥ Be happy, for your reward will be great in Heaven. Now do you believe Me? How many times have I said that you are going to be persecuted as I have been persecuted? My Message will entice hearts, but some, in spite of this, will turn against you, not knowing they are condemning Me since they are condemning My Message. Have I not said that they will scrutinize you to find a fault as they have done to others whom I have sent? Bless your persecutors, pray for your accusers, forgive them all with all your heart. Learn My Vassula that I am Love. ♥ Love Me, I need this love to give it to others. Love My brothers as I love you.

But Lord, some are completely blinded!

Trust Me little one, with My Light I shall enlighten and shine upon many. Blessed one of My Soul[2], have you forgotten My Passion? I suffered out of Love, be now one with Me. It is I who allowed everything to come as it is so that you taste of the same Cup I have drunk in My Passion[3]. I love you, and it is because of this love I have for you, My child, that I have allowed you to drink this time from My Cup. ♥ I rise little souls to form them and look like little images of My Passion. ♥ Happy are you, you who have offered Me your heart and soul to form with My Divine Hands into another little crucifix. Rejoice soul! Rejoice and be glad with My Gift! but remember little one, under this same sky you live in, are also to be

---

[1] Our Holy Mother and Jesus.
[2] When I hear these words from God's Mouth, I simply melt and His Majesty makes me feel this "tent" covering my body more than ever. I feel that this exile I am in is endless.
[3] Jesus sounded here as if He was offering me a treat! and I am happy that He has offered me His Cup.

found ravenous wolves, hidden under the skins of sheep, they are those false prophets I have been warning you about. ♥

I asked the Lord to give me an answer about these people, and from the Bible this time. I opened the Bible to have my finger on Jeremy 23:10. This passage speaks of false prophets.

Beloved, fear not, I am before you. Be happy that they talk all sorts of calumnies about you; My Eyes watch these people and I hear their tongues and I feel their heart.

Yes, but You are with me and I have nothing to fear.

Courage, I shall give you My Strength to carry on. ♥ *We, us?*

Forever and ever.

Like all these persecutions were not enough, the big hall we rented to have our meetings was refused to us. Just like that. In spite that we had it reserved long ago. They said that they did not want religious movements in their place. There I was, stuck with 200 people on my back with no one wanting us, only a week before our reunion. But the Lord came to our rescue. The Lord made it possible for us to be in His Church. A little church which belongs to the Capuchins. Yes, His Majesty chose the most humble and poor from all the brothers, as a sign, for those who are persecuting Jesus' Message.

I RESCUE ALL THOSE WHO CLING TO ME

April 23rd, 1989

After the reunion of prayers and the reading of Messages in the little Church of Saint Maurice. The little church was full.

Blessed be my Lord who has not deprived us to meet in His Name. The Lord is good even to those without merits. My Lord, You responded to our prayers, You responded to the fasting and to the sacrifices Your beloved children offered You. I bless Your Name. We bless Your Name. "My[1] Lord is good, His love is everlasting, His faithfulness endures from age to age." Let us serve the Lord.

---

[1] Psalm 100:5.

I am the Lord who loves you. Before the eyes of your persecutors I shall feed you. Be blessed all you who heard and recognized the shepherds call; be blessed all you who offered Me sacrifices. ♥ *I rescue all those who cling to Me and My Arms are your cradle, My Sacred Heart your Refuge. I am your God and you My people. Rejoice! Rejoice beloved. Seek not to understand why My Voice is carried by this weak instrument; believe with simplicity of heart; avoid testing Me; be favourable in My Eyes like innocent and pure children.* ♥

Look at My Sacred Heart, I am before you exposing My Heart to you all. ♥ *Feel My ardent Love for you, do not resist Me, do not resist My plea. Come to Me and allow Me to thrust you in the depths of My Sacred Heart.* ♥ *Let My Heart be your refuge.* ♥ *How would I not come to your rescue, My beloved ones? I, who am the Sublime source of Love, would I ever fail you? Your cry of distress resounded in all the Heavens, I heard your plea from earth. No, beloved ones, do not fear, My Eyes see everything. I hear everything and I tell you truly that I shall guide each step you take and bless it. I am your Devout Keeper and My Vineyard shall be watered and kept by My Own Hand; I shall watch over It lest intruders penetrate My Vineyard by night. Let all those who want to come and see My Vineyard approach by daylight, only foxes will come by night. Arise then like sensible men at daybreak and visit My Vineyard. I, the Lord, am It's Keeper and it is out of My Infinite Love and out of great pity I come to restore My Vineyard.* ♥ *Be happy and let the Heavens hear your praises! Rejoice and acclaim the Lord's Glory. Be the little mouthpieces who carry My Word. Let those who sleep awake at your sound, proclaim My Love to all nations. Let those who wandered away from Me, return; I will not refuse them, though their hearts are arid and their sins scarlet-red; I will show them the Richness of My Forgiving Heart. Sing and rejoice for I will remain among you till the end.* ♥

BE AT MY SERVICE

April 28th, 1989

Lord?

I Am.

I thank You. I thank You and praise You for Your marvels You are literally showering us with. My heart rejoices and exults Your Holy Name. You are my shield that protects me. You are the Righteous Judge. I offer You my will.

My Vassula, offer Me your will always; be at My service; be willing to be My tablet, allowing Me to use your hand. ♥ *Refuse Me nothing and I shall act in you, allow Me to tighten My grip on you. Dearest soul, realize how useless you are without Me. I am Wisdom. My Message, even after your death will be read by many, it shall reach each corner of this earth to augment love, faith and hope.* ♥ *Trust Me My child, I am your Teacher, your Saviour, your Peace, your Creator and He-Who-Loves-you-Most.* ♥ ⫷⟩✕ *IXθΥΣ*

LOVE IS THE ROOT OF THE TREE OF LIFE
SCRIPTURES ARE BEING FULFILLED

May 1st, 1989

Lord, would You like to write Your Message for the reunion of 19th May?

Are you ready?

I am never ready, but You can make me ready.

Ask and it shall be given to you. ♥

I ask You, my Lord, to make me ready to hear Your Voice and write.

Open your ear then and listen carefully. Write:

Peace be with you all. I am the Lord, Emmanuel, the Holy of Holies who manifests Myself through this weak instrument. ♥ *I come to you little ones, a nation so highly favoured, to you I come exposing My Sacred Heart before your very eyes.* ♥ *My Sacred Heart is Holy, Pure and filled with Love, so awake as in the past. Awake from your lethargy, awake and feel Me. My Spirit is constantly poured out ever so generously among you, yet so many of you have still not understood... I, the Lord, have formed prophets ever since I have created you but My Own repeat what they have always repeated... they are still persecuting all My prophets, hounding them from town to town. Abel's Holy Blood is being shed without cease. These people ask Me for laws that are just, they long for Me to be near them but when I send them My Holy Spirit of Grace, they close their eyes and refuse to hear and allow their hearts to turn into granite; they gather together, chasing away My Holy Spirit of Grace as one chases away an evil bird.* ♥ *My*

Sacred Heart is in pain... <u>Open up! Open up!</u>[1] Do not block My Way! Remove those blocks that only hinder My people, whom you have starved, from reaching Me. I have come to <u>you</u>, to heal <u>you</u> and console <u>you</u>; I have come to bring you Peace and Love; I have come to fertilize My land and cultivate it's soil. <u>My Name is Holy</u> and holy are My precepts and My laws. ♥ *Yes, I will water this thirsty soil with My Love and <u>I, the Lord, will keep pouring out My Spirit upon My children, blessing them</u>.*

Have you not noticed? Have you not noticed that I am preparing you to receive a New Heaven and a New Earth I had promised you long ago? Have you not <u>yet</u> understood? Have you not seen how I work? I beckon all of you from one corner of this earth to the other to <u>listen to My Voice</u>. ♥ *Ah beloved ones, I have come to heal your sores, your wounds and your infirmities, which were all so savagely inflicted upon you in this darkness. No, beloved ones, your sores are not past healing, your injuries <u>are</u> curable for I-Am-With-You and ever so near you. <u>So come to Me with love, ask Me with love and you will receive, invoke Me with love and I shall hear you</u>. I will rise you to My Bosom and cradle you, comforting you. Hear My Cry of Love and Peace, Love loves you.*

Love is the Root of the Tree of Life so let it be LOVE that comes out of your heart. When Love manifests Itself where there is evil, Love effaces all wickedness, dissolving it like mist is dissolved with the first warm rays of the sun. ♥ *For the sake of My devout ones I will revive all corpses, I will not keep quiet; I will rise you all with My Word; I shall not be silent until I will Glorify My Body and renew My entire Church. Learn, all you who want to suppress My Spirit of Grace and who want to muffle down My Voice, that your evil efforts and your evil intentions are all in vain. I will keep stretching My Hand to everyone, even to the rebels, even to those who provoke Me night and day, see? You are all My people, no matter what creed or race, remember I am LOVE and I have created you all. Today My Salvation Plan covers the entire world.* ♥ *I have been, and I am, sending you messengers in every nation to progress you in your faith, to convert you, to establish peace and love, to unite you, so do not try to muffle down My Voice and My Mother's calls; Our Voices will keep coming upon you like a hammer shattering the rocks[2] until the Day of My Glory.* ♥ *Rejoice and acclaim My Fruitful Vineyard, for it is by My Own Hand the soil is overturned and toiled; by My Own Hand the thorns and briars pulled out and burnt; with My Own Cape I shelter It from the dry winds and storms that arise from My enemy. I am Its Devout Keeper who fervently and forever watch over It.* ♥ *This vineyard is My Gift to you and Its Grapes will be offered freely to you and fill the whole world, feeding it.* ♥ *Ah My beloved of My Soul, listen closely to My Words and try and*

---

[1] Jesus was crying out loudly.
[2] Rocks = hearts out of stone.

understand them, do not doubt, testing Me without cease... I, the Lord, am telling you most solemnly: <u>Scriptures are being fulfilled</u>. ♥ *So why are so many of you surprised at the outpouring of My Spirit? Why are you surprised when your young ones see visions? I come before you to revise your knowledge of My Word; I come with great love to revive the corpses of My sons and daughters; I come to convert you and remind you of My statutes; I come to call the sinner to confession; I come to call to repentance all those priests, bishops and cardinals who have so wickedly wounded My Sacred Heart and betrayed Me their Friend and God. I do not come as a Judge, not yet, I come to you as <u>The Beggar</u> in rags and barefoot with parched lips, imploring and lamenting for some love, for a return of love. Today you have in your sight a Lamenting Beggar with His Hand constantly outstretched, begging you for a return of love. <u>"I beg you, come back to Me and love Me; learn to love Me, learn to love Me; make peace with Me, make peace with Me, I will not reject you. I Am Love and I love you everlastingly."</u> Come to Me when the Hour has not yet come, do not wait for My Justice to arrive, do not let My Justice take you by surprise and unaware. Remember then that I shall be in this terrible, awesome Hour, standing before you as a Majestic Severe Judge and My Voice which was that of a lamenting beggar shall turn into a glare of a Devouring Fire, in cloudburst, downpour, hailstones. My Breath will be like a stream of brimstone which will set fire everywhere, to purify you and renovate you all, uniting you into <u>One Holy People</u>.*

Happy are all those who hope in Me and who welcome My Spirit of Grace I outpour so generously now on all mankind, for you shall see Me your God. Blessed are the poor in spirit for theirs is the kingdom of heaven; happy are all those who have ears to hear and are simple at heart, welcoming My Spirit of Grace with a child-like-faith, for in these little hearts My Word shall take root. Blessed are those who are persecuted in the cause of right for theirs is the kingdom of heaven. ♥ *In just a little while, My little doves, and I shall be with you - have My Peace. I bless each one of you. I, Jesus Christ, bless and forgive your persecutors, for they know not what they are doing. I, the Lord, love you all eternally.* ♥

The Lord then indicated where in the Scriptures I should read for them. It's in Hebrews 3:7-19 and Hebrews 4:1-17.

Yahweh, my Abba, remind me of Your commandments so that I may follow them and be faithful to You. I know that Your rulings are righteous my Abba, and I know and believe that You make me suffer out of faithfulness. It was good for me to taste and drink from Your bitter Cup. Now Lord, please, let Your Love comfort me, come and treat me tenderly and I shall live, since Your Law is my life and my delight. Direct my steps towards Your Home as you have promised me. I desire You, Father in Heaven. I am waiting for You, Yahweh, my Abba. I am waiting for You.

Love loves you My child ♥ *and I will allow no one to separate you from Me. You are part of Me now.* ♥ *Let us work.*

HAND OVER YOUR WILL TO ME

I saw in a dream-vision in the night Jesus' portrait. I noticed that Jesus' Eyes were filling up with tears and before they would drop on the floor I hurried up and opened my hand. With the palm of my hand full of Jesus' precious tears I started to walk away. I was considering to drink His Tears.

♥ *Daughter, have My Peace. Come, I am with you! Are you happy to be with Me?*

Oh yes, my Lord Jesus!

And are you still willing to hand over your will to Me and work for Me?

Yes Lord, please name Yourself again to me.

♥ *I am the Lord Jesus Christ, your Saviour.*

Yes Lord, if this is Your wish.

It is My wish, offer Me then your will and I will use it.

I offer You my will, take my will and do as You please with me.

Take My Hand then, I and you together. I love you, love Me. ⊂✕ *ΙΧΘΥΣ*

Here I was trying to recollect myself before the Lord, I was trying to feel His Holy Presence and be one with Him.

Little one, every time I feel how you try, My Sacred Heart rejoices profoundly. I am the Highest and I love you, will you recollect yourself and pray with faith?

I will try my Lord. Help me pray as You want it.

Abandon yourself then entirely to Me; please Me and tell Me, "Jesus I love You." Make Me happy with spontaneous words of love that come with sincerity and from the heart. My Sacred Heart is your refuge, rest in Me. Come, augment your love to Me, I want you perfect!

I want to do Your will and please You fully.

I will help you. My Vassula, we, us?

Forever.

Come, rest in My Heart.

Rest in mine, Lord.

I will. ♥

TO BE CONVERTED IS TO DESIRE TO BE WITH GOD

May 12th, 1989

Jesus?

♥ *I Am. Feel Me and contemplate Me. I am Love and Holy. Love Me and be holy. I will teach you, for I am Wisdom. Come, My Mother loves you. She will write now the message:*

Message for May 19th at Martigny.

♥ **My child, I, your Holy Mother, bless you, here is My Message:**

Peace be with you all. I love all of you and bless you. Listen and pay attention to Our Calls of today, realize how time is pressing. Jesus and I call you night and day for your conversion. Our Calls for your conversion are all over the world now and shall multiply. The time is pressing My children.

Today My Heart is in pain because so many of you do not seem to understand the urgency of Our Calls. I ask you to meditate and examine yourselves; test yourselves to see whether you are converted and in God's Way. My beloved children, it is not just to believe in God and pray. To be converted is to please God, to be in full contemplation with Him. To be converted is to be holy and live in holiness. To be converted is to <u>make peace with God and love God with all your soul</u>. Think of the love Jesus is pouring on you. Live in Christ; purify

yourselves and open your heart entirely so that Jesus heals you. To be converted is to <u>desire to be with God, to long for Him with all your heart</u>. Many forget that the biggest spiritual gift is love. ♥ I remind you again of Jesus' commandment: love one another as I love you. Please Me and live Our Messages, be Our little mouthpieces, scattering Our grains everywhere. Let those who have ears hear, realize the urgency of Our Messages. ♥

I am happy to see you here tonight, all assembled together. We bless all your religious objects you have with you. Tonight let it be a special night of meditation, a thorough examination of your soul. Jesus and I are present always to help you, so speak to Us <u>with your heart</u> and We will listen. ♥ I bless you all in the Name of the Father and of the Son and of the Holy Spirit. Amen.

I AM KNOWN TO APPROACH SOULS WHO ARE POOR

May 13th, 1989

Jesus?

I Am. Discern Me fully and in the capacity I have given you. ♥

Blessed are the poor in spirit for theirs is the kingdom of heaven. ♥ *Be blessed. Beware of evil who is redoubling his efforts to discourage you. I am helping you not to fall in his traps; I am levelling your path, have you not noticed?*

Yes, my Lord, I have and I bless You.

Remember, it is I who promotes you, dearest soul, never forget your incapacity and your inability to even breathe without Me. Remember always the way I work. ♥ *I have chosen you among others too, to receive My Messages. I am known to approach souls who are poor, heal them and through them make My Word known.*

Lord? May I dare say something?

♥ *Love is listening.*

Lord, many a times Your Word is given, but also many a time never listened or believed.

I know, yet everything does not go in vain, for even if many do not listen, there are a few who do, thus even if just one grain takes root, all these sacrifices are worthwhile.

Lord, with Your grace and out of pity You give us all these Messages, but there could have been masses reading them and getting converted, but it is not that way. Your Messages are fought down and many times ignored by Your very own.

This, My flower, is the great apostasy in My Church. My Church is filled up with Cains, enthroning themselves in My sanctuary, they pay more attention to formalities rather than My teachings of Love. I have entrusted them with millions of souls to lead to Me with love but they have taken the key of knowledge away, neither they go in themselves, nor allow others in who want to.

Lord, for how long yet are we to suffer?

Not for very long, put your trust in Me. Come, I will read to you a passage out of My Word.

Jesus indicated to me Jeremiah 4:5-31.

Creation, do not delay, convert and hear My Word. ♥ *Come, we, us?*

Yes, my Lord and I never seem to say it these days.

And I want you to say it Vassula... smile at Me.

You <u>are</u> really?

I Am. Flower, how often will I have to tell you?

I know, Jesus, but I like to hear You confirming it.

Realize then how I too love hearing you repeat My Name. I never tire of hearing you call Me; have always My Name in your mind, in your heart; utter My Name always and everywhere; speak of Me, it glorifies Me.

Ah Jesus, You have given me so much, blessed be Your Name. Glory be to God.

Have My peace. Will you kiss My Feet?

Yes my Lord.

I kissed the Lord's feet in spirit and on a crucifix.

Glorify Me by keeping faithful to Me. ♥

HEAVILY PERSECUTED
MATTHEW 10:34

May 15th, 1989

Lord?

♥ *I Am. I have not come to bring peace to the earth; it is not peace I have come to bring, but a sword.* (Matthew 10:34) *Evangelize with love, My angel, for Love, I shall help you. It is I, Jesus Christ, and I love you.* ♥ ⟁⟩✕ *IXθYΣ*

I, THE LORD, NEED LOVE AND ADORATION AND UNITY

May 16th, 1989

Jesus?

I Am. Never fail Me. Desire Me more than ever. Grow in your trials.

Let them[1] learn to love Me their God. Let them learn to prostrate themselves and adore Me, their Holy One. What use are to Me their lip-prayers? I need love and adoration. ♥ *Pray, My beloved of My Soul, for My priests, bishops and cardinals to discern My Will. I, the Lord, need LOVE and ADORATION and UNITY, all together around one single Tabernacle.* ♥ *If they sought My interests, they would understand how My Sacred Heart longs and desires this unity under the leadership of My Peter, Peter whom I Myself have given the keys of the kingdom of heaven. So pray with fervour all of you, that they may all understand, that I, the Lord, call them to unite. I call all those under My Name to return to true unity, under Peter-of-My-Lambs. I will later on call all other nations too to accept My Name as the Anointed, I shall speak in their heart.* ♥ ⟁⟩✕ *IXθYΣ*

---

[1] Everyone.

May 22nd, 1989 - Medjugorje

Lord?

I Am.

I love You. I adore You, Holy of Holies, Holy Jesus.

Love Me and adore Me, welcome Me always in this way. ♥

COME AND ADORE ME

May 24th, 1989 - Medjugorje

Jesus?

I Am. Beloved, love Me. My child, let this day be a joyful day. Rejoice, for I the Lord-Am-With-you all the way. Come and adore Me; come and feel My Sacred Heart; come and be one with Me little ones. I bless each one of you. Love is with you, Love loves you. ⟨ᴪ⟩ *IXθYΣ*

This message was given for our little group in Medjugorje. Jesus was asking us this morning to come and adore Him. Later on, at lunch-time, the priest announced in Church that in the evening there would be an evening of adoration. We ran there since Jesus was calling us!

LOVE IS SO LITTLE LOVED

May 25th, 1989 - Medjugorje

Lord?

I Am. Daughter, do not write in haste, open your ear and hear Me. I am Love but Love is so little loved, Love is so misunderstood! Come, we, us?

Forever Lord.

FEAST OF THE SACRED HEART

Sacred Heart of Jesus?

I Am. Today My Sacred Heart is calling all nations to hear My Voice. I am Love;
♥ *I am peace; I am the Way, the Truth and the Life, there is no other refuge for
the salvation of your soul than in My Sacred Heart.* ♥ *Daughter, write with Me
the prayer I had dictated to you last year.* ♥

O Sacred Heart of Jesus,
Teach me Your Ways
Sacred Heart of Jesus, lead me in
the Way of Integrity,
Keep me away from the evil one
and do not abandon me at his will,
Sacred Heart of Jesus
Be my Sheltering Rock
for You are my Refuge,
Assign Your Love and Peace
to guide and guard me. Amen

June 1st, 1989

Sacred Heart of Jesus, You rain on us a downpour of blessings. Sacred Heart of
Jesus You give the lonely a permanent home. Your family has found a Home.
Blessed be our Lord day after day who saves us and brings us one after the other into
His Sacred Heart. Blessed be our Lord who bears our burdens and shares our
sufferings. Lord?

♥ *I Am. Feel My Presence, recollect yourself and hear Me.* ♥

I AM IN SEARCH OF YOUR HEART

Message for the prayer meeting:

*Peace be with you all. I am the Lord, your Saviour, and He who seeks your heart.
I am He who stands untiringly outside each door, knocking. I am He who pursues*

the sinner and he who leaves the wise stupefied; I am He who increases My blessings and who prepares you gently to enter into My New Jerusalem[1]; I am the Holy Trinity, all in One and the Same, who with My Salvation Plan am preparing you all to unite into one holy single fold; ♥ *I am He who stunts the tall trees and allow the small ones to grow. Do not fear beloved ones, for in this wilderness I shall sow new grains of Love and Peace; I shall revive My garden so that those who are godless and wicked see and know that My Divine Hand is upon you all. The stone-hearts will understand My Boundless Mercy and that I, the Holy One am among you.* ♥

I am holding you by your right hand, feel My Presence; I shall not forsake you so do not fear. Yes, I shall take each one of you by the hand and form you so that you are called children of the Light and serve the cause of right. ♥ *I, the Lord, have said from the very beginning that I want you to be holy like I am Holy. Since I am your God and you My people, you will have to follow My Law.* ♥ *My Law is a Law of Love; learn how to love Me; learn how to adore Me.* _I am in search of your heart_. *Do not listen to the world, listen to My cry of Love; listen to My Heart-beats, every single heart-beat is a call for a soul. Come to Me in My open Arms, thrust yourselves into My embrace and _feel_ this Love I have for you, _feel_ this Mercy I have for you all! Return to me and I will heal you; treasure and engrave My Words in your heart, do not leave My Words be carried off by the four winds. Come and fix your eyes upon Me and do not let anyone take your eyes off Me.* ♥ *Realize the Graces I am offering you when I the Lord, flower, overcome your apathy.*

Lord Jesus, help me out of it!

Please Me and hear Me.

Help me hear You my Lord.

Am[2] present. I solemnly ask all of you to confess your guilt and desire Me. My Spirit of Grace is poured upon you _all_, to take you away from this spirit of lethargy, that lies heavily upon you, and revive you before you start decaying. So open your ears and hear Me. I know how most of you are dead now, although you believe you are alive but it is because of your resistance from abandoning yourselves entirely to Me. Trust Me and do not resist Me; abandon yourselves to Me, surrender, surrender. Allow Me your Loving God to be your captor of your little heart, do not fear. I am Love and Love desires to embellish your heart, so be attentive to My Words, they may appear simple to you but I am a God of

---

[1]That is: in our new state after having been purified.
[2]Jesus continues His dictation.

Simplicity, I am Meek and Humble. I know that many of you never cease thinking that I am repeating Myself but this is because My Words do not seem to penetrate you at all! If I do repeat Myself, it is because of your lethargy, because of your deafness, it is because so many of you do not put My Words into practice. I come offering you My Heart into My Hand; I come offering you My Peace and My Love; I come to unite you all back into one single Fold; I come to raise this dead era into a living one. Come and praise Me your Lord, I, who stoop to you from My Celestial Throne to pull you up to Me and revive you. Praise Me, all you who have been waiting for My Spirit of Grace to come upon you; go and proclaim My Righteousness to all nations and let My Message reach the ends of this earth, let them hear My Cries for Love.

Be joyful and be glad now all you who thirst for Me for I shall fill you; dry your tears all you who are oppressed day and night for I am here to console you and guard you.

My Sacred Heart is calling you all to come to Me in holiness. Lean on Me and I shall guide you to My Tabernacle, where I am waiting for you day and night. I offer you Myself every day. Come, come and receive Me in holiness and in purity; do not offend Me. Be pure and holy when you receive Me; recollect yourselves and recognize My Living Presence in the little white Host, let Me feel your holiness and purity. Oh if you only knew what a Grace I am offering you! Come, please Me by meditating upon My Message; please Me and live My Message; please Me and change your lives. ♥

Happy the man who meditates on what I am offering him today and studies his heart and examines his soul for I shall raise him. Happy are My priests, bishops and cardinals who come to Me like the publican[1] admitting their guilt, for in these hearts My Word shall take root and prosper. I shall then unveil their eyes so that they may see and understand with their heart that all what I need is love, Love and adoration. But alas! so many of these ministers have fallen into the charms of Satan! How can I endure their formalities and their pseudo-humility when inside them love is missing? Who is there left to adore Me? Who, among all these, will be the first to give the example to My children and come with his heart full of love to Me, fall prostrate in My Holy Presence and adore Me in silence? All I ask, beloved ones, is love in holiness; I am in search of your heart. ♥ *Come and offer Me your heart and I shall imbue it with My Love so that you in your turn may fill My children's heart too.* ♥ *I am your Holy One who asks you this simple question: where is the flock once entrusted to you, the flock that was your boast?[2] Purify yourselves, repent. Obey the Vicar of My Church, John-Paul II, who never*

---

[1] Luke 18:9-14.
[2] Jeremiah 13:20.

fails you, but whom you push aside and ignore. <u>All you who are still scoffing at him are weighing ever so heavily in My Sacred Heart</u>... Betrayed I Am, and by My own. For how long still are you to be like a deceptive oasis for My flock? A mirage of an endless desert? Brothers, all I ask from you is love. Come and adore Me, spend no time in seeking Me where I do not exist. Be the example to My flock. Love is waiting. Come and adore Me; come and adore Me your God and your King; come back to Me brothers of Mine and I, your Jesus, with My Sacred Heart palpitating with an everlasting love, I shall pity you and will let your sins pass Me by never reminding you of a single one. ♥

Seek Me while I am still to be found in My Mercy[1] and I shall come and open the eyes of the blind. And the ears of those whom I have made deaf I shall unseal. I will allow you to see My Light and hear and understand My Word so that you may be converted and be able to praise and extol and glorify Me your God from the very depths of your heart. ♥ *I, the Lord, place My Hand on your head and bless you.* ♥ *Be one.* ⊂⟩< *ΙΧΘΥΣ*

I bless you My child. Come, hear My Mother.

Flower, feel Me. I love you. Remember that I shall defend you as a lioness defends her little cubs. Be blessed and hear My Message.

My little children, do not resist God's Calls; surrender, lean on Him and let Him capitulate your heart; listen to Him and do as He says. I am your Holy Mother who reminds you all that the Lord's Word is Life, God's Word is Light. Many of you hear His Plea of Love, yet, as soon as you leave these premises the world draws you back in itself and thus His Plea of Love is forgotten. ♥ I have been asking you in My latest Message to meditate and examine your consciousness; today I ask you, "why do so many of you who heard My Message, arrive today to listen to a new Message, when the previous one was neither meditated nor read again?" My Immaculate Heart loves you all, dear children, and that is why I ask you today to read again My Message of before and <u>put it into practice</u>. I love you all. Never forget that My Immaculate Heart is your balm to your sorrows. I bless you all, in the Name of the Father and of the Son and of the Holy Spirit. Amen. ♥

Scriptures to be read were 1 Timothy 4:1-16, 1 Timothy 6:20-21, 2 Timothy 2:14-26 and 2 Timothy 3:1-17.

---

[1]Before His Justice comes.

ADORE ME IN SILENCE

June 5th, 1989

My Lord?

I Am.

Glory be to God. I must fulfil the vows I made you my Lord, to be faithful to You and seek only Your interests and what gives You more glory, for You came to my rescue. From Your Throne above You have stooped to look upon me in my disgrace. You have lifted me to walk in Your Presence, in the light of the living.

Flower, My own, glorify Me by loving Me. Come and adore Me in silence, look at Me in silence, love Me in silence. Have My Peace, daughter.

I will intensify My Celestial Works on mankind. ♥ *Enter into My Sacred Heart and find your rest in there. Come.* ♥

ADORE ME, THIS IS THE WAY TO ME

June 10th, 1989

Jesus?

♥ *I Am. Have faith, Vassula, for these are My Works of Wisdom; be receptive to My Voice and do not worry about the rest. Every single person who shares this Work, is sharing My Cross of Peace and Love. Never let the wise deceive you, so have confidence in Me till the end. Adore Me, this is the Way to Me.* ⊂✕
IXθYΣ

WILL YOU REMEMBER MY PRESENCE?

June 12th, 1989

Jesus?

I Am.

Jesus, it's difficult.

(I meant, all this supernatural approach, I still cannot realize...)

Flower, believe like a child.

Oh it's beautiful!

Around Me are My angels, I have come with My angels.

It's beautiful Lord!

Delight Me and always seek Knowledge; let My Commandments fill you with delight and you will be blessed. Delight My Soul and say Abba to Me every now and then. O sanctified by My Own Hand, be My reflection, be holy, let your heart be My Head-rest. I, the Lord-Am-With-You, will you remember My Presence? Have Me in your mind to be aware of your actions, thoughts and words. Have My Peace. ♥

PADRE PIO

June 12th, 1989

♥ *It is I, Jesus. Come, I am with Padre Pio.* ♥

Sono con te Vassula, ascolta nostro Buono Signore.

Padre Pio is encouraging me.

I AM YOUR SPIRITUAL DIRECTOR

June 14th, 1989

Jesus?

♥ *I Am. My Will is to improve you, is it yours too?*

Yes my Lord it is, but my surroundings are difficult.

Accept your surrounding and all that I have given you. My Will is to have you near Me, leaning on Me and no one else. I am your Master and I am your Spiritual Director.

Lord, when You say this, You make Father James flee and hide!

My Vassula, allow Me to read you a passage from My Word. ♥

Jesus made me open the Holy Bible on Ecclesiasticus, (Book of Sirach) chapter 4:11-22, Wisdom as educator. I had opened at random.

See? I am Wisdom and I am your Educator.

Lord, verse 19 bothers me.

That means if you refuse Me totally, but do not worry, I will lift you every time you are bound to fall. I have you placed in a special part of My Sacred Heart. My Vassula, allow Me to educate you fully. Love loves you. I am pleased every time you remember Me. ♥ *Will you meditate upon all of this? Have My Peace.* ♥

My God, how is it possible all this, God talking to me?

I Am. Flower, be with Me.

Glory be to God.

I NEED VICTIM SOULS

June 15th, 1989

My God?

♥ *I Am. Discern Me. Be prepared to receive Me. My angel, repeat after Me these words:*

> *O Sacred Heart of Jesus,*
> *My Lord whom I adore,*
> *I offer You my will.*
> *Make Me your instrument*
> *of Your Peace and of Your Love,*
> *make me Your victim*
> *of Your Burning Desires*
> *of Your Sacred Heart. Amen.*

♥ *Yes, and now abandon yourself to Me entirely, I need victim souls so offer Me your will. Vassula, be one with Me, I, who am the Supreme Victim of Love. My remnant, My own, My myrrh, My altar, I will embellish your soul by letting you share My Cross of Peace and Love till the end, I and you, you and I, united in Love.* ♥ ⊂⊃✕ *IXθYΣ*

LOVE DESIRES LOVE

June 19th, 1989

Message given for the prayer meeting at Fribourg at the Soeurs du Bon Pasteur.

Lord?

I Am. Peace be with you. Dearest souls, feel Me, feel My Presence, I am among you all. ♥ *Come and remove this veil that lies heavily on your eyes and see Me in My Glory. I know how weak you are and that the slightest tempest risen by My enemy, you shake and fall, but do not despair in these Rebellious Times for I the Lord, who am your Refuge and your Consoler, am ever so near you; I am a Refuge for the needy and the desperate; a Shelter from the storms raised by My enemy; an Everlasting Spring for those who are thirsty; a Shade to protect you from the scorching heat of this desert you are now living in. My Sacred Heart is wide open to welcome you and rest you. ♥ I am Love who seeks every heart to console and love; I am Love who loves you eternally. ♥ See? I descend from My Celestial Throne, stooping over you to lift you to Me and nourish your soul directly from My Heavenly Store. I come to you My starved lambs; I come to assemble you all in the warmth of My Arms. ♥ For your sake I shall multiply My Graces upon you all and your dead I shall raise with My Burning Flame of Love. ♥ I come with My Sacred Heart in My Hand, offering It to you, will you receive It?*

My beloved ones, the Day is near when every vision will come true, every vision will soon be fulfilled and in your own lifetime too. So open your hearts and try to understand why My Spirit of Grace is poured on this generation so generously. The Day is drawing near, when all generations shall be one, under one Shepherd, around one Holy Tabernacle and I, the Lord, shall be Unique for them. So pray My beloved ones, pray for this Unity which I, the Lord, am in full preparation on it. ♥ <u>Now you are scattered and your pastures barren. The wailing of My shepherd[1] is heard in all Heaven, for the Cains have broken his staff in several pieces, union in splinters to break the brotherhood between them[2]</u>, but the Day of the Glory of My Body is near and what joy that will be! It will be a day of wonder and the Wounds that I received in the house of My best friends shall heal. ♥

My Sacred Heart today desires love in purity, all I need is a return of love. Have I not out of love offered Myself as a Fragrant Offering and a Sacrifice? Is it too much to ask of you your abandonment to Me? Is it too much to ask of you for some recognition and a return of love? <u>Love desires love, Love is thirsty for love, Love is begging you for a return of love</u>. Revolt not against My Law which is a Law of Love. O beloved ones how I love you! Why have so many of you stopped adoring Me? I am reminding you that I am present at this Holy Hour, encircled by My seraphs and cherubs I stand in silence before you. I, the Holy of Holies, have given you your name <u>"Beloved"</u>. Although you have sinned against Me, I have forgiven you. You are My seed! Will I at the appointed Hour of Adoration see you My beloved? Will you rise and come to Me, I, who will be waiting at My Tabernacle? Come to Me. Come to Me. Do not deny what the Spirit is offering you these days, keep yourselves within My Love and accept My Mercy. ♥ Remember how everything will vanish and remain no more and that all will wear out one day, but your soul remains forever. I, the Lord, bless each one of you, giving you My Peace so that you may give it to others. ⊂⟩✕ ΙΧθΥΣ

---

[1] Our Holy Father, John-Paul II.
[2] Here I felt God sorrowful to the point of death.

I AM WISDOM AND YOUR EDUCATOR

June 21st, 1989

Lord?

♥ *I Am. Never cease praying. Follow My instructions, beloved, remain always available for Me, your God. I am always near you to provide your soul what it lacks. Wisdom? I shall instruct you freely with Wisdom. Perseverance? and I shall infuse your soul to be full of zeal. Patience? I will give you Mine. Endurance for atoning for yourself and for others? You will absorb from Me.* ♥ *Love? I will fill your heart from Mine. Peace? My Peace is yours. Ah, my child,! Why have you stopped asking Me these Graces that can nourish your soul?*

I do not really know.

Remember, I am Wisdom and your Educator, so depend on Me, have I not nourished your soul so far and those of others? I shall continue to pour on you teachings like prophecy. Trust Me, seek Me, walk with Me, obey Me, love and adore Me, I am Present at all times, so feel secure. ♥ *I am the Authority and Discipline that descend upon you. Ah, My child, I love you everlastingly. Do not trouble your soul seeking to understand My Ways, for in doing this you only allow yourself to be drawn into winding ways that never end. Know that My Ways are not your ways and the difference of this is, I tell you, immense! Accept what I give you in Peace, allow Me to keep My Finger on you.* ♥ *I and you, united in Love.*

Come, we, us? ⤳ ΙΧθΥΣ

COME AND EXTOL ME AND ADORE ME, FOR I AM HOLY

June 29th, 1989

Blessed be our Lord, the Almighty, who alone performs marvels. My God, You taught me Your Word and I am still proclaiming your marvels. Full of compassion You forgave my guilt and You brought me back to my senses. You have made me understand and perceive Wisdom's words:

They who eat Me will hunger for more, they who drink Me will thirst for more. (Si

24:21).

Similar to a woman who has been widowed, so am I roaming in this desert looking for Your Eternal Source and Your green pastures where I may lay my head and rest.

Daughter, instead of a barren tree, I have made you flourish and bear fruit; instead of a hostile pagan, a fervent worshipper; instead of apathy, I have given you zeal for Me your God. Come, stay in My favour and be one with Me. ♥

Lord, I was wondering about our meeting of yesterday.

♥ *I, the Lord, will give My couriers My news. Look, today I am having your hands unchained. Feel free... if you like to come with Me and share My Cross of Peace and Love, then come, I will look after you, feel free... you know very well that I am Self-sufficient. I am the Most High.* ♥ *I love your innocence and I shall not deprive you from my signs, I shall give to the poor and needy so that they may praise My Name. Come to Me in purity of heart, I mean to progress you. Come and* extol *Me and* adore *Me, for* I Am *Holy.* ♥ *Love loves you eternally. Come.*

Lord?

I Am. Pray and let Me hear your prayer, the prayer I have given you in dictation.

> O Sacred Heart of Jesus, My Lord, whom I adore,
> I offer You my will,
> make me Your instrument of Your Peace and Love,
> make me Your victim of Your burning desires
> of Your Sacred Heart. Amen.

Stay small and grow only in My Spirit. ♥ *Forsaken you shall never be.*

ALL I WANT IS YOUR WILL

July 4th, 1989

My Lord?

I Am. Recollect yourself at each meeting, recollect yourself. Do not fear, My teachings are sound. Allow Me to educate your soul, allow Me to continue My

Divine Plan. All I want is your will[1]. I am giving you My Peace, My Love, for all Eternity. I shall never fail you. Peace My child, hear My Mother.

Yes Lord.

St Mary, Our Holy Mother:

Vassula, let your soul rest in Jesus' Sacred Heart and leave the rest to Him. Come, I will dictate to you My Message.[2]

Peace be with you. I am with you all in this assembly with My hands outstretched on you, blessing you all. Listen to Wisdom's Words. All that the Lord is seeking is your heart, do not refuse Him. If you offer Him your heart, He shall give you the Gift of His Love to lead you and take you into His Sacred Heart, which is your Home, the Home of your soul. Return to the Lord and offer Him your will; come back to the Most High and He shall fragrance you with His Love. I am calling you to encourage all of you today; Our calls are all over this dark world, this world of distress and anguish that your era has become.

I solemnly request each soul to meditate why Jesus and I are urging you all in various ways and in so many parts of the world, calling out for your conversion. We are like distracted Parents Who take all means to reach you and warn you, you who are Our so beloved children. Take Our Warnings and Calls to heart. Repent. Pray with your heart; come with love to the Lord. Come and adore the Lord. Accept the Love He is offering you. Delight His Heart and let Him see you come all at the Hour of Adoration. ♥ Love desires love, Love is seeking your heart; come then to Love, come to the Holy One who cries out to you for a return of love. I am your Holy Mother who loves you, have no doubt. I bless you all in the Name of the Father and of the Son and of the Holy Spirit. ♥ Amen.

---

[1] I saw interiorly Jesus stretching His Hand to me while saying "all I want is your will."
[2] Message for our prayer reunion for July 14th for Fribourg.

ST MICHAEL

Saint Michael is giving us a message.

I am Saint Michael. I am your Saint Michael to whom you pray for protection and for defending you against the evil one. Have no fear, your hardships will be redressed by this prayer. ♥ Allow the Spirit of Love to expand His calls of Grace, listen to the Spirit of Grace, listen to the Spirit for His Mercy is Great; do not suffocate those who receive the Holy One's Messages like your ancestors by saying to the seers "see no visions" and to the prophets "do not prophecy to us for we are in the Truth." Instead, lift up your eyes and look around, all are assembling and coming back to God, your sons from far away and your daughters being tenderly carried, for the Lord has announced this, "though night dominates your era, My Light shall pierce it and will cover this earth and all nations shall come to Me and My flock I will gather again into one Holy Fold under My Holy Name." Pray, O children of the Lord, and allow the Lord to redress His people by accepting what comes out of the babe's mouth and the lowly. Have no fear, salvation is near and at your very gates. ♥ I bless you in the Name of the Father and of the Son and of the Holy Spirit. Amen.

Allow the Lord to use you Vassula, yearn for the Lord. Love Him for He is most Compassionate. ♥

Later on, still thirsty for God, I come to Him in this special way He has given me, even if it meant to be for ten seconds. I needed just an exchange of intimacy, a conversation with my Redeemer. Lord, I love You.

I Am. Flower, love Me, you rejoice Me. Approach, I am near you. ♥

YOUR SUFFERING IS NOTHING COMPARED TO MINE

July 5th, 1989

My Lord?

I Am. Peace be with you.

Lord, sometimes it is difficult.

My Vassula, I know it is hard to live in a desert, but remember how My Eyes never leave you. Lean on Me. My Words do not differ from the past; I have never ceased to call every generation to convert; with great love and pity I will always hold out My Hand to you. Are you willing to proceed with My Works of Love?

Yes Lord, I am willing, if this is Your wish.

It is My wish. My wish is to embellish every soul on earth; My wish is to let everyone taste My Bread, I love you all. My wish is to fill you and at no cost; My wish is to bring back to their senses the godless. ♥ *My Vassula, feel My Sacred Heart, never has It been torn and pained as much as in this dark era.*

O God.

Yet, how much greater My pain to see so many souls heading for the eternal fires. Understand My child how your suffering is nothing compared to Mine. Allow Me to rest in you, be in Peace. ♥ ⟨⟩< IXθΥΣ

THE ROOT OF MY CHURCH IS LOVE

July 6th, 1989

Lord, these past days surely You are hiding Your Face from me. I do not feel Your Light as much as before, why are You abandoning me? Lord?

I Am. Never cease praying. ♥ *I am your Redeemer, the Holy One. My love for you is great and I am teaching you what is good for your soul. It is I who forms you, do not think that I am abandoning you. Grieve not, you are not toiling in vain. Listen My Vassula, I love you and I shall never cease feeding you My Bread.*

Hear Me, I am, out of great pity, preparing for this generation a delightful Vineyard. ♥ *I am like a Vine, putting out graceful shoots[1], My Blossoms bear the Fruit of Love and Peace. Approach Me, you who desire Me and take your fill of My Fruits[2]; they who eat Me will hunger for more, they who drink Me will thirst for more[3].* ♥ *Ah daughter, how I wish that every soul would hunger and*

---

[1] Ecclesiasticus 24:17.
[2] Ecclesiasticus 24:19.
[3] Ecclesiasticus 24:21.

thirst for Me! Ecclesia would not have been in ruin as it is now, for of what use are to Me their formalities and their ceremonies when love is missing? Can a tree survive without a root? The Root of My Church is Love, if then Love is missing how can My Church survive?

Jesus, I want to console You.

Repose My Head with your love, love Me and allow Me to rest in you. I rejoice profoundly that I shall see you all at My Tabernacle[1]. ♥ Love loves you. I Am the Lord, so feel secure. ⊂⊃⤬ ΙΧθΥΣ

INFATUATE ME WITH YOUR SIMPLICITY

July 7th, 1989

Teach me to obey You since You are my God and since it is You who educates me. My spirit is failing me and I feel unconsoled in this exile. Lord, listen to my pleading, where are You?

Flower, peace be with you, I am near you. From now on I want you to have more faith in Me, am I not your Educator? So why have you to worry? Be in Peace, I am Forgiveness. Remain faithful to Me and leave the rest to Me, I will never deny you My Bread, nor My Love. Care for each other. Pray often to Me, even for just one moment. I am always before you and I am the Only One who will guide you, feel then confident since your hand is in Mine. I know you are poor, but am I not Infinite Wealth? You need not worry, for it is I who will provide you. Never think for one second that I shall leave you in the dark; I will fill your lamp with oil, I will never cease feeding you. Little one, I am caring for you. Pray without ceasing, allow Me to be your Educator till the end. ♥ Caress Me with your love, adorn Me with your prayers, infatuate Me with your simplicity. Seek me and you shall find Me in simplicity of heart. Desire Me; thirst for Me and never weary to evangelize for Love with love. I, the Lord, love you to jealousy. ♥ Remain in My Sacred Heart, My Sacred Heart will give you all that your soul lacks; I desire this love since I am the Source of Love. Love loves you all.
⊂⊃⤬ ΙΧθΥΣ

---

[1]Jesus was referring those who would be present at the hour of adoration.

LET MY SHOULDER BE YOUR HEADREST, MY SACRED HEART YOUR HOME

July 8th, 1989

Lord, my soul lacks Wisdom, perseverance, fervour, patience, I need Your Strength to go on, but I know I need only to say: "I'm failing You, I'm slipping away from You" and Your Love immediately comes to support me, Your Hand to lift me. Lord?

I Am. Never doubt, I am the Lord and your Refuge. When you need Me in times of dangers, remember to call out My Name and I will rush to your rescue. Cling on Me, beloved, for I am your God who protects you. ♥ I answer to all those who invoke Me. Trust Me and I shall never fail you; lean on Me. Let My Shoulder be your Headrest, My Sacred Heart your Home. Forsaken, you shall never be. Have I not out of My Infinite Mercy lifted you to Me? Have I not rained a downpour of blessings upon you? Arise then and do not be afraid. I know you are fainthearted but I shall give you My Strength to face My oppressors, they shall fall one after the other. ♥ No one shall touch you, for I am your Refuge. You need not fear while passing through this exile, remember how I have redeemed you from the evil one. I am the Source of your hope. ♥ I will always share with you till the end, so come and unburden your heart to Me, I and you, together. Realize how I lead your soul, without any merit from you daughter. Everything I give is freely given, write with Me and be one. I give you My Peace. Sin no more.

α Ω Alpha and Omega?

I Am.

Glory be to God. Blessed be Our Lord.

Flower, remember, when you see Me, smile at Me, I am Love and am at your side. Allow Me to be your Educator. It has already been said that My sons and My daughters will be taught by Me and that Love will be your Educator, your Teacher and all discourses will come from Wisdom Herself. I it is who will guide you till the end. ♥

Come, you who err still in this wilderness saying,

> *"I have sought My Redeemer but have not found Him",*
> *find Me My beloved in purity of heart,*
> *by loving Me without self-interest.*

Find Me in holiness,
in the abandonment I desire of you;
find Me by observing My Commandments;
find Me by replacing evil with love;
find Me in simplicity of heart.
Sin no more;
cease in doing evil,
learn to do good;
search for justice, help the oppressed.
Let this wilderness and this aridity exult;
let your tepidness inflame into an ardent flame.
Relinquish your apathy and replace it by fervour,
do all these things so that you may be able to say,

"I have sought my Redeemer and I have found Him. He was near me all the time but in my darkness I failed to see Him. O Glory be to God! Blessed be our Lord! How could I have been so blind?" I shall then remind you to keep and treasure My Principles, <u>so that you may live</u>. ♥

Thank You my Lord that You are now going to turn this wilderness into flowing springs.

Remember My Teachings. Come, remember My Presence at all times. Love loves you[1]. ♥ *Shall we share?*

Oh yes Lord!

Then let us share with love. Be one with Me. ♥

THE WALLS OF MY SANCTUARY WILL BE REBUILT

July 9th, 1989

The Lord gave me to read a passage in Scriptures about how He will rebuild Jerusalem. Lord?

♥ *I Am. All that you have read will come true, My Church, I shall rebuild. My Church today lies in ruin and in terrible havoc, but the days are soon coming when*

---

[1] I suddenly remembered my household work.

every man shall follow My Law because of the Seeds of Love I am sowing now in their heart. They shall carry My Law deep inside their heart, and they will be called "Witnesses of the Most High." ♥ *They shall be My People and I shall be their God, and Knowledge they shall learn directly from My Own Lips; I will be their Master and they will be My Pupils. I shall then establish Order that will never pass away and they shall all know Me by My Holy Name, even those without any merits, since I am Infinite Mercy, Forgiveness and Pity. Yes, the Walls of My Sanctuary will be rebuilt, layer after layer, brick after brick, all will be rebuilt by My Own Hand.* ♥ *I shall then go in each street corner in search of the dead and I shall raise them one after the other, so that they may become My new mouthpieces and I shall send them with My Spirit to minister before you and when you will ask them "who gives you this authority?" they will answer that they were given the authority by Authority Herself; and you, My beloved ones, you who suffer in this wilderness, will become like a watered garden, like a spring of water whose waters never run dry. Love will be living among you and I shall be surrounded by My Own, praising Me, glorifying Me, all united under My New Holy Name; and Rebellion shall cease and will come at its end, pierced by My Word It shall be dead, never to rise again. I mean to deliver you from the hands of the Evil one, fortifying you in My Light[1]. Only for the sake of those who love Me and immolate for Me, I shall reduce My Fire. For your sake, beloved ones, My Hand shall not fall as hard as you were told. Your era's guilt is still great and her sins innumerable, her iniquity so grave that your trees hardly bear any fruit. Are you surprised to see no grapes on the vines? no fruits on the fruit-trees? and no green leaves anymore? Are you surprised that they no longer bloom and do not exhale any perfume? it is because My enemies have poisoned My springs that water My garden, to dry up the little fruit that was left on them. I have seen them extirpate flower after flower. Treacherous and vicious as vipers, they come by night into My Sanctuary, unfolding without fear their despicable inclinations, such abetting of evil men that no one renounces his evil-doing.*

But Lord, they must know that You are watching them!

They are rebels, rebelling against My Law. It is those that Scriptures say of them, "they dress My people's wounds without concern. Peace, peace they say, but there is no peace. They are without shame and without love, they are heartless"; but I shall overthrow these rebels with one blow of My Breath; I shall overthrow all of those Cains that have enthroned themselves into high seats of Falsehood. Of what use are their thrones to Me? I have been warning them and the more I warned them the more they refused to hear lest they should turn to me and be converted. These Cains have persisted in apostasy for several decades, never leaving their grip from their evil-doings; they cling to illusions and to falsehood; they trample on My

---

[1] I suddenly remembered the purification by fire.

devout ones and on those who keep faithful to My Peter, yes, they ridicule all those who still believe in him. These Cains harm My Church to the extent that they made My Eyes turn into a Spring of Tears, weeping all day and all night long.

My God, what pain You give me. Your decrees are so wonderful, why should anyone do this to You? Your decrees are my eternal heritage, oh Lord, ever so loving and tender, my eyes stream with tears too, because others disregard Your Law.

This is why I am sending you[1] these very ones you call weak, worthless, contemptible and foolish, I mean to shame all you who call yourselves wise. You shall be caught unaware, for I mean to confound you to the point that you would not know your own name and where you come from.

Beloved, rest now, I hope to spend some more time together with you. Be awake to all dangers; stay firm in the faith; let everything you do be done in love. I bless you, we, us?

For Eternity My Lord.

Come, rest in My Sacred Heart, your Home. ⊂>< IXθΥΣ

I AM LIKE A WATCHMAN

July 15th, 1989

My Lord come, lift me and allow me to meet You, let Your Light shine on me. I try not to forget Your statutes though the nooses of my persecutors do not seem looser where I live in this wilderness, but remembering Your Presence in my heart I take courage, I rejoice at Your Presence, Holy of Holies.

Vassula of My Sacred Heart, love Me, amend for those who do not. Please My Sacred Heart and learn this little prayer:

> *O Sacred Heart of Jesus,*
> *Restore my soul,*
> *Hide my heart into Your Sacred Heart,*
> *so that I may live.* ♥ *Amen.*

---

[1]That is; our generation, our era.

Devote this prayer to My Sacred Heart. Daughter, your toiling will not be in vain. Ah, My remnant, never cease praying, never cease looking at Me. Fix your eyes on Me, have Me always Present in your mind for I Am Holy, Holy, Holy. ♥ *Your persecutors My child, are My persecutors as well, they are those who come by night into My Vineyard to destroy It; but do not fear, I am like a watchman on guard against those prowlers. I shall allow no man touch the fruits of My Vineyard.* ♥

I AM THE GREAT SHEPHERD OF MY FLOCK

July 17th, 1989

Lord?

♥ *My child, hear Me and write.* ♥ *I am the Great Shepherd of My flock. I had trained shepherds to look after My flock, but many of My companions have taken the gear of incompetence, not bothering for the lost, not bringing back to the fold the strayed. My best friends are giving Me the greatest sorrows, and the deepest Wounds on My Body are inflicted by the staff I Myself had given them. They are My best friends, yet I am Wounded beyond recognition from their own hand. I am incessantly scourged on My back; My whole Body shivers from pain; My parched Lips tremble. Without fear they cry out for Peace, but there is no peace because they have allowed themselves to be captured and seduced by Rationalism, Disobedience and Vanity. What sorrow they give Me and what Wounds they inflict on Me!*

Lord? Why is it so difficult for some?

It is difficult to leave the sceptre of Falsehood once they hold it; it is difficult to give up their human doctrines and regulations; it is difficult to die to their own greed; it is difficult to accept the self-abasement-robes. To these I say, "howl, shepherds, shriek, roll on the ground you lords of the flock, for the days have arrived for your slaughter. Like the finest rams you will fall one after the other. I had offered you the fairest heritage among My friends; I had ranked you with the elect; My House, I trusted you with, but you have not followed My precepts, you have apostatised, you did what I consider evil. I called you, but you would not listen, you disobeyed Me[1]."

---

[1] This was said with great bitterness.

Ah my God, mercy on us, wash these shepherds clean of their guilt, purify them from their sin.

My little bride, allow Me to share My sorrows with you.

I love You Lord, my God, ever so tender and merciful. I live only for You, my gaze is only upon You and no one else, I adore You!

Ah how your words of love appease My Justice! Every drop of love counts. Innumerable souls can be saved by love. Allow Me to use you as My tablet, I come to you to show you My Wounds and like a friend tell you of My sorrows. ♥ I am showing you the Wounds of My Sacred Heart. ♥

Blessed be our Lord.

My Vassula, I am in the Age of Mercy now, have you not noticed how My Spirit of Grace is poured upon you? It is now that you have to repent, it is now for you to change your lives. Pray without ceasing, pray with love. ♥ Do not persist in rebellion, for the terrible Hour of Justice is soon with you, be ready to face Me then as a Judge. ♥ Daughters and sons of Mine, long ago I freed you from your chains that linked you to death and with great Compassion I have taken you back; I redeemed you from the evil one; I showed you My Heart and how it was pierced by your ancestors; I sacrificed Myself in order to set you free. Your era provokes Me incessantly and yet I, out of great pity, I let My Spirit of Grace remind you of My precepts. My Mercy today reaches from one end of the earth to the other. Listen to My voice of today, accept My Mercy of today. I solemnly ask you to pray with your heart. Fast, repent, love one another, renew yourselves into a completely new batch so that I may show My Glory through your transfiguration. ♥
ΙΧθΥΣ ✕⊂▷

FROM ALL ETERNITY I LONGED TO BE WITH YOU, IN YOU AND YOU IN ME

July 19th, 1989

Holy One, my soul yearns for Your Sacred Heart. Happy are all those who live in Your Sacred Heart and can adore You all day long; happy those who receive graces from You. Call back to life again all those who still lie dead so that they may rejoice in You, show them Your Love, show them Your Sacred Heart so that they may sing a New Hymn of Love to You.

Beloved of My Soul, take My Hand and evaluate all that Wisdom instructed you with. ♥ *I have instructed you with the language of Love; I have instructed you to discern and to listen to My Voice; I have instructed you how to find Me your Lord. I have enlivened your soul. I reminded you of My Beauty and that I am the Sublime Source of Love. From all Eternity I longed to be with you, in you and you in Me.* ♥ *Perhaps now you are beginning to understand this ardent Love of Mine? and how eager I, your God, am and how I thirst for Love? Flower, I am always with you and will be till the end and forever.* ♥ *Make My Sacred Heart your Home, like a dove that has its cote, have My Sacred Heart to be your Home.* ♥ *My Love for you all is everlasting.* IXθΥΣ ⤓

PATMOS - THE APOCALYPSE ISLAND
Where Saint John was exiled

July 25th, 1989

I brought you to a fertile country to enjoy its produce and good things. ♥ (Jr 2:7)

My Lord, I ask Your permission to give me the grace to "receive" Your Word if it is possible in the cavern where St John received also Your Word. Lord, from the depths of my heart I call to You. Listen compassionately to my pleading. I rely on Your answer. Amen.

When your pleading began, a word was uttered and I have come to tell you what it is, "you are a man specially chosen." ♥ *(Dn 9:23)*

What does it really mean Lord?

Hear Me, come near Me anytime so that they may know that I Am He. I, the Word, descend among you to forgive you and to bring you all back to Me. ♥

Message given to the Greek young group who came to Patmos to pray and learn the rosary. Some came from Athens, others from Rhodos. All joined together in a pilgrimage to Patmos.

Awake! Beloved ones, I am your Saviour, the Crucified, your Redeemer. Feel My Love. For your sake I have come to increase love and diminish evil; I come to provide your soul with all that it lacks. Have no fear little ones, am I not Bountiful? Am I not the Highest? So have confidence, for your are in your Father's Arms. I, the Holy Trinity, am One and the Same. ♥ *Abandon yourselves entirely into My Arms and allow Me to form you into Living Columns of Light; allow Me to share all that I have with you. ♥ I love you! Beloved, the light in this dark world flickers, for the evil one is extinguishing the little light that is left now in this world. Your generation delights unmercifully to call evil good and good evil. Without any pity they ceaselessly blaspheme My Holy Name, ever so ready to face evil and kneel at his feet. How I suffer to watch all this! Feel My Sacred Heart how It is lacerated, how It bleeds to see this dead era struggling to cut off their umbilical cord attached to Me so that they may delightfully call themselves "Godless", ♥ so that they may say, "no need to think about whom we belong to; see, we are freed. We shall now go out and construct a Tower of Babel, have we not done this before? Why be attached to God? What do we gain by His Law?" They are doing all these things because they have never known either the Father or Myself, most of this generation are worshippers of Baal. Yes, they are the descendants of their ancestors who worshipped false gods. All they do is wither their soul, for they have snapped their navel string attached to me and that nourished their soul. They are heading willingly in the eternal fires; they are assailing My Holy Name and deliberately are provoking Me. Come, I have called you and you have heard Me. I Am your Lord and you My People, My Own. Accept Me with love and peace. The earth is defiled under this generation's feet, this is why My Cleansing Fire shall descend from above on them to clean the tarred soil. Lift your soul to me and be one with Me, have My Peace. I bless you all and all that you have brought to be blessed. My Sigh is upon each icon and religious object. ♥ Be one. ΙΧθΥΣ ✕◗*

The above message was given after the "ship incident." While sailing from Rhodos to Patmos, someone started to talk religion; in 15 minutes the 12 of us found ourselves surrounded by a big crowd of young people, most of them atheists and arguing with us. They were fighting God's Word. But in spite of this violent attack and mockery, one of them got converted there and then.

My Lord, let them see Your Jealous Love. You are our Peace and Hope. We do not deserve Your Love nor Your Mercy. Be with us for we are weak and frail like flowers and we need Your Sap to nourish us.

Be holy, like I am Holy. Read My Word, live for Me and Me only. Repay evil with love. Be like shoots which sprout from the Vine, soon you will bud and blossom and you will fill the world with fruit. ♥ Have My Peace. Stay on My Bosom. Holy is My Name, so remember to be holy. Come. ♥

PATMOS

July 26th, 1989

Inside the cavern of the Apocalypse just where the scribe's feet were standing to write I lay down my copy-book and receive the Lord's message. Lord?

I Am. Never doubt. ♥ *I am with you now and until the end of times and forever.*

Lord?

I Am. Love is near you, do not fear. Come, all I ask from you is Love, a return of Love. My Peace is yours, take My Peace so that you may give It to others. ♥ *Cease to do evil. Unite! Unite and be one, as I and the Father are One and the Same. Peace. Peace, come and make Peace with Me. Love is calling you now.*
ΙΧθΥΣ ⋈

LACK OF DISCERNMENT PRODUCES UNIQUE FRUITS

July 28th, 1989 - Rhodos

Lord?

I Am. Little one realize how I am Present.

And will I hear You my Lord?

Little one I want you to hear Me and feel Me. Allow My finger to rest on you, allow My Spirit to breathe in you.

O Lord, how I do not deserve all this!

Be one with Me. How I the Lord love you! See? My Sacred Heart is open and he who wants to step in It is welcome, you are all free to choose. ♥ *If you choose My Sacred Heart, I will fill you, I will let you live in My Light, you will absorb from Me. I will nourish you, then I shall ask you if you are willing to share with Me. Like a Spouse and a Bride we will share, and I shall renovate you entirely with My Love.* ♥

Lord, make everyone come back to You. Renew our generation as in times past.

Come then, come back to Me. I am not rejecting you, I am all Merciful and ever so Compassionate. Acknowledge your sins, repent and be Mine. ♥ *I-Am-He-Who-Saves; I am your Redeemer; I am the Holy Trinity, all in One; I am the Spirit of Grace and although your generation calls herself fatherless I am ready to forgive and forget and take back all those who have apostatised. My Holy Spirit of Grace is ready to lift and renew you.* ♥ *Why continue to reduce your lands into deserts? Are you not weary in having to live in wilderness? Return to Me, be one of those who have sought My Wells and have found them. I shall renew you with My Perfection, with My Beauty, with My Glory. I mean to rise you in perfection so that your soul may live.*

I wish to speak to My beloved children[1], I love them and My Love for them is eternal. I have called to show them My Heart and they have heard Me, they heard My cry from My Cross. I always desired to seduce their soul since they are My offspring. ♥ *I desired this closeness to Me since the beginning of times and from all eternity I wished them to love Me and adore Me, their God. Come, I wish to remind them how I can manifest Myself in different ways and in devout souls, revealing My secrets, revealing My Wisdom. I wish them to learn how to discern what comes from the Spirit and what comes from their subjectivity.* ♥ *Since the beginning I have never ceased advising them to watch My Lips; lack of discernment produces unripe fruits, folly, presumption; it can only aggravate their hearts. I have raised them from their lethargy so that they may live and I had waited for this Hour ever so impatiently.* ♥ *With Me they will learn. Understand how My Spirit works.*

I love you all and I do not wish you to fall into folly, I do not wish you to be misled by your own subjectivity. Be humble, stay small and allow Me to feed you in the way I have chosen. I shall never cease watching over you. ♥ *I, the Lord, give you My Blessings, My Love and My Peace.* ♥

July 29th, 1989

I ran to the Lord for just a moment.

Love is near you. Stay small so that My Spirit can grow in you. I am the Truth, the Life and the Way. Glorify Me by loving Me. ♥

---

[1]The group of Athens.

HERESIES ARE DEVOURING MY BODY

July 30th, 1989 - Rhodos

The reading of today was from Col 2:1-15. This was after I had met a man belonging to the evangelists. He said that all the messages were beautiful but that surely the devil intervened, taking Our Mother's name! He said that the demon will be the one who will unite the Churches! It's amazing how Satan can mislead good people...

Lord?

I Am. Have My Peace, My Peace is yours. Truly do not get deceived by rational philosophy and unsound teachings, fulfil your mission for My Glory and repeat all these things I have been teaching you. I am Wisdom and your Educator, from My Own Lips you are learning. Repeat after Me these words:

> *Lord, take me in soul, take me in spirit.*
> *My Lord Jesus, take my heart, all is Yours.*
> *Your Love is better than life itself.*
> *I put my hope in You. Amen.*

Little one, Love will remain always near you. ♥ *Will you remember always who is your Redeemer? Heaven is mourning all day and all night long for these heresies that infiltrated into My Body, heresies that are devouring My Body. Like cancer they develop inside My Body,* ♥ *their yeast has infiltrated into My Bread. I tell you most solemnly that these people will bear the weight of their faults and the fault of those following them, this will be as grave as the faults of their ancestors who worshipped Baal.* ♥

Flower, remember My Holy Presence, My Eyes never detach from you. Come. We, us?

Forever.

BE PRUDENT

August 4th, 1989
Back in Switzerland

Last night while waking up in the middle of the night I realized that the Holy Spirit was praying for me the Credo, I followed the voice which was in the middle of the prayer and finished the prayer. Later on again that night, I woke up and realised that the voice of the Holy Spirit was praying Saint Michael's prayer, I had woken up somewhere in the middle of the prayer. I finished the prayer with the Holy Spirit. The Holy Spirit is praying in me without ceasing, even when I'm asleep.

My Lord and My God, Sacred Heart of Jesus, is it Your Will for (...) it will be for those who love You. Please give me Your answer in Your Word. Later on the Lord showed me Col 3:1-4.

I will write it: "since you have been brought back to true life with Me, you must look for the things that are in heaven, where I am, sitting at God's right hand. Let your thoughts be only on heavenly things, not on the things that are on earth because you have died, and now the life you have is hidden with Me, but when I am revealed, and I am your life, you too will be revealed in all your glory with Me. For all the good you do under My Name, glorifies Me. I am Love. We, us?"

Yes, we, us.

We, us?

Yes, Holy Mother, we, us.

Lord! Please help me know where I'm standing, for as it is now I feel as though the ground I stand is moving. You made sure that no one would be my spiritual director and that it will only be from You that I will receive sound teaching and counsel. Now my heart grieves for not knowing (the big problem I am facing.) You said that You will expound discipline to a nicety and proclaim knowledge with precision. Now I am being jostled harshly because I was trying to warn and correct someone. I need Your counselling. First, I plead You Father to tell me if I was wrong, reassure me, by giving me Your confirmed answer to my question from Your Word then speak to me my Lord.

Keep as your pattern the sound teaching you heard from Me, ♥ *in the faith and love that are in Me.* ♥ *You have been trusted to look after something <u>precious</u>,* ♥ *<u>guard it</u> with the help of My Holy Spirit who lives in all of you.* ♥ *(2 Timothy*

54

1:13-14) Vassula, let Me write this too: you must live your whole life according to the way you have received Me your Lord ,you must be rooted in Me and built on Me and held firm by the faith you have been taught and full of thanksgiving. ♥ *Make sure that no one traps you and deprives you of your freedom by some secondhand, empty, rational philosophy, based on the principles of this world instead of on Me, the Christ.* ♥

I want to ask the advice of Our Holy Mother too. Holy Mother of Perpetual Succour (Perpetual relief) come to my help again like in the times of persecution, intercede for me. I feel wretched for not knowing whether I was wrong in correcting this person. Maybe I was too harsh? or wrong? Please give me your advice from the Lord's Word, when I open. (I opened the Holy Bible on Philippians 4:4-6). It read: Last advice, "I want you to be happy, always happy in the Lord. I repeat, what I want is your happiness. Let your tolerance be evident to everyone. The Lord is very near."

Thank you Holy Mother, always advise me, I depend on your advice. (Our Holy Mother gave me three extra passages from the Holy Bible to encourage me and these are the following:

"It is to you, then, to preach the behaviour which goes with healthy doctrine." Titus 2:1

"Do not let people disregard you because you are young but be an example to all the believers in the way you speak and behave, and in your love, your faith and your purity." 1 Timothy 4:12

"…your zeal has been a spur to many more…" 2 Corinthians 9:3.

Lord?

I Am. My teachings are sound, so do not worry, worry about those who replace good with evil and insinuate to do good when in reality they are doing evil. Worry about the dispersions and the divisions in My Church; worry about those who ignore the Works of the Spirit, for on such I will pour out My wrath, they are the cause of the downfall of My children. ♥

My Lord, do not hide Your Holy Face from those who love You, bend down to us and come to our rescue, come back to us. Return to us. Be quick and return! Let Your children see what You can do for them, let them see Your Glory.

Pray and amend. Amend for the sins and the iniquity of this era, I need victim souls. Enliven this dead era with love. Although you are nothing, you can appease My Justice by loving Me. Glorify Me by loving Me. ♥

Remember how I lead your soul towards sanctity. Beloved, come to Me, why look elsewhere? Be prudent daughter with words, with gossip, with remarks, replace all these with silence, My Silence. ♥ **IXθYΣ** ⤜⊃

Sono con te, Padre Pio. ♥ *Recordatilo sempre.*

BY YOUR DISCIPLINE, THEY WILL LOOK UPON YOU AS HARSH

August 7th, 1989

Lord?

I Am. Look around you and understand. My Word is given to you. Recognize My Signs and fear not, blessed one. I remain in you because of your nothingness. I freed you from your chains, let no one[1] trap you. Remember, I have showered upon you learning and discernment. Beloved, let no one deceive you. Little one, I give him[2] My Peace and My Love, bless him and forgive him as I, the Lord, have forgiven him. ♥ *My Vassula, I have said that all I have given you is to cover My interests, eating directly from Me was to embellish your soul. Remain in My favour, remain in My Arms. I, the Lord, guarantee to you that I shall never fail you. By your discipline, they will look upon you as harsh, they will contradict you because My Ways are not their ways[3], but these people will be only striving against the current of a river.* ♥ *Be in Peace daughter. I bless you.*
⤜⊃ **IXθYΣ**

---

[1] This was said when I asked again the Lord about the same person whom I corrected, I knew not anymore if my discernment was just "feelings" as he had put it, or was my discernment real.
[2] That particular person.
[3] This was due to a decision inspired by God but that was received in horror.

WHERE IS THE FLOCK OF YOUR BOAST NOW?

August 9th, 1989

Message for prayer meeting of August 18th in the Catholic chapel of Caux.

Lord?

I Am. ♥ *Hear Me, beloved. I am Holy and I am preparing you to walk into the Way of Sanctity. My little children, remember not to cling on earthly possessions, cling on all that comes from above and is heavenly and holy.* ♥ *I am Holy and since you are My offsprings I desire you to live in holiness.* ♥ *Hold My Name Holy.* ♥ *Hallow My Name.*

My own, come to Me and find Me in Silence, feel Me. Allow yourselves to open entirely to Me and when you do, I then shall begin to rear you in great joy. I shall shower upon you learning and I shall rise your soul to Me, embellishing her. ♥ *I am the Constant Reminder of My Holy Word. I am Discipline and Wisdom; I am the One and Unique who rear all those who abandon themselves to Me.* ♥ *Live in My Light and find your Shelter under My Wings. Eat from Me, do not try and snap-off your navel string prematurely; allow Me to prepare you fully and feed your soul to maturity and to perfection, so that you will be able to live. Do not turn away from Me, walk with Me.* ♥

All day and all night long, I call again and again all those who still err in this wilderness seeking Me. <u>*Come!*</u> *you who err still in this wilderness saying, "I have sought My Redeemer but have not found Him." Find Me, My beloved, in purity of heart, by loving Me without self-interest; find Me in holiness, in the abandonment I desire of you; find Me by observing My Commandments; find Me by replacing evil with love; find Me in simplicity of heart. Sin no more; cease in doing evil; learn to do good; search for justice; help the oppressed. Let this wilderness and this aridity exult, let your tepidness inflame into an ardent flame. Relinquish your apathy and replace it by fervour, do all these things so that you may be able to say, "I have sought my Redeemer and I have found Him, He was near me all the time but in my darkness I failed to see Him. O Glory be to God! Blessed be our Lord! How could I have been so blind?" I shall then remind you to keep and treasure My Principles <u>so that you may live</u>.* ♥

O come to Me, all you shepherds, who have strayed from the Truth, how could you say that you have left no path of lawlessness or ruin unexplored? How could you boast that you crossed deserts without any tracks? What has boasting and arrogance conferred to My flock? Yes, where is the flock of your boast now? Can you say now that you have governed justly? Have you ever asked yourselves in sincerity if you behaved as I, The Shepherd, would have you behave? Listen then to Me and understand and take these words as a warning, you who have exchanged your shepherd's staff for a sceptre of Falsehood and who have thousands under your rule. Was it not I who relieved your shoulders of the burden? Was it not I who atoned for you? Could I have still watched you eat on the bread of tears? All I have done was to relieve you and to come to your rescue, and with great tenderness I have named you:

My shepherds.

The time is short now; I am giving you Wonders and Signs and filling the skies with Portents; I am giving you warning after warning; I am giving you Great Signs of My Love and My Mercy but you are not aware of these. Is your heart today ready to receive Me? Are your mouths ready to speak and acknowledge My Spirit of Grace that I outpour on you these days? Are your eyes willing to see? Are your ears ready to recognize My Cries of Love? Are your hearts willing to open and acknowledge My Graces of today? Are your feet ready to walk and come and prostrate yourselves at the Time of Adoration, just like the first shepherds who came to adore Me in My Nativity, glorifying Me? Are you ready to glorify Me with your heart this time and show to My flock your love and your faithfulness towards Me?

You claim you are alive and not dead, then how is it that I hear no sound from you? How is it that I hear no blessings? I am the One who reproves and disciplines all those I love. Come and repent. Fill My Sacred Heart with joy today and set your eyes on Me your Shepherd so that you may no longer err aimlessly in this desert. ♥ I am present to guide your feet into the Way of Peace, Love and Unity. I implore you then to take the Key to My Kingdom and use It, the Key to My Kingdom is, LOVE. ♥ Love in all its Glory. ♥ Love and Humility will be the other key for UNITY. ♥ Take those keys and use them, use them My beloved and be one, be One Holy People. ♥ I bless each one of you, leaving My Sigh of Love upon your foreheads. ⋗⃝ *IXθYΣ*

I want to add this to My Message:

Anyone who claims to be in the light but hates his brother is still in the dark. Forgive, forgive, as I the Lord am forgiving. Be holy, just as I am Holy. Meditate on My Message. Meditate, absorb My Message. Love loves you all.
IXθYΣ ⋗⃝

Our Holy Mother now is giving us her message:

♥ I bless each one of you. ♥ I want from you to constantly praise the Lord, thanking Him for His Message. It is still a living power among you who believe It and follow It. Be confident then in approaching the Throne of Grace, for you have His Mercy and His Love, for He is ever so Compassionate. Follow His instructions and live His Messages. Do not read Them, only placing Them aside, waiting for the following One; put Them into practice, for this will please His Sacred Heart. Listen to His Voice. ♥ My children, offer Him your problems and your sufferings and He will bless you. Keep His Name Holy. Love is among you. Come, I bless each one of you. ♥

I AM JESUS

August 12th, 1989

Jesus?

♥ *I Am. Flower, unity, bondage to Me, faithfulness, zeal, will raise you to Me. Adore Me, I am your God. Rest Me, I am your Holy Companion. Console Me, I am your Spouse. Hope in Me and Me only for I Am He-Who-Saves.*

I am Jesus. ♥

I SHALL NOT STAND ASIDE IN YOUR MISFORTUNES

August 13th, 1989

My child, My Spirit is upon you, My Hand on your hand, My Word on your lips. My Proverbs are your lamp, guiding your step. Should you keep your love for Me always and follow My precepts and keep My Commandments, Love and Faithfulness shall never fail you. ♥ I shall remain your Hope and you will remain My hereditary child. ♥ I shall overpower all evil, My child, that surround you. I shall not stand aside in your misfortunes. And you My child, will proclaim My Righteousness and My Power which save even the corpses that lie in decay. I Am The Resurrection and every nation shall glorify Me and praise Me. ♥ I will be with you till the end. ♥ We, My child? We?[1] Always remember that I, your Mother, am always near you. Pray without ceasing. ♥

---

[1]The second "we" was from Our Holy Mother.

THE DAY BEFORE ASSUMPTION

August 14th, 1989

I am the Lord, My child. Scarcely had I passed this exile, then I found you, you whom My Heart loves. I held you fast and led you back to the straight road. Nor would I leave you go? not until I bring you into My Mother's House, into the Room of Her Who conceived Me. ♥ Devote your day tomorrow and be My incense and perfume your surrounding. My Spirit rests upon you. ♥ Courage! I shall not desert you, My blessings are upon you My child. ♥

I HAVE COMMISSIONED YOU FOR THIS MISSION

August 16th, 1989

Peace My child, love Me as I love you. Feel Me, discern Me and touch Me when you see Me. Have I not asked you to do this My child?

Yes, You have Lord.

Will you do it? Now? Yes, take My Hand. Recognize Me by this Peace I am giving you. Recognize Me by the Love I am giving you. ♥

Why should I still wander in this exile? It seems endless my Lord.

I know, but I have commissioned you for this mission which you will accomplish soon. ♥ I will not abandon you and I will see to it that you glorify Me. Vassula, stay near Me, would you do this for Me?

I want to obey You my Lord always.

I shall never fail you, hold on to Me. Remember that I am your Educator. We, us?

Yes Lord, forever.

I AM MULTIPLYING MY FRUIT

August 22nd, 1989

May Your Name be praised. Let everything that breathes praise You my Lord!

Love loves you. My transcending Love and Mercy is upon you. ♥ *Lean on Me, I am your Guide. Do not doubt, My beloved, I shall always fill you. Have I not been sending you a flow of My Peace and My Love like a river? Rejoice then, for I the Lord-Am-With-you. Read My Word.*

I then open at random at Isaiah 49:6.

Later on:

My Vineyard is being cared by My Own Hand now, for I have heard the cry of distress from the needy and the just. I heard them asking for fruit so I, the Lord of Mercy, am multiplying My Fruit as I had multiplied the loaves and fishes and fed the crowds. ♥ *This fruit shall be the beauty and glory of this earth. I shall build a wall to surround My Vineyard, not to let My enemy trample on It.* ♥ *Beloved I, the Lord of the Vineyard, am among you. Courage My beloved ones, I know how you have been deprived of light and I know how you were imprisoned in darkness but I am descending to contrast this darkness with My Blazing Fire of Love. The whole earth will shine with brilliant light and I, who am Love, shall live among you.* ♥ ΙΧθΥΣ ⤝⟩

I AM FEEDING YOU WITH MY SPIRITUALITY

August 23rd, 1989

Vassula, be still, receive Me in peace. ♥ *My ways with you are in silence. Proclaim My Word left and right and never hesitate. I have given you, out of My Infinite Love, a gift to all humanity. Praise Me, love Me, keep My Name Holy, My grace is upon you.* ♥

Hear Me, once the Vintage is ready, to Me you shall come. I will annihilate you entirely into My Body. I, the Most High, will never abandon you, knowing you are a nothing. So you see how I want you? Remain nothing and you will abide in

Me. Be complacent and obedient to Me, your God, who am surrounded by thousands of myriads of angels of each order. Feel My Holiness, feel My Divinity. Let your eyes be fixed upon Me, upon My Sacred Heart. Be My flower. Come, lower your eyes when I bless you. ♥ Will you do this now? Accept this Way I have chosen for you. Be simple in heart, for this is what pleases Me. Ask Me for Wisdom and I shall multiply Her on you, ask for Discernment and I shall pour Her on you, ask these things in your adoration to Me. Come, evaluate all that you have learned from Me. I am your Teacher, your Educator, you are learning from Wisdom's Lips, see? I am feeding you My Vassula and do you know with what? Spirituality, ♥ My Fruit. My Fruit of the Tree of Life, see?

My Yahweh is good to me, His Love is everlasting, His Faithfulness endures from age to age. He has pulled me out of the pit and has healed me. He has settled my feet on a rock and steadied my steps. How many wonders You have done to us, My Lord!

MY NAME IS LOVE

August 24th, 1989

Jesus?

I Am. Little one, one kind look, one little smile from you and My Heart rebounds with joy!

Later on:

Vassula, bless Me and praise Me. Flower, are you happy to be with Me? Learn that My Name will be glorified again.

Yes, my Lord. I am happy at what You have done and Your great achievements are a blessing for us all.

Then, My child, proclaim My Name around the globe so that everyone may know that My Name is LOVE. ♥

Lord, allow me to read to You a Psalm of David called, (I opened at random) 'Hymn of Praise to Yahweh the King.' Psalm 145.

I have chosen this Psalm so that you read it out to Me. Read, My Vassula, looking at Me. I am listening. ♥

I read to the Lord the Psalm.

Come. Pray, fast, read My Word. Receive Me in Holy Communion. Pray the rosary. Adore Me. We, us?

Forever.

Later on that night:

Shall we go and rest my Lord?

Yes, let us rest, but with one condition, that I rest in your heart and you in My Sacred Heart. ♥

This made me smile and bounce with joy.

Yes, my Lord! I bless You Jesus.

I bless you, flower. ♥ *Come.*

MY WORD IS LIKE A LAMP

August 28th, 1989 - Paris

My Lord please give me Your response to this question from Scriptures, how do You wish Your Message transmitted, since You have chosen Your servant for this work already. Do You wish it to be parted or given whole as You have dictated it to me? (Answer in St Mark 4:21-25.)

My Vassula, My Word is like a lamp to give light and shine so that every soul may see Me, feel Me and return to Me, see? I wish to remove this darkness which lies heavily in this world. ♥ *I am giving you My lamp so that you place It on a lampstand and not under your beds.* ♥

Thank You my Lord Jesus.

Come flower. I bless the house that received you and bless My children, I love them infinitely, I shall never ever abandon them. Carry My Cross too on your shoulders, share My Cross too, will you do this for Me? Love loves you.

✕◯▷ ΙΧθΥΣ

A SMILE AT MY HOLY FACE
AND I SHALL FORGIVE AND FORGET

August 29th, 1989

Make my heart ready Lord to hear Your Word. I pray to You, Lord of Love, Lord of Mercy. In Your great Love answer me. God, shine on me and revive me with Your Light! Amen.

I am the Lord of the Harvest and since you have asked for labourers to reap this rich Harvest, I shall send you those helpers. ♥ Come nearer to Me now, approach. I[1] Am The Resurrection and The Life and I promise you that the Day of Devotion is not far now. Your dead will come to life again and all who still lie underground and buried by their sins, I will rise to life again. I will enlarge My Kingdom and I will restore your lands which lie now barren and deplorable to look at. I shall repeat those Words from Scriptures, "does a woman forget her baby at the breast, or fail to cherish the son of her womb? Yet even if these forget, I will never forget you[2]." I am preparing you a New Heaven and a New Earth and Love shall return to you and live among your remnant as love; and all these corpses you meet at each street-corner, I shall resurrect and like the wind I shall blow your shepherds back to New Pastures and with their shepherd's crook they will lead My flock to pasture as in the days of old. For even though their wickedness entered into My Own House and have deceived many and even though their sins made godlessness spread throughout the land, I am ready to forgive and forget and My anger would turn aside and would be as though it never existed, if even today they would recognize their fault. ♥ But, still to this day, My Sacred Heart is broken from the lack of love and by the immense number of your era's sins; sins that have pierced My Heart and blushed Heaven; sins that defiled My Sanctuary and profaned My Holy Name. Yet, if you only knew how I am ready to forgive your era's crimes by just one kind look at Me, a moment's regret, a sigh of hesitation, a slight reconsideration, a smile at My Holy Face and I shall forgive and forget. I shall not even look at My Wounds. I will efface from My sight all your iniquities

---

[1] Message for the prayer meeting.
[2] Isaiah 49:15.

and sins, had you one mere moment of regret, ♥ and all Heaven would celebrate at your gesture, for your smile and your kind look will be received like incense by Me, and that slight moment of regret will be heard like a new song by Me. Today I descend upon you full of Mercy to redeem you for the sake of My Love. My Holy Spirit of Grace will be like mist and will cover this earth. I tell you most solemnly that I shall multiply My Graces upon you. My Word shall be revealed and heard by many and I shall multiply your visions. So all those who ignore My Holy Spirit of Grace and try to suppress It will be only kicking against a goad, all their efforts will be in vain, for I, the Lord, mean to resurrect you and cultivate this desert you are living in and make oasis out of your deceiving mirages.

I, your God, stand before you and ask those who still suppress My Holy Spirit this, "how is it that you cannot tell The Times? How is it that you have decided to leave My Signs and My Wonders unacknowledged? Why are you repeatedly muffling My Voice and repeatedly persecuting My prophets? Why are you fearing and ever so eager to extinguish the little flame you see that lights _your_ darkness? Why do you rush to trample and annihilate every flower that grows with My Grace in _your_ wilderness and aridity? How is it that you want Me, your God, silent and dead?" Let Me tell you then and remind you Who I Am,

I Am The Word and Alive
I shall Act.

While I was on earth, I had multiplied My Bread and My Fishes and fed multitudes, and when Moses crossed the desert with thousands, and had nothing to eat, the Stores of Heaven opened and fed them all with manna, ♥ and so it is today. Since the earth lies in desolation and cannot produce sufficient Bread to feed you, I, with My Spirit of Grace, shall multiply My Bread to nourish you, beloved ones, you who are starved and neglected. In your days, this is called, "_The effusion of My Holy Spirit_." You will be nourished directly by Me for I mean to keep multiplying My Bread and leave no one hungry. ♥ _Woe to those who try and prevent My children from coming to Me in these times of Grace!_ So open your heart, you who still doubt, not your mind. ♥ My teachings are sound and healing. Do not fear, believe in simplicity of heart. Do not judge and abuse My angels sent by Me with My Spirit, not even the Archangel Michael when he was engaged in argument with the devil about the corpse of Moses, dared to denounce him in the language of abuse. ♥ All he said was, "let the Lord correct you[1]." Hope in Me, have Faith and Love Me. Live Holy for I am Holy. Fast and amend. Repent and offer Me your abandonment daily to Me; abandon yourselves into My Hands and I shall make out of you living columns of light.

---

[1] Jude 9.

Pray without ceasing, pray with your heart. Receive Me[1] in purity and My Graces shall pour upon you. Come at adoration time and adore Me. Confess your so many sins. Please Me, your God, and walk with Me. Follow My precepts and do not look left or right, be perfect! <u>*Be My Heaven!*</u>

O creation, if you only knew how I your God love you, you would not hesitate to follow Me in My Footprints! Why look elsewhere for consolation? My Sacred Heart is the balm to your wounds, My Sacred Heart is <u>your</u> Home. My Eyes are upon you all. I bless each one of you, I bless your families, I bless all those who read this Message leaving My Sigh of Love upon your forehead. Love loves you all. Be one. ♥ ⤳⊃ ΙΧθΥΣ

Thank You my Lord. I bless You.

PERSECUTED - IN TIMES OF PERSECUTION

September 4th, 1989

In You my soul takes warm shelter,
until the raging storm ceases again.
I bend my ear towards Heaven
to listen to Your Tender Love, ever so consoling.
I need not fear,
beside me Your Holy Presence consoles me,
there is no one who can replace Your Faithfulness.
You are my Master now, The Highest, the Lord of Lords, my Redeemer
and so I fully abandon myself to You.
My soul and my heart I commit into Your Divine Hands. Amen.

Wisdom, My child, is your Teacher and Educator. ♥ *Come, fall into your Abba's Arms for consolation, you will not find better. Put your trust in Me. Offer Me your sorrows, I make good use of them. Come and let Me be a hiding place for you. I said, "I will watch over you", I shall not leave the torrents of your persecutors, who in reality are My persecutors, sweep you away in their turbulent waves. The more they persecute you My child, and all the more I, the Lord, shall rise you and bless you, never forget this. Rely on Me. Let your prayers be like incense. Allow Me to use you as My bait for the godless, all these sacrifices will not be in vain.* ♥ *Remember, My Sacred Heart is your Home.* ♥ *We, us?*

---

[1]Holy Eucharist.

We, us, my Lord.

Be Good. ♥

COME TO HIM AS YOU ARE

Our Holy Mother's Message for the prayer meeting:

♥ Peace be with you all. God alone is Wisdom. Listen to Wisdom's Voice that calls out to you in this desert, open your ears and recognize His Voice. Jesus is calling you all, one after the other to return to Him, to return to Love and follow Him in His Footprints. My Son is aware of your weakness and your faults but you need not worry if you abandon yourselves entirely into His Divine Hands and trust Him. Come to Him as you are and offer Him your will; offer Him your love; offer Him your sufferings, your sorrows, your anguishes, your problems; offer Him everything. Trust Him. Allow Him to lead you into the depths of His Sacred Heart where you will find His Peace, this Peace your soul needs so much. ♥ I want you always to be on your guard against the evil one who encourages trouble, divisions and confusion and more than ever is fighting God's Plan of Salvation. ♥ He is deceiving even the elect, confounding them, but anyone who will call in the Name of the Lord will be heard and saved from falling, but those who will be listening to the evil one's voice will be failing to recognize the righteousness that comes from God, they will fail to recognize Love's Voice.

Remember always that the footsteps of those who bring good news is a welcome sound. ♥ Pray, beloved children, with your heart and welcome the Spirit that is now being outpoured on many nations. ♥ Feel how the days of Love's Return are approaching and that Grace is shed unsparingly upon so many of you. ♥ I will end up My Message by reminding you that you were created out of love for Love, to love your Creator, and that everything that was made to exist is made by Him and for Him; so praise Him and give glory to the One Who created you. ♥ Please Me, your Mother, and meditate Our Messages and live Our Messages. I bless you all. I bless your families. ♥ I, your Holy Mother, love you all. ♥

BE MY ECHO

September 5th, 1989

My Lord, I have spent hours meditating upon the fruitless conversation I had last night. I was too distraught to even approach You later on, I did not dare face You, out of shame. What have I said on Your behalf? Nothing, I failed You... I have neither honoured You nor praised You and yet, I delight in nothing but in You my Lord. I am pining away with love for You Lord. God keep my heart pure and away from temptations.

My Vassula, feel this love I have for you. My Mercy is Great and My Tenderness has overcome My anger. My Ways are Holy, daughter, so be holy for I am Holy. May your conversations be like music to My Ears. Wisdom, My child, is your Teacher and Educator. Avoid empty talk; avoid useless conversations, be fruitful. Speak from My Teachings. I am your Counsellor and advice shall always come from Me. My pupils I want perfect, so be perfect! Resent all things that pull you down, like gossip, empty talk. I love you and I want you perfect. Feel My Presence and glorify Me by being My reflection, speak for Me. A pupil who is in My Hands should remain pure and listen to His Master's Voice. My Grace is upon you. I desire you to keep and follow My precepts. Understand how I have placed you in My Sacred Heart since the beginning. ♥ My Spirit is upon you, I blessed you beloved. Courage, all this is not in vain; all you have to do is to love Me, adore Me and allow Me to use your hand. I wish you to be My Echo. ♥

What do You mean Lord?

I mean you to read out My Messages in prayer meetings. I feel glorified. Meditate often and accept all that I give you. Flower, I come to you with My Cross, I need to rest for a while, will you bear My Cross for Me?

My Lord, willingly.

Do remember what I am giving you, My Cross is precious. Lift My Cross, I shall return to unload It from your shoulders later on. My child, I delight in souls who are available for Me, never deny Me whatsoever. <u>Be always ready and available</u> ♥ *for Me your God.* IXθYΣ ⋉⟩

FIRE OF LOVE

September 6th, 1989

Lord?

I Am. Before you I stand, realize this Grace My Vassula.

Somehow Lord I do not realize fully, I am unable to realize but I believe.

Believe, yes. Believe in a child-like-faith, for this is what pleases Me and the Father. Do you wish to write? Yes?

I realized that I have forgotten to write.

About My Cross?

Yes Lord.

Then write it now.

Thank You my God. Later on after Jesus left with me His Cross, in a mystic way, it was like I received on me till late at night a <u>rain of sorrows</u>, it was like the world with its sins was closing upon me, sins of every kind. I suddenly among this torment, remembered Jesus in Gethsemane, I wept bitterly, on the other hand I was pleased to relieve Jesus for just a short while. Jesus later on came and took His Cross.

♥ *I am sharing It with you now, beloved.* ♥

Lord, I am listening.

Listen and hear. Have you ever heard of anyone who tried to live in devotion to Me and was never attacked or persecuted?

No Lord, some of them even died as martyrs.

Yes, so you see little one we have now confirmation of what was said in the prophecies, ♥ to this day whoever comes forth from My Mouth and raises his voice to deliver My Message is sure to be persecuted by the Cains. I call them but they refuse to listen; I beckon, but no one takes notice. They are spurning all My warnings; they make fun of the promise. Have I not said that in your days I shall *pour out My Spirit on mankind? And that I will put My Laws <u>directly</u> into your hearts and write them on your minds? <u>No prophecy</u> comes from man's initiative, how could it? My Word is given by My Holy Spirit, thus making men speak of Me. ♥ I, the Lord, have promised you New Heavens and a New Earth and My Vassula, I am in full preparation of these! but people are self-centred in your days, irreligious, heartless, preferring their own pleasure to God, but the days are fleeing and soon all this wickedness will come to its end, swept away and cleaned by My <u>Fire of Love</u>. So courage little one, hardships there will always be, but My Strength will always sustain you. Soon you will see My New Heavens and will live on a New Earth, for My promise is soon to be fulfilled and a renewal of My Church is on its way. Already you are living in the beginning of its birth-pangs, so courage, My beloved ones, you who bear My Name and are My offspring, do not despair, My Word is being fulfilled. ♥ I have said that I-shall-be-with-you and live among you, you shall eat directly from Me and I shall offer you water from the Well of Life free to anybody of you who is thirsty. ♥ My Fire is already coming down on you from Heaven and consuming you with My Great Love; I will spread this consuming Fire from nation to nation, transfiguring your wickedness into love, enticing your petrified hearts leaving them ablaze, and your lethargy into zeal for Me your God. This Sacred Hour of My Fire will be spreading among you like a burning furnace and you will be filled with My Fire of Love, the Fire of My Holy Spirit, similar to the last Pentecost. I shall renew you, enlarging My Kingdom of Truth, Unity, Justice, Peace and Love, so rejoice! Exult with all your heart My beloved, I will come and remove all your proud boasters who were one of the reasons of your dispersion and your downfall. They who muffle down My Spirit, shall be overpowered by My Breath, you shall be purified by My <u>Fire of Love</u>. ♥ Daughter, love Me, adore Me, please Me. Love loves you. I bless you My child. ♥*

We, us, Lord?

We, us My child. Come. IXθYΣ ⟩⟨⟩

APOSTASY, THE FRUIT OF RATIONALISM

September 13th, 1989

My persecutors cluster round me, my Lord, they are determined to see me crushed. Lend an ear to my prayer, guard me from the arrogant claims and from the lying tongues. My Protector allow me to take my shelter in Your Sacred Heart.

My child, leave everything into My Hands. Your accusers are in reality <u>My</u> accusers, your condemners are <u>My</u> condemners, your persecutors are <u>My</u> persecutors. My children perish for want of knowledge yet, when Knowledge is freely given from above, they reject It.

But Lord You can always spread Your Message of Peace and Love through souls who are open to You and willing. (I suddenly felt pains in the palms of my hands.)

Flower, your pains are invisible to the eye. Listen, My Divine Works will cover this earth, I shall see to it that they cover this earth and no man will be able to interfere in My Plan. Flower, be certain, for this is My Will, allow Me to use you as I wish. I love you and because of the greatness of the love I have for you, I allow you to drink from My bitter Cup. The greater My Love I have for you, the more I will allow you to drink. I, as your Spouse too, offered you My most precious jewels - have I not entrusted you with My Cross, My Nails and My Thorned Crown? See how I love you? My Ways are not your ways. I am purifying your soul, leading it into perfection and into the road of sanctification. My bride, allow Me to adorn you with My Jewels, allow Me to show you My Passion. Self-abnegation will lead you to perfection, so leave Me free to do what is best for your soul and remember, even though you do not understand fully My Words and My Ways, remember that Jesus means Saviour. ♥ ΙΧθΥΣ

Lord, those who refuse all private revelations have as an argument that the only true revelation is the Holy Bible, this we all know, but what do You say my Lord?

The Holy Bible is indeed The Truth, the True Revelation, but I have not ceased to exist. Look, I am The Word and I am active in Spirit. My Advocate is with you all, the Spirit of Truth that many tend to forget or ignore, for all that the Spirit tells you is taken from what is Mine, He is the Reminder of My Word, the Inspiration of your mind. This is why My child, I am continually recalling you the same Truths. Understand the reasons and why I am constantly stirring you up with The Reminder. ♥ *Accept My Holy Spirit of Truth. I come to remind you of My Word, I come to call you to repent before My Day comes. Child, evangelize with love for love. Beside you I am, never fear. Ecclesia will revive, since Love is the Root of the Tree of Life and is among you. I shall feed this dying generation with the Fruit of My Tree, placing It directly into their mouths.* ♥ *Allow Me to use you as My tablet.* ♥ *Eat from Me. Come, we, us? Yes, I am together with your Mother. I love you, aghapa me[1].* ♥ *Pray* ♥ *Vassula, please Me and come often to Me in between your daily work.*

---

[1]Love Me in Greek.

I often leave whatever I am doing at home to come and be with Our Lord even for two minutes, the nostalgia for God is such.

Delight Me and show Me that you are linked to Me. ♥ *Remember the ransom that I paid for you, so come to Me anytime and talk to Me. Stay small. Understand how I, out of Love, will call every soul to Me. I want you to understand that the heart of your wise is in the house of mourning, they tend to forget in their so-called great stature My Power and My Divinity; their corruptibility blinds them leaving in them an open space for Satan to speak to them, for they have shut their heart to Love; their mind and their heart are closer to the rational world than My Spiritual World. This plague has infiltrated into My Church; many of My shepherds are like those crows in the parable that I have given you* ♥ *- they are the cause of so much discordance in My Church. Their speeches and sermons lack Spirituality, faithfulness to My Word and My precepts; they repudiate My Mysteries in My Presence; they flout piety. Remember the deeds performed by their ancestor Cain? They have adopted his language, serving vice instead of virtue, immorality instead of purity. They have submitted without reservation to the slavery of sin - these Cains are alive to sin, but lifeless to My Spirit of Truth. When My Day comes they will have to answer Me and give Me accounts for not having guarded the Traditions of their Shepherd.* ♥ *Today, their mouth is condemning them and their own lips will bear witness against them,* ♥ *it is the fruit of their apostasy.*

But Lord, listen to the cry of Abel, do not let us lie alone here with no one to lift us! Your House is in ruin, Your House is our Shelter, and we have nowhere else to go. Thousands will die from lack of bread, we are living among the rubbles. Hear our voice and Your children's laments, hear Your Abel!

My child! Be praying, never cease praying. Daughter, I promise you that I shall enter into My Temple unexpectedly and with a loud Cry I shall say to Jerusalem[1], "be rebuilt!" and of the Temple[2], "let your foundations be laid" ♥ *and She will be My New City[3], alive with My Spirit, and Love shall dwell among you all My beloved remnant* ♥ *and I shall fill Her with My Trees of Life, and you, My beloved ones, will eat to satiety. I am the Light of the world and He who shines on you. Be alert and do not sleep for the days are counted.* ♥ *Have My Peace My child. I, Jesus, love you, allow Me to feed you and this starving generation. Rest now in My Sacred Heart, I shall never fail you. Love is near you.*
ΙΧθΥΣ ✝

---

[1]That is: us.
[2]That is: our soul.
[3]That is: us.

EXALTATION OF THE CROSS

September 14th, 1989

Vassula, pray more, never doubt of My Love. Respect My Law always. Make a place for My Mother, take Her into your arms. I shall wait for you in My Mother's House, into the Room of Her who conceived Me. ♥ Work for Me with untiring effort and with great earnestness of spirit. Work with love for Love. Worship Me your God and allow Me to educate you, even though it means through suffering. I am offering you My Passion. Your lips now should utter only holiness and righteousness, and for My sake adorn Me beloved one, with words that come from your heart. Adorn My Cross with wreaths of love, adorn My Cross with every drop of love in you. ♥ Endeavour and please Me now, I have given you so much! Have Me as First ♥ Let Me now feel your zeal and fervour which pleases Me. I am your Teacher and from Me you will learn. ♥ Vassula, pray and ask for My Strength, do not allow Satan to take advantage of your weakness to tempt you. ♥ Weary not of writing, remember My precepts and follow them. Come, I will enlighten you in those things that trouble your soul, am I not your Spiritual Director? so have faith in Me. Even in your awesome weakness I will be able to complete this Revelation. ♥ Understand My child that by choosing you in your poverty and your weakness, My Holy Name shall be all the more glorified. ♥ I bless you. Come, love Me. ♥

Today it was like all hell broke loose. I was constantly attacked by the demon. I am going through another trial, my soul is tormented. Later on, in the evening.

Jesus?

I Am. My angel, do not fear, just wait and see how I work. I Jesus, love you.
>< ⸓ IXθΥΣ

I adore You Holy of Holies.

Still later on: I come back to Jesus for reassurance and consolation. I feel attacked and miserable, how I fear that I'm in error!

My Lord guard me from evil and his attacks on me, keep me out of Satan's traps before my spirit fails me. Come!

"Be my Saviour again, renew my joy,
Keep my spirit steady and willing
and I shall teach transgressors the way to You,
and to You the sinners will return."

Psalm 51:12-13

Flower, have My Peace. ♥ Pray, My Vassula, so that the demon does not find you sleeping. Pray without ceasing[1]. How I pity you... To love Me is to give Me everything, I want everything you have.

Jesus, take everything You want.

Are you willing to sacrifice more for Me?

I am willing, even if the flesh is weak. I had asked You my Lord to drag me if You must. Please do it.

Ah Vassula, I want you to do things willingly. I love you.

Lord, I am willing.

Allow Me then... stop resisting Me. Abandon yourself to Me and have no fear. Peace My child. The demon hates you and is persisting his attacks on you - do not release your grip from Me, hold on to Me. ♥

KYRIE-ELEISSON

September 15th, 1989

I then went to bed to rest, it was after eleven. I prayed and prayed and before this horrible word, "sleep", overcame me. I managed to say several KYRIE-ELEISSON, CHRISTE-ELEISSON, suddenly a <u>loud</u> Voice inside me that made me startle and jump said: "I WILL HELP YOU!", Several times in the night The Voice inside me was in constant prayer for me, sometimes I repeated some of The Voice's prayer-words, although I was not understanding them. (Next morning).

---

[1] I thought Jesus wanted me awake the whole night praying. I knew out of exhaustion I would be unable. When Jesus said "how I pity you", His Voice was <u>extremely</u> tender.

74

Vassula, I want more from you. ♥ *Are you willing to give Me more?*

Jesus, take everything You like from me.

Even your life?

My life <u>is</u> Yours.

Flower, I shall make you suffer out of Love. Remember, sanctification proceeds from suffering, allow Me now to read to you a part from Scriptures. ♥ *(Hebrew 3:1-6) Remain faithful to Me. Remember, I am The All Faithful, so have confidence in Me, do not resist Me. Abandon entirely yourself to Me, I know what is best for your soul. I am Love.* ♥ ΙΧθΥΣ ⤜⚬D

MULTIPLICATION OF VINEYARDS

September 20th, 1989

My Lord and Saviour?

I Am. ♥ *My Peace I give you. My Vassula, hear Me and write. I am happy to have you near Me. I, the Lord, bless you. Are you ready?*

Beloved ones see Me your God as the Most Compassionate Holy Companion, Who sits enthroned in Glory up in the Heavens, yet at the same time, in My Divinity, I bend all the way down to you on earth to allow you all to feel Me, hear Me, understand Me and thus get to know Me, your Lord. Yes, I bend from My Throne all the way to you to lift your soul to Me and enliven you in My Light. ♥ *See Me, beloved ones, as your Spouse who will provide for you with great abundance all that you lack. I will remove your mourning veil and the shroud enwraping your nations; I will wipe away your tears from your cheeks, consoling you. I love you all with an everlasting love and out of Great Pity I will restore you. I, your Spouse, will share all that I have with you. I have here with Me, to adorn you if you wish, My most Precious Jewels, My Cross, My Nails and My Thorned Crown. I am ready to share with you, are you willing and ready to share with Me My Cross of Peace Love and Justice?* ♥ *See Me as your Redeemer.* ♥ *I rescue all those who cling to Me, I answer everyone who invokes Me. Compassionately I look upon you all, for I know how frail you are and how easily you are tempted by The Tempter. I have redeemed you all for the sake of My Infinite Love, this Love so misunderstood. I am Love and anyone living in Me lives in the Truth.*

I am the Root of the Tree of Life and the Source of Life. I have got with Me both, the Fruit of The Tree of Life and The Living Water from My Everlasting Wells. ♥ Come then to Me; come and have your fill; come and eat; come and drink from My Living Water all you who thirst, I shall never deny you. I, God, shall wean you to real Food, Food that will last in you so that your poverty-stricken soul may be able to live.

Your lands have turned into wastelands and the scorching winds have dried up your throats, but I, who am your Saviour, see from above all these iniquities, so do not say, "the Lord has forgotten us". I am The-All-Faithful and My elated Love I have for you is saving you. I have never turned away My Holy Face from you. (One agio omga elneah rima, rima, purdripgara nedro ha unu Amen rima[1].) Write; ♥ I shall spread Peace and Love in the lands of your dead, I mean to spread My Peace and My Love all around and in all the nations Without-Love. ♥ I mean to overthrow all Injustice and this dead era will be resurrected and shall follow Me into the New Earth I am preparing for her, and under New Heavens she will glorify Me and praise Me all day and all night long. Have you not yet understood how My Holy Spirit of Grace is preparing you, Vineyard after Vineyard, spreading Them gently and with so much love in every nation? Have you still not understood how your Holy Mother and I are stretching out Our Arms over you, covering you with Our Blessings, and preparing you, Vineyards. Vineyards which We shall keep multiplying, Vineyards which will produce enough fruit to feed a multitude. My Spirit of Grace is like a Vine putting out graceful shoots, My blossoms bear the fruit of Love and Peace. Approach Me, you who desire Me, and take your fill of My fruits, for memories of Me are sweeter than honey. Inheriting Me is sweeter than the honeycomb. They who eat Me will hunger for more, they who drink Me will thirst for more. ♥ Whoever listens to Me will never have to blush, whoever acts as I dictate will never sin[2]. ♥ Have I not said that in the days to come, I will put out shoots that will bud and blossom and fill the whole world with fruit? This fruit will increase by My Light and Heaven will pour upon you Its Dew to refreshen your dry throats. ♥ I am bestowing all these blessings on My People. ♥ Feel loved by Me, My little ones. Love loves you and blesses each one of you, leaving My Sigh of Love upon your foreheads. ΙΧθΥΣ ⋉⊃ *Be one.* ♥

---

[1] I suddenly had a language unknown to me.
[2] Ecclesiasticus : 24:17-22

I AM THE ROOT OF THE TREE OF LIFE

September 20th, 1989

My Lord, You who are the Root of the Tree of Life and Love in Itself and that from Your Fruit, You are giving us an Everlasting Life, be blessed. Your leaves that never wither or dry are made out of pure white gold and from them emanate a vivid light. I adore, I hope, I believe and I love You, please forgive those who do not adore, do not hope, do not believe nor love You. Look after us Immanuel. I bless You, I bless You, You who are my Counsellor during the nights, filling me with ceaseless prayers, praying over me. I know that You will not abandon my soul, since You are revealing **Your Path** of Life to us, our hand in Your Hand. Save us in Your Love. You are the Source of our hope to see the New Heavens and the New Earth, Lord.

I am the Root of The Tree of Life and from Me emanates Everlasting Life. ♥
Flower, read the Scriptures.

PETER'S CHAIR

Jesus means that I open at random the Holy Bible and I shall come upon what He desires me to read. I open on Isaiah 40:9.

Read it and write it. "Go up on a high mountain, joyful messenger to Zion. Shout with a loud voice, joyful messenger to Jerusalem. Shout <u>without</u> fear. Say to the towns of Judah, "<u>Here is your God!</u>" Your New Jerusalem is at hand. I, God, am descending in this era, stumbling on corpses. All that I had been dreading has come true. I descend to find no faith, no hope, no love and My lambs that I left to graze in My Green Pastures, I find starved and lamentable to look at. Living among the rubbles they seek for some shelter and some food, but find none. With hope they lift stone after stone looking for a crumb, or perhaps a seed they could sow, but instead of a crumb or a seed they find scorpions ready to sting and fill them with their venom. My lambs err from town to town, to only find the remains of what was once a Great City. Yes, I am speaking of Jerusalem, but only a few are ready to hear Me. I call each one of My shepherds by their name, but very few hear My Voice. I stifle, I suffocate to see them filled with dead words.

Hear Me, I have, daughter, called you to serve the cause of right; I have taken you by the hand and formed you to witness; I have shown you the Truth and I have unveiled your eyes to see whom I had chosen to sit in Peter's Chair and to whom I once said, "you are Peter and on this rock I will build My Church. And the gates of the underworld can never hold out against it. I will give you the keys of the kingdom of heaven: whatever you bind on earth shall be considered bound in heaven; whatever you loose on earth shall be considered loosed in heaven[1]." I had given this man this Authority, and today you are trying to overthrow him and steal his shepherd's staff so that you rule with the sceptre of Falsehood and Vice. Peter? Peter-of-My-Lambs, My beloved shepherd, I know how your heart lacerates and bleeds in rivers for this ungrateful and unfaithful generation, I know how they have turned your eyes into a spring of tears, I know how many of your brothers have turned their backs to you. These are, My beloved, those shepherds who know nothing, feel nothing, they all go their own way, each after his own interest, serving Folly instead of Wisdom, Lust instead of Poverty, Disobedience instead of Obedience. I gaze from My Cross on all who inhabit the world, and I am telling you who people many nations, that soon the Hour is with you, the time is almost up and the days will not last long before you pass your nights weeping. You unfaithful shepherds, shepherds who sin against Me by faithlessness, you who cry Peace! When there is no Peace. Return to Peter all you who have strayed away in different direction. Serve Me, why serve Unholiness? Be Mine, not the Rebel's. Why are you so willing to serve the Rebel? Even foreigners, even these have listened to My Voice and have understood My Words. My Principles are Holy and I tell you most solemnly that Holy They shall remain forever and ever. ♥ *Daughter, read My Word.*

The Lord indicated to me where. Again in Matthew 5:18-19.

Read and write, "I tell you solemnly, till heaven and earth disappear, not one dot, not one little stroke shall disappear from the Law until its purpose is achieved. Therefore the man who infringes even one of the least of these commandments and teaches others to do the same will be considered the least in the kingdom of heaven; but the man who keeps them and teaches them will be considered great in the kingdom of heaven." Child, rest now, delight My Soul with your child-like faith. Come, rest in Me. I, the Lord, bless you. Love Me. ♥

Praised be our Lord!

---

[1]Matthew 16:18-19.

I WILL INCREASE MY CALLS

September 22nd, 1989

Our Holy Mother's Message:

Beloved daughter, Abba loves you all. ♥

Praised be the Lord.

Tell My children this: peace be with you. My sons and daughters, allow yourselves to open so that Jesus enters into your heart and heals you. My Message today shall remind you who is Jesus. Jesus is the Source of Sublime Love, the Light of the world. To save you He endured the Cross, disregarding the shamefulness of it. He is meek and humble. Come and acknowledge Him as your God, for acknowledging Him is the perfect virtue. Feel Him; feel His Holy Presence. Learn how to count Him among you; learn to say "we, us". Do not forget Him in between your prayers; have Him constantly in your heart, have Him locked in your heart. ♥

Do not take Our Messages as threats, Our Messages are Messages of Love and Peace, coming out of God's Infinite Mercy. Delight God by reflecting before opening your lips to utter whatsoever. Do not allow your lips to condemn you, all that you utter let it prove that you are God's children with a spirit of holiness, submission and purity. Be zealous to serve the cause of right. Today I shall ask you this question, you who hear Me, "do you love your neighbour as yourself?" I want to remind you that even in your weakness you can achieve perfection if you allow yourselves to be guided by the Lord. Abandon yourselves to Him daily, offer Him your will without fear, He knows your capacity and will never ask from you anything that can harm you. ♥ Elevate your souls by praying. Grow in holiness, grow in the Love God is offering you so abundantly. Never listen to the Rebel, leave no empty space in your heart for the demon to be allowed to tempt you. Abide only in Faith, Hope and Love, let these be your fruit filling your heart. ♥ God-is-among-you to provide your soul all that it lacks. The Vineyards of the Lord shall multiply and They shall yield enough fruit to feed thousands. The Creator is preparing you to enter into the New Era of Love. See your Creator as your Holy Companion, your Father, your Spouse, your Redeemer, your Advisor. Praise the Lord for His Merciful Calls, for He says, "I will increase My Calls and will not diminish them. I will draw My children very close to Me to nourish them by My Own Hand. I shall place My Law in their heart and they shall abide and be sheltered in My Love. I will comfort them as I lead them back to Me, back to the Truth. I shall wean them

79

to real Food, dead will be the days where no blessings were welcomed. I shall unwrap the shroud covering the dead and with My Light resurrect them." Love will return to you as Love and live among you. ♥ Meditate on Our Messages and live Our Messages. Feel secure, for We are with you all. ♥ I bless you and your families. Pray and I shall be praying with you. ♥ Come daughter. ♥

THE WAY TO ME IS NARROW AND DIFFICULT

September 24th, 1989

My soul glories in the Lord, come and help me hear You, feel You, so that my soul can delight in Your Light.

Beloved, feel loved by Me. Sin no more. Evaluate all that you have learned from My Mouth. Courage daughter. Remember, I am beside you and I tell you truly that My Word given to you shall spread like morning mist. Allow Me to use you daily, allow Me to infuse in you My Burning Desires, I want My altar constantly ablaze for Me your God. You are bound to Me, yet never more free. ♥ From the beginning I never imposed on you anything, I have always respected your liberty. Remember how I led you step by step, closer and closer everyday to Me? Pray My Vassula and I shall give you My Strength and the will to continue in perseverance, for My Shoulders are weary carrying My Cross and I need willing victim-souls of My Love to rest Me and share My Cross with Me. I love you all to folly and would not want to see any of you lost. I need to share My sufferings with generous souls. ♥ Do you now understand Me, My Vassula? The Way to Me is narrow and difficult, it will require from you many more sacrifices than you are giving Me now, but I shall help you carry on. Do not fear as you do sometimes, I am leading you to sanctification. I am before you all the time, so do not resist Me. Abandon yourself to Me, remember how My Love saves. ♥ Desire Me and have Me as first. Never cease praying. Do not give a foothold to the devil to tempt you. Cease doubting, for how long yet are you going to doubt? Flower, I know that you are frail and weak but believe Me, I bear your weakness on My Shoulders, I will carry you all the way to My House. I, your God, have adopted you, have I not? So will I leave My "adopted child" just because you lack strength and are still being wretched? Never. ♥ I have adopted you to be My Own and you are now truly Mine, feel My joy! I have raised you in tenderness and I have accepted you as you are, with all your sins, your weakness and your faults to show, through you, to all the world how My Mercy reaches from age to age and how in spite of your sins and your imperfections I am forgiving you fully and I am ready to adopt you all as My children so that you can all share My Kingdom in Heaven. My Love reaches from generation to generation and always will. Take My Hand then and allow Me to lead you all to My House, come now to Me as you are. I love you, My child. Come as you are to Me and I shall carry you all on My Shoulders with love into My House. ♥ IXθYΣ ⤢⟫

I HOLD THE KEY

September 26th, 1989

My Lord?

I Am. Never doubt. ♥ *Remember, it is I who hold the keys to many doors.* ♥ *I will open them one after the other, each one at the right time. Do you understand this, My child? You need not worry, you need not haste, I, the Lord, will bring up everything on the right time.* ♥ IXθYΣ ⤢⟫

ADORE ME IN SILENCE
HEAR MY WEDDING SONG

September 28th, 1989

My Lord, it is not so easy to grasp Your thoughts, I want to be pleasing in Your Eyes, sometimes I feel You are hiding away from me. Is it my sins that make You hide?

Vassula, My love for you shall never exhaust. Pray more, let Me remind you to pray now and then the prayers I have given you. Pray the psalm I have chosen for you[1]; ♥ *allow Me to use you now and then and when I wish; allow Me to be free and reign over you.* ♥ *So do not fear, depend now fully on Me. I have elevated you to be with Me and no one else. I will always extirpate all My rivals who approach you, never will I leave them distract you, taking your mind away from Me. You are now Mine and forever. Come to Me and adore Me in Silence.* ♥ *Depend on Me fully now, it rejoices Me; depend on Me just as I have taught you.*

---

[1] Psalm 86.

Meditate in silence, thirst for Me, I like it! Desire Me, be in constant thirst for Me, your God. Cease to wonder all the time, am I not the Lord of Lords? Never doubt of My Works. I know your capacity, so love Me boundlessly, willingly immolating yourself for others. Remain faithful to Me. My Spirit is upon you and will always guide you. Speak to Me, why neglect Me? Are your worries more important than My Presence? Lean on Me, I am offering you millions of times My Shoulder for you to lean upon. ♥ Come, I want to see your face up and lit with joy, look what I have given you! Be like a sunflower, turn your face towards Me and follow My Light, I am not hiding My Face from you! Flower! If you stop drooping your head only, and look up at Me, your worries will leave you. ♥ Have confidence in Me, offer Me everything and I shall help you. Come, all these sacrifices will not be in vain, your Jesus loves you[1]. Have you nothing to tell Me now?

Yes my Lord I have. I want to tell you that You are constantly in my mind all day and all night long, I meditate on You all night long; I end up my day with You on my mind and begin my day with You on my mind. My soul clings on You.

Then rejoice! Let your heart and soul rejoice! Your King came to you in your bareness and your poverty, your King has covered your nakedness with His Love and His Peace and in His Tenderness adorned you majestically with His most precious Jewels. Have I not adorned your head with My Thorned Crown? Have I not entrusted you with My Nails? Are we not sharing My Cross as our matrimonial bed? Have I not revealed to you My Beauty? I have espoused you to Myself. Speak daughter!

My Lord, whatever I say will never be enough! Have mercy on my misery, I trust in Your love, I will be glad to sacrifice more.

Then open your ears and hear My wedding song. I know what you are made of: dust and ashes. Come out of your gloom by lifting your head, look at Me. I am He who has risen you and He who keeps your soul tranquil and quiet. Enveloped in My Arms I guard your soul. I have given you everything so that I raise your soul to Me. I have shown My Infinite Mercy and I have favoured you, giving you to drink from My Cup, have I not? Seek to please Me daughter; seek My Ways, My Ways are Holy. So beware of complaining about nothing, I have always been near you guiding you. Come always to Me in simplicity of heart My Vassula, for your days on earth are but the passing of a shadow, a superficial passage that will fade away. Nothing on earth lasts forever, keep then My precepts and follow My Commandments. I have entrusted you with My most Precious Jewel, guard It, embrace It and hold fast on to It; My Cross of Peace and Love shall be the sweet

---

[1] There was a moment's silence.

torment of your soul. Your eagerness in sharing My Cross should be an ardent flame in you as it is in Me; your thirst for My Cross should grow like Mine. By now you must have realized how I show My Love, yes, by allowing you to suffer. Soul! I have turned your aridity into a flowing spring; your hostility towards Me into tenderness; your apathy into fervour for My Cross; your lethargy into nostalgia for your Home and your Father. Rejoice soul! Your King has unwrapped the shroud covering your body and has risen you as He has risen Lazarus, to possess you.

Oh Jesus! You <u>are</u> not very discerning in selecting!

My choice is Mine. ♥ I want you to inherit and share My Kingdom in Heaven with Me. Every Work I do is for My Glory. ♥ Look! You are free now My dove, I am your Master and to Me you will always come and in My Sacred Heart you will always rest. My Sacred Heart is your cote and your refuge, see? I have trained you to recognize Who your Master is and what He requires of you; ♥ <u>your Master and your King requires love from you now</u>. Come, return My Love, like a mirror reflect My Love. I have created you out of Love to love Me, never ever forget this. ♥ ♥ ♥ ΙΧθΥΣ ⊂▷

PRISONER OF LOVE
HONOUR MY HOLY SACRAMENTS

September 29th, 1989

Alleluia! The Lord bends down to listen to me every time I call. My gaze is fixed upon You my Lord. I meditate on You without cease, You are my food, my bread and my wine. I need nothing more in this hostile world, my soul is thirsting for You, my lips are parched for You. You are my God who sought me and founded me in my wretchedness. Allow me to abide in Your Sacred Heart.

Rejection you will never have from Me. ♥ Every time you come to receive Me, My Sacred Heart rebounds with joy. I have made Myself ever so tiny in the little white Host. In taking Me you are accepting Me, and in accepting Me in this way you are acknowledging The Truth. I and you are then one, you are in Communion with Me, what more delightful to be together with Me your God? What more pure and holy meeting? I, your God, meeting you My creature, ♥ I your Redeemer and you My redeemed one. I, Jesus, love you to folly, how could some of you doubt of My Love, defiling this pure and holy Love? How could so many of you doubt of My Holy Presence in the Host? My Holy Eucharist should not be spilled or treated as though It was not holy. If you only understood fully what I am offering you and Whom you are receiving in you, you would be blessing Me without cease. Look! Even My Angels gazing at you from above desire this Meal you can have, but not they, yet many of you do not seem to perceive Its Fullness. I am the Prisoner of Love behind each Tabernacle, waiting and hoping to see you come.

Approach all you who err still in this wilderness, come to Me pure and clean, let Me rejoice in you. So please My Heart further by repenting, recognizing your sins. Do not say, "why confess? I have nothing to tell My confessor." Do not be one of these who have lost the sense of sin. You are far from being perfect, yet some of you behave as though you are unsullied and have reached perfection. Be humble, be humble. Your sins can easily be detected if you pray in sincerity of heart and ask Me to help you detect them. Blessed are those who obey My Law and follow My precepts, honour My Holy Sacraments; blessed are all those who come to Me in full Faith to eat Me and drink Me. ♥ I am Holy, so treat Me with Holiness so that I pour on you at this moment ever so Holy, My graces which will enliven your soul. I do not hide My Riches away, I give Them freely even to the least of you. Come, I am so eager to be with you, so do not hurry and do not be impatient in your prayers; do not flout piety; reflect and meditate on My injunctions. Although you cannot see Me, I tell you that My Hand is upon each one of you, blessing you, leaving My Breath upon you all. Be one. ♥

✝ ΙΧθΥΣ

RATIONALISM IS DEADLY

September 29th, 1989

It is good for me to have to suffer, the better to learn your statutes. (Psalm 119:71) I <u>know</u> that You make me suffer out of Love. You are <u>lavishing</u> Your love on me because You have made me Your offspring. I know that You train those You love, <u>You are Lord a consuming Fire!</u>

My Vassula, every day that goes by brings you closer to Me. Day after day I give you proofs of My Love and that it is I, who manifest Myself to you in this way, ♥ but your generation is plaguing you, the plague of this generation is called Rationalism, and Rationalism is Deadly. ♥ Rationalism descends from the Prince of Darkness and all those that live in Darkness have this disease among other diseases; ♥ but all that comes from Me comes from Light and when I descend to My chosen souls to enlighten this dark world you are living in, through them, <u>My</u>

Light is disturbing all those whose deeds are evil. _My Light is disturbing them so much that they are ready to kill because their wickedness is exposed and their nakedness is revealed for every eye to see. Their reaction does not so much differ from Adam's and Eve's, who were trying to escape and hide from Me._ ♥ _Yes, My child of light, you belong to Me and this is why Darkness is your enemy and your persecutor, the offsprings of Darkness will always persecute My offsprings._ ♥ _My Light is disturbing them, the Hour of Light upon your nations is terrifying these peoples, since they spent a lifetime conceiving mischief and breeding rationalism. The Hour of Light is an unceasing torment for these dark souls who rest in tombs, but I shall let My Light shine on them. My Light shall pierce this Darkness and with My Warm Rays revive everything that has been lain waste. Darkness will no longer cast her shadow over the nations. My Light will flourish their tender buds and My Rays will open their blossoms and the earth's branches will turn green again._

Never cease praying. My child, Love loves you eternally. ⤚⤑ IXθΥΣ

FALSEHOOD IS PERSECUTING THE TRUTH

September 30th, 1989

I will rejoice in Your Love for ever, My Jesus, every hour of the day I shall not cease in proclaiming Your Love and Faithfulness because Love _is_ built to last forever and firmly rooted in the Heavens and on the earth. There will come a time when no one will be able to deny this love!

My child, lean on Me and let Me savour the love you have for Me. ♥ _Ah daughter.... all I ask from you is love, acknowledge My Love. Let your prayers be like incense; let your heart be transformed into an incense bowl, pleasing Me, appeasing My Justice and My Wounds I receive from My best friends. Feel the love I have for you all. Believe with a child-like-faith, never try to rationalize, for in doing so you will only be removing the Veil-of-Childhood that covers your eyes. My Mysteries should be respected as Mysteries, and My Presence in this way I have given you is also a Mystery._ ♥ _My desire is that you give Me every drop of love you have in your heart and I in My turn I shall keep filling your heart from Mine._ ♥ _Bear My Cross for a while now and allow Me to rest. I want My children to know that in mortifying your senses and your body, all is used by Me in Celestial Works. I use your sacrifices to deliver souls from Purgatory; I warm up hearts on earth for their conversion; I purify your soul. All that you offer Me is used for reparations; it appeases My Justice from flaring up and striking you; it relents Me,_ *it relents Me. My Mercy is Great.*

I felt the devil rage, attacking me.

Do not fear. I, the Lord, am with you, I never leave you a second alone. It is normal that the devil is raging. If you knew how he hates those I love in a special way. Understand then, My child, why he attacks you; but I am protecting you under My Cape, I will never have him touch you and because of this then he penetrates ever so maliciously into souls who listen to him, placing these victims on your path to hound you and persecute you[1] to reduce you to total silence. Satan, by using these people as his weapon is determined to silence you because you are like a trumpet on the roofs of all houses, crying out loud The Truth given to you with all My Authority. My child, keep on crying out, keep on shouting at the top of your voice. Be My Echo, for your voice is My Voice, you come from My Mouth so keep on shouting. Shout to the Nations The Truth! You need not fear. ♥ My persecutors will all be blown away, because in reality they are My persecutors and not yours. Falsehood is persecuting The Truth, Obscurity the Light, but in the end I, the Lord, shall prevail. ♥ Stay near Me, little one, devote yourself to Me; allow Me to breathe in you always, be My headrest. Have My Peace; augment your faith, it pleases Me. ♥ Come. We, us?

Yes Jesus, we, us.

THE DESIRE OF GOD

October 2nd, 1989

Jesus?

I Am. Come, My child, take My Hand and we shall work together. I am Wisdom, your Teacher, so depend on Me only. Learn that no one is able to give you better knowledge than I, who Am the Lord. ♥ Listen and write: ♥

Creation! Soul! You who read Me, you who hear Me, praise Me, glorify Me, praise Me from morning till night, praise and extol Me without ceasing; amend for those who never praise Me nor glorify Me; bless Me, worship Me and desire Me. Have no one told you of the Song of the Three Young Men?[2] Then learn and

---

[1] This reminded me of my vision (29.1.89).
[2] To be found in the book of Daniel 3:52-90.

proclaim this among the nations, the Spirit of Truth is with you all.

My little children, I will remind you that I am God whom you come to meet and pray. Since I am a living God, I feel if you come to Me with a lip prayer. I want you to desire Me, desire Me, desire Me; thirst for Me, seek Me eagerly. Have no other desire but Me; desire to be in constant link with Me; desire to please Me; desire to feel Me and hear Me; desire My Presence, let nothing of this world deceive you ♥ for if the world hates you, remember that it hated Me before you. <u>Place Me as First</u>, do not wound My Sacred Heart by neglecting Me. Near Me you will feel My Love, My Peace and this harmony of Heaven that I have with My Angels can be yours too if you come nearer to Me. I love you all with an eternal love, a love you are unable to understand on earth. Come and I shall show you, if you are willing, what <u>True Life in God</u> means. <u>I tell you solemnly that anyone who lives in Love lives in Me, your God, and I live in him</u>. Wake up from your sleep, wake up from your lethargy and do not deceive yourselves saying, "but I love the Lord and He knows it, I always have and so my conscience is clean." Today I am telling you to return to Me. If you ask, "but how are we to return?" I will tell you, by converting yourselves, and if you say, "but we are converted, how are we to convert?" I will tell you then, by desiring Me, by thirsting for Me. Seek Me the Holy One; come and adore Me. Let your portion be Me, your Holy One. Let your eyes dissolve in tears of love in My Presence. Be alert, be alert, if you knew how much more alarming it is not to know the cause of your sins, not to feel your sins and to have lost the sense of what is good and what is evil! Resist the devil's tactics; be awake in your praer; be in constant prayer to Me. Pray without ceasing. Let Me feel you are in a constant desire for Me, a constant prayer. A prayer coming from your heart is, <u>The Desire of God</u>.

My beloved ones, if you wish to grow in My Love do away with your lethargy and your lip-prayers. <u>To be in constant prayer is to desire Me your Lord</u>. ♥ Try and understand My Message. Desire Me with joy; desire Me with your heart and not with your lip, let Me hear you cry out "<u>Abba!</u>" So come to Me as little children again, return to Me and <u>ask Me with your heart, seek Me with your heart</u>. Come to Me, offering Me your heart. Devotion will embellish your soul. Do not stray from the Truth, for the Truth is Love, so come to Me full of Love, drawing from My Heart. <u>Be in the Truth, live in the Truth by desiring Me without ceasing</u>, do all these things so that you may live. ♥

In these last days I am outpouring My Spirit of Grace on all mankind. Have you not noticed that I give even to the least? My Spirit of Grace is being poured on your generation to teach you to love Me. I come as the Reminder of My Word; I come to brighten this darkness with My Light; I come to warn you and wake you up from your deep sleep. I do not come with wrath, I come with Love, Peace and Mercy to unveil the shroud of death enwraping your nations. I come to remind you that I am Holy and holy you should be living; I come to remind you and teach you how to pray. I have given you everything to rise your soul to Me and share My Kingdom. I am coming to you as a Beggar pleading you. I am coming to you as Wisdom, teaching you all over again the knowledge of Holiness, ever so ardently. I offer you My Heart. Ever so humbly I offer you Myself every single day as your daily Bread; I give you Food to eat to your heart's content, eating your fill. So come to Me, return to Me and praise Me your God. ♥ *I bless you all, leaving My Sigh of Love on your forehead. Love loves you all. Be one.*

✠⟩ ΙΧθΥΣ

I AM THE GOOD SHEPHERD

October 5th, 1989

My Jesus?

♥ *I Am. Peace My child, together we shall work. Have My Word[1], then write it. (I open at John 10:14-16). Write, "I am the Good Shepherd, I know My own and My own know Me, just as the Father knows Me and I know the Father and I lay down My Life for My sheep. And there are other sheep I have that are not of this Fold, and these I have to lead as well. They too will listen to My Voice and there will be only one Flock and one Shepherd."* ♥ *At this the earth will grow radiant, I will spread integrity and peace and the earth shall grow once as before with fresh things.* ♥

I got up and kissed Jesus on His right cheek. I did this on the Sacred Heart statue in front of me. I saw Jesus with my heart sitting near me and just after I kissed him, He had lifted His Hand to touch His cheek just where I kissed Him, looking like a Happy Child. Jesus asked me to write down this episode.

My beloved, it is to show you how I feel everything. ♥ *Come, My child, let us be together, let us be inseparable.* ♥

---

[1] Jesus means through Scriptures.

TURIN - DAME DU ROSAIRE

October 7th, 1989

Peace be with you. ♥ *Say after Me this, "Jesus I love you, Jesus forgive my sins, Jesus relieve me from my doubts, Jesus do not allow the evil one to approach me."*

Our Holy Mother:

Flower, by loving Jesus His Wounds are soothed. Love loves you. ♥

TURIN - SUNDAY

October 8th, 1989

I visited the Basilica of the Holy Shroud. After having prayed and talked to Jesus, we went out and I felt an immense joy in me; I praised the Lord for showing me His Great Love, a love I never knew all those past years. Just then I was covered by a strong incense fragrance. My joy doubled, for His Sign.

We walked to San Domenico Church, where two years ago my cousin saw an apparition of our Holy Mother, above the church's side door, to call us in, since it was the Feast of Our Lady of the Rosary and we did not know then. We were early for Mass and so while sitting I was in adoration to Jesus. I was speaking to Him in French, realizing this I said to Him in English: "why am I speaking French to You? I'll speak to You in English," and immediately Jesus said to me: "I would rather you speak to me with your heart." And He showered me with His Incense fragrance.

I NEED VICTIM SOULS

October 9th, 1989

Peace be with you. ♥ *Pray for those who still attempt to destroy My Vineyard by night. Pray My Vassula that My wrath decreases on these souls.* ♥ *I have Wounds that make My Father's Justice flare up by all the crimes of this generation.* ♥ *When He sees how they treat My Atonement and how bruised, scourged and torn My Body is, His urge to scatter the nations, reducing them into a heap of dust is great, even My angels tremble upon what can come on the whole earth. My Abba is relenting only because of those few souls who immolate and who love Me. Ah Vassula! My pains are great. Little soul, I love you to passion. I refine and purify generous souls, souls who are willing to amend and expiate for others. I need victim souls to become victims of love, victims of My Passion, victims who die to their own self, victims who are willing to share My Cross. I need generous souls who are willing to be formed by My Own Hand into living crucifixes, how else would I keep My Father's Hand away and from striking you? The world has to change, convert and live holy. I will no longer allow My Holy Name to be profaned.* ♥ *My Passion is being repeated in My Mystical Body and I suffer as much as I had suffered in My Passion. I tread, daughter, repeatedly on the same Path to Calvary, every single hour I am re-crucified. I who Am Love, do I deserve all this?*

Breathe on us to become victims of love and be able to expiate for others Lord Jesus.

My Own. ♥ *You can relieve Me with your love. Love Me and repair, fast and sacrifice, all these things withhold My Father's wrath. Vassula, allow Me to fill you, allow Me to use you, aahh daughter... your tears are consoling Me. My flower, let your tears dissolve in Mine and be one, when My Father will see your tears in Mine He will be appeased.* ♥ *I, Jesus, bless you. I bless all the sacred objects you have in your home.* ♥ ¹ *Repeat this!*²

Oh how I want to console You!

Ah Vassula, you are consoling Me by desiring to console Me. I have created you to console Me; I have created you to rest Me, to love Me and to share with Me My sufferings. ♥ *Remember, I am soon with you.* ΙΧθΥΣ ><D

---

¹I said to Jesus: "Oh how I want to console You!"
²Jesus like taken by surprise exclaimed, "repeat this!" I felt His Sacred Heart rebound with joy.

PRAY IN SILENCE
THE GREAT APOSTASY

October 10th, 1989

My souls yearns for You today. I have given You my heart and my soul to form. My Lord has come to me in all His splendour and majesty to lift my soul to Him to show me His Great Love and Mercy. He has lifted me with tenderness to acclaim to all nations His Infinite love and His Mercy. His Love is everlasting.

Beloved, stay small so that you may easily creep into My Sacred Heart. ♥ *Love loves you. Listen and write:*

Peace be with you all. ♥ *I am Peace, I am Love, I come to your nation out of My Boundless Mercy to stretch My Vineyard in your land too so that its Fields yield enough fruit to feed your dying nation. My Divine Works are spreading all over this earth and all are good since they supply every want in due time.* ♥ *Listen to My Voice devout children and blossom like the flowers blossom when spring comes, blossom with My Rays of Pure Light shed upon you. I am filling your nation's darkness with blessings; I want to healr your poor soul; I want to rest your weary soul, so thrust yourselves into My open Arms, I am your Saviour who calls you to* <u>return to Me</u>. *You see My children, the spirit of lethargy has veiled many nations leaving many of them in deep sleep and I, from above, watch all this with agony and with pain.* ♥ *Today I, the Lord, am in search of your heart since what I need is love, a return of love. Come, come to Me with simplicity of heart, as a child approaching his father with confidence. Come to Me too, showing Me your weakness and telling Me your problems,* <u>let your Father in Heaven hear you</u>. *I am love, the Sublime Source of Love, who thirsts for a return of Love, do not refuse My plea. Refuse the temptations surrounding you, My child, refuse to give Satan a foothold.* ♥ *If you only knew how near you I Am and how eager I am to lift your soul to Me and wean you to real Food! Try and understand Me, try and perceive My Will, do not be here only to satisfy your curiosity, be here to learn. Widen the space of your heart only for Me to allow Me to make My Home in you.*

Do not suffocate My Spirit in you with immorality, rationalism, egoism and other sins; do not suffocate Me, leave My Spirit to breathe in you and <u>lift your eyes to Heaven and pray in silence as I have been praying to My Father</u>. *Pray with your heart and He will hear you, pray with love and He will not refuse you, pray with Faith and He will not deny your plea. All that you do, do it with love for Love* ♥ *and I will not remain silent or unmoved or unresponsive to your plea, for I am full of Mercy and full of Tenderness.* ♥

*I am the Good Shepherd who seek among the rubbles My lambs and My sheep.
I come to seek you with My Heart in My Hand to offer It to you; I come to seek
you in your poverty to remind you again that you are not fatherless and that you
all belong to Me; I come to remind you that in My Father's House there is a room
for you My child[1], a room which belongs to you. My Soul is yearning for you.
My Soul is in unspeakable distress when every time a room is left void for eternity.
I, the Lord, bring to you Heaven in My Hands[2] as a gift for you, to offer It to you
but My enemy wants to prevent you from receiving It. So many times he is using
poor souls to reduce My Voice into silence, rebuking the Graces of My Holy Spirit
and thus injuring My Body beyond recognition. Hiding behind a Cloud of
Darkness these souls become Masters of Evil and Vanity, refusing to grasp My
Ways, these people weigh heavily in My Heart. Fearlessly they come to Me void
and empty handed; they make fun of the Promise. They are once again placing
in My right Hand a reed, jeering at Me, then remove it from My Hand to strike My
Head with it; then they go down on their knees to do Me homage so that people
outside the Church should speak well of them. ♥ Those sacrileges are re-
crucifying Me every single day; they are dragging Me to calvary repeatedly; they
hate Me for no reason. Ah, My children... these people have turned My Eyes and
the Eyes of My Mother into an eternal waterspring.*

*Listen to My Cry from My Cross, for innumerable multitudes are constantly falling
into the eternal fires; listen to the Spirit that brings life. Your nations have grown
coarse at heart and have forsaken the fountain of knowledge. ♥ Turn your eyes
to Me! Lift your heads to Me! Come and absorb My Light, allow Me to remove
your shroud, enwraping your nation. I am the Guardian of your soul and of your
heart who implore you for a return of love, a love without self-interest. Die to
your own self and allow your heart to be directed by the Spirit and the Spirit will
lead you to the Truth, acknowledging Me. Listen to My Voice, the Voice of My
Spirit. Augment your prayers and live holy, be holy for I am Holy. ♥*

*If My House lies in ruin today and atheism reigning in so many hearts[3] it is
because your generation refuses Me a place in their heart. I come to find no love,
no faith and no hope. My House lies in ruin, reduced into rubbles by rationalism,
disobedience and vanity. My glorious pastures of the past are now barren because
of the Great Apostasy which penetrated into My sanctuary. Obedience is missing.
I have given My shepherd's staff entirely to Peter to guide My lambs until My
Return, but in their wickedness and for their own self-interests and not Mine they
have broken My shepherd's staff in two, then in splinters. The Brotherhood was
broken, fidelity shattered and, dead by the Fountains of Love, Peace and Unity,*

---

[1] Jesus said this very moved.
[2] I saw in an interior vision Jesus holding in His Hands a most sparkling and
luminous globe, reminding me of the luminosity of St Michael the Archangel.
[3] Jesus in saying this was extremely sad.

92

Fountains that once were, lie in heaps, My Flock. All I ask from these shepherds who turn their back to Peter is to bend their neck and acknowledge their Error. I want them to reach the place of rest I have for them, I do not want them to fall like stars one after the other; if only they would listen to what the Spirit says to them today, I shall not remind them of their apostasy nor the Wounds I am receiving from them. ♥ *Pray for these priests, My love for them is Great but so are the sorrows they are giving Me today. Pray that they may bend and wash each others feet with humility and love.* ♥

I, your Lord Jesus Christ, am leaving My Sighs of Love upon your forehead and with Great Love I bless each one of you to unite and be one as the Holy Trinity is One and the Same, you too be one under My Holy Name. ΙΧθΥΣ ⊱⊙

CONTEMPLATIVE ADORATION

October 12th, 1989

Lord, I thank You for saving me. I love You and I adore You and <u>You</u> only, my God.

Ah, let Me hear this often, let your heart speak to Me. Come and meditate on Me, meditate on He who is the Way, the Truth and the Life. Come to contemplative adoration, for this is what pleases Me. I and you, you and I, face to face in total silence; I, revealing My Beauty to you, and you, praising Me. ♥ *Learn that My Heart languishes after every soul, I have now taken you back to Me, but how many more souls will I have to bring back! Come and rest in My Heart and allow Me to rest in yours. Love loves you.*

Lord! How I love You. How I desire You. How I thirst for You. How I need You!

Free at last![1]

(Here I squealed with joy!)

---

[1] Jesus said this with great joy.

GREECE - RHODES

October 17th, 1989

My Lord?

I Am. Remember who leads you. Synchronize with Me. Ask always with your heart and it shall be given to you, prayers coming out of your heart are like sweet melody in My Ears. ♥ ΙΧθΥΣ ⤳⊃

October 22nd, 1989
Rhodes

Somehow in that single week I was in Rhodes, people following these messages, arranged two prayer meetings with the local Catholic and Orthodox priests. Let us say, Saint Francis and Padre Pio together with Saint Basil led by our Mother of Perpetual Help arranged those unexpected meetings. One was held in the Saint Francis Church and the other in the Greek Orthodox Church of Annalypsis.

Dad? I've done the shouting as You've asked me to do on the message of the 30th, September. I've shouted out the Truth.

Look My child, bewilder not, for I am the Highest and from above My Word descends to you. I come to revive My Church. Remember always this: no power or height or depth can ever destroy My Church, My Church shall be restored by Me again. ♥ *My Vassula, you are nothing, nothing at all, and yet I can use you. By eclipsing what is "you" My Spirit can speak and act in you, My Spirit in you should not meet any rival. Have no fear, even when My Spirit meets with a rival, I always make sure to extirpate this rival.* ♥ *Abandon yourself to Me every day, be willing to do My Will* ♥ *and leave the rest to Me, your God.* ♥

BE SLOW TO ANGER

October 23rd, 1989

Lord?

I Am. Never doubt. How I love you! This little faith you give Me is like a bunch of flowers offered to Me daily by you, ♥ *I receive it in this way[1]. My little one, refuse Me nothing, be slow to anger, just like Me your God; be quick only to do good; be faithful to Me. Beloved of My Soul, you who willed to offer Me your will, your soul and your heart, fear not for you are in your Father's Hands and what more wonderful than being linked together? Refuse Me nothing. Efface yourself entirely so that I may be seen completely; stay small so that My Power occupies every part of you; die to your self daily and be nothing so that I may be everything. Believe in Me with a child-like faith so that I may glory in this way and use you when I please.* ♥ *All I ask from you is love, love, love. All that you do in My Name with love, glorifies Me and purifies you. Evangelize with love for love. Enter into My Sacred Heart daily and allow Me to rest in yours; be in Peace for I am Peace. I promise you that I shall offer you daily My Bread. I, Jesus, love you and count every minute now to bring your soul to Me[2]. I, the Lord, bless you.* ♥

I bless You too my Lord and Redeemer.

GOD WANTS YOUR DAILY ABANDONMENT

October 25th, 1989

Our Holy Mother for the prayer group:

My Peace is with you. ♥ **Ecclesia shall revive. Come, be pleasing to the Lord and offer yourselves daily to Him, allow Him to change you into devout children, into children of Light.** ♥ **Change your lives by detaching yourselves from the worldly things for, My little ones, you are only passing by in this world. I am constantly reminding you that your soul will live forever and I am repeatedly warning you to change your lives. What does God want from you?**

---

[1] Jesus means when I come daily to Him and let Him use my hand.
[2] Here Jesus means in Heaven.

and what is the perfect thing to do? God wants your daily abandonment, a full abandonment to model you into a perfect being. ♥ The perfect thing to do is to obey God's Will by offering Him your will; seek Him, seek all that is Him. I beg you, do not listen to the demon's whispers, elevate your soul by a constant prayer. I love you, children and My Eyes do not leave you an instant alone. Learn to do good from Our Messages; let Our Messages nourish your poor soul and lead you back to knowledge, let them lead you to the Holy Bible and to the Truth and the Life. ♥ I want to save you from the nets of the devil; I want to elevate your soul into a higher level of prayer.

Tonight My children, I shall intercede to the Father for all of you in a very special way, you should know that through His Goodness you can obtain many graces. You should know how infinitely rich He is in Grace. Desire the Lord, be hungry for the Lord always; unload all your worries, offering them to Him. Trust Him. ♥ Enlarge His Kingdom with your love to Him and to your brethren, repay evil with love. Let love be the principal of your life, let love be your root. Be aware of your thoughts, do not judge each other, for your ways are NOT as the Lord's. Endeavour to please the Lord by being humble, without any judgement for others. God's Love is revealed even to the least of you all. Go in peace, beloved ones; enter your homes without leaving Us behind, take Us with you. Learn to feel Our Holy Presence; learn to say, "we" instead of "I", "us" instead of "me". I bless you all. Be one, like the Lord desires it, do not be divided for in Heaven you are one. ♥ Be in Peace and live in Peace. ♥

I DO NOT USE YOUR WILL
UNLESS YOU OFFER IT TO ME

October 26th, 1989

Lord? I feel like a boat without oars.

I Am. Flower, My Path is straight but narrow, and very few find It. My child, do not make a whole fuss every time I prune you, I prune you to grow stronger so that you may produce many more fruits. I want to multiply your fruit. I know that you are trying to tell Me, "that I prune you too often",[1] I know what is best for you My child, after all have you yourself not offered Me your liberty?

Yes, I have offered You my liberty for eternity.

---

[1] This made me smile.

I am using what you have offered Me, soul, I do not use your will unless you offer it to Me. Trust Me. Have faith in Me always for I am most Gentle. Persevere My child and be zealous to serve the cause of right; be ardent to convert other souls; remain small and ask My advice always before taking any decision, help will always be given to you from above. ♥

THE THREE IRON BARS
COME HOLY SPIRIT

October 26th, 1989

My Vassula, draw three iron bars with a head on the top, ▯▯▯ *these represent the Romans Catholics, the Orthodox and the Protestants. I want them to bend and unite but these iron bars are still very stiff and cannot bend on their own, so I shall have to come to them with My Fire and with the power of My Flame upon them they shall turn soft to bend and mould into one solid iron bar, and My Glory will fill the whole earth.* ♥ ΙΧθΥΣ ⤳ *Pray often to the Holy Spirit this prayer:*

> *Come Holy Spirit, come through the powerful intercession of the Immaculate Heart of Mary your Beloved Bride. Amen.*[1]

With this prayer My Holy Spirit will haste and come upon you. Pray for the effusion of My Holy Spirit to come upon you. ♥ ΙΧθΥΣ ⤳

EMBRACE MY CROSS

October 30th, 1989

Flower, My Love offers you Its Gift: My Passion, My Passion. Go through it and please the Father as I have pleased Him, I love you passionately and this is My Way of showing My Love to souls. ♥ *Allow Me to be your guide, guiding you in*

---

[1]Prayer shown to me.

the Path of My Passion; I teach souls to endure It without complaints and to each one I give according to her capacity. Vassula, learn: to reach perfection there is one road, the Road of My Passion and that is, <u>My Cross</u>. ♥ *Endure It with love, endure It with patience; embrace My Cross My child, all will soon be finished and near Me you shall be. Adore Me, adore Me. I bless you.* ♥

BONDED TOGETHER FOR ETERNITY

October 30th, 1989

Lord, save us in Your love, let Your Holy Face smile on those who love You. Our Protector <u>come</u> to Your Abels. We need You.

Come My child, remain near Me. ♥ *Espoused to Me, understand what I have offered you, I have offered you My Heart and My Love; espoused to Me, I offer you all that I have; I offer you My Cup now and then; I offer you My bread to keep you alive and I offer you My Fragrance to remind you of My constant Presence. Daughter, I and you shall remain bonded together for eternity. Come.* ♥

I CHOOSE POVERTY TO SHOW MY RICHES

October 31st, 1989

Beloved, peace be with you. ♥ *Hear Me: I teach with love, I have taught you with Wisdom, I have elevated you and formed you. Remain in My favour and My discipline, all will come from Me. Stay unshaken to My Teachings. My Vassula, appease My Father's wrath by pleasing Him, repaying evil with love; appease His Anger on this evil generation with your love. Reveal Me in you so that you evangelize with love for Love. God-is-with-you, My child, you have been commissioned to evangelize. <u>I choose weakness to show My Power and poverty to show My Riches and Wisdom</u>. Never make any claims for yourself; stay nothing; reduce yourself even more now so that I may accomplish My Work.* ♥

A NATION CONSECRATED IN YOUR HOLY NAME WILL RESURRECT

October 31st, 1989

My Lord and Saviour?

I Am. Peace My child, do not fear, never fear My Presence, fear Me only if you rebel against Me. ♥ *He who is not with Me, scatters. Think of this: My Revelation to you does not scatter, It gathers; My Revelation unites you into one Body. Have My Peace, My child. Remain nothing, remain in Me. I the Lord, bless you.* ♥

This was said because of the doubts I have now and then that I might be in error.

I lean towards Our Lady of Fatima's statue I have on my little table on which I write. I go close to Her right ear and whisper in Her ear, "you know, Jesus gave me something <u>very precious</u> to guard. It has to do with the Glorification of His Body. It also is for the salvation of souls! So I come to You dear Mother and ask you if <u>you</u> could keep It, guard It and defend It for me. Yes, it is the Lord's Revelation, <u>I transmit It into your hands, entirely.</u> In the meantime I must carry on the work of the Sacred Heart of Jesus, He Who has risen me for this mission and He Who formed me."

Soon the dead will leave their graves at the sound of His Voice, all for His Glory. <u>Soon a Nation will resurrect, a Nation consecrated in Your Holy Name, for this has been made known so long ago[1].</u>

My child, nothing will interfere between God's Love to humanity, even if you are persecuted, worried and attacked, be prudent and obey God. No one has the right to accuse those that God chooses. I will guard the Revelation as I guard all other Revelations from God. Have confidence in the Holy One, He watches over His Works. Reveal God's Love, My Vassula, without fear. Come, be in constant prayer to the Father. ♥

I thank You and I bless You Holy Mother.

---

[1](Note added later in 1992) Without me knowing I was prophesying about the fall of communism in Russia.

A HEAVENLY CHURCH

November 2nd, 1989

The Lord is constantly these days showing me the "three iron bars." This time I see them a bright orangy colour, because they seem to be very hot.

My Vassula, with My Fire and with the power of My Flame, not only will I soften these iron bars, but with My Breath, I shall melt them altogether and form them into one solid bar forever and ever, then you will all reach the fullest knowledge of My Will and My Understanding. ♥ This will be My Gift to you, a heavenly Church. It will be radiant with My Glory and your hymns shall be sung around one Single Tabernacle and your land of ghosts shall revive again, <u>transfigured and resurrected</u>. Come daughter, Wisdom shall instruct you. IXθΥΣ I bless you, love Me. ⤳◗

YOUR BEAUTY SHOULD BE INTERIOR

November 3rd, 1989

Let us join the procession of Your Angels who are <u>around You</u> my God, for You are <u>Unique</u> in the Holy Trinity, and as they praise You without ceasing and sing to You hymns, let us too proclaim all Your wonders around <u>One Single Tabernacle</u>. I love Your House, my Lord. Make haste to unite us all in Your House, let Your Angels and Your Saints be the example for us, let us learn from them how to adore You around a unique Tabernacle.

My flower, everything shall be fulfilled in its own time. In the meantime be pleasing in My Father's Eyes, let your ornaments and your beauty be <u>interior</u>, for I look and search scrupulously in each heart. So rejoice Me and be agreeable in My Eyes by ornamenting and embellishing your soul. Draw from Me, all that I have is Precious and Life in Itself; draw from My treasury, I give freely. Be thirsty for My Riches and draw from My Heart and fill up yours. ♥ My Vassula, keep doing all the things that you learnt from My Wisdom and have been taught with My Gentle Mastery and have heard from the Voice of the Truth. ♥ Be in Peace. Remember My Presence.

Yes my Lord, I bless You.

I bless you and each step you take. ΙΧθΥΣ ✕◯▷

Lord?

I Am. Vassula, plead for faith, remember I can give you faith in its fullness.

I do not even know how to properly ask You for a stronger faith Lord!

Even if you do not know, try, My Mercy is Great. Flower, be confident. Rejoice Me My flower and extinguish a few more fires from the souls who are in purgatory. Love extinguishes their purifying fires. Remember always this, learn that I use the essence of your love to Me to extinguish their fires and remove them upwards, some can even come to Me finally. I, the Lord, have given you My Word, this is your spiritual Food. Slow down and hear Me[1]; even in your absolute weakness I will be able to give you all My Messages. In spite of your nothingness and your inability to do whatsoever I, the Lord, shall accomplish My Work. ♥ *Stay small, My child, remain faithful to Me. I, the Lord, love you with all My Heart. Glorify Me and honour Me. Receive Me for it pleases Me. Allow Me to use you. Pray always with your heart. Come, we, us?*

Yes my Lord and my mother. ΙΧθΥΣ ✕◯▷

CONSOLE MY WOUNDED HEART

November 6th, 1989

Daughter, peace be with you. ♥ *Every soul who <u>loves</u> Me is amending for her past sins. The love and the repentance I receive from these souls, console My Wounded Heart and appease My Father's Justice and relent Him. Relent Him, for He sees your efforts and indeed takes in consideration all your good intentions. You are not many, but even for those very few ones My Father's Hand is relenting. Have <u>faith</u>, pray and believe in what you ask.* ♥ *Have <u>hope</u> in Me; I have Resurrected and your salvation comes from Me. Desire Me always. I bless you.* ♥

---

[1] Jesus means not to let my hand "run" before I hear His words.

IT IS WRONG TO BELIEVE THAT THIS
IS MY HANDWRITING

November 7th, 1989

My Jesus?

I Am. Peace be with you. Receive Me in the way I have taught you. Flower, love Me, absorb Me, receive Me and be My reflection, My dove. ♥

My Lord, do let me understand why there are spelling mistakes?

Vassula, these are your own, not Mine. I have chosen you because you are imperfect and with many weaknesses. I God choose My instruments weak because My Power is at its best in weakness.

Yet, You do now and then give me new words unknown to me.

I do. When the need comes I have you under dictation and it is wrong to believe that this is My handwriting.

Why then the difference of writing Lord?

I like it this way. I use My instruments as they are with all their imperfections and all their weaknesses to dictate to them My Knowledge and to feed them and others My Word. I know how many of them take My words, which many a time are symbolic to the word, but this again is reflecting their weakness, their obedience and their child-like-faith ♥ *to Me and their desire to please Me. Happy the man who stands firm when trials come[1]. Come My child, allow Me to use you as I please, all your sacrifices will not be in vain.* ♥ *Be one with Me. Love loves you.* ♥

---

[1] James 1:12.

MY VINEYARDS, I SHALL SPREAD EVEN MORE NOW
I AM ON MY WAY BACK TO YOU

November 8th, 1989

My Vassula, lean on Me, please Me, and renew your vow of fidelity.

I renew my vow of fidelity to You my Saviour and Lord. Help me keep it. Help me be faithful to You. Lord, You have done great things to me. You have lifted my soul to You and You allow me to live under Your Light. You have covered my nakedness with Your Majestic Gifts. You have renewed me. You have risen me as You have risen Lazarus. You freed me and I love You and adore You.

Beloved of My Heart, lean on Me, I and you, you and I, together we shall share My Cross of Peace and Love. Ah Vassula, you are My own now, freed and alive! Listen and write: My Vineyards I shall spread even more now, since this generation is so unspiritual, unable to tell their right hand from their left. Since they are veiled and living in darkness, I am coming in this way to visit you all. I am returning soon and no man can stop Me, even when those who abide under the beast's power are sent as a holocaust to trample on My Vineyards, I shall with My Power keep expanding these Vineyards even more. This is a Holy battle between the Holy Ones and the fallen angels from the Pit; besides, the earth feels the weight of this Battle. No one shall stop Me from feeding My lambs. I am not just words, I the Lord am Power. ♥ I do not come to your generation with menaces, I come to ask for your conversion, I come to shine upon you. I descend to you, all Merciful, and with Great Love I come to take you back to Me. I, the Lord, am a God of Love and Mercy, do not be slow in understanding that it is I the Lord who shall transform your arid lands into vineyards. Only a little while now, a very little while and the One you are waiting to come will have come. I will not delay, My Hour is prominent. I have given you My Promise not long ago of My Return and I tell you all most solemnly that I am on My way back to you. Love is returning, Love shall return to you as Love. I the Lord, Am Love and I shall dwell among you. Try and understand, try and perceive the Times. I tell you most solemnly that unless you repent, fast and pray without ceasing, you will be unable to see My Light. Eat My fruits while there is still time, convert and live holy. Never cease praying. My Holy Spirit shall continue to spread on mankind. Read the signs of the Times, I am Present at all Times. Come daughter, Love loves you infinitely. ΙΧθΥΣ ><>

LEARN TO BE PATIENT
TRIALS AND DOUBTS

November 9th, 1989

I come in this way to the Lord with fear of being in error again. I somehow do not seem to grasp and understand all this, I'm again going through a trial yet I come to You in this way You've taught me. Jesus?

I Am. Be in peace. ♥ *My Vassula, let no one take away the gift I have given you.*

Do not allow this to happen my Lord!

I shall not allow this to happen but keep in mind My Teachings, keep in mind how I the Lord came to you.

Jesus, You know my fears.

I know them.

You know my anguishes.

I know them.

Sometimes I fear of being in error.

I know. My sympathy is with you and I am yearning even more to press you closer to My Heart. Fear not and be in peace. Today I tell you that I shall show you that what you have, comes from Me. Learn to be patient, learn from Me. Hear Me, lean on Me, devote your time for Me, never cease praying[1]. Vassula, since when do you love Me?

I love You since the time of the "writings" when You approached me in this manner, just after my guardian angel Daniel.

I have come to you by "the writings" and I have risen you through "the writings", I have formed you through "the writings", I have instructed you My Knowledge through "the writings", I have transfigured you through "the writings", I have converted many Godless people through "the writings", I have shown you the state

---

[1] There was a pause here.

of My Church again through "the writings", I have shown you My Sacred Heart through "the writings", <u>how could you ever believe that this fervour I am giving you</u> is yours or comes from you!? <u>Flower!</u> I have chosen you <u>because</u> you are so wretched and <u>because</u> you were so far from My Church; I chose you <u>because</u> you were dead, to show the world that I need no power from man nor their holiness to accomplish My designs[1]. It is as Scripture says, "it was to shame the wise that God chose what is foolish by human reckoning and to shame what is strong that He chose what is weak by human reckoning: those whom the world thinks common and contemptible are the ones that God has chosen, those who are nothing at all to show up those who are everything." ♥ And to this day I thank the Father for hiding these things from the learned and the clever and revealing them to mere children (Matthew 11:25). Be in peace My child; My Cross of Peace and Love cries out to the world for <u>conversion</u>, for <u>love</u>, for <u>peace</u> and for <u>unity</u>. <u>My Works are to bring to divinity again this human race</u>. My Works come from My Mercy. Enter into My Sacred Heart and rest My Vassula. Freedom is to love God, <u>I freed you</u>. ♥

Glory be to God! Praised be our Lord!

I, Jesus of Nazareth, am beside you. Today I shall come to you by My "visiting statue."[2] I never fail the graces you ask from Me. Be blessed. I will help you pray, for this is talking to Me and I then am listening to you. I am with you too, My little angel[3]. We, us?

Forever and ever.

I SHALL OVERTHOW ALL THE IMPOSTERS
IN MY CHURCH
MY RUSSIA SHALL BE THE LIVING EXAMPLE OF
YOUR TIMES

November 13th & 14th, 1989

Peace be with you, My child. Evangelize with love for Love. ♥ Ecclesia shall revive because I the Lord shall overthrow all the imposters who have placed

---

[1] Jesus said all this maybe in one breath.
[2] A pilgrim statue of the Sacred Heart. A statue that stays nine days in each house.
[3] This was our Holy Mother.

themselves in high seats, within Her. Daughter, remove these thorns that pierce My Head, thorns that cause so much bleeding, do not fear them daughter for I am beside you and I tell you truly that with My Power and My Great Mercy I shall overthrow each one of these.

You see My child, <u>all Heaven was too long in mourning</u> for your Sister-So-Unloved, for years We are swallowing Our bitter Tears. "O Russia! Mere creature of flesh! Evil coiled in your very womb, creature of mere dust and ashes, I the Most High shall resurrect you <u>for I am the Resurrection</u>. I shall nurse you back to Life and I shall with My Finger upon you, transfigure you into a glorious nation as I was transfigured. You shall be majestically dressed in dazzling white robes and all Heaven shall thrust away Its mourning garments and Heaven's bitter Tears shall turn into joyful tears. All Heaven will celebrate your Resurrection and all the martyr-saints, who prayed without ceasing by the Feet of your Holy Mother for <u>Her</u> intercession , shall in this day too, together with My Mother and Her innumerable holy angels, all descend in your children's homes and make their home together with them. I then shall feed them My Body and offer them My Blood to drink". Russia shall eat Me and drink Me with great love, praising Me. My Russia shall be the living example of your times and for generations to come, because of her <u>Great Conversion</u>. Your Sister-So-Unloved by many, shall renounce all her evil behaviour and shall call Me her God with all her might.

Vassula, can you hear? Listen, listen to your Sister's children's laments[1], her children are lamenting and there is wailing. It is My Russia's children who are weeping, all Heaven plainly hears their grieving. Heaven is deeply moved by their distress and I, who have never ceased loving her, now am near her dead body. My Hand upon her cold heart and her bones will flower again from her tomb and her name shall be well spoken of for <u>I</u> shall adorn her and her sons and daughters. ♥ <u>Hence a covenant of Peace and Love shall be signed and sealed between Me and her</u>. ♥ I love her and always have, even in her disloyalty towards Me and even in her wickedness I blessed her and blessed her. ♥ <u>This shall be My Glorious Miracle</u>, just wait and see. Those who have fallen asleep in hatred, hating Me for no reason, those too I shall bring back to life since they are her sons too and still live in her womb. All these things shall soon take place. ♥

Daughter, I am the Holy One, the Most High, I am the Most Holy Trinity. Please Me and hear Me as you heard Me today. ♥

God seemed satisfied.

---

[1] Here I started to weep not only for Russia's children who suffer, but also because God sounded <u>so sad</u>, beyond description.

"Alleluia our Anointed One![1] Delight the Lord and seek Him in purity of heart, seek Him in simplicity of heart, we are your angels who guard you without ceasing." *"God loves you and I, Daniel,[2] am always with you. Stay small for this is what pleases the Lord!"*

Ahh Daniel... how can I avoid the meetings where people start to know the revelation and me. How can I stay "small"? You know how I dislike being exposed!

Vassula, stay small means remain humble and pleasing to the Lord. Remember, it is the Lord's wish you assemble[3]. Have no fear, His Message should be known, the world ought to come and meet the <u>King of Peace</u>. Your generation should recognize God and be converted. Give thanks to God for His Merciful Works. I, Daniel, pray without ceasing for you, God wants you to be good. Reveal His Love to all mankind without fear. ♥ The Most High blesses you and all those who commit themselves in this Message to announce It to the nations. Love loves you all. ΙΧθΥΣ ⪢⟨⟩

NEVER DEMAND, ASK

November 14th, 1989

My Lord? I want a bigger faith, I need it.

♥ *My Vassula, never demand, ask.* ♥ *Realize My Infinite Mercy and Love, so say these words,*

> *"my Saviour, augment my love;*
> *augment my faith;*
> *augment my hope;*
> *let all this be done according*
> *to Your Divine Will.*
>
> > *Amen"*

---

[1] This came from angel's voices.
[2] Daniel, my guardian angel.
[3] The monthly prayer meetings.

♥ *Do not be in a hurry, you seem to be always in a hurry, why?[1] I am listening, but you seem to think that I shall leave and so you hurry, why? Do not rush, I hear you as much when I am with you in this special way. Reduce your speed and meditate on each word of prayer. Why the rush? I am your Educator and you My pupil, I have taught you to discern. I am your Teacher who formed you, I will now and then remind you when you tend to forget My precepts ♥ and shall continue to pour in you abundant revelations. Come, let us work. ♥*

ΙΧθΥΣ ⊱⊰

SAINTLY HUMOUR

November 15th, 1989

Just before I rest[2], I asked Jesus to give me just one more word but from the Scriptures. I open at random after asking Him and Jesus said to me through Scripture:

"I still have many things to say to you but they would be too much for you now." (John 16:12)

In saying this to me, I noticed a trace of saintly humour.

IT IS ESSENTIAL TO PRAY AND ASK MY FAVOURS

November 16th, 1989

Lord? I lift my eyes to You, I lift my soul to You. I long for You my Saviour, Your Holy Presence is my delight, oh take my cause and defend me.

My flower, Love is near you. In spite of seeing Me only with the eyes of your soul, do not diminish your faith. Smile at Me, it pleases Me. Ah My child, come take up My yoke, My yoke is easy and My burden light. ♥ Pray the way I have

---

[1] I sometimes get tempted to hurry up my prayers so as to come quickly to the notebooks and be with Jesus in "writing".
[2] I use the word "rest" instead of "sleep". I became allergic to the word "sleep", because I was sleeping for years before Jesus came to wake me up.

108

taught you, <u>with your heart</u>. It is essential to pray and ask My favours, this is My Law. ♥ *Enter every minute into My Sacred Heart; I long to console you; I long to rest you. Allow My Mother to teach you.* ♥

Our Holy Mother:

My Vassula, I am near you, be sure of this. Console My Son by loving Him, console Jesus by speaking to Him and having Him as First. Never leave Our Hands, never seek to look beyond His shoulders. Keep pace with Us; adore Him and evangelize for Him with love; trust Him, do not worry about tomorrow, tomorrow will take care of itself. Do not look to your left nor to your right. The Lord wants your full abandonment to make out of you a perfect being reflecting His Divine Image, this Divine Image your era has lost. Jesus and I do not 'descend' by means of Our Messages to judge you; We do not come to judge you nor do We come to condemn you, We come to you with great Love and Mercy to bring you all back to Us and make out of you all divine beings. ♥ **I bless you. I am with you.** ♥

I bless You too Holy Mother. Amen.

November 20th, 1989

Ah Vassula! Realize, realize what I have given you! Come, I and you, you and I, have Me as First. Daughter, all I ask from you is love. I, Jesus Christ, Beloved Son of God and your Saviour am on My way back to you, see? I am already on the Path of My Return, soon you shall start hearing My footsteps clearer and clearer, for I am approaching you all. I love you all. ΙΧθΥΣ
〉⊂▷ *Be one.*

MY PRESENCE IS ALSO A MYSTERY

November 22nd, 1989

Please Lord, speak to me through Scriptures. I open the Bible at random and it reads: "The Holy Spirit will come upon you." Luke 1:35.

Daughter, remind the world of My Presence, announce My Message to the ends of the world. ♥ *Pray, I am listening[1]. I shall help you:*

> *Please Father reveal to me Your Love,*
> *for in revealing Your Love,*
> *You are revealing me Your Holy Face.*
> *Shine on me, let no one deceive me.*
> *Be my Guide, my Master and my Educator.*
> *Let me learn from Wisdom's Lips.*
> *Amen.* ♥

See? Just ask for My help and I shall not wait. Come, you are still learning, but stay near Me. Remember My Presence that I so much insist for each one of you to learn, My Presence is also a Mystery. ♥ *Do not neglect Me nor shall I neglect you. I am still talking.[2] Let Me be your Consoler. I the Lord shall guide you till the end, even though you do not realize fully what I am giving you as Graces. I, out of My Infinite Mercy, shall fill you with My Spirit without ceasing and pour into you My Words and My Law and raise you to Me.* ♥ *I, the Lord of lords, keep a close eye on you. Have My Peace and My Love. I bless each one of you. Be good.* ΙΧθΥΣ ⤳

DEAREST SOUL GIVE ME YOUR LOVE

November 23rd, 1989

My King, lead every soul to the Truth that they may glorify You around one single Tabernacle. Let those who hear and hear again but not understand, understand <u>this</u> time; and those that see and see again, but not perceive, perceive <u>this</u> time, entering into Your Mystery. Soften their heart so that they may understand with their heart and not their mind and thus be converted and healed by You, praising You my King.

My child, I shall raise even the dead. Pray for these souls who have not understood My Will. Be steadfast in My teachings; be firm in My Ways and discourage those who inflict wounds on My Body. Treat your enemies, who are My enemies, kindly but at the same time teach them firmly. I shall guide each step you take My child. Love Me with all your heart, with all your soul and with all your mind for in doing so you shall see Me your God. Daughter, come to Me even for a few moments of the day to meet Me as I have taught you, it pleases Me.

---

[1] I hesitated to find the words so the Lord came to my rescue.
[2] I had tried to interrupt and say something.

Dearest soul give Me your love, have I not given you Mine? I am your Spouse who feeds you, who fills you, who consoles you, who defends you, who cares for you and who lifts your soul to Me. I am He who loves you most, dearest soul. I know[1] but I have trained you and formed you for this mission. Lean on Me when you are weary and I shall lift you. Flower, all you do in My Name, glorifies Me. Eat from Me. I love you and I have created you to love Me; I have created you to rest Me; I have created you to share with me all that I have. Pray to the Father to relent His Justice that lies heavily upon you[2]; relent His Anger by loving Him, by praying with your heart, by fasting, repenting and confessing your sins. Enter into the world of Peace and Holiness. Live holy, reflecting My Divinity. My Vassula, are you happy now that I have liberated you?

Glory be to the Lord, YES!

Then gratify Me by allowing Me to use you for My Glory, see? Understand that I shall require from you sacrifices, sufferings, and great patience, but nothing shall go in vain. Remember, I have formed you to become another little crucifix for My Glory, each little crucifix becomes a column of light, thus diminishing the darkness that surrounds you. Treat Me now as a King and offer Me souls, I am thirsty for souls. I shall help you and Wisdom shall instruct you. Keep near Me and remember My Presence. I, Jesus, bless you. Love Me. IXθΥΣ >⊂D

I LOVE CHILDISH FAITH

November 26th, 1989

Child, peace be with you. Hear Me, be prudent, do not mention things that do not come from this revelation; use My Words from this revelation and from Scriptures. I am your Teacher, be prudent. ♥ *Rely on Me. Your Saviour I Am; your Holy One I Am; I Am Who I Am.* ♥ *So why not rely on Me? You please Me when you smile at Me. I love childish faith.* ♥ *Vassula, courage, I shall overthrow all My enemies, courage daughter, I know it is hard to live in exile and in the valley of death, but be assured of My Love. I am by your side and I shall help you even in the tiniest of things. Love loves you.* IXθΥΣ >⊂D

---

[1] I said something to Jesus.
[2] Our generation.

I BLESS YOU FOR THIS LITTLE FAITH
YOU ARE GIVING ME

November 27th, 1989

Lord, be my Strength. I shall embrace Your Cross till the end. I thank You for all that You are giving me.

Have My Peace, Vassula of My Sacred Heart. Fear not, the charisma I have given you shall remain with you until the day I come to fetch you. Be happy that I am willing to feed you in this way! Be happy that I am willing to leave this gift with you till the end! Be happy that I have favoured you so highly! Be happy daughter that I gave you life again! I bless you for this little faith you are giving Me. Take My Cross, hug My Cross, My Cross is your Life. I, Jesus of Nazareth, bless you and all those who work on My Message diffusing It. I bless each one of them. Come, we, us?

Yes Lord.

We, us?

Yes Holy Mother.

November 28th, 1989

My Jesus?

I Am. Love is near you. Take My Cross and rest Me My child. Love is weary and needs rest. Ah, My child, do not abandon Me. I shall infuse in you learnings and discernment but I want your full abandonment daily, for how else would I then activate in you My Will? Come, remember My Presence. Love blesses you. ♥

November 29th, 1989

My heart is ready my God to receive You, I am listening. Here I am. (Message for the prayer group for December.)

My Vassula, I am well pleased for allowing Me to use you. Listen and write. ♥

Peace be with you. I am your Saviour, the King of Peace. I am your Consoler, I am Love and it is to Love you are lending an ear to and it is for your King of Peace you have travelled from far to come and listen to, and it is your Saviour who redeemed you that you shall hear today. It is Peace that you come to seek and I tell you, I give you My Peace. Is it consolation that you seek My beloved ones? Come, I shall lavish on you consolation. Is it Love that you are thirsty for? Oh come! Fall into My open Arms. <u>I am Love</u>! My little children, do not let your hearts be troubled, I have never abandoned you. I, Jesus, am always by your side, Therefore, the reason why I descend in this way is to console you is <u>to remind you of My Law</u>. ♥ *I want to call you all back to Love, to Peace and to Unity.* ♥ *I do not come to judge you nor do I come to condemn you, I come out of My Infinite Mercy to remind you that I am Holy and that you ought to be living holy. I am a God of Love, not a God that drives you to despair. I am a God of Hope and I come to give you hope.* ♥ *Blessed ones, I am He who loves you most; I am he who laid down His Life for the sake of His Love to you. Will I then not take all possible means to come in these days of darkness to warn you and draw you away from evil and to pull you closer to My Heart and show you that your Abode is indeed My Sacred Heart?*

I come to ask those who have still not reconciled with Me, to reconcile and make Peace with Me. All I ask from you is LOVE. My Spirit is being outpoured lavishly upon your generation, all out of My Infinite Mercy, and it should not seem incredible to you that I should speak in this way since I Am the Almighty. ♥ *My Messages are to bring many of you who have strayed back to your senses and remind you of the Truth;* ♥ *and for those who still do not believe in these Divine Works of Mercy, I shall ask the same question I had once asked the Pharisees, "which of you here, if his son falls into a well, or his ox, will not pull him out on a sabbath day without hesitation?"[1] Beloved ones, I am an Abyss of Mercy, I am Infinite Wealth and My Voice shall be heard all around the globe and even underneath, in the dark belly of this earth where lie the dead. My Voice shall be heard and I shall go to them and raise them, making columns of light out of them, and to those who continue to condemn My Works I say, "seek the Lord in simplicity of heart."* ♥ *My priests, My priests... all you who are the reflection of My Divine Image, allow Me to remind you at this end of the year to come to Me and draw from My Heart which is an Abyss of Love and fill up yours. Listen to My Words and act upon them.* ♥ *Do not be like a house built only on soil and with no foundations, then with a gushing of a river upon you, would collapse! Be firm and put into action the lessons learnt from Me.* ♥ *I shall draw all men to Myself and the Spirit of Love shall reveal to you all My Holy Face. I come to you*

---

[1]Luke 14:5

to encourage you, My beloved brothers. Remain in My Love. Continue to shepherd My people with love for Love. Walk in My Light and I shall guide you; I am the Light of the world and you are My friends, My chosen ones. Enter into My Sacred Heart; enter into this Furnace of Love and allow Me to enkindle your heart so that you, in your turn to go and inflame other hearts. Come to Me, imperfect as you are, and share My Great Love. Your love should not be just words or mere talk, but something real and active. ♥ *Repay evil with good. Repay injustice with righteousness. Repay hatred with love. Forgive, forgive. Let love be always present in all your acts.* ♥

Children of My Sacred Heart, in these days you are living in difficult times where My foe has stretched out his dominion like a veil, this is why I come to ask you to double your prayers, prayers of the heart that reach Me. ♥ *Come, repent... confess your sins My child, do not come unworthy to receive Me in this little white Host. Come and drink Me, come and eat Me and remember Whom you are receiving in this Sacred moment, you are receiving Me, your are receiving Life. Be pure to receive Me. Yearn for this Holy moment as never before, yearn to receive your God. Even My angels from above look at you, yearning after this Meal, desiring to be one of you! Let your heart be stirred by a noble theme, say to Me: "Jesus, I the sinner ask to be forgiven, I am not worthy of receiving You, yet I know that by just one word from You I can be healed." Keep saying these words, they please Me, they make Me your God run to you, they fill My Sacred Heart with Compassion.* ♥ *Call out to Me, "Kyrie Eleisson! Christe Eleisson! Forgive me, the sinner!" Humble yourselves and I shall raise you. Efface yourselves, and I shall lift you to Me and hide you in My Sacred Heart. I ask you from now on to live in constant faith, love and holiness. Let My request be your motto for this coming year.* ♥ *Come, be one under My Holy Name as I and the Father are One and the Same.* ♥ *I, the Lord Jesus Christ, bless all of you, leaving My Sighs of Love upon your forehead.* ♥ *ΙΧθΥΣ* ⟩⟨⟩ *Love loves you.*

Message of Our Holy Mother:

LET YOUR PRAYERS REACH HEAVEN

Children of God, peace be with you. I, your Holy Mother, need your prayers to realize God's Salvation Plan, I need prayers from the heart. Let your prayers reach heaven, let them be as incense. Fill your hearts with God's Love and rejoice for a Saviour was born for your salvation, a Saviour meek at heart who descended on earth to serve and to call the oppressed; "He has come to open the eyes of the blind, to free captives from prison and those who live in

darkness from the dungeon."[1] Beloved children, it is the same Saviour who calls out to you today; it is the same Saviour who calls each one of you by his name to return to Him; it is the same Jesus who reminds you of His teachings; it is the same Jesus whom I, as His Mother, held in My Arms and had Him wrapped in swaddling clothes, born to serve, born to redeem you and now it is the same Jesus always who calls out to you for your salvation; it is the same Saviour who reminds you that you all belong to Him. He was made visible in the flesh and He sacrificed Himself for you, My children, in order to set you free. Come then and rejoice and be filled with happiness! Come and proclaim the greatness of His Holy Name! Come and be the joyful messengers carrying His Word. ♥ I love you and believe Me, My Cape is large enough to hide you all inside it![2] Come to the Lord, do not fear to show Him your weaknesses. Come to the Lord and offer Him your heart and He will receive it like myrrh, incense and gold. ♥ We love you. We love you without measure. Abandon yourselves to Him. Jesus comes to each one of you. He comes to free the captives of this world and give them their freedom, captives who like doves have been caught and caged by the evil one; but Jesus untiringly goes from cage to cage and frees every single captive.

My children, live according to the Lord's Heavenly Commandments and Law, for the Law of Heaven is resumed in one single word and this word is <u>LOVE</u>. ♥ I, your Holy Mother, intercede and pray for you, day and night. I give you My Love and I bless all of you and all your families. ♥

BE MY HEAVEN

November 30th, 1989

I heard again the Holy Spirit praying for me without ceasing during the whole night and in the end, very early in the morning the Holy Spirit asked me to repeat after Him this prayer: "Pere aide moi, car Ta Puissance est Amour" it was given to me in French, and it means: "Father help me, because Your Power is Love."

Lord, in spite that many nations have sunk into a pit of their own making, and caught by the feet in the snare they set themselves, have pity on them. Lord, grant them a hearing, make out of them a completely new batch of bread, glorifying You my King. I shall ask You again Lord of Love, Lord of Mercy that those who heard and

---

[1] Is. 42:7
[2] Our Holy Mother was smiling.

heard again but never understood, to hear this time for the sake of Your Love and that those that saw and saw again but never perceived, to perceive this time, for the sake of Your Great Mercy, entering thus into Your Mystery. Soften their heart so that they may understand fully with their heart and not with their mind, and thus be converted and healed by Your Divinity; then they shall realize how wonderful Your decrees are, and their soul shall not resist but respect them.

My child, I shall glorify My Name again, just wait and see. This is only the beginning.

Lord, You are like a consuming Fire and I know You are working in many hearts. Lord I live for You, be very near me in this exile.

Saturated by Me, live for Me, live under My Wings. Imbued by My Love, flourish now and grow, spread your branches like a terebinth. Tell Me that I am He whom you love most. Be My song little one, be My Heaven and glorify My Holy Name again. ♥ Lean on Me when you are weary, oh yes! Delight Me and feel My Presence! Oh yes! Hunger for Me, thirst for Me, look at your King! Behold the One who saved you! Look flower at My Beauty! <u>Free</u> My dove, free at long last. Enter now into My Sacred Heart and let It consume you entirely and make nothing else out of you but a living flame of Love's jealous Love. I am an Ardent Flame of Love and My Love is indeed a consuming Fire. ♥ Desire Me. I am being glorified. Stretch this love for Me, My Hand is upon many nations. All shall be accomplished soon on the right hour and the right time. Love Me, desire Me. Come, we, us?

Yes Lord, for eternity. Glory be to God.

MY OWN KNOW ME

December 4th, 1989

My Lord, do not abandon me to the will of my persecutors. False witnesses have risen against me. Since the day I am trying to make your ways known to the youth of today and teach them your paths, the Evil one has doubled his fury upon me. Yes Lord, since the day I announced your Message and showed your sweetness of your Holy Face, the Evil one is manupilating my accusers, deceived and blinded by him, they are persecuting me and hounding me.

My Vassula, be strong, My Sacred Heart is your Fortress; come My child and hide in its depths; exempt by My Hand, Love loves you. You see My child, these men do not talk My language, My language of Love has really never penetrated them. You are fully aware now that anyone I lift to Me, talks My language and tries to live close to Me in devotion, is cetain to be attacked. My language is a language of Love, but they have not understood if they call you heretic[1], they call Me heretic and My entire Kingdom, since My Kingdom is based on Love. These ministers need many prayers followed by sacrifices. Every soul who condems My Message shall have to face Me in the Day of Judgement, giving Me his accounts and believe Me, I shall judge them severely. Remember nevertheless that I am always by your side, think constantly of this My Vassula. Come, let us pray:

> *Father! You who lifted my soul from this dark exile and placed me under Your Wings, take pity on me. Raise me up when I am fearing, grant me Your Peace and Your Love. Establish me in greater Faith so that I may glorify Your Holy Name again. Amen.* ♥

Love is near you ♥ *and I know My own and My own know Me, but I shall take away the sight from those that see and give sight to those that are blind. Come, be My incense and please Me by refusing Me nothing.* ♥ *Wisdom shall instruct you, come.*

We, us, Lord?

We, us, My beloved. ΙΧθΥΣ ⪦⬭⟝

OBEDIENCE TO ME YOUR GOD COMES BEFORE OBEDIENCE TO MEN
EVERY DEVOTION GIVEN TO MY MOTHER PLEASES MY HEART

I felt Jesus was calling me, I had to rush to Him.

Daughter, you are the apple of My Eye, let no one deceive you in thinking otherwise. Your weakness incessantly infatuates Me; your incapacity reminds Me of My first disciples where they had to constantly depend on My Mastery.

---

[1] A priest called me heretic because Jesus is so gentle with me and calls me "betrothed". He forgets that all nuns get "married" to Christ and that He is the spouse, so why not be betrothed to Christ!

Daughter, worship Me and cling on Me for I am the Life. ♥ *IXθYΣ* ⤚⟨▷

My Vassula, obedience to Me your God comes before obedience to men. Meditate on these words. ♥

Lord, I have problems in concentrating today.

Elevate your soul to Me by reducing your external thoughts. Recollect yourself and feel My Presence, let your soul rise from meditation into contemplation. Reach Me your God in silence. Come to Me in contemplative adoration, see? Pray the rosary now.

Jesus means while on dictation.

I am listening together with My Mother.

I prayed the beginning of the rosary up to the first mystery. They are the glorious mysteries today.

I resurrected. ♥ *Shall we pray? I shall help you meditate, come.* ♥

After finishing the first mystery.

Beware not to loose your concentration. ♥ *Come into the next mystery when I ascended to the Father. Beloved, pray.* ♥ *Amen. Enter now into My third mystery when My Holy Spirit descended like tongues of Fire. Pray for the coming Pentecost, already your generation feels the pangs of Its birth. The night is almost over, dawn is soon to break and when it does, evil who prowled with ease in the night, shall flee at daybreak. Yes indeed, My Spirit of Grace shall be poured out on all mankind and your generation shall be fed directly by Me, you shall be taught and guided by Me and even My saints and My angels from above shall meet you at each street-corner. I will shower upon you My Bread. Rejoice and be glad! I, the Lord, am the Light of the world, let those who have ears hear.* ♥ *Take courage, dawn is soon with you. Come, meditate.* ♥ *Now comes the fourth mystery, My Beloved Mother's Assumption.* ♥ *Be blessed and meditate.* ♥ *Blessed one, let us now enter into the fifth mystery where I the Lord crown My Mother and name Her Queen of Heaven. Daughter, I desire you to contemplate upon this glorious mystery.* ♥ *Come, every devotion given to My Mother pleases My Heart. Come, write. I am near you. Rejoice soul, take your pencil and copy all this.* IXθYΣ ⤚⟨▷

THEIR PRUDENCE BECOMES IMPRUDENCE

December 6th, 1989

My Lord, teach me if it pleases You, to be patient, like Job was patient and clinged on You.

Depend on Me, I shall teach you My own patience. ♥

My Lord, if it is Your wish, infuse in me courage just like Your disciples.

My flower, I shall remind you how I endured My Cross disregarding the shamefulness of It, then you will not give up for want of courage. ♥ *You are guided by My Spirit. My aim is to bring atheism at its end.* ♥ *Ah, My child! Not many will listen to My Voice because your generation* lacks humility; *each time I approached My children through weak instruments, My own, many of My own muffle down My Voice; daughter their prudence becomes imprudence since they do not recognize the fruits of My Divine Works and refuse to believe; but as I have said before, they do not believe because they are no sheep of Mine. The sheep that belong to Me listen to My Voice, I know them and they know Me and follow Me, so in their case these prophecies are being fulfilled, "at the end of time, there are going to be people who sneer at religion and follow nothing but their own desires for wickedness. These unspiritual and selfish people are nothing but mischief-makers"[1]* ♥ *and "you are reputed to be alive and yet are dead". "Wake up" I tell you, "revive what little you have left: it is dying fast."[2] Not only they are dead but in their fall want to deprive My children from eating My Heavenly Bread too, they are forgetting that I rule over them and that I confer My Spirit of Grace on whom I please and raise the lowest of mankind. In their wickedness they shut the door at My Face. Resentful to My angels, they abolish all hopes from this generation, they treat My Holy Spirit of Grace no less better than the Pharisees treated Me on earth. My Vassula, beloved of My Soul, courage, let Me tell you this: I have placed you* all[3] *on My Path to share My Cross of Peace and Love.*

Lord, what about 'X'?

He too is a victim of My Love, a victim of My Soul, a victim of Love's jealous love. Rejoice! for already you feel My anguishes of Gethsemane[4] but have faith in Me and trust Me for I am near you to share My Cross with you till the end.

---

[1] Jude 1:18-19.
[2] Revelation 3:2.
[3] All those who one way or another participate the diffusing of these messages.
[4] This is referred to "X".

I and you My beloved ones, you and I, together we shall strive and I tell you, mountains can be shaken and valleys transformed but My Love shall never ever fail you. ♥ My Love for you is unshakeable and My Faithfulness unalterable, see? Lean on Me and I shall rest your soul, but allow Me too to ask you for rest when My Soul is weary, allow Me to unburden My Cross on your shoulders to rest. I, the Lord, shall remind you of My Presence. Peace upon you. Yearn for Me. Love loves you, love Me. **ΙΧθΥΣ** ⤳ *Evangelize with love for Love.* ♥

I AM QUICK TO FORGIVE AND FORGET

December 7th, 1989

Since You are One Lord, bring us to One Faith and One Baptism. Lord, You are <u>One God who is Father of all</u>, over all, through all and within all, we are incapable to come all of us to an understanding, we are unbending... will You leave us in this way?

<u>Pray</u> for all of you to come to an understanding. I have created you, giving you the freedom to make your own decisions. To be faithful to Me and keep My Commandments is within your power, I have never commanded you to sin, so <u>pray</u> for Wisdom to enlighten this generation to start telling their right hand from their left. ♥

This message is for the youngster group I have:

Reveal Me to mankind the way I have taught you. I am a God of Love and Mercy, I am not a complicated God and I never hound anyone to death. Realize that I give and ask accordingly; I shall never demand from a soul more than what she can offer, I do not ask more than her capacity offers. I am asking from each one a small return of love, a smile, a thought, a kind word, just one word coming from their heart would be received like a million prayers. ♥ This is of considerable importance; even a mere thought, I shall take it ever so preciously. I love each soul to folly. I am a God ever so Tender and Meek. I am Gentle with My offsprings; whosoever presents Me to My offsprings as a demanding and quick to anger God, is damaging My Church. I am patient and slow to anger but I am quick to forgive and forget. No one should say that I am only after holy people; I am known to go and find the sick and wretched, their wretchedness attracts Me, their incapacity to reach Me makes Me all the more eager to pull them up to Me and press them to My Heart. ♥ I am Jesus and Jesus means Saviour and I come to save and not to condemn. ♥ **ΙΧθΥΣ** ⤳

BE PATIENT LIKE I AM PATIENT

December 7th, 1989

My child, do you believe it is I, Jesus, meeting you in this special way?

Yes I do Lord.

Do you believe it is I, Jesus, you see around all the time?

Yes I believe Lord. Why are You questioning me Lord?

To hear you say it child. Be happy then and bless Me, for you are under My Father's favour, you must work though and elevate your soul constantly. I have given you the grace to see Me with the eyes of your soul and to discern My Voice, do not allow the world to monopolize you now that you do not belong to it. ♥ My Wisdom shall enlarge your learnings. ♥ Be gentle with the poor like I am gentle with you, plead for their cause. No father deserts his child in the desert, so be patient like I am patient with you. Daughter, do not try to discover things that are beyond your power, for you can be misled by your own presumption and thus mislead others too. Trust Me and I shall give you learnings that you can absorb and for your capacity. Listen to My Words and never to others; lean on My Shoulder when you are weary, let My Shoulder be your Headrest and My Sacred Heart your Abode. ♥

Later:

Eat from Me, learn from Me, console My children. Will you write now?[1] I am happy to feel you cling on Me, devotion shall keep your eyes open and your soul far from sleep. ♥ Come, be glad that I have risen you from the dead and from those who lie years dead and are decomposed.

Jesus, I have asked You this before and I am asking You again, if it is Your Will, do unto the dead and even the decomposed as You have done unto me, raise them to Life and allow them to live under Your Light.

Death shall be swallowed up in victory before the Resurrected One, for I am the Life. ♥ I am the Resurrection and Life in Itself and anyone who comes to eat My Flesh and drink My Blood shall have eternal life. ♥ Come, I shall dictate to you further revelations on My Holy Eucharist. I the Lord bless you for joining Me in

---

[1]I was "clinging" on Jesus, I did not want to leave this instant and let Him "go".

this way and for allowing Me to use you to write My Words. Work hard My Vassula, all will not be in vain. Come, I shall guide you in all your undertakings, be firm! ♥

To "be firm" was said just because while I was under dictation, the evil one tried again, suggestions, that all this might be coming from my subconscious mind! and so Jesus said to me to "be firm". Satan is a real nuisance, as for the other demons I do not pay much attention to them, they are also a nuisance but are more or less like flies buzzing around and are fearing me although they'd have liked it to be the other way round. Still, they are malicious and one has to be on guard. These demons are at their best the minute they notice a soul slumbering or weakening, or hesitating. Prayers just "kill" them and keep them off. Faith in the Lord's Love and Mercy destroys these demons who are "buzzing" close to one's ears so as to "suggest" us evil disguised as the Truth and far from Love. This is why the Lord wants us to be aware and in constant prayer. A constant prayer keeps these demons away and Satan himself too. Prayers become a safe barrier around us, keeping away Satan and all other demons. Yes, it's a constant fight.

YOUR MERITS ARE NONE

December 13th, 1989

My Lord and Saviour?

Beloved, love Me. Remember Vassula how I favoured you above many; this Grace I am giving you is a great gift, to be annihilated in Me your God. Little seedling of Mine, your merits are none, yet My eagerness to lift you to Me and be within Me is such that I overlook what you are, even your sins I overlook and pardon. Now do you understand My fervent Love? Stay small, never cease calling Me, never cease thirsting for Me. Lean on Me when you are weary, remain in Me for this is the way I like it. ♥ *Love loves you.* ΙΧθΥΣ ><>

THE SOURCE OF LIFE FLOWS OUT OF ME

December 14th, 1989

Glorify Me by loving Me and by adoring Me your God, see? Now you know what it is like to be in your God and to live in Me. ♥ *I am your Beloved Father who keeps you glued on My breast; just like a mother who keeps her infant upon her breast, nourishing it, warming it, so am I too with you. I feed you and I comfort you.* ♥ *You need not worry since your source of life flows out directly from Me, you need not fear since you are enveloped by My Love and in My Arms, I am your Protector and near Me you are secure.* ♥ *I the Lord developed you, just like a mother who takes good care of her infant. Beloved, the Source of Life flows out of Me, be blessed.* ♥

SANCTITY DOES NOT COME IN A DAY

December 16th, 1989

Peace be with you. Sanctity does not come in a day, you need to persevere in this road full of obstacles and little crosses. Do not let go of Me, will you continue? Will you continue with Me in this road up to the end of it?

I shall not let go of You my Lord. Help me so that my fists which are tightly closed on Your Garment do not go loose.

Cling on My Cross and My Cross shall lead you all the way to Perfection. Near you I Am, united to you I Am. Pray My Vassula, for devotion is primarily what comes out of love. I the Lord, have impregnated you with My Love. ♥ *I ask each soul to come and thrust herself in this Ocean of Love so that they too may be saturated and feel this Love.* ♥ *I, Jesus, love you all. Enter into My Sacred Heart, I long to hide you deep in Its Depths, hide you for always and keep you just for Myself.* ♥ *Flower, love Me, love Me, adore Me, adore Me and I shall do the rest. Learn to say, "Jesus make my heart Your resting place, come and rest Lord."* IXθΥΣ ⋊◯▷

December 17th, 1989

I felt the Lord far away. I panic when I feel this way, I know it is entirely my fault and it is a heavy trial again. The Lord immediately came to my rescue and said, writing:

"I want you to <u>listen</u>; I am near you, but your spirit is far from Me. <u>Listen</u>, I the Lord, want you to <u>listen</u>! Unite with Me, be one with Me, I and you, you and I, then WE could work in one, see? Be careful Vassula." *"By being united WE could join in the work."*

I had panicked, because by receiving revelations and having been guided in an extraordinary way, and having tasted Heaven and the Presence of God without any merits from my part, suddenly it had appeared as though Heaven slightly had closed Its doors and I did not feel His Presence.

Fear not, I had been eagerly waiting for these moments where I would be together with you, so never ever believe that I am closing you out. I simply challenged you to recover from your lethargy, and I shall work together with you till the end. ♥ Let your heart exult with joy in My Presence. I still have many things to say to you but you would then be unable to take everything down, you are frail and I know that you are also weak. Come, you need not speak to Me with words to tell Me you love Me, speak with your heart. To desire Me, to love Me, to contemplate Me and you are then doing My Will, because My Will is to love Me and to adore Me, so by just doing this, <u>ALL</u> is then done in Silence. ♥ Offer Me your will, offer Me all that you have, will, self, pleasures, everything.

I offer You my Lord, my will, self, pleasures, and all that You want. Feel FREE my King to just take and take from me as You please.

In return, do you still want My Cross of Peace and Love?

Yes, my Lord, entirely; even if by Its size I fall flat on the ground, I'll carry It even if I have to crawl on my knees.

Daughter, My Cross of Peace and Love shall sanctify many of My children, let Me enter and rest in your heart. I the Lord bless you. Beloved, wait and you shall see. ♥

I like it so much when You say "wait and you shall see!"

I know little one. ♥ We, us?

Yes, my Lord.

We, us?

Yes Holy Mother. **IXθYΣ** ⊃⊂ (Our Mother was present too.)

I AM NEAR YOU TO BE THE THREAT TO YOUR ENEMIES

December 18th, 1989

My Vassula, I the Lord shall feed you before the very eyes of your persecutors, feel My pain to see you My child among these wolves. My Soul is disconsolate and My Heart grieves to the extent that I have mobilised legions of angels to come and console Me. Your persecutors are giving you poisoned water to drink, but I shall ceaselessly keep curing you with My great Love I have for you. ♥ *I shall overthrow all these blocks who despise you My angels[1], all you in whom My Heart rejoices to be with and in whom I find My comfort and My rest.* ♥ *My lambs, you who receive My Messages by My Grace; My lambs, you who rest My Heart, you who are My predilected souls, I shall not see you attacked by these Cains, these Cains who are drenched in sin and who never stopped aiming for your throat, My Abels.*

Lord! The Cains are without pity attacking us. They have killed Your prophets in the days of old and today they want to repeat their crime, <u>their aim is to break down all Your Altars</u>, one after the other. They want to annihilate us from the surface of this exile!

My remnant. My altar. You whom I have risen from dust to shape and form into a living altar for Me, the Most High. You are one of My altars, altars that I place in different corners of the globe and in which I pour My Burning desires from My Ardent Flame of Love. I tell you this, Cain shall have to face Me this time, he who still thirsts to kill, because he continues to sow in the soil he has tilled his evil seeds and today eats what his harvest offers, he shall have to face Me. ♥ *Listen My dove: he shall neither drag you by force nor by sword to the desert to shed your blood again, nor will I let him blow away the Flame I have given you.* ♥ *My little altars, you <u>who make My Joy</u>, take courage, do not fear. Every sin of his will recoil on his head and the prophesy of Isaiah still stands for these Cains to this day, that I, the Lord, will give them "a sluggish spirit, unseeing eyes and*

---

[1]Today's messengers.

inattentive ears, and they are still like that today" and forever will be. ♥ *I deported Cain from his land into the desert, a country where I do not live, a country where wickedness flows in rivers and waters its banks and irrigates its soil. Justice had cast him out of My sight, yet, even when Mercy today comes to his rescue and stretches out Her Hand to lift his veil from his eyes, he refuses. I even went down into the countries of underneath the earth to the peoples of the past to lift your life from the pit Cain, but to this day you are not hearing Me nor are you willing to recognize Me your God.*

Vassula, My dove, do not be afraid to speak up for I have endowed you with My Spirit. ♥ *Crossing this exile is hard, but by your side I am to provide you with speech, friendship and consolation. I am near you to be the threat to your enemies; I am near you to calm down and appease any whirlwind that tends to rise and frighten you; I am near you to chase away the wolves who come to hound you; I am near you to shelter your head from the scorching sun; I am near you My beloved, to chase away with My Light all the vipers and scorpions that come on your path. I lead you in the way that you must go and with My Incense I cover you daily and all those who accompany us, blessing each step they take. My Eyes are upon you My doves, you whom I had gone out to seek all the way from the desert. My Love for you is a Living Fire and my jealousy relentless as never before, so listen to My song, My resting Place is not far from you now. I am He who loves you most and I am giving you the Gift of My Love.* ♥ *Come and listen to My teachings; My teachings are Light; teachings that the world have forgotten, these very teachings that should have been the apple of their eye.* ♥ *Come, we, us?*

Yes forever Lord.

We, us?

Forever Holy Mother.

I love you[1]. ♥

---

[1] Our Holy Mother.

WHEN TRIALS COME DO NOT PROTEST

December 19th, 1989

O Holy Spirit of Instruction, do not allow my soul to be confounded. You are my Divine Teacher and it is You who instructed me, and it is from Your Mouth I have been taught. I am here to listen to you my Lord and Master.

Little one, when trials come, do not protest, do not give your opinion, My Peace should be the only thing that ought to come out of you, the Lord's Peace. Spontaneous answers to disputes can become irreparable mistakes. Take what I have given you out of My Heart, nothing less, nothing more; take from what I have given you, do you understand Me now?

Yes my Lord. Lord tell me again who You are.

Hear Me then: it is I Jesus, Beloved Son of God, the Word made flesh, who came to live among you, it is I, your Saviour, who speaks to you[1]. Flower, courage. Repose on My Heart and listen to My Heartbeats, just like the Dove in your vision. Listen, ♥ *I love all of you to folly, now you know Me better.* ♥ *The Pantocrator.* ♥ *I am your Educator and I shall maintain you by faith, faith, faith. I love you and it is by faith and in faith I want to educate you and raise you up. Locutions you shall always have. To hear Me you shall have to recollect yourself to be able to enter into contemplation that will remind you of My Presence, accept these things since they come from Me, I like it this way. Have you not noticed that all you have learned came from Me? I shall guide you till the end in this way. Rejoice pupil!*

You leave me speechless my God.

Be happy, for you have not merited any of those graces. Come, Love loves you. ♥

---

[1] Jesus was saying this as if He was saying it to someone for the first time.

TODAY, THE HOLY SPIRIT OF GRACE IS INDEED
THE KEYSTONE

December 23rd, 1989

Peace be with you daughter, touch My Heart. Feel how lacerated My Heart is.

With my spirit I felt Our Lord's Heart.

Remove the thorns that now pierce My Heart,

Show me how to remove these thorns Lord.

♥ *Thorns can be removed by love. Love Me, love Me. Vassula, be My balm; console Me and bring to Me small souls, show them My Heart, tell them of My Love. Remove each thorn and replace it with a small soul. Tremendous reparations have to be done to My House but I shall rebuild It, brick after brick, layer after layer. In spite of the tremendous attacks My House receives, I the Lord shall prevail in the end.* ♥ *I shall then fill up My House with pure souls; like doves that fill up their cote so will it be too in My Own House and I shall allow these pure souls to eat directly from My Hand so that they learn to say, "Abba". Divinity shall conquer corruption, corruption that through the world's vices made out of My children atheists.* ♥ *I intend to make out of these pure souls divine beings, reflecting My Divinity, this is why I am in these days reminding you without ceasing the Truth. Even though I am repeating Myself, even when some of you get annoyed because I repeat Myself, I shall continue to remind you of the same truths, this is the only way to stir some of the sluggish spirits.* ♥ *Today My Holy Spirit of Grace is rejected by the unbelievers, but they do not know what they are rejecting. It is as Scripture says, "the stone rejected by the builders has proved to be the keystone, a stone to stumble over, a rock to bring men down[1]."* ♥ *These unbelievers stumble over the corner stone because they do not believe in the Works of My Holy Spirit. Yes, today My Holy Spirit of Grace who descends to show you the Way, the Truth and the Life* <u>is indeed the Keystone</u>, *the Corner Stone that you do not recognize and reject altogether.* ♥ *Daughter, even in your imperfection I shall be able to accomplish My Messages. Take your sufferings as blessings, think of what I had to suffer to accomplish My Work and through My Wounds healed you all. I the Lord need generous souls who are willing to immolate themselves for others and become little crucifixes, all these sacrifices shall not be in vain. Tremendous reparations have to be done and the time is pressing. So little one lean on My Shoulder when you are weary, do not fall. Lean on Me, united we*

---

[1] 1 Peter 2:8.

are. Pray My Vassula for the cause of your era's salvation. ♥ *Caress Me your God with your littleness, caress Me with your prayers coming out of your heart. I want sincerity, I do not want obligations. I want your heart.* ♥ *Be perfect! Come, My Eyes do not leave you, you are all[1] My Joy, My Happiness.*

ΙΧθΥΣ ⌑◁▷

PROPHECY ABOUT RUSSIA

December 24th, 1989
Christmas Eve

Jesus?

I Am. Glory be to God. ♥

Glory be to God.

Pray My child. Devote yourself to Me, love is near you and was always from your crib days to this day and will forever be. ♥ *Stay near Me and reject all confusing thoughts, lean on Me alone, be one with Me, satisfy My insatiable thirst for love.* ♥ *The Pantocrator.*

THE FALL OF COMMUNISM IN ROMANIA

♥ *My flower, I am the Light of the world. Sing and be happy, sing for joy for it is I, Jesus, who performs these marvels. My Cross shall be erected again on every church, do you see?[2] A universal peace is soon to come. Peace is about to be born, pray for this birth of Peace and Love. Today the earth feels the beginning of its birth-pangs; these, My beloved ones, are My early Signs of Love[3]. I am the Master of heaven and earth and I shall with My Power demonstrate to every nation that I am all-powerful. I have said that I shall overthrow with My*

---

[1]Small souls.
[2]I saw in an interior vision the roof of a church, and two to three men on it, struggling to put in the right place a heavy cross, back again in its place.
[3]On 29th November, a month before Romania events, Jesus and our Holy Mother gave us a Christmas message so that I read to the prayer group on 22nd December. Our Holy Mother's message was alluding to Romanias freedom.

Breath all those who reduced you to slavery, let your nations realize that everything is subject to My Power and what I did with one breath is for My Glory. No man is able to efface My Law. ♥ *Let the nations realize that it is I, the Lord, who came to free these captives from prison and lift them to Me; it is I who reduced your enemies into everlasting shame and this is not all, I shall, with your sister Russia, sign a covenant of Peace and Love and her crimes shall be forgotten by me and I shall make her My Bride again and out of her heart shall come out this song:*

> *I will keep my love for Him always, and my*
> *covenant with my God shall stand.*

My Soul is thirsting for this glorious moment. <u>I mean to show My splendour and My glory to every nation living under these skies, through your sister Russia.</u> I shall dress her with My beauty and with My integrity and I shall parade her to your brothers[1] so that they may see My beauty and My integrity through her and in her. ♥ *Daughter, the wedding of your sister's conversion is soon to come. I have said that I am He who descends in your era's misery to console the oppressed and free her captives from prison and those who live in darkness from the dungeon. It is I your Saviour who comes to rescue you from the red dragon's jaws; it is I your Jesus My doves who comes to break your cages and free you.* ♥ *It is I, your Holy One, who never abandoned you and I tell you truly your[2] gates shall not be closed to Me. Vassula, I shall overthrow with disgrace and humiliation all these evil powers, these powers who knocked down My House and made out of It gaping graves. My Light shall resurrect your sister Russia and all her neighbouring countries. <u>I shall break all your cages and set you free</u>.* ♥ *Learn that salvation and liberation comes from Me alone. Pray for your sister, pray for her neighbours.* ♥

My Lord, You have said that a trouble will be coming to the man who amasses goods that are not his and loads himself with pledges, will not his creditors suddenly rise, will not his duns awake? Then he will be their victim. Hababak 2:7. This is exactly what happened in Romania but innocent people paid it with their blood.

Be assured that <u>I have with Me all the martyr-saints of your season</u>, victims of Satan's <u>fury</u>. I have with Me all those who perished as victims. I tell you that his fury was such that knowing he was loosing his grip he intended to annihilate every single flower of Mine.

Jesus then looked from above on Romania.

---

[1]The Lord here means the Roman Catholics.
[2]Romania's gates.

Do not weep little one[1] for I the Lord shall rebuild your ruins and I shall increase you to bear witness on My Name. I shall make you see great things under My Name. Free at last! Free to come to Me your Saviour and live in My Sacred Heart. I shall pursue your enemies, who are My enemies too, with My Light. Do not weep for your children that are no more because today I tell you that I have placed each one of them in the depths of My Heart.

Blessed be our Lord, the God of Mercy, for He has visited His people. He has come to their rescue, He has come to give Light to those who live in darkness and the shadow of death. Glory be to Him who comes to guide our feet into the way of Peace and Love. Amen.

I AM HE-WHO-SAVES

December 29th, 1989

Lord, my God, whom I adore in silence day and night. You who looked down from heaven and from Your Holy and glorious place took pity on Your children who were kept in captivity like doves in a cage, starving and broken, oppressed by the enemy, praised be Your Name that is full of kindness.

> The people that walked in darkness
> has seen a great light;
> On those who live in a land of deep shadow
> a light has shone.
> You have made their gladness greater,
> You have made their joy increase;
> They rejoice in Your presence
> as men rejoice at harvest time,
> as men are happy when they are dividing the spoils.

Epiphany - Isaiah 9:1-2

Salvation comes from Me. ♥ *I am He-who-saves.* ΙΧθΥΣ ⊃

---

[1]Jesus means Romania.

ADORE ME AND LOVE ME IN MY HOLY EUCHARIST

December 29th, 1989

Peace be with you. Adore Me and love Me in My Holy Eucharist. Come and receive Me in My Sacrifice as an unblemished lamb, you must come pure to Me. If you only realized how I am present in Body and in Blood in which I have won an eternal redemption for all of you, you would approach Me without blemish and with respect. I have out of My Infinite Love offered Myself as the perfect Sacrifice to purify you all from sin. ♥ *I want you all to fully understand this Sacrifice, yes, I want to encourage you by understanding what I am offering you and thus stir in you a response of love.* ♥ *This Sacrifice can lead you into sanctification and into divinity. My child, It can achieve in you My purpose and bring you to eternal perfection. My beloved, My Sacrifice is for eternity and you whom My Soul loves, have It every single day.* ♥ *My sanctuary at this Holy moment is filled with angels of each order ready to meet Me their God; prostrated they lie in adoration for Me, consoling My Heart, and you who are ready to receive Me, will you not adore Me? Will you not worship Me? Be aware of My Holy Presence, do not sleep in My Presence. Do not allow your spirit to flutter elsewhere in My Presence, would you have allowed yourselves to be lethargic were you to be by the feet of My Cross on Golgotha? My beloved ones, how would you feel had you been assisting My Crucifixion on the mount? Would you have allowed your spirit to fill with insignificant events of the day? or would you have fallen prostrate at the feet of My Cross and adore Me your God? I have died for you on the Cross, disregarding the sufferings I had to undergo, would you allow yourselves to become inattentive and careless in front of My Sacrifice then? I am present in My Tabernacle as I was present and nailed on My Holy Cross.* ♥ *Come then to Me this time with full awareness of Whom it is you are receiving, and Who it is who unites Himself to you to purify you, giving everlasting Life. Daughter, be patient like I am patient.* ♥ *Come, rest in My Sacred Heart and allow Me to rest in yours. Love loves you.*
♥

O Jesus Christ, our Lord and Saviour
thou didst promise to abide with us always.
Thou dost call all Christians to
draw near and partake of Thy Body and Blood,
But our sin has divided us and we have no
power to partake of Thy Holy Eucharist together.
We confess this our sin and we pray Thee,
forgive us and help us to serve the ways of
reconciliation, according to Thy Will.
Kindle our hearts with the fire of the

*Holy Spirit, give us the spirit of Wisdom
and faith, of daring and of patience, of
humility and of firmness, of love and of
repentance, through the prayers of the
most blessed Mother of God and of all the
saints. Amen.*

Prayer of Fr Sergius Bulgakov

JESUS IS LOVE

January 5th, 1990

Lord?

I Am. Lean on Me. Realize how weak you are. Allow Me to guide you, without Me you are lost and in the dark. I am the Light, the Light to guide you. ♥ *Be careful for the demon is always and all the more determined to make you fall and confuse you. Come My bride, be one with Me. I know your weaknesses, I know how by the slightest attack your spirit is left shaken and your soul in anguish.* ♥ *I am Peace and it is in Peace I lead you and it is with Love I guide your steps, do I not know all these torments beloved? Allow Me to work in you, then all will be accomplished.* ♥ *My Message[1] shall be dictated to you very soon, be ready. Jesus is My Name and Jesus is Love. Grow in My Spirit, how else are you to witness? I am preparing you in all ways to witness and glorify Me. I love you. Enter into My Divine Heart and absorb from Me; caress Me, your Lord, with integrity and humility, I am your Master and Educator who never abandons you even though you often feel it that way.* ♥ *Remember that without Me you are unable to make one little stroke.* ♥ *I am the One who leads you and instructs you, by your side I am. Let Me guide you in this way. Pray and you shall obtain strength in your faith. I shall help you to observe, come.* ♥ *I, Jesus, love you![2]*

Later on:

Be in peace now My child. Leave your worries behind in My Presence. Look at

---

[1] For the prayer group.
[2] I knew Jesus wanted to tell me this but I did not want it to be written because some people had criticized that there were too many "I love you", but Jesus wrote it anyway with great speed before I have the time to lift my hand from the paper and added an exclamation mark with Holy Humour.

Me in silence. Be in peace, feel My Peace. I am near you but you cannot see Me with your physical eyes; I am near you and I have taught you to discern Me My child, just like I have taught others. Even today I am still teaching a few chosen souls to hear Me and discern Me. ♥ *Rest. Come, we, us?* ♥

Forever and ever. I bless You Lord.

I WANT YOU INDULGENT AND DEVOUT

January 5th, 1990

Jesus?

I Am. My Love for you is everlasting, My Faithfulness to you is everlasting. Abandon yourselves to Me daily and I shall do the rest. Pray without ceasing to Me, I am always eager to hear your prayers. Never forget Me, I never forget you, so think of Me constantly. If you only knew My child how near you I am! Treat Me as a King. Realize how naked you were and how I covered your nakedness with My Graces; realize how I your King looked upon you, who are nothing, and formed you and lifted you. So have patience with those I have not given as much as I have given you, implore My help and I shall give it to you. I am not blaming you, I love you and so I do not want you to fall. I shall always remind you of My Presence to conquer evil; I shall always remind you of My precepts, take them and cherish them. ♥ *Remember it is love speaking and it is in Love you are working. I want you perfect. I want you indulgent and devout. Always remember My Presence, be one in Me.* ⊃〇⊂ **ΙΧθΥΣ**

THE FIRST COMMANDMENT

January 8th, 1990

My Lord?

I Am.

Its unbelievable all this!

Ah Vassula, I Am! I wished you to become My bearer. I give even to the least of My creatures. ♥ Beloved, My Love for you is more than anyone can understand. I desired that you love Me, giving Me rest, I had asked each one of you to love Me with all your heart, with all your soul and with all your mind, this is My Law and the greatest and first Commandment. ♥ I bless you, bless Me. ♥ Love delights in you.

I bless You my Lord. ΙΧθΥΣ ⊱⊙⊰

IN EVERY WAY BE MY REFLECTION

January 9th, 1990

I am the One who loves you most, stay in My favour by loving Me and by doing My Will. Set your heart in completing My Work. Understand all this My child and allow Me to use you. I love you. Devote yourself to Me and I shall raise you, feeding you, impregnating you with My Blood. Act with love, speak with love, think with love, in every way be My reflection. All I ask from you is devotion, love and sincerity. Treat Me as your Holy Companion, count Me among you. Tell Me often how much you adore Me. I am a Jealous God and I want ceaseless prayers, see? Flower, I am the vigilant Keeper of My Garden and although I find it neglected and dry, I promise you that I shall revive it and all by Myself. I shall reveal My Face to you all and many shall acknowledge Me and worship Me with sacrifices and prayers. Yes, many will turn to Me and in seeing Me they shall understand My Love and I shall heal them. ♥ Love loves you all. I am the One who performs marvels and listens to everyone of you, small or great, just or unjust, devout or pagan. I listen to everyone. I bless you all. ♥

THEY NO LONGER COUNT THE FRUITS OF OUR HEARTS

January 10th, 1990

Jesus called me to dictate to me His Message for our prayer group, prayer meeting held for 27th January.

Peace be with you. Feel My Presence. I am among you. Set your hearts to listen and understand My Words. ♥ Beloved children, it is now a little bit more than a year that I the Lord have been with you in this special way, giving you My Messages and in this way I have shown you the Wounds of My Sacred Heart. I have made known to you the state of My Church of today and the cause of the bitterness of My Soul. I have shared with you all My Cross of Peace and Love. I have made known to you My most intimate desires and my Holy Spirit has been reminding you of My precepts. I have been reminding you the teachings of My Church, I have assembled you because you are My Own and it is to My Own I come to show My Glory. I am in you and you are in Me. I am the Light of the world and you My little ones are the vessels carrying My Light and My Message of Peace and Love. ♥ *I have assembled you as a shepherd gathers his sheep back in their sheepfold and have encircled you with My Arms, yet there are other sheep I have that I have to lead as well.*

I am preparing you to live under the New Heavens and the New Earth because the time is drawing near now when Love is to return and live among you. Soon you shall be hearing Love's footsteps on the Path of return and it is for this reason all around the earth My Voice is heard, and it is for the same reason your young ones see visions. I have said that I will pour out My Spirit on all mankind and that your sons and daughters shall prophesy and that even to the least I will give My Blessings. Yes, My Voice today cries out in the wilderness. I am calling each one of you, yet some have failed to understand what My Spirit meant and have neither understood My Signs nor the visions of your young ones, they no longer count the fruits of Our Hearts but treat My chosen souls as imposters. ♥ *I shall remain with you in this way for only a short time now, but I shall not leave you without making sure that you have shelter and pasture. I am your Good Shepherd who cares for you. I am the Lord who, like a watchman, watches you from above, how could I resist and not descend and take any means to reach you when I hear your laments and your agony? How could I resist and not rush to you when I see so many of you heading into the eternal fires? I am coming to you in this way not to condemn you, but to alert you. I come to save the world. I do not come to condemn the world but the world will misjudge the Times again, as they had misjudged the Times of My Coming as the Messiah and have not recognized Me but treated Me as they pleased, handing Me over to the pagans. The world again misjudged the Times of he who was put to straighten the path before Me, they did not recognize John the Baptist who came in all righteousness as Elijah, but treated him too as they pleased* ♥ *and today your generation shall misjudge the Times once more, because these Times are not in their favour. I have said that in the last days to come I shall be sending you Moses and Elijah on earth but your generation shall not recognize Them, they shall neither hear Them nor understand Them but they shall abuse Them, rejecting Them as they rejected John the Baptist and Me as the Messiah. I have said that in the last days many false Christs shall arise and I have advised you to be alert for these false Christs who, in your days, are the false religions. I have given you My Word and I have warned you not to set off in pursuit after these sects. I have given Peter the charge of My Church and I have asked him to feed you, to look after you and to love you.* ♥ *I tell you solemnly, before this generation has passed away* <u>all that I have been telling you will have taken place,</u> *so do not be deceived but resist to your opponents, resist to those who oppose Peter. I Myself shall give you an eloquence to recognize what the Spirit today is saying to the Churches,* <u>so do not prepare your defence.</u>

The fig tree has ripened and My Kingdom is near you now.[1] Pray for those who do not understand, to believe is also a grace given by Me. I have chosen you and this is why you will be persecuted but do not let your hearts be troubled, love one another and do not judge. Let this love I have shown you be the <u>emblem</u> *of My new disciples so that they may recognize that you come from My Fold and that you are children of God and in God.* ♥ *My little children, love one another as I love you. Do not ask for signs, be content to what the Spirit is giving you now. I tell you solemnly that soon there will be One Single Fold which shall be led and guided by One Single Shepherd.* ♥

I am Spirit and I desire you to worship Me in spirit and truth and not by dead words, therefore learn to pray with your heart. ♥ *Pray for the whole Church. Be the incense of My Church and by this I mean that you pray for all those who are proclaiming My Word, from the Vicar who is representing Me to the apostles and prophets of your days, from the sacerdotal souls and religious souls to the laymen, so that they may be ready to understand that all of you whom I mentioned are part of One Body,* <u>My Body.</u> ♥ *Yes, all of you make one body in Me. Pray for those who refuse to hear, to be ready instead of reluctant, to hear a sermon or a revelation inspired by the Spirit. Pray that they may understand how My Spirit works in different ways and how My Spirit teaches you, reminds you, warns you. Pray that they may let My Spirit speak out.* ♥ *I reveal nothing new. I have told you all this beforehand so that your faith may not be shaken when harder times shall come. Remember little ones that someone who has never had his trials, knows very little.* ♥ *I, for My part, shall constantly keep watch over you but I desire that you too offer Me your full abandonment so that I mould you as I please. I want you to be like clay in the hands of a potter; I mean to mould you all back into My Divine Image; I intend to give you back the divinity you once had, but lost.* ♥ *Flowers of Mine, I am He Who Loves you most. I bless you all, leaving on your foreheads the Sigh of My Love. Be one.* ⳹⳺ *IXθYΣ Come, hear My Mother.*

---

[1]Jesus said these words very majestically and as though speaking to himself.

UNITY CAN ONLY BE TO GOD'S GLORY

Have My Message Vassula, flower I bless you.

I bless you Holy Mother. I am listening.

Peace be with you. Jesus and I bless you all, the Holy One is among you and Wisdom is your Teacher.

Hear Me, Our Love for you is such that no man on earth can ever come close to it in understanding (no one has ever seen God).[1] The Holy One has revealed to your nation His Holy Face, He has uncovered His Love and has shown you the Wounds of His Sacred Heart. ♥ God has so much loved the world that He has sent His only Son to be the Sacrifice that takes away your sins, He who has His place at the right Hand of God, the Father, and has out of His Infinite Mercy descended to be in this special way with you and to be present among His Own. The Holy of Holies has come <u>to remind your nation to live holy since He is Holy</u>, He has come to remind you that all flesh is grass and its beauty like the wild flowers. The grass withers, the flowers fall, but His Word remains for ever.[2] ♥

My little children, the Vineyard of the Lord is in your days spreading in many parts of the globe and His Voice is heard more and more in your wilderness. He shall keep multiplying these little oasis of His Kingdom so that His Kingdom on earth shall be as it is in Heaven. Do not be astonished nor amazed, on the contrary, rejoice! Rejoice that His Holy Spirit is being so lavishly outpoured upon every nation and raising new disciples. If only you would listen to Us today and not harden your hearts as in the time of Rebellion. The time is fleeing and I implore you to listen to Us, because in a short time you will no longer see Me. ♥

My dear children, live in Christ, live in Him, be prepared always to meet the Lord, for the Lord is among you. Be happy and rejoice with Me, keep doing all the things that you learnt from Us. Live Our Messages and God shall make them clear to you, meditate on Our Words so that in the end God's Plan will come into realization. His intention is to transfigure your bodies into a copy of His Divine Image, He intends to bring you back into divinity and make out of you all One Pure and Holy Body.

---

[1] No one has ever seen God. No man has ever understood fully God's love, so we have not seen Him.
[2] 1 Peter 1:24-25. Isaiah 40:7-8.

Unity can only be to God's Glory, so come and praise the Lord, <u>do not be like the pagans differentiating yourselves in Christ</u>. You should, all you who are in Christ, help each other and thus fulfil the law of Christ, <u>this is an appeal to all Christians from your Lord's Mother</u>. The Lord is preparing you, all you who are under His Name, for this Glorious day. Yes, the Lord will unite His people and deliver them from all the evils. Mercy and Justice is working with such wonders as has never happened among many generations, and Unity shall come upon you like Dawn and as sudden as the fall of communism, it shall come from God and your nations shall name it the Great Miracle, the Blessed Day in your history. ♥ This Miracle shall be all for God's Glory and in this day all Heaven shall celebrate and rejoice profoundly. This is why I implore you children of Mine to be in constant prayer and to love one another. Give your full abandonment to God and He will do the rest. ♥ I bless each one of you. My Presence shall be felt by many of you upon entering your homes. I love you all.

GROW IN MY SPIRIT

January 15th, 1990

To live in You is wonderful!

♥ *Flower, this is a delightful moment for Me. I elevate your soul to Me, reaching contemplation, and these moments delight My Soul. Are you aware of the difference? I lift your soul to attain the peak of awareness, you are aware of My Presence in this minute[1] more than most of the time. Abandon yourself to Me and grow in My Spirit. Have Me as first.*

My God it's fantastic to be with You. Lord?

I Am little one[2]. Will I ever abandon you?

I mean this is INCREDIBLE to be with You like this, Moses' God, Abraham's God, You Jesus!!

Flower, surely you have heard of My Wonders even greater than this one? ♥

God means this wonder of being in communication with Him in writing.

---

[1] In writing.
[2] I sighed.

Love is near you and it is Love you hear and it is Love who consumes you. Love Me and I shall do the rest. Have My Peace. I the Lord bless you, the saints are with you. ♥

LIFT YOUR EYES TO ME

January 17th, 1990

Peace be with you. Flower of Mine, allow Me to use your hand today to write down My Message[1]:

I give you My Peace. Beloved ones, I have raised you up to use you as a means to make My Messages known throughout the world; I have raised you up to make out of you living altars, giving you My Flame; I raised you up to transfigure you into living temples. My Grace is upon you, My Eyes never leaving you. Come and draw from My Riches, come, please Me and say these words:

> *May You be blessed Lord*
> *all Merciful.*
> *All the greatness, the power*
> *the splendour is Yours.*
> *Yours is the sovereignty and You*
> *are Ruler of all and above all,*
> *And it is by You and through You*
> *that Unity shall descend as*
> *lightening*
> *To honour and Glorify*
> *Your Body.* ♥ *Amen.*

and I tell you that in Unity you shall be like vessels carrying My Light, proclaiming My Kingdom and teaching the Truth with complete freedom and without hinderance of anyone. ♥ *(Take down a few more lines for My chosen ones). Be prepared for a few more tribulations, I am before you to open your way, so do not fear. Many shall be scandalized, but he who proclaims the Truth never goes without trials. Your oppressors are surrounding you, but have your felt any? I tell you, before they even reach you I scatter them away. I the Lord walk by your side.* ♥ *Hear Me: to unite you shall <u>all</u> have to bend, <u>there must be no competition among you</u>, no conceit but everyone has to be self-effacing. I am Divine and*

---

[1]Message for 18th January, first day of the feast of Unity and my birthday as well. This message was given to be read for the 18th.

divine I wish you to be. You should, My beloved ones, <u>all bend</u>, since you all share My Spirit. I the Lord bless you. IXθΥΣ ⤳⟝

Jesus?

I Am. I Jesus love you. Daughter, tell Me, had I not come to you in this way to save you, would you be waiting for Me, serving Me? and had you not been lifted by Me would you have been aware of all that is happening in My Church?

No, no Lord, but I'm no good to have been given all this.

Flower, even if you are no good, I am here with you to bless you and to draw you deeper in My Heart. ♥ *Eat from Me in this way.* ♥ *Have My Peace.*

Lift your eyes to Me

and My Holy Face shall shine on you. I have anointed you to be one of My brides, I have elevated you to be Mine. Love loves you. I have imbued you with My delicate fragrance, I have spread My fragrance all the way to your friends, I have adorned you with My jewels to resemble Me. I have fastened you to Me.

Lift your eyes to Me

and see My Holy Face, I am your Saviour who loves you. Accept the way I lead you, I have laid out My Plans long before you were born. Fast, My beloved; mortify your senses, amend for those who wound Me.

Lift your eyes to Me

and feel how My Love covers you and consumes you, expiate for others to please Me. Look! I am He who loves you most, would you resist My call? Would you resist Me? I who called you by your name and fashioned you to My Image, I who lifted you from the dead and your soul I delivered from the countries underneath the earth.

Lift your eyes to Me

and look at your King who adorned your nakedness with His Blessings. I have espoused you to Me and brought you up with Wisdom. Ah Vassula, My pupil, rejoice Me and share with Me.

Lift your eyes to Me

and look at the One who saved you. I am He, He who created you.

Lift your eyes to Me

and look at Me. I am He who revealed to you My Holy Face, I am He who flourished your senses, I am the Lord who looked on you and assessed you and poured on you My Teachings. Watch My Lips[1], from these very Lips of your God you have learned all that you know today, from the Lips of your God you were dictated and all the Knowledge you have comes from Me. I am your Educator, are you willing to let Me draw you in My Footprints till the end? Will you allow Me to do this?

From Your very Hand I have been given food, without any merits. Who am I to have been poured with graces? All comes from You. From Your own Hands I have been given gifts. I bless You O Lord. I will exult and rejoice in Your Love and follow You feverishly till the end and even more determined.

Then take My Cross of Love and Peace and together we shall proceed. ♥ Remember My beloved that I am near you all the time, remember My Holiness so that you may walk in holiness. Offer Me your wretchedness and My Soul shall soothe you, your Saviour is by your side. I am He who raises the poor from the dust. You see My Vassula, it is by faith and through faith in Me that I have made you enter this state of grace. ♥

The Lord means that I approached Him with His grace by faith and through child-like faith.

I Jesus love you. Delight Me always. ♥

THE JESUS PRAYER

January 18th, 1990

Lord Jesus Christ Son of God, have mercy on us.
Lord Jesus Christ Son of God, have mercy on us.

I tell you if anyone prays this rosary[2] to Me, heaven will open to him and My

---

[1]Jesus said this indicating with two fingers His Lips.
[2]The Orthodox rosary.

Mercy shall save him. Make your peace with Me, make your peace with Me. Ask Me every day, "Lord Jesus Christ, Son of God, have mercy on me the sinner." ♥ Daughter, teach your brothers[1] this prayer, teach them to be in solitude and in silence while praying this rosary. Embellish My Church, daughter. ♥ Come, advance in purity of heart. ΙΧθΥΣ ⋗◯Ð

BE IN A CONSTANT PRAYER AND AWAKE

January 19th, 1990

Peace be with you. Meditate upon the mystery of My Presence. O Vassula, there are so many temptation in the world that souls cannot afford to be one second asleep, they should be in constant prayer and awake. These temptations arise from almost nothing, the traps that Satan puts are so cunningly disguised that souls fall instantly inside them completely unaware they have even fallen! but if souls only listened to Me and would pray more often and feel My Presence more often, talking to Me as their companion, or praying to Me as their Father, then they would be more aware of these traps. ♥ Incessant prayers keeps the devil far and their soul closer to Me. Come, praise Me daughter now and then, it glorifies Me and it pleases Me too. Say these words:

> *Glory be to God the Highest*
> *Blessed be His Name.*

just these words and I am glorified. Then say this:

> *My Jesus, You who favoured me,*
> *I bless you.* ♥

Come, these lines please Me. We, us?

Yes Lord.

We, us?

Yes Holy Mother.

You are My flower. ♥

---

[1] The Catholics.

CREEP IN THE DEPTHS OF MY SACRED HEART

January 21st, 1990

Peace be with you. Never stop desiring Me, I am being glorified and you little one are being purified. Creep in the depths of My Sacred Heart and let Me hide you in there, I want you just for Myself. I love you to jealousy. Your God loves you in spite of your nothingness, your incapacity to follow My precepts and to adjust yourself into My Law. I love you to folly in spite of your imperfections, I love you because you want to follow Me. My little lamb, I shall lift you on My Shoulders and you will come with Me wherever I go[1]. ΙΧθΥΣ ⋈⊃

I AM THE WAY, THE TRUTH AND THE LIFE

January 22nd, 1990

Message for France, in Nice for our prayer meeting for 11th February:

Peace be with you. I am the Spirit of Love, of Peace of Reconciliation. ♥ I am He who loves you most, I am your Creator. I tell you solemnly that I shall keep spreading My Holy Spirit on your sons and daughters as has never happened among many generations, to nourish you directly from My Own Hand and to place My entire Law on your hearts. ♥ I am in your days revealing My Holy Face to you all, yes, My Holy Face shall shine on you My beloved ones. I shall reveal to you My Glory and you who might not know Me yet, I shall come to you too and take your hand in Mine and place it on My Sacred Heart. I shall make you feel My Heartbeats and if you would then allow Me, I shall entice your little heart and consume it with My ardent Love and make you Mine entirely. ♥ I shall, if you abandon yourselves to me, form you into My Divine Image, I shall give you back your divinity and make you holy as I am Holy. So come to Me, your Saviour, why look elsewhere? Why seek what the world offers and does not last? Seek what is Holy and Eternal, why rely on what the world offers when what it offers does not last? Have you not heard before that I have said how all flesh is grass? The grass withers, the flower fades, but My word remains forever. Turn to Me and rely on My Love.

---

[1] Jesus' love covered me. I cannot describe in words His Great Love.

My little children I am the Way, the Truth and the Life. Do not listen to the Tempter who seeks the ruin of your soul, his dominion is in the world, but listen to Me your God, who offers you My Hand today and who bends all the way to you to lift you from the dust and make you holy in My Heart. ♥ Listen to Me and you shall inherit My Kingdom. Come to Me and make peace with Me, My Peace I bequeath to you, a peace the world cannot give you. Come you who have not acknowledged Me yet as your Redeemer and detach yourself from the elemental things that can neither lift nor feed your soul, why be enslaved to them? Come back to Me. Even in your wretchedness and your guilt, I accept you as you are and tell you that I have forgiven you already. Let Me tell you My child that no man has greater love for you than Mine. Lift your eyes to Me and behold Who is pleading you, it is I, Jesus, your Saviour, who comes to you today speaking through the mouths of even the least among you. I come bare-foot[1] and like a Beggar to ask from you a return of love. I am in search of your heart, do not refuse Me. Day and night I stretch out My Hands to you, when will you come to Me? When will I hear your response? Will I find an answer in this wilderness My child? or will Silence cover My Soul? Listen, listen to My plea, this is the consolation you can offer Me. Do not be afraid, I will help you, see? I shall renew you entirely if you shall abandon yourself to Me. I have come all the way to your door and today, if you are assembled together here to listen to what My Spirit says to you, it is because I chose it to be this way.

I have come to give you Hope, I have come to give you Light, I have come not to condemn you but to awaken you My child and to show you My Sacred Heart and Who is standing before you. ♥ You are Mine, though not all of you are, because some of you put honour from men before the honour that comes from God. ♥ So I tell you solemnly :

> *receive My Holy Spirit today*
> *receive My Holy Spirit today*
> *receive My Holy Spirit today*

Return to Me. ♥ I mean to deliver you from evil and rouse your love for Me; I mean to show Myself to you and give you the sign of My Holy Presence as I give to others, covering you with My delicate fragrance of incense. Come then to Me and talk to Me. Talking to Me is praying, praying from your heart. ♥ I have in the stillness of the night come to remind you of My precepts. Do you not know that since time began and man was set on earth, a room in Heaven has been prepared for you? Your Home is in Heaven with Me by My side, let this room be filled with your presence. Do not grieve Me to see your room empty for eternity.

---

[1]Bare-foot = in simplicity, without necessary choosing holy souls, to manifest Himself through them.

Return to Me. Cease erring in this wilderness aimlessly, seek Me My child. Cease in doing evil. Learn to forgive, learn to do good, be confident in Me your God. Learn to love your enemies, make peace with Me. I tell you solemnly that if the earth is covered with disasters today, it is the fruit of its apostasy. ♥

Ah My friends, all you who love Me and devote your entire life to Me, you who freed the needy when they called and with the orphan who had no love, gave him your warmth; you who are sensitive to the poor men's needs and console the widow and open your doors wide to the fatherless, and you, who seek to serve the cause of justice, never raising your hand against the guiltless, rejoice! for you are indeed My children. I am today, beloved ones, asking you to pray fervently and amend for those whom My Heart loves, but have turned against Me.

I am asking you to immolate yourselves for all those who severe My Wounds, by watching them kill their child before even its birth. Pray for the womb that shape these children but forgets them, and their names are recalled no longer. Invoke Me in your troubles and I shall rush to you.

Count your blessings and praise Me, have you not heard before, that I rescue all those that cling to Me? You are not fatherless, you have a Father in Heaven who loves you infinitely and His Name is like myrrh, pouring out of Him to anoint you and bless you. Beloved, I am giving you the gift of My Love. Take courage all you who immolate for others, I am near you to console you; take courage My children, your God is very near you and many heard My Footsteps. Love is returning to you as love and shall dwell among you. ♥ *I bless each one of you, leaving My Sigh of Love upon your forehead. Be one.* IXθΥΣ ⤜◻▷

THE WORLD IS UNGRATEFUL TO LOVE

January 26th, 1990

Peace be with you. ♥ *Love loves you. Evangelize with love for Love, repeat after Me these words:*

> *My Lord and King*
> *Keep my spirit steady*
> *and willing*
> *and I shall teach transgressors*
> *the way to You,*
> *and to You the sinners shall return. Amen   Psalm 51:12-13*

146

Later on:

Delight Me and stay in My Light, I am the Light. Pray My Vassula that those souls who wound Me, may see the Light and get to know then their left hand from their right hand. Hear My Mother:

♥ **Today My Heart is in tears because of so many sins. The world is ungrateful to Love. I appear to many and call out,[1] pleading them to return to God and change their lives but only very few really do. So many do not change, daughter, pray for these stubborn souls.**

I shall pray Holy Mother.

I bless you and all those who pray for these. ♥

A PRAYER FROM JESUS

January 29th, 1990

Lord?

I Am. ♥ *Little one let us pray:*

> *Lord my God*
> *Lift my soul from this darkness*
> *into Your Light.*
> *Envelop my soul into Your*
> *Sacred Heart;*
> *Feed my soul with Your Word;*
> *anoint my soul*
> *with Your Holy Name,*
> *make my soul ready to*
> *hear Your discourse.*
> *Breathe Your sweet fragrance on*
> *my soul reviving it.*
> *Ravish my soul*
> *to delight Your Soul.*
> *Father, embellish me, Your child,*

---

[1] To humanity.

by distilling Your pure myrrh
upon me.
You have taken me to Your
Celestial Hall,
where all the Elect are seated.
You have shown me around
to Your angels,
ah, what more does my soul ask?
Your Spirit has given me life
and You who are the Living Bread
have restored my life.
You have offered me to drink
Your Blood,
to be able to share for eternity
with You, Your Kingdom
and live forever and ever.
Glory be to the Highest!
Glory be to the Holy of Holies
Praised be our Lord,
Blessed be our Lord, for His
Mercy and His Love
reaches from age to age and
forever will.

Amen.

Good, My child. ♥

Jesus was happy for my dictation.

I WANT YOU TO TRUST ME

January 30th, 1990

My Lord?

I Am. Lean on Me every time you feel discouraged and weak. I love you and it is out of love I allow certain situations and events to happen to show you that without Me you are nothing. I allow these events to happen to keep you near Me, and to make your soul depend on Me and lean on Me. I want you to trust Me. I am He who holds the foundations of the earth together. Tell Me that you love

Me flower, lean on Me. Listen to My Voice and follow Me blindly. Set to work with your God. Come, it pleases Me. I and you, you and I. See?
IXθΥΣ ⪧⎯⫐

GOD HAS GIVEN YOU THE GIFT OF HIS LOVE

January 31st, 1990

Yesterday I was for seven hours under the Lord's dictation, today, around six hours, and in the end I asked Jesus, "Jesus shall we go now and do some other work?" (I had in mind to start cleaning the kitchen.) And Jesus, without the slightest hesitation said, "Then let us go!" He sounded very eager to have me up and start cleaning the kitchen. He behaved as though I had to do a very important and urgent work.

Message for Nice to be read on 11th, from our Holy Mother:

Peace be with you. ♥ My little children, I am your Celestial Mother, the Mother of your Saviour, the Mother of your Redeemer. Today I invite you all to look for the things that are in Heaven. I ask you to detach yourselves from the principles of this world and lift your heads towards heaven. Seek all that is heavenly, seek the Light and the Light shall not fail you. ♥ Please God and turn to Him, do not cling to the world, cling to the One who shall guide your step to heaven.

Ah beloved children, have you not yet understood? Heaven is your Home and earth is your preparation, your preparation to meet God. God has given you the gift of His Love, will you not respond to His Gift? Many of you have seen many signs. These signs are to be observed, they are the signs of the end of Times, they are not the signs of the end of the world, they are the signs of the end of an era. ♥ Jesus and I are preparing you all to enter into the era of Love and Peace, the New Heavens and the New Earth that has been promised you long ago. I therefore implore you for your conversion before the day of purification because the time is pressing and I tell you that before this generation has passed away, all that I have been telling you through my chosen souls will have taken place, ♥ from the time at Fatima to this day. ♥ Beloved children, remember that Our Presence is also a mystery and you should always remember that you are NEVER alone. ♥ Learn to pray without ceasing and with your heart; learn to fast and do penance; learn to go and confess once a month, do not weary to do good and practice it with regard to others. Live the Lord's Law. I love you children and it is out of Love that I prepare you to meet

the Lord. I bless each one of you. Enter your homes with Our Peace and never forget that We are with you. ♥ (Reading from the Bible : St Luke 18:1-8)

Lord?

I Am. I give you My Peace. Reveal My Holy Face in Nice, before many I shall stand. My child, be dauntless. Love loves you. ♥

Jesus was encouraging me for the prayer meeting in Nice.

Heaven is made out of Light and when Heaven's doors open even slightly in front of you, this Light covers you entirely. I have given you the possibility to have "tasted" a bit of heaven, let Me be then your theme of your praises and proclaim My Name to your brothers in My sanctuary. Praise Me in full assembly, entice the hearts of My children, give all glory to your God. ♥ Love is with you. ♥

I want to fulfil the vows I made to You, my Lord. I shall indeed try and pay You my thank-offerings. Give me the right words to speak and honour You. I bless You my God for spoiling me and for allowing me to walk in Your presence, in the Light of the living.

February 9th, 1990

Message for Sion. Monastry of the Capucins:

Peace be with you. ♥ All I ask from you is love. Beloved children it is I your Jesus who was giving you so many messages to remind you of My Law, to remind you who I Am. If you make My Word your home, your soul shall be lifted to Me and you will reach Me. Come to Me before your spirit fails you, come and reflect on all that I have been giving you, come and ponder on My desires. Seek Me, be thirsty for Me. Come and meditate on all that I have given you and take My Words at heart. I desire that you actively put everything I have given you into practice and treasure them. ♥ Ah beloved children, if you only knew how My Sacred Heart is wounded every time one of you postpones for later on My desires. If you only knew what I have been and am offering you, your joy would be complete. Praise Me your Saviour day and night, praise Me for feeding you by My Own Hand. I have listened to you from above and so I came to your help, will you then not listen to Me? Accept and submit to My Teachings and My Desires which like seeds I have planted in you. So do what I your Saviour ask you and do not just listen to my messages and deceive yourselves. Beloved ones, you whom My Soul loves, I tell you solemnly that I desire prayers coming from the heart. I desire you to pray for all the bishops and priests; I desire you to listen to all the teachings of those who represent Me; I desire you to fast and do penitence; I desire you to receive My Holy Eucharist as often as you can; I desire you to go to confession at least once a month; I desire you to read daily a part out of Scriptures; I desire you to amend for others by sacrificing; I desire them to pray the rosary and if possible all three mysteries. My goal is to bring you back to divinity and live holy for I am Holy, these are My Principles. ♥ *I desire your abandonment daily. I am the source of Love and you can all draw from My Heart to give this Love to others. Then I want you to learn to adore Me and to remember My Presence constantly, My Presence is also a mystery. You should always remember that you are NEVER alone, I am always with you. Reach perfection ... let this dry land prosper ... I am not asking you things unknown to you nor out of your capacity. I am asking you all that is holy and all that I have is Holy, My Body is Holy, so come and eat My Flesh and drink My Blood for whoever comes to Me I shall not turn away. I am the Bread of Life. Pray so that the evil one may not deceive you, do not let My Eyes grow dim with grief. Proclaim My Love on the roof of your houses.* ♥ *Proclaim that My Love is more delightful than wine. I shall remind you that you all have a Father in Heaven who loves you infinitely and His Name is like myrrh pouring out of Him to anoint you and bless you, His Name is Love.* ♥ *I bless each one of you, leaving my sign of Love upon your forehead. Love loves you and is with you every single day. Be one.* ΙΧθΥΣ ⤳

Our Holy Mother's Message:

Peace be with you. ♥ My beloved children, do as the Lord asks you to do. Pray for My other sons and daughters who are far from Us, pray for their conversion. Seek always what is holy. Be like sunflowers who seek and turn towards the sun, following the light. Look on what the Lord is offering you and praise His holy Name. Approach all you who desire Him to be so near you and take your fill of His Fruits, God is your creator and He can be your Educator too. Do not cease praying when everything goes well for you, pray even in your joy. Come and praise Him. Come and exult Him, God is your Guardian too. Depend on Him and He shall never fail you, for His Light is your guide in the darkness. Observe His commandments, beloved ones, be docile in the hands of your Father. Be fervent to take Wisdom as your Educator and Guide. Grow in Wisdom, grow in the Lord's Spirit so that you may be in peace and in perfect union with the Lord. One more advice for today: follow the <u>path of Faith</u>, keeping the Law. Please live Our Messages, meditate on our messages. Realise what great joy Jesus and I have teaching you, but Our joy will be at its fullest the day you shall overcome <u>completely</u> your lethargy and abandon yourselves entirely to God, trusting Him. I bless each one of you. ♥ Remember Our Holy Presence, do not leave us behind ... Pray My beloved children, fill your days with Love's Presence. ♥

LIVING THE PASSION

February 13th, 1990

Today while praying the rosary with Fr James and while we were on the 4th mystery, the carrying of the Cross, I suddenly went into a sort of rapture. I lost my voice and had to whisper and every word I pronounced came out of me with great difficulty. I found myself in the Passion sharing Jesus's sufferings, while on the 5th mystery, the Crucifixion, I seemed to go slowly out of it again. When it was over I felt heavy and my speech and movements were slower than usual, my spirit still under His agony.

Jesus ?

I Am. Dearest soul, My agony is great, let Me share it with you. Make My heaven in you. Bless Me. Love loves you. Peace upon you. Look at Me .. are you willing to go through My Passion? Are you willing to sacrifice more ?

I'm willing to do Your Will.

Then I and you shall share greater things. Vassula, eat little today and tomorrow fast strictly. Please Me and devote your day for Me, do no more writing for now. I want you to remember My Presence fully today. ♥ *I love you and I bless you. We, us, remember? Pray.* ♥

I AM THE RESURRECTION

February 15th, 1990

Jesus?

I Am. Lean on Me entirely, summoning My lambs to feed them My Bread glorifies Me. Come, let me give you a few words of Light. I am the Resurrection who brings the dead to Life. Go on your way now and remember? Go on, say it!

Your Presence Lord.

Yes, My Presence and My Mother's too daughter. ♥ IXθΥΣ

THIS GIFT IS NOW GIVEN TO YOU

February 16th, 1990

Early in the afternoon Fr James and I knelt in front of my small altar to pray the rosary, the sorrowful mysteries. As soon as we started the sorrowful mystery of Gethsemane, I had great difficulty to pronounce the words. I found myself unable to utter any word and it seemed that my spirit went again into a sort of rapture and in this way I entered Jesus's agonies in Gethsemane. I was in this way until the last 'hail Mary' then when Fr James, who went on anyway, started the second mystery, the scourging, I found myself violently thrown on to the rug, prostrated, and arms slightly above my head. I went through the scourging. My body shook violently every time the 'whip' fell on me. For this first time Our Holy Mother was preparing me for every mystery and thus I went through the whole Passion until the Crucifixion, going through the agonies and suffering of Jesus. I had no physical pains, all pains were interior. Later on, like one hour later, I went through the whole Passion once more. Then at around 18.30 again, I succumbed once more through the whole Passion more violently than ever.

This Gift is now given to you out of My Love. You have not merited My Gift nevertheless I am your God and I overlook all your weaknesses and your sins I have forgiven. IXθYΣ ⋈⊃

February 19th, 1990

Ah Vassula ... My Spirit of Love shall invade your whole being. Let My Spirit rest on you and you shall experience great wonders. ♥ *Love loves you.*
IXθYΣ ⋈⊃

MY PASSION IS REPEATED EVERY DAY

February 20th, 1990

Today again, while praying the sorrowful mysteries, I experienced part of the Lord's Passion. I experienced part of Gethsemane and part of the Crucifixion.

Child, penetrate deeper into My Wounds, listen to My Heartbeats ... My fondness for you has become folly to the extent that I want you now to participate with Me My Passion. Love Me as I love you. My Passion is repeated every day. Every single day I am dragged on the road to Calvary by those who do not follow My Path any longer. My agonies are multiplied when I see My children heading into eternal fire; My Heart sinks into intolerable pain to watch so much ingratitude on this earth; My Body is scourged unmercifully. I suffer, yet I had filled their houses with good things, I had given them My Peace. I love them and still love them to Passion and yet from these very ones I am crowned with a crown of thorns. I stand before them like a Beggar with My Heart in My Hand, pleading them, but instead of a kind look they mock Me, they spit on Me, they jeer at Me, they strike My Head and they lead Me with violence to the Mount where they recrucify me, to waste away slowly and My Blood is poured out without cease. I am re-crucified every day by sinners. I need to rest, will you let Me rest? Take My thorned Crown, My Nails and My Cross ... Have you nothing to tell Me ?

My Lord, my Beloved One, You who entrusted me with Your most Sacred Jewels, You who covered me with Your Love and Tenderness, You who poured on me like myrrh Your Teachings and who fragranced me with Your Perfume, I delight in Your Presence. You have given Me the Gift of your Love, You have given Me the Gift of Your Passion and I in my poverty cannot offer You but my blessings, my will, my soul, and my heart.

February 23rd, 1990

At 15.00 hours without fail I went to the appointment with Love to meet Jesus in the Passion and His Cross.

154

WE ARE SHARING MY PASSION

March 2nd, 1990

Jesus met me again in His Passion and Cross.

♥ *We are sharing My Passion for the following reasons, My child: for the conversion of souls, for reparations for all those who distort My Word; for these teachers who assume that I have not risen with My Body; for those who stifle Me differentiating themselves in Me; for the insincerity that reigns around those who surround My Vicar; for the insincerity that reigns among those who cry out for Peace and Unity but remain lifeless to their word; for those who suffocate the Voice of My Holy Spirit and for all those who continue to live in great wickedness under these skies. Beloved amend for all those souls who lead Me hour after hour on the road to Calvary, all these reparations are not in vain.* ♥ *Love will assist you too.[1]* ♥ *Come.* ΙΧθΥΣ ⤳⬭*

I, GOD LIVED IN YOUR WILDERNESS

March 3rd, 1990

Jesus?

I Am. Never be flagrant, despise all that does not come from Me. I am Pure and Holy, how else does My Spirit work in you as I wish?[2] Vassula, there is nothing you can do without Me, it is I who shall glorify My Name again. Sinners shall return to me; My Name shall be held Holy and what I have said I shall fulfil.

My child, I am the Revealer of Mysteries and I am disclosing to many what is to take place. You are one of my chosen souls to whom I have revealed My Holy Face and My intentions, all you have to do is to keep transmitting My messages. You are not to convince anyone. Flower, do everything you can and I shall do the rest. I know how limited you are, but do not worry, beside you I am to hearten you. Multiply your prayers, delight Me and remain near me. Remember, you were dead and I lifted you; you were cold towards Me and I enlivened in you My Flame to consume you with My Love; you were apathetic towards Me but I have made you

---

[1] Jesus meant when I shall be living that afternoon His Passion.
[2] Jesus is reproaching me for certain things I was saying about someone.

fervent and thirsty for Me. For years I, your God, lived in your wilderness, finding no rest and no consolation from a creature I have created with so much love. With great dismay I could see you slipping away from Me. I had but to say, "let this wilderness and dry land exult!" but I wanted your co-operation, I did not want to violate your liberty. To free you beloved, I had to drag you all the way to the desert and leave you on your own ♥, only then you came to realize how naked you were and how stained your soul was, and so with great terror you came flying at My Feet. ♥ You realised how insufficient you were on your own. I then made you understand how I had suffered in your wilderness and how you had turned My Lips dryer than parchment for thirst of love. Then I made you see your insides as having become the perfect wasteland for the viper to nestle and lay its eggs without fear, within you.[1] ♥ I then allowed your veil to fall so that your eyes see My Beauty and with My Finger I touched you, transfiguring you. I went in all directions seeking by what means I could make you Mine for eternity and make out of you an initiate in My mysteries. I transformed your desert into a spring and I made out of your wasteland rivers.

Yes! I am the One who soon out of your[2] scorched earth will make lakes, and out of your parched lands springs of water. I shall not leave you to die, I will stir up many of you and shall make My Voice heard from My Holy dwelling place. I mean to display My Holiness and My Mercy to many nations so that they may acknowledge Me. I am Holy and I mean to make you all understand that you too must live holy. ♥

"Late have I loved You, O Beauty ever ancient, ever new. Late have I loved You! You were within me but I was outside and it was there that I searched for You. In my unlovliness I plunged into lovely things which You created. You were with me but I was not with You. Created things kept me from You, yet if they had not been in you they would not have been at all. You called, You shouted and You broke through my deafness. You flashed, You shone and You dispelled my blindness. You breathed Your fragrance on me. I drew in Your breath and now I pant for You. I have tasted You, now I hunger and thirst for more. You touch me and I burned for Your Peace." (St Augustines Confessions, Book X)

My Lord, my thoughts are for unity, are they sincere My Lord to unite ?

There My child, have I not told you and shown you how rigid some of them are? They cry out for peace and for unity but they do not mean one single word out of what they say, their heart is as hard as rock and they are unyielding as a millstone, yet I shall bend them all with My Flame, just wait and see ..

---

[1] In the very beginning of this revelation God had given me a vision to see the interior of my soul. I saw that I was feeding a viper.
[2] The entire world.

MY CUP TASTES BITTER

March 5th, 1990

Peace be with you. ♥ *Hear Me, I am the Most High who favoured you. Pray.*

I prayed.

Remember Vassula, you are clay and I am able to mould you into anything I want to. Daughter, allow Me to mould you every Tuesday and Friday into a copy of Myself, giving you my agonies of My Passion. My Cup tastes bitter but will you share it with Me? Tell me My child, will you undergo My Passion like I please?

Yes Lord, as You please.

My Grace is upon you. I shall shape you into a little crucifix. My Body is covered with innumerable marks given to Me by those whom I love most. Will you share the marks of My Body?

Yes my Lord, as you want.

The Love I have for you is unmeasurable. Come. ♥

THEY PIERCED THE HANDS THAT CREATED THEM

March 10th, 1990

Message for the March 31st, 1990 to prayer group:

Peace be with you. I the Lord Jesus love you. Dearest children, learn that I am the Eternal Truth. I am the Way that leads you to Eternal Life ♥ *are you ready in these days of lent to follow My Path? Are you ready to recognize that I am He who marked My Path with My Blood? I am the Crucified with the Five Wounds who speaks to you today. I am the Victim of Love who seeks your heart. Com, approach, you whom My Heart loves, you who still hesitate. Come to Me and penetrate into the Wound of My Heart so that I may entice you and make you understand that therein you shall find your Peace and Joy. Come nearer to Me soul and let Me breathe on you My sweet fragrance, reviving you. Abandon yourself to Me and I shall envelop your soul into My Sacred Heart; call to Me and*

I shall answer you; seek Me fervently and you shall find Me. Abandon your evil ways and place your feet into My Path and I shall lift you and ravish your soul to delight My Soul.

My Love is like a Fountain, a Well of Living Waters, so come and draw from this Fountain and you will live. Do not be like the world, because the world fails to appreciate My great Love. ♥ My child, have you fully understood My Passion? I am the One who delivered you from Death. Persecuted I was for your sake, disfigured from the blows, spat upon, despised, mocked and jeered, I was, for your deliverance. Scourged without mercy, I was, for the sake of My great love for you. I have carried your sins on My Shoulders without uttering one complaint, like a lamb that is lead to the slaughter-house, like a sheep that is dumb before its shearers, never opening its mouth.[1] And to free you my beloved one, I allowed Myself to be pierced by those very ones I had created. Yes, they pierced the Hands that created them and through My Wounds I healed you... For your sake I have endured hours of suffering to lift your soul from the pit. I am your Holy One, yet I allowed you to stretch Me on the Cross until My Bones were disjointed. Feel today My agony, feel My thirst for lack of love, a love no flood can ever quench and no torrents can ever drown. ♥ Will I ever see you, you who still err in the desert? Come back to Me and reconcile with Me and live holy, abandoning your ways. In sorrow and tears I watched this unholy generation go away following Vice instead of Virtue, Death instead of Life, because this generation relied on falsehood, thus conceiving rationalism which gave birth to atheism. So for how long must I have stayed bereft and lonely behind each Tabernacle while tears of Blood stream down My Cheeks, leaving every fibre of My Heart broken? My agonies of Gethsemane are repeated in My Soul every hour. Enter into My Wounds and you will understand My agonies.

I had foreseen from the very beginning how, in spite of My Sacrifice, clans would rise against Me and divide My Body causing so many new doctrines, and once their sense of right and wrong dulled in their own dissension, would lose the sense of brotherhood. And the wailing of My Lambs since then have pierced My Ear .. and now as an echo My Cry comes from the Cross to different nations to call you all back and make you one. So if anyone asks Me "why are these Tears of Blood streaming down Your Cheeks?" I shall reply: "these are shed for you My child, they are Tears caused by sins and impurities." And if you ask Me "and what about these marks on your Body? Why are your Wounds wide open?" I shall reply, "these My Child are being given to Me daily without Mercy for those I love most but have now turned against Me, leaving My Wounds wide open," yet they were the ones who once said, "we would like to learn Your Ways and follow You." ♥ Intellectually they are in the dark and not until they die to their self will they

---

[1] Isaiah 53:7.

be able to see the Light.

Today again, in these days of lent, I come to you My child, sinner, just or unjust, or repelled from humanity, or tossed around one way or another in this world, I come to ask you for reconciliation. Go and reconcile with your brother, for in reconciling with him your are reconciling with Me your God. Offer Me your peace as I offer you My Peace, imitate Me and be holy, sacrifice and fast so that you may grow in My Spirit which is: Love, Holiness and Truth.

What I need is holiness from you, do not be like jackals who run their lives by night! because your intentions I knew them long before you were born. In these days I am pouring out My Spirit on your nation so that you grow like grass where there is plenty of water, I descend in this way to fill your stores with My produce. I come to awaken you from your lethargy and draw you away from your evil ways; and now I make a special appeal to all those who are under My Name and are working for Unity and Peace, I ask you to come to Me like a child and face Me answering Me these questions:

brothers, have you done everything you can to preserve the unity of My Body?

Tell Me brothers, where is the Peace I bequeathed to you, the Gift I have given you?

Why are you continuously differentiating yourselves in Me?

Are you sincerely trying to be united again in your belief and practice?

I tell you solemnly to renew your mind with a spiritual revolution, a revolution of love. Forgive the grudges you have against each other and come to Me renewed, come to Me pure. Wake up from your sleep! I am at your very doors knocking. Do not be like salt which has lost its flavour, be like a tree putting out graceful shoots and bear the fruits of holiness. Fulfil My Law by uniting and helping each other ♥ *like yesterday. I lift My Eyes to the Father and pray to Him:*

> *Holy Father, keep those you have given Me true*
> *to Your Name so that they may be one like Us.[1]*
> *May they all be one.[2] Father, Righteous One,*
> *remind them of My docility, My humility, My*
> *sincerity and My great Love, so that they may*
> *end My Agony, this Agony which is the cause of*

---

[1] John 17:11.
[2] John 17:21.

so much bleeding in My Body. Let them recognize their errors and reconcile so that when they come to receive Me, they come worthily. Father, call the shepherds and teach them to be yielding and docile towards each other, self-effacing and humble. May they realise My Atonement this time of lent and seek true Wisdom in Me. Amen. ♥

Happy the man who listens to Me, happy those who follow My Ways, happy the man who humbles himself, happy the poor in spirit theirs is the kingdom of Heaven. I, your Lord, bless you and your families, leaving My sigh of Love on your forehead and My Peace in your little hearts. Never forget that Love is always with you, be one. ΙΧθΥΣ ⊂▷

COME AND DRAW FROM JESUS' SACRED HEART
COME AND ADORE HIM

Message from St Mary:

Peace be with you. ♥ Feel My Presence among you, let this grace be given to you all... Beloved children, I ask you today to purify your soul. Prepare your soul in these days of lent so that you understand and fully penetrate into Christ's Passion. Understand how He sacrificed Himself for you in order to set you free from all wickedness and to purify you so that you could be His adoptive children. ♥ God asks your reconciliation and to do penance. Repent and believe the Good News, be reconciled to God and you shall become His Heirs for the Eternal life. ♥ God wants you perfect and to reach perfection. I will remind you that you cannot reach it without having reconciled through Him and for Him. ♥ Self-abnegation will <u>lead</u> you on the road to perfection. ♥

I your Holy Mother, am without ceasing interceding for all of you to the Father for your voluntary abandonment and for you to be made perfect. Jesus and I are coming to you in this way to warn you and wake you up from your sleep. The time is fleeing and although many of you woke up, Satan redoubling his malices and traps made a good part of you fall back into deep sleep. His aim is to divide you, create quarrels among you and cut you off from the Vine. <u>Resist</u> all temptations, <u>resist</u> evil and conquer it with love. Conquer egoism with sacrifices; conquer malice with good. Prove to God your love to Him with good acts, love your neighbour as yourself. Our Messages are to be followed and not just read, they are to be lived. **Prove to God that you are His children by being pure, humble, obedient and self-effaced.**

My priests, I love you, you who are the sheep that Jesus gathers in His Arms and instructs. Come and draw from Jesus' Sacred Heart to enliven your love into an ardent flame and thus transmit it to Jesus's lambs. Follow the King of Peace and you shall learn to know Him. Jesus who is the Sacrifice will help you sacrifice more of yourselves. Find Him, beloved ones, in simplicity of heart, God is not complicated. The Holy of Holies first speaks in one way and then in another to make you understand that the time is pressing. I am filled with pain and choked by Tears and My Heart swells with sorrow to watch so many of My children in deep sleep, rejecting all Our Merciful warnings. I call all day long, I appear all around the globe, pleading you to convert and approach God. I do not come My beloved children to reproach you, I come out of love to warn you, to help you and educate you in your spiritual growth. Being your Mother I observe how you grow, I love you and My aim is to educate you to grow in God. Accept with joy these days of grace, God has not deserted you nor has He condemned you. He has never turned His Holy Face away from you ♥ so receive His Holy Spirit of Grace with joy and with song.

Rejoice Our Hearts and spread Our Messages at the ends of the world and through them convert other souls. ♥ I desire to see all churches full, alive and warm so live Our Messages. I am pouring out on you graces to encourage you, be blessed and come nearer to the Cross of Jesus' Feet, as I was with John and the Holy Women. Come and adore Him, come and adore Him, let the Spirit of Holiness dwell upon you for ever and ever. I your Holy Mother bless you and your families. ♥ (Biblical reading from Matthew 5.17.26)

ALWAYS REMEMBER MY GENTLE MASTERY

March 29th, 1990

Flower, I give you My Peace. Carry My Cross till the end. Never ever forget My great love for you, a love no human can ever give you. ♥ Always remember My gentle mastery, I am delighted to have you near Me in this way. I have favoured you so rejoice! Vassula, you had not prayed nor had you any love for Me. I did not accuse you for your aridity nor for your hostility towards Me, yet out of Compassion I lifted your soul from the pit, this, my child, should be branded on your mind.

I the Lord love you. Come, one day you will understand fully. Lift now your eyes to Me and say: "Praised be the Lord! Glory be to God!" I the Lord bless you.
ΙΧθΥΣ ⤜◗

Later on in the evening:

My Lord where are You ? I do not see You!

Little one I am in your heart. ♥

THE LEAST YOU ARE THE MORE I AM

April 2nd, 1990

I want to keep my love for You always. I know I cannot detect my own failings, this is why I came to ask you to preserve me from any wicked tendencies. Free me from grave sin, allow me sweet Yahweh to take my shelter in You.

Beloved of My Soul, I will grant you the safety you sigh for, be glad. Always choose what pleases Me. Never fear, by your side I am. I desire from you love, obedience, self-effacement, humility, docility, and thus you shall disarm hatred, disobedience, pomposity, vanity, and wickedness. Rejoice soul! Do not look behind you, look at Me, face Me and abandon yourself to Me. My coming is near, anyone who fears Me the Lord will understand. ♥ My Spirit is upon you My well-beloved, I who reared you shall always remind you of My Love. Feel happy! Feel happy! Rejoice, rejoice I tell you! Allow My Spirit to work in you. I am able, in spite of your extreme weakness, to accomplish everything. The least you are the more I Am. Accept My grace and efface your passivity. Peace be with you always. Caress Me with your Heart, never neglect Me. I will teach you many more things. I will acquaint you with real Knowledge, from My Mouth you shall learn. Wisdom comes before you and is your Educator. All you do, do it with love. Embellish My garden, embellish My Head by replacing The Crown of Thorns by a Crown of Roses. I the Lord wait ever so impatiently for the day of My Glory. ♥

LET ME HEAR YOUR VOICE BEFORE NIGHTFALL

April 3rd, 1990

I long for You Jesus, my Saviour, You who snatched me from the pit. I know that you treat me tenderly and that You made me suffer so as to better educate me. Be my Saviour again! Renew my joy, uproot all evil from me since You love Holiness and sincerity of heart!

Be in peace My child. Suffering is My Gift to you to sanctify you. I shall be the sweet torture of your naked soul, the torment of your mind[1], the insatiable thirst of your mouth, the throb of your heart. Open your eyes soul and proceed on the way to sanctity, offer Me your will. ... Open your eyes and look soul! look at the trace I left behind Me. My Path is marked with My Blood, follow these marks and they will lead you to Me. Seek no ally and do not ask what is this? or what is that? My strength shall sustain your falls. Come all the way to Me soul and I shall offer you My Cup, Vassula do not refuse My Cup. Although My Cup tastes bitter, drink, drink and give Glory to Me and I will pour on you like myrrh My Blessings. Listen Vassula, My daughter, though you are surrounded by my enemies you yourself will remain unscathed so do not fear but advance. Follow the marks of My Blood and do not look to your left nor to your right, I am before you waiting for you to sanctify you. Come, come alone, I do not wish to find in you rivals. For the sake of My great Love I have for you, eat less in these days of purification. ♥ I am your Redeemer who stands at the end of this road. Open your eyes and look at the marks of My Blood I shed for you, let these days be memorable to you. Wake up soul, why are you asleep? Come and find your strength in Me, come and I shall appease your thirst if you appease My thirst for Love, this, my daughter, is your due since it was I who came to deliver you from the pit and since it was I who came to your rescue, displaying My great Love for you. Come now and offer Me your will, show your eagerness to quench my insatiable thirst for love by leaving a few drops of your love on My parched Lips, I will welcome them as the wild flowers of the desert welcome the morning dew.

Soul! you were neither blameless nor faithful, yet I have forgiven you in My Purity and My Light. I blotted out every sin of yours; so gratify Me now, lift your eyes to Me now, lift your eyes and look at the banner I am displaying above you ... Among many I have chosen you to show to mankind, through you, My banner of Love and Mercy I am displaying it now above your heads. Generation! like a lover who pursues his well-beloved, I go in all directions seeking by what means I could make you Mine for all Eternity. Show Me generation that behind your wall I can

---

[1]That is: to thirst for God and suffer for not being in heaven already with Him.

still find a faithful friend, even if I find none, a hesitant friend .. and I will turn your deceitfulness into sincere speech so that the Day of disaster does not strike you. Friend! you who still hesitate between evil and good, do not be tepid! Have you not yet understood that My Heart is sick with Love? Come and feel My Heartbeats, every single Heartbeat is a beautiful song of Love. ♥ *Come to Me before the sun sets and before the shadows of the night fall like a veil on you. Come to Me, do not leave Me in dismay until tomorrow. Come before the Gale and Fire come to scatter you like chaff.* ♥ *Come to Me and I shall watch over your soul in the days of distress. Let Me hear you soul, let Me hear the sound of your step, let Me hear your voice before nightfall..* ♥[1] *The fig tree is ripe and soon you shall be eating its first fruits... happy you who are hungry now, you shall be satisfied.* ♥ *Love loves you, My House is your House. Fall into my arms and I shall fill your aridity with My flow of Love. Come, I Jesus love you without measure.* ♥ ΙΧθΥΣ ⤳⊃

MESSAGE FOR LENS

April 10th, 1990

Peace be with you... I am your Holy One who watches you from above. Recollect yourselves and feel My Presence... feel My Presence. Feel My Eyes upon you. ♥ *I tell you truly that no man has greater love than Mine. I am He, He who loves you most, the living God.*

Today My beloved ones your nations are living in darkness, but I descend out of My Infinite Mercy to restore My House and bring you back to Me. I am indeed pouring out My Spirit on all mankind to feed your starving nations with My Word and <u>remind you that I am Holy</u>.

I come to you to encourage you in doing good and discourage your evil tendencies. I am standing at your very doors soul, knocking. I am the One you are looking for, I am the One who lifts your soul and exalts it. I tell you most solemnly that Love is on His way of return. ♥ *My return is soon with you, so pray for the conversion of souls, pray for them to convert before My Return. Pray with fervour that My Cry in this wilderness may reach their ears and break through their deafness. Pray to the Father that His Chalice of Justice does not brim over before your conversion generation! Call out to Me and I shall hear you!*

---

[1] Jesus from pleading suddenly changed His tone.

O generation, generation... defiled beyond words, impure beyond description, your guilt is killing you. Your perversity generation and your disloyalty have pierced all Eternity, leaving the pillars of heaven trembling. Your iniquities have made destitute your spirit from all wisdom. If you knew how My angels tremble to see what is awaiting you... earth, that will be covered with your own blood by your apostasy! earth, who will tear yourself to pieces before the very eyes of My angels! If you all understood the tremor that is to come you would not waste, as it is now, you breath in empty words and in godlessness. I, the Lord, pour out My Spirit to prepare you, to teach you from heaven and call for your repentance and call you for your conversion. I am a God of Mercy who bends all the way down to you in these days of grace to save you, listen to My Cries of distress. Beloved ones, I come to wake you up, I do not grow tired of repeating My pleas ungrateful generation and I shall continue to repeat My Pleas to you. My Lips shall never grow tired calling you but while I am speaking My suffering remains... yet the Light is near you to chase your darkness generation... Open your eyes, open your eyes and you will see Me in My Splendour. ♥ I am ready to give your eyes the light to see so that you may not sleep yourselves to death.

Your generation's deeds are corrupt and vile, far from being My Image, far from Love, far from Holiness. ♥ I am your Holy One but you recrucify Me every single minute. I am He who today with so much Love embrace you with My Arms around you and with My Hand nourishes you gently with My Word to restore you back to divinity. Generation, ever so weak, I come to deliver you from evil, I do not come to menace you, I only come to warn you out of My Infinite Mercy. My very core yearns to possess you and make you Mine for all Eternity and invest you in dazzling white robes! My Heart seeks desperately to drag you away from your abominations. I am calling but so many of you today would not answer. I speak through weak instruments but many of you would not listen, instead these people treat My messengers as imposters. These people would rather choose to do what displeases Me most: take their life .. ♥[1]

Thinking they are doing Me a holy duty; their spirit in the dark and unaware does not recognise My Holy Spirit of Grace not more than the Jews recognized Me as the Messiah! They provoke Me they do not exult Me, they block My way with thorns and briars, promoting impurity and promiscuity in this godless and senseless

---

[1]"take their life.." just three words mean much more they mean that by suppressing the messages of God they are in reality attacking the Holy Spirit, (see Acts 9:4 Jesus asked St. Paul: "Saul, Saul, why are you persecuting Me?" Jesus did not ask: why are you persecuting the Christians) the Holy Spirit who speaks through them. Because of this these people will be held responsible for souls that will be lost but that could have been saved if they had a chance of hearing the Divine Message. The Holy Spirit of Grace today has chosen to wake us up with what our generation needs: multiplication of revelations, messages through apparitions. Fatima's call was not taken seriously, it was ignored for 13 years, it was a warning, the result was the 2nd world war and communism.

generation. Feel My Agony, feel My Sorrow, My Eyes grow dim and are wasting away with weeping. I come all the way to you with great love to offer you the gift of My Love, the gift of My Spirit, the gift of My Divinity. I come to remind you of My Holiness. Tell Me then, let Me hear you, you whom My Sacred Heart loves and throbs for you, will I ever see you coming from this desert? Return to Me so that I may no longer lie in agony in wait for the sound of your step. ♥ I shall not reprove you, no, I shall only let you thrust yourself on My Bosom and I shall cradle you with Tears of Joy My child. I shall wrap you with the flow of My love leaving your soul in My Peace. I will take care of you, am I not your Shepherd? See, you are living in the beginning of those days promised you. I have said that My Spirit of Grace shall breathe on your dead. I mean to raise you from your graves and lead you back to your domain, My Sacred Heart, and I shall fill you with My Spirit, healing you and you will acknowledge Me your God. You on the other hand open your eyes and your heart, abandon yourself to Me, offer Me your will and I shall do the rest. ♥ Remember My Holy Presence. Be My vessels of Light carrying My Word and diffuse My Messages. I the Lord bless each one of you, leaving My Sigh of Love on your forehead. Be one. ΙΧθΥΣ ⤨⊃

THEY LEFT ME MAIMED IN THEIR BATTLE

April 12th, 1990

Message for Paris and Italy

Peace be with you. I am the Resurrection, if anyone believes in Me even though he dies he will live. ♥ I am the Holy Spirit of Truth, I am the Reminder of My Word who comes to you and stirs you up from your deep sleep. It has been said that My Spirit of Grace shall be poured out lavishly on all mankind and that your sons and daughters shall prophesy, all that Scripture says is being fulfilled. I am preparing you from Heaven to acknowledge the Truth; I am encouraging you by displaying portents in heaven and on earth; I am giving to the poor and the small visions; I am sending you My Mother to instruct you as a teacher in different nations; I am displaying My Infinite Mercy like a banner above your heads, generation, to educate you and bring you back to divinity. If you would listen to Me today I shall lift your soul and you will reach the place of rest. Generation! You have been worshipping long enough unnamed idols, lifeless idols, inventions that harm you to death. You accorded divine honours to these, corrupting your life. For years I have not heard the sound of your voice, nor of your step, you have not invoked Me nor praised My marvels. Ah generation, why have you rejected Me your Holy One? Come and listen to Me again. Love will be coming back to you as Love, ♥ *this is My Promise.   So be prepared to receive Me and I shall give you the gift of My Love and the gift of My Holiness.* ♥

Beloved ones, you who are gathered here today learn that it is I Jesus who sought you and called you all the way from the desert to enter My delightful Garden, My Assembly. ♥ *I am the Sacred Heart ever so sensitive who asks you to make peace with Me and reconcile with Me.   Let those thorns encircling My Sacred Heart bloom into a wreath of flowers.   Open your heart to Me and welcome Me, offer Me your heart and I shall ravish you to delight My Heart.   Speak to Me with your heart and I shall not remain unresponsive.* ♥ *Realize that I, who am your King and Sovereign of all, descend all the way to you in this world drenched with sin to seek you My friend, how much longer do I have to seek?   My Eyes are worn out looking for your welcoming response to My Spirit of Grace.   I open My Mouth, panting eagerly for your response, but the word is not even on your tongue.   My Spirit of Grace cries out to you to lead you in the depths of My Sacred Heart but today My Spirit of Grace gets no gratitude for Its Mercy.*

I bend all the way down to you from My Throne to your door.   I come to you weary and as a Beggar in rags, wounded beyond recognition, barefoot and forlorn. Hear My laments, it is I the Christ.   I am thirsty.   I am thirsty for lack of love; My Lips are parched for thirst of love; My Mouth dryer than parchment from repeating My pleas; My Heart is sick with love.   I love you to distraction in spite of your awesome pride and wickedness. ♥ *I come to you My little ones with My Heart in My Hand, I know how poor you are but can I share your meal with you? Will you quench My thirst?   Will you appease My Wounds?   No, you have not sought Me, it is I who sought you and found you naked in this desert you are living in,   Allow Me to enter your heart and I shall adorn you majestically.* ♥ *If you allow Me to enter your heart I shall make you see My Wounds given to Me in the house of My best friends, you shall be awed by their depth and struck by the numerous marks savagely inflicted on My body.   The Wounds of My Body are such that they left Me maimed in their battle.*

I tell you solemnly, anyone who does not welcome the kingdom of God like a little child will never enter it.   Seek Me in simplicity of heart and you shall find Me. Do not put Me to the test and you will see Me, recognizing My Omnipotency; do not stay aloof and cold to Our Calls; do not be deaf to Our Calls, hear Our supplications, open your ears and recognize the Shepherd's Call.   If you are weak I shall lift you and I shall carry you on My Shoulders.   I am ready to blot out every sin of yours in My Purity and My Light.

O friend! Why do you still waver with hesitation?   Your navel-string is still attached to Me.   I am the Source of your breath, I am the Bountiful all-nourishing Source and it is with My Word that I give you life and preserve you from death.   It is not the various crops you eat My friends that give you life, it is I who gives you life.

Lift then your eyes to Me and treasure My Word in your heart and you <u>shall</u> live! Come and ask Me to open your eyes and I shall come eagerly and pull away your veil My friend; come and ask Me to bring you back from your exile, where many of you strayed and I shall come flying to you. Even if you have built a wall across My Path in the time of your wickedness, to divorce Me from you, I shall with one blow of My Breath pull down that wall. Then I shall remind you of My Love, I shall remind you that I am He who loves you most and that your abode is My Sacred Heart; I shall remind you not to differentiate yourselves in Me; <u>I shall remind you to be united in heart and soul</u> and love one another as I love you. Yes, it is I, the Constant Reminder of My Word who speaks to you to refreshen your memories. ♥ Receive My Holy Spirit. I bless each one of you and at this very instant I shall leave on your forehead the Sigh of My Love. Be one.

ΙΧθΥΣ ⋊⃝⃟

THOSE THAT FAIL ME SHALL BE REPLACED
PRAY, PRAY, PRAY, THIS IS MY RECOMMENDATION

April 13th, 1990
Holy Friday

Message for all those who work and diffuse these messages:

Peace be with you. I am the One who stimulates My instruments. Cease worrying, I am beside you My child.

Lord? Invade me.

I shall, if you let Me. ♥ Make space for Me. I love you. Do you realize that through Me My Message shall be known? I hold the keys to all doors, if there is any hinderance remember that I allowed it for My Glory. Be subtle with My Work and this I say to everyone whom I have chosen to spread My grains, those that fail Me shall be replaced. Be clever as snakes but harmless as doves. Fear no one; be alert to the dangers; confide to each other; share with each other; remain all of you in My Love. Remember you have not sought Me, it is I who chose you and it is I who formed you, transfigured you and made you zealous. I have given each one of you a task so that you go out and bear fruit, it is I who have commissioned you for this work. ♥ I love you and I shall guide you till the end. Persevere until the end, do not sleep to give Satan a foothold, stay awake. Rest when you must but do not neglect My Work. Do everything you can, I shall do the rest. I am the Door and no one can enter into My Kingdom unless he passes through Me.

Please Lord, name these people you are talking to.

Vassula, everyone who carries My Word carries My Light, I have chosen them and they know themselves. ♥ *I bless you all, all you who diffuse My Message. Vassula, My lamb, I always knew you weak and this is why I have chosen you, weakness attracts Me.* ♥ *My Power is at its best in weakness, trials you shall always have but these are for your growth. I want you strong, I want you to be able to face difficulties with prudence, I want you to glorify Me.* ♥ *So My Vassula, do not allow the serpent to tempt you, he is prowling near you and trying desperately to make you fall. Be alert always, I am with you and I shall sustain your falls. Pray without ceasing so that the tempter has no opportunity to approach you. This is My recommendation, pray, pray, pray and remember always My Presence. Fast, confess and adore Me, eat Me and drink Me. Repay evil with love and rejoice for all I am giving you. Ahh Vassula... delight Me and stay small.*

Lord, crush me if you must but keep me small.

I shall keep you small. Take now My Hand and let us climb. ♥ *I Jesus love you all, remember, I am the Resurrection.* ΙΧθΥΣ ⤝⟆

THE OUTPOURING OF THE SPIRIT

April 22nd, 1990

It was the stone rejected by the builders that proved to be the keystone, Psalm 118:22. My Lord Jesus, You were rejected then as the Messiah because their spirit was not prepared, their hearts were closed and hard, yet You proved to be The Keystone. In our generation my Lord, the effusion of Your Holy Spirit is also rejected by the "builders" and yet one day Your Holy Spirit will prove to all of us that He was the Keystone. By denying and suppressing Your Holy Spirit that comes to us as the Reminder, "the builders" are preparing again their own downfall.

See how former predictions have come true? Indeed, I have said that the Advocate, the Holy Spirit, whom the Father will send in My Name will teach you everything and <u>remind</u> you of all I have said to you, but I knew all along that only a remnant would listen and return to Me. On these very ones who would listen to Me I shall invest with My Holy Spirit of Wisdom and Insight, yes, I shall invest them with My Spirit of Counsel and Knowledge and the flickering light that now is left in this world will become a vivid fire. I repeat that My Holy Spirit of Grace is being sent out to the four corners of the earth to teach you to be holy and raise *you up again into divine beings. The earth shall turn into a copy of heaven and thus My Will will be done, the prayer I have taught you to pray shall be fulfilled.*

Lord! Turn then all of us away and quick from the path of delusion. May we be one, united and live holy as your angels in heaven, like all souls who live in heaven and undivided in Your Love, may we too share like them Your Love in unity, so that the earth becomes a reflection of heaven. Let Your Kingdom come and renew the earth with fresh things, let Your Holy Spirit in this second Pentecost come quick to renew us with a new spirit of love and transfigure us all into divine beings! Maranatha!

Peace be with you. I tell you truly that the days are coming when My Kingdom on earth shall be as it is in Heaven. You shall not remain divided for long now under these skies, soon you shall all be one and Love will be dwelling among you, this is My Promise. But, My beloved ones, this renewal shall not come without tribulations, like any birth, this renewal will have its birth-pangs too, but the pains will also be quickly overtaken by joy.

I am pouring out My Spirit on you generation to water your desert and to make rivers out of your dry soil. Yes! I shall water your desert and turn it into a Garden, eventually you will see the force of My Words and the splendour of My Beauty. I intend to bring you all back to divinity one after the other, I am your Hope, I am your Refuge, I am your Consoler. Almighty I Am. ♥ *Recognize the Times, recognize the gentle Breath of My Holy Spirit of Grace upon you, I am blowing now on your nations, raising up with My Breath your dead, turning them into a reflection of My Image. I am raising new disciples every single day to glorify My Name again and evangelize with love for Love. I ask you then My beloved ones to pray daily for My Second Coming which is the second Pentecost. Pray for the conversion of souls that they may convert before My Coming.* ♥ *Come to Me as you are and lean on Me, as John My beloved one leaned on Me; you too, place your head on My Bosom and listen to Love's Heartbeats, every heartbeat is a call for Love. All I ask from you is a return of love. Love Me, adore Me, rejoice Me your Lord. I bless you, leaving My Sigh of Love on your forehead. Be one.* ΙΧθΥΣ ⇒<

THE SECOND PENTECOST

Messages for prayer meeting for Lens from Our Holy Mother. Also message for Italy and Paris.

Peace be with you little children. I am your Holy Mother of Love, the Mother of the Word made flesh. I come to you in these days of darkness to educate you in the path of divinity. Be vigilant and fully aware because Satan, the enemy, prowls around you like a roaring lion and seeks any opportunity to make you fall. Stand up to him and combat him together with Me, combat him with your prayers. Your prayers are the most powerful weapon against him. Obedience and humbleness makes the demon flee. God is offering you the gift of His Love, respond to his Merciful calls. God is speaking and He and I call you from the four corners of the earth for your conversion because time is pressing. My little children, stay small and simple, be the salt of the earth by remaining small, for you are the light of the world, you are the predilected souls of Our Heart and the Kingdom of Heaven belongs to the children and to the very little ones.

I appear today in various nations to turn your heart towards the Divine Light, I want to restore your soul, I want to remind you that you all belong to the Father and the Father is Holy so you ought to live holy too. But do not get discouraged because I am here with you to teach you step by step and I can assure you of Our blessings. Every step you take We bless.

I want to, if you allow Me, make you a reflection of the Eternal Light so that when you meet God you would look like an untarnished mirror of God's active power and an image of His Holiness and His Goodness. Today I invite you all to pray with fervour for the renewal of the Church, for the second Coming of the Lord, for the second Pentecost. This is why Jesus and I come today in various countries to prepare you all for this Coming. Pray and lead a life of adoration, pray for the conversion of souls so that everyone may be ready for the Lord's Return. ♥ Love is on the Way of Return, listen and you will already hear His Footsteps. ♥ This is why I implore you to change your lives and live only for God and in God. Remember Scripture says, "anyone who claims to be in the Light but hates his brother is still living in the dark." (1 John 2:9). Reconcile with your brother, reconcile with God, make Peace with God. Beloved ones, remember Our Presence. I bless each one of you. Be in Peace. ♥

YOU ARE MY ALTAR

April 24th, 1990

I rely on Your Love. Let Your love rest on us, let it live in us as never before.

Beloved one, all that I have given you was to draw you closer to Me and adapt you to being with Me. I have given you this grace because it pleases Me - I wanted to comfort you. This, My child, is for your salvation and I shall remain near you in this way till the end, you are My altar and I want My altar pure. I want to fill you with My ardent flame, My Fire, My Holy Spirit. ♥ It was, daughter, only yesterday that I had found you caught and ensnared by the evil one, and today see? you are free. ♥ I, your Saviour, freed you and not only have I freed you, I have also given you Life. You were imprisoned and I have liberated you. You were naked but I have adorned you majestically. You were barren but I have prospered you and flourished you. Your knee had never bent to praise Me nor worship Me your Lord, yet I bent all the way to you to reach you and anoint you, blessing you. I had never heard your voice acclaim Me nor had I seen you in My House coming consciously for Me, yet I came all the way to your house, in your room, to let you hear My Voice. I sang a song of Love to you, so that you in your turn go out to the nations and teach them My Song. I have dispelled your faults like a cloud, your sins like mist, rejoice then in My Presence soul! I shall continue to show to humanity My great Love and Mercy through you so that they may at last believe that it is I. I am LOVE. This is how I shall summon My people and surround them with My Love. I shall be to them like a wall of Fire surrounding them and I will be their glory in their midst. Come, My Vassula.

O God, how I love You!

These words are like flashing jewels of a diadem. Yes, love Me your God, follow My first commandment without nevertheless neglecting the others. Rest now, without forgetting My Presence. We, us?

Yes my Lord, we, us, forever and ever.

I bless you, bless Me too.

I bless You my Lord and I thank You for all that You are giving me.

THE SONS OF RUSSIA SHALL BE RESCUED BY ME

This was a message given to a Russian Orthodox friend of mine concerning Russia.

I will give Russia My Restoring Peace, an everlasting covenant shall be sealed by Me. Like a shepherd rescuing his lambs from the wolves mouth, so will the sons of Russia be rescued by Me. I intend to rise her and make her holy and make out of her sons holy men who will teach incorruptibility, for within her My Spirit shall be living and shall govern her with holiness and justice. ♥

WISDOM IS GIVEN TO MERE CHILDREN

April 30th, 1990

Lord, my God, save us in Your Love. Raise us in Your Light and with Your Infinite Mercy forgive us. Make us strong in faith; unite us to be one so that we may say together, around one Holy Tabernacle, "there is one Lord, one faith, one baptism, and one God who is Father of all, over all, through all and within all."[1]

Try then to imitate Me. ♥

Give us the wisdom then to imitate You.

Wisdom is given to mere children. Unless they seek Me in simplicity of heart, Wisdom shall not be given to them ♥ *and as long as their intellect is at work, wisdom will remain hidden and as a riddle to them.*

Tear away Lord their intellect so that they may at last <u>see</u> with their intellect so that they may at last <u>see</u> with their eyes Your Beauty and Your Splendour!

Little heart, pray for them then, pray in these godless times, let your prayers be like blended incense. ♥ *Pray that I may give them back their sight.* ♥ *Pray that I may go over to them and wake them up from their everlasting sleep. Pray My little one, you who had the Law brought to you by Me and directed by My Holy Spirit, pray that they die to their sin and resurrect to Holiness, Love and Faith, and if there are any wise men let them show their wisdom by their simplicity of heart towards Me. Their zeal to all that is holy and by their ardour to draw souls to Me,*

---

[1]Ref: Ephesians 4:5-6.

may all these things be done with humility and love. Remember that if you do not get what you ask it is because you do not pray hard enough and with your heart. ♥ Come now, never forget My Presence, I am your Holy One and the One who loves you most.

Lord, You are good, patient and forgiving, most loving to all who invoke You. Hear our prayers my Lord, although they may be of extreme poverty, have mercy upon us and open Your Ear. We are sinners and not saints, but You were known to go to the sick and heal them with Your Love. We are all sick, a sickly generation drenched in sin, come to us and heal us, helping us to believe in our unbelievable unbelief!

My Righteousness is eternal; My Love I have for you all is Infinite; My Compassion for the wretched and the sick is Great and beyond human understanding, ask and it shall be given to you. I open My Mouth panting eagerly for your prayers.

I ask and on behalf of my brothers too, that You come and save us Lord in Your Love. Return to us, purify us!

I shall return to you as Love and My Fire shall purify you all.

You have promised us a New Heaven and a New Earth Lord.

I have promised you more than that little one, I have promised you a new Jerusalem and I have promised you that I shall be living among you. I will make My Home among you, see? Very soon now I shall be with you.

Then hurry Lord, hurry, we are all waiting eagerly for the second Pentecost and the outpouring of Your Holy Spirit. The Second Coming.

Are you all prepared to receive Me? Why are you silent?

Because my Lord it is difficult to say these words, "many are not prepared to receive You."

Pray then for those who ignore Me, pray for the godless, pray for those who are not ready to receive Me, prepare yourselves! The fig tree is ripe and soon you shall be eating its fruit. ♥ Come, we, us?

Yes my Lord, we, us.

COME AND VISIT ME IN MY HOUSE

May 12th, 1990

Jesus?

I Am. Peace be with you Vassula. Let Me hear the sound of your step tomorrow in My Church, I shall be waiting for you impatiently. Are you as impatient as Me for this hour when I shall be united to you? Vassula[1], leave Me write it. I love you, are you still willing to answer Me?

Yes Lord. I shall go to the Greek Church but I always have a problem of language, I can hardly follow what the priest says.

But I am there and I do listen to your heart. Speak to Me. Come, listen to this: suppose you go and visit a friend of yours who eagerly is waiting to see you. Would you, upon meeting your friend, remain erect and distant? or would you go towards her and warmly greet her with a kiss? Then, would you not sit together and talk? or would you sit and keep silent? You would talk of course! This is the way I want you to be with Me when you come and visit Me in My House, I want to feel your heart rejoicing every time you meet Me. I want to hear your heart talking to Me. To talk to Me, your God, is praying. My Ear then shall be stuck on your lips and I shall receive each word as drops of honey. Daughter, then comes My great moment, the moment I am so much looking forward to, the moment I had given Myself to you on Golgotha, the Holy Hour of My Sacrifice, the Holy Hour of your redemption, the Holy Hour when I unite Myself to you. I shall wait for both of you to eat Me and drink Me. I bless you My child, do not deny Me these moments of love, these moments of Holy Communion. ♥

My Lord, praised be the Lord, glory be to God, blessed be the Lord!

Peace be with you little one, please Me and discern Me. These very minutes you are with Me are a delight to Me, they are like a welcomed rain on a thirsty soil. I delight to hear you.[2] Take and read what I have given you. Tell Me, are you happy in spite of all these trials?

Yes!

---

[1] Jesus said, "I love you" and I stopped Him from writing it.
[2] Jesus was silent for a while, He then asked me, "Would you like to write?" I said "yes".

Flower, when one of your petals is torn out I make sure that another petal t̤ *its place. With My Light I reinforce your stem, if you only knew how I guard yc̤.* *and with what care I treat you. Lean on Me when you are weary and I shall rest* *you.* ♥ *Come.* ΙΧθΥΣ ⊰◯▷

THE GREAT APOSTASY

May 12th, 1990

Message for Lens, above Sion:

Peace be with you, beloved children. My Heart sings with joy to have you all united here in My Love, your prayers are like music in My Ears. Come to Me and I shall fill your spirit with My Spirit; come to Me as you are and I shall lift you to make you holy beloved ones.

My Cross today calls out for Holiness, My Voice resounds in the four corners of this earth to remind you all that I am Holy and that you should be living holy. O generation, do I not know how weak you are? Your era has created images unpleasing in My Eyes and not according to My Mind, and in this Babylon you have created I descend to find most of My creation imprisoned, yes, captive, by the evil one who feeds them godlessness, rationalism and iniquity. Do I not see all these things? The supplications of the saints have reached My Ears. I tell you that I am now like on Fire and I shall not wait much longer, I shall not leave you much longer in this darkness. I will come back to you. In a short time the world will see Me again, yes, Love shall descend on you and live among you. But before your trees start blooming with noble branches, thick set leaves and lofty trunks, and before the birds of heaven start nesting in their branches and before I spread rivers to water your thirsty soil, I shall send from heaven Columns of My Purifying Fire, I intend to purify you all. Dead will be the days when the dead rejoiced in the presence of the dead. You shall, after this purification, be talking one language, My Own language, called LOVE, DIVINE LOVE. ♥ *I mean to extinguish all evil and wickedness, this is why in these days, My Veil will be thrown over the sun, the moon and the stars. I will cover the sun with dark clouds and the moon will not be giving you its light. I will dim every luminary in heaven for you and I will cover your countries in darkness so that Babylon will cease intermarrying with sin. She shall then adopt My Law of Love, because her renegades I shall put up in flames. If your era has failed to appreciate My great love and has defiled My Holy Name, it is because of the great apostasy that penetrated in the core of My Sanctuary.*

...ion, My Spirit of Grace comes to help you more lavishly than ever ... am raising in each corner of the earth new altars to sanctify your ...tify you all. It is by Grace that I intend to rise you and make out ...tars carrying My Flame. For within you will be living My Spirit of ...irit unique, subtle, unsullied and Pure. Then I shall send you out throughout the earth and your message will be to proclaim My Infinite Love, and I promise you, you who love Me, that in those days of darkness which will come on the whole world, I will keep you safe and I will lock you in the depths of My Sacred Heart, I shall be with you. But alas for all those who spend their time breaking down and trampling on My altars! Alas for those who kill My prophets! Alas for these souls! Alas for those who follow the black beast! Alas for all those who reject My warnings, spurn and ignore them! They shall in these days of darkness call to Me, but I will not answer. Five of My Wounds are wide open and My Blood is gushing out all over again. Repent generation, repent. Think twice before you open your lips to speak, seek Me with your heart and not with your mind. Imitate Me your God, follow Me in My Footprints. Ask yourselves this before you speak, "what would have Christ said in this situation?" or "what would have Christ done in this situation?" Think twice before opening your lips, do not let your lips be the cause of your downfall, do not let your spirit err you. Imitate Me and be the perfect reflection of My Image.

Even if you are unable to pray properly, My Spirit will pray for you, see? I never abandon you even when you fail to appreciate My great Love. For the sake of My Holy Name I stoop even more towards you to lift you to Me, and in My loving kindness I forgive your sins. The minute you open your mouth to invoke Me, I come flying to you and place My Ear on your lips and every word you utter consoles My Heart and rejoices Me.

Come back to Me with all your heart and let your prayers reach Me because it is not those who say to Me, "Lord, Lord who will enter the kingdom of heaven, but the person who does the will of My Father in heaven."[1] So speak with love and I shall hear you, give with love and I shall know you, pray with love and the doors of My Kingdom shall open for you to receive you, act with love so that I may say to you, 'you are Mine, you are My seed, come to your Father!' I am Love and anyone who lives in love lives in Me and I live in him. ♥ Do the Will of My Father in heaven so that you enter My Kingdom.

Remember that the Root of the Tree of Life is Love, pray more with your heart My Children and feel confident that My Ear is near your lips. I bless you and bless every step you take. Love loves you, remember My Presence. I leave My Sigh of Love on your forehead. Be one. ΙΧθΥΣ ⋈

---

[1] Matthew 7:21.

Later on:

Men have lessened and degenerated, if only they renounce their folly. Pray daughter. Nevertheless, even in your state of degeneration I love you and I weep on your atrophy.

I had been with Jesus in dictation. When He had finished dictating, I hurried up to do other things without blessing Him or praising Him. In my wickedness I treated Him as if He was any human being who dictates a message, somehow forgetting His Divinity. I felt very ashamed and so I came flying back to Him and I asked Him to forgive me. When He told me all this, He was like someone not surprised, calm but sad.

I WILL FILL YOUR MOUTH

May 14th, 1990

Lord and Redeemer, hear my prayer. Listen Lord all Merciful, my prayers indeed are atrophic. I am poor and needy but I am here and from this desert I call for Your help, You know our needs and You have surely heard the supplications of the dying. With just one Blessing coming from You Lord and they shall be healed!

I, who brought you out of Egypt, you have only to open your mouth for Me to fill it and I shall do the same to all of your brethren. IXθYΣ ⤬⬭

PRAY TO THE FATHER IN THIS WAY
THE WORLD IS DEAD TO LOVE

May 15th, 1990

Our Holy Mother's Message for Lens/Sion:

Peace be with you children. I, your Holy Mother, am preparing you to meet the Lord, I am educating you in your spiritual growth, I am covering you with graces to help you and encourage you. Realize that these are special days you are living in your times, these are the days preceding the Lord's Coming, they are the opening of the path where the Lord will come. These days are a

preparation for the descent of your King, pray so that everybody will be ready. Pray My little children fervently for those souls who refuse to hear and refuse to see, pray to your Father who is in Heaven in this way:

> Father all Merciful,
> let those who hear and hear again
> yet never understand
> hear Your Voice this time and
> understand that it is You
> the Holy of Holies.
> Open the eyes of those who see and
> see, yet never perceive to
> see with their eyes this time
> Your Holy Face and Your Glory.
> Place Your Finger on their heart
> so that their heart may open
> and understand Your Faithfulness.
> I pray and ask you all these
> things Righteous Father,
> so that all the nations be
> converted and be healed through
> the Wounds of Your Beloved Son,
> Jesus Christ. Amen.

Ask the Father to forgive the stubborn souls who refuse to hear and see, the Father is all Merciful and He will look on all His children. Yes little ones, <u>you are the incense to God</u> when you pray for the salvation of your brothers, the harder you pray all the more powerful your prayers become. ♥ Thank the Lord who called you and with His grace made you hear His call, so pray for those who refuse to hear.

The time is pressing and many are still unaware and in deep sleep, the days are fleeing and My Heart plunges in deep sorrow when I look from above at the youth of today. Love is missing but they never met with love either, many of them never even received their mother's warmth or love since she had none to give. ♥ The world has grown cold, icy cold, and the parents turn against each other. The child turns against his parents for lack of love, the mother refuses the child's pleadings for love, <u>the world is dead to love</u>. It lies in deep obscurity because hatred, greed and selfishness dominate the entire earth all the way to its core. I am shaken by terrible sights, with the iniquities of this dark world and the apostasy that penetrated in the sanctuary itself. The disasters, famine, afflictions, war and plague, all these are drawn by you. All that comes from the earth returns to earth, the earth is auto-destructing itself and it is not God who gives you all these disasters as many of you tend to believe. God is Just and all

Merciful, but evil draws evil. Pray hard, pray with your heart for the conversion and the salvation of your era. Children of Mine pray with Me, I need your prayers. Pray and I shall offer them to God. ♥ I assure you that I am with you wherever you go. I never leave you, you who are My children. I bless you all. ♥

BLESSED ARE THOSE WHO DO THE WILL OF MY FATHER

May 16th, 1990

Peace be with you. I, the Lord, come to open hearts and deliver you all from evil. You are living in a period of grace. I said that My Spirit will be poured on all mankind. Blessed are those who receive My Spirit of Grace without doubting; blessed are the poor in spirit for theirs is the kingdom of heaven; blessed are the simple in heart for Wisdom shall reveal Herself to them; blessed are those who do the Will of My Father in Heaven for the doors to My Kingdom shall open to receive them; blessed are My vessels of light who carry My Word and diffuse My Messages given to you by My Holy Spirit, for many of your sins shall be forgiven. ♥ Come.
ΙΧθΥΣ ⌖

DO NOT COUNT THE HOURS YOU SPEND WITH ME

May 22nd, 1990

Peace be with you flower. Delight Me and meditate more. Pray more. Be pliant so that I form you to My Image, fear only when you do not speak My language. Can you recognize now the Voice of Your Master?

Yes my Lord, I can.

Why?

Because you are teaching me good things and Your language is Love.

Share then all these teachings with the others, all that you learn from Me share it together with your friends. Glorify Me, delight Me and share My Passion. On Fridays enter into My Wounds, sacrifice more of your time for Me. Live holy, sacrifice by giving all that you have received from Me. Do not count the hours you spend with Me, I want you generous. I want you to offer Me your will daily, offer Me your pains, offer Me your sufferings, offer Me even the slightest scratch so that I may use what you offer Me to efface your sins and to deliver souls from their purifying fires. Do not let these things go by in vain, offer them to Me and I will use them. Come, before you rest, pray the Salve Regina. I am listening. Rejoice My Heart and your Mother's Heart too. ♥ (I prayed it.) Good. Come daughter, go and rest. I bless you and your child. ♥ Rest in My Heart like I will rest in yours. Feel confident in all you receive. Love loves you.

LIVE FOR ME

May 23rd, 1990

Peace be with you. It is I, Jesus. Never cease calling Me, never cease praying. I give you My Peace and My Love. Daughter? Have you nothing to say?

I give You my poor love and my nothingness Lord.

Ah, I desire your love even if it is poor and as for your nothingness little one, always remain nothing. Efface yourself entirely, annihilate all that is <u>you</u> by absorbing all that is <u>Me</u>. Fill your spirit with My Spirit so that your soul becomes a living torch of light. Be transparent, yes, limpid, so that your light shines through you without any blemishes but in purity only. If you ask Me daily to forgive you your sins and if you allow Me to purify you, even if this requires sufferings and trials, I will do it without hesitation. I know your needs, I do not allow you to sin. I never commanded you to sin and I have no pleasure hearing your tongue slip. Have I not asked you to be My incense appeasing Me with your fragrance? I adorned you with impressive vestments and I gave you a tongue to praise Me and remind My people of the Love I have for them. Be attentive then pupil and listen to Wisdom's instructions. Keep My Name Holy and keep scrupulously My Law and My Teachings and I shall never desert you. ♥ I am your God and with Me at your side, who can be against you? Be certain that after such a charism given to you without you meriting it, <u>not</u> to refuse Me anything, and I <u>mean</u> anything. <u>So live for Me</u>, do penance and fast. Fast on bread and water. Do not reject with disdain the trials I am giving you, rejoice when persecuted! Rejoice when threatened for My sake! Rejoice when attacked by My enemies! These My child are the trials with which I shall perfect you. ♥ Pray without ceasing. Pray, pray, pray without counting the minutes. I shall not spare you Vassula from suffering, as the Father did not spare Me from suffering. I want *you to be a living crucifix, a memory of Myself. Did you not know that the gift of suffering comes out of My Infinite generosity and out of My Infinite Love? Do not hesitate then to embrace My Cross, let your arms grasp My Cross with fervour and It will lead you into the Path of Life. If your feet wander from the rightful Path, be certain that My Love and Faithfulness will preserve you, I will come quickly to your rescue. Let your soul be in constant thirst for Me, let Me hear and feel your sighs of love. Your forehead, soul, I have deeply marked with the Sighs of My Love, those Sighs I have been giving you incessantly. I have branded your forehead with My Holy Name and made you Mine for Eternity. Lift then your eyes to Me and find True Peace in My Presence. ♥ Tell Me then My daughter, you whom My Heart loves, will you return to Me this Love I have for you?*

My love is poor, how will I ever replace Your Crown of thorns by a garland of roses? My spirit ponders this continually and sinks within me. Explain then to me without tiring of me and I shall learn. Teach me to love You as You desire us to love You; teach me to observe Your Law scrupulously for ever and ever so that I walk in the Path of Righteousness. Direct my steps in the Path of Love as You promised.

Ah daughter. I have strained My Eyes waiting for your lips to utter your vows of faithfulness.

Sweet Jesus ever so tender, Beloved One, draw me then in Your Footprints of Faithfulness, let me be sick with love for You, let me taste Your Sufferings, they shall be in my mouth as the rarest fruit of Your Garden.

Open to Me then so that I may breathe on you, My Breath is of the subtlest odours, My fragrance is a blend of incense and myrrh. Open to Me soul so that My Spirit of Love breathes on you. My Breath is Life. Open to Me My beloved, My daughter, I have been panting for this moment to show you My Divine Heart. I came all the way from Heaven to your doorstep to meet you and now that I have found you I shall not let you go. Speak soul! Respond to Me. ♥

Come, come to us Lord and multiply Your Seal of Your Holy Spirit's Love on our forehead, the seal of the Promise. God, create a clean heart in us, I know that You are at the doorstep of every soul, waiting for their response, Your Eyes languishing for their door to open. Your Vineyards are flowering now my Lord and soon they will give enough fruit to feed every desert. The dead will not come to life unless You breathe on them arousing them with Your sweet fragrance. For the sake of Your Love let this land of ghosts come to life again.

I shall then smile on them and My Light shall penetrate through the hinges of their door and through every key-hole, even below their door My Light shall penetrate!

Alleluia, glory be to God!

Yes! Shout little heart for joy, your barren lands will bear fruits! Break into tears of joy, all you who hear Me, with everlasting love I have taken pity on you. ♥ *Vineyards will grow instead of thorns and briars, I mean to show My Holiness and My Wisdom to efface this era's hostility on My Divinity and their so-called wisdom.* ♥

I AM SENDING MY MOTHER AS A TEACHER
MY PARABLE OF THE DARNEL

June 8th, 1990

Lord, the vow I have made help me fulfil.

Peace be with you, I shall help you dearest soul. Receive My Holy Spirit of Grace. Remember My Teachings; remember that My Ways are not your ways. Pray for discernment.

I pray You Lord to offer me the gift of discernment to protect Your Word and be able to know the right from wrong, evil from good, the Truth from the lie.

I shall feed you with discernment, I shall not leave you unaided. Remain in My Love. Hear Me: cry out to the nations that My Return is near you, all those who have ears let them hear and those who have eyes let them see. I the Lord descend out of My Boundless Mercy to warn you and call you back to Me. ♥

Listen, just before My Return I shall give mankind still greater Signs than what I am giving you today. Be vigilant, for the greater My Signs become the greater Satan's fury will come upon you. I have risen prophets to announce the End of Times and I am sending My Mother as a Teacher to teach you all around the earth. I am sending Her to prepare in this wilderness a path for My Return, a levelled highway for Me your God across your wilderness. Stay alert because the more I multiply My mouthpieces, all the more Satan shall multiply false-prophets to confuse you all. Pray My beloved ones to discern one from the other, pray that you may not be deceived. I have warned you not to run after these false prophets. Remember, he who sows good seeds for My Glory shall be later on recompensed. I want also to remind you that among the good seeds that have been sown and are growing to produce a good harvest, My enemy never loses his time, he too sends his false prophets to sow his seeds among My good seeds, let them be until the time of My Harvest. As I have said in My parable of the darnel[1], do not try to weed out one from the other lest you weed out My crop too, let them both grow till the harvest and at harvest time I shall say to the reapers: first collect the darnel and tie it in bundles to be burnt then gather My crop into My barn. ♥ *Stay vigilant though and you will always be able to tell and know the difference.* ♥ *Be prudent and ask Me to guide you, may everyone listen to My advice.* ♥ *Be alert, My enemy is like a wild beast which has been injured thus becoming wilder and more dangerous, for the Hour of My Return is soon with you and since I shall be giving you greater Signs than these of today Satan already spreads in My Holy places, before the eve of these Great Signs, confusion among you to lead you to dissension. Be in peace all of you, trust Me and lean on Me. Do all you can and the rest it is I who shall accomplish by My Works. Remember, I have all the keys to all the doors and I shall open each door on the hour I choose. Love loves you. I bless you, bless Me and love Me.* ♥ ΙΧθΥΣ ⊱⊙⊰

YOU INFATUATE ME WITH YOUR "YES"

June 13th, 1990

My Jesus.

I Am. It is I your Jesus. Ecclesia shall revive by Me! Not by you mankind! I am He who shall lift My Bride. Do you want to continue being My bearer in spite of the persecutions?

Yes. I am willing my Lord.

Feel how I rejoice every time you say "yes!" I do not need you, as you know, I suffice by Myself but you infatuate Me with your "yes" in your weakness! Your incapacity provokes My Strength and delights My Soul, your weakness and your wretchedness overwhelms My Pardon and from My Heart you release Forgiveness in its fullness. Stay near Me My child, you delight My Soul. I am your Fortress. Be on your guard My little one because among those who approach you are diviners and false prophets.

What shall I do Lord?

Keep My Principles.

---

[1]Matthew 13:24-30.

Will You guard me from these Lord?

You will live secure and I am guarding you safely. I shall continue My lamb to carry you on My Shoulders, be in peace. ♥

June 14th, 1990

I am the Rock. ♥

WHAT I WANT IS ADORATION

June 19th, 1990

My Jesus?

I Am. Peace be with you. Honour Me by imitating Me; glorify Me by loving Me. Sanctify your body, since I live in you, by eating Me and by drinking Me. Adore Me, thirst for Me, amend for those who do not love Me and are blinded by their intellect and who cannot tell their right hand from their left. Pray that they may realize that they need perception so as to not deviate, like many of them do, now from My Words. Pray that they may understand that what I want from these wise men is adoration, I want them to come and do Me homage like the first shepherds and like the Magi. I know that I have in My Hands a mere child. Do not fear, do I not know where I am sending you? I have brought you up to be My bearer, to witness for the Truth. Pupil, you are My Own and from My Mouth you have learned. Take your Master's Hand and allow Me to guide you where I wish you to be, lean on Me when you are weary and discouraged My child and I shall comfort you. Ah Vassula, every time you feel wretched My Heart becomes a Burning Furnace of Love ready to consume you. Listen, rejoice! For what greater than receiving the gift of My Love? ♥ *Understand My child that I am He who loves you most and forever will.* ♥

FROM NATION TO NATION, I LET MY SPIRIT BLOW

June 19th, 1990

Lord all Merciful, we have deviated from Your Path, yet You never stopped acting towards us with mercy and with great love. Today I call on You Lord: do not desert us in the days of ordeal, save us from destruction, deliver us from evil, unite us in Your Love and Peace!

I give you My Peace and My Love My child. Ecclesia shall revive in spite of all the tribulations she is undergoing. My Church will be one and holy and My People shall speak one language, all these things shall soon take place. Vassula I shall rise again My Church out of My Everlasting Love and Mercy, I am going to give you all back your vineyards and make out of this valley of death a gateway of Hope and you shall all respond to Me as once before as you did when you were young and pure. ♥ *You rejected Knowledge for quite some time now, offering Me sacrifices that never reached Me, but in My Mercy I shall say to each valley of death: Rise! Let every dark valley be filled with My Word, every mountain and hill be laid low to pasture and let everyone who has been branded on the forehead with the Sigh of My Love come forward and eat from the Tree of Life. Today I am giving everyone a chance to hear plainly My Voice from My Holy dwelling place, My Voice sounds like an echo from Jerusalem and reaches all the inhabitants of the earth. No one can say later on that I have not been warning you, from nation to nation I let My Spirit blow. I am sending you all My servants, the prophets, so persistently to remind you who is your Father and to turn you away from your evil doings and amend your actions. I come to stop you from idolizing theories that are godless, I am sending My messengers to you to remind you of My precepts and to remind you to live holy as I am Holy so that you will all be worthy to face Me on the Day of My Return.* ♥

My daughter be My incense, I shall always feed you.

Lord, I have so many things to tell You!

Things?

Yes! To start with I'm not worthy of anything You have given me.

I know, but I give Wisdom to the poor and simple. Let My Love envelope you. Come, never forget My Presence.

May Your Good Spirit guide us on to level ground. Yahweh, for the sake of Your Name keep Your Promise to save us. Amen. (Psalm 143:10-11)

DO NOT JUDGE

June 27th, 1990

Peace be with you. Daughter, pray, giving Me glory for having lifted you from the world of the dead and having allowed you to enter and live in My World of Peace and Love and having taught you through My gentle mastery the Knowledge of the ancients. ♥ *So do not condemn anyone who still cannot tell their right hand from their left, be compassionate as I am compassionate. Do not judge and you will not be judged yourself;* ♥ *do not condemn and you will not be condemned yourself. Resist evil and conquer it with good.* ♥ *Do not give the Tempter a foothold, do not say that I your Lord have abandoned you. Out of My Five Wounds I nourish you soul! Pray for discernment.* ♥ *Look My daughter, I am Hope, I am Life and I am near you! I am the Crucified and your Redeemer who tells you: My love for you is eternal.* ♥ *Bless Me and love Me.* ΙΧθΥΣ ⤫⊃

Later on, to a priest visitor:

Tell My servant this, write: My peace I give you. Take this token as a gift of My Love, take My Word and prophesy to the nations, tell them that once more there will be poured on you My Spirit from above, then shall your wilderness be fertile land. Integrity will bring peace[1], a peace the world had never known before. "My people will live in a peaceful Home." Yes, they shall live in My Sacred Heart, for I shall "keep them safe" but before this desert turns into a fertile land and into fine vineyards, My Breath shall come and blow in this dark world, like a stream of brimstone which will set fire everywhere, to purify this era and renovate her entirely, uniting her into One Holy People. Your renegades I shall turn into holy people and their apathy into fervour for Me your God. I shall make you holy as I am Holy. Remember that My City shall be rebuilt on its ruins. Be blessed. ΙΧθΥΣ ⤫⊃

---

[1] Isaiah 32:15-16.

BRING MY PEOPLE TO THE OBEDIENCE OF FAITH

June 30th, 1990

Lord, they have failed to appreciate Your Great Love, this Love no flood can quench and no torrents can drown; and now I am telling You, my strength is gone and my soul is shut out from consolation. I think You have given me my fill of bitterness, is there yet more to come? I have offered my cheek to the striker to be overwhelmed with injustice. Your lambs You have gathered lie now scattered. I have trodden the winepress alone; of the men of my people not <u>one</u> was with me.

Look, who is coming from Heaven all the way to your room? It is I, Jesus, your Spouse, so do not be afraid, I will rescue you again. ♥ *Your flesh is weak and your spirit these days has been taken by a hurricane. I am near you by your side, do not be afraid My daughter, My bride. My Pity is stifling Me to see you taken in this hurricane but I shall take you out of it. My enemies[1] are nursing My Father's Justice again, to become even greater now, how can He relent? How can He relent when wickedness is the only bread they eat!*

My God do not desert me!

Hold on to all that I have given you My child, cling on Me. These people cannot sleep unless they have first wronged you, I watch them and My Father's Justice flares up to hear them coming to Me with lifeless words. Have they not read in Scripture, "Some I have blessed and made more important, some I have hallowed and set near Me"? (Ecc 33:12) But when My Day comes, I shall spare not one of them! and as for you My child, you are <u>My property</u> because you are poor but they have not understood. Daughter, daughter weep not. Come, <u>they have been the trade of rich merchants - like expensive material they have been bought</u>. Hope My Vassula, hope. Faith My child, have faith in Me. I shall never abandon you, never... never. Blessed one, My Pardon has already been given to them, yes, to these very ones who do not sleep unless they do evil. So let Me hear your pardon too for them.

I forgive them Lord, for they know not what they are doing.

My Eyes watch over you. I am your powerful protection and your true support, nothing therefore can come between you and Me, even if you are persecuted, threatened or even attacked. Was there any prophet who was not persecuted, threatened or attacked? They are ranging second in the rank of My Church, after

---

[1] Here Jesus changed tone, from being tender to severe.

the apostles, yet they have always been mistreated and abused for out of their mouth they hear the truth and the truth disturbs them. ♥

What am I to do now?

<u>Bring My people to the obedience of faith</u>.

Broadcast My Message. Come I will give you the means of diffusing My Message. ♥ I will supply every want in due time. Flower, spread My fragrance of incense abroad. ♥

May Your Will be done, use me as You please, make out of me Your instrument of Peace and Love.

MISERY ATTRACTS ME

July 4th, 1990

Smile on us Lord and every face on earth shall grow brighter. Hope shall creep back in our hearts, and the whole earth, from end to end will remember and come back to You.

My Heart is pining with love even for the deserter, have you not noticed? Have you not heard My Sighs of Love? Have you not read My theme of Love I have written for all My creation? Come to Me and let Me see you stretch out your hands towards My Sanctuary. Adore Me and bless Me day and night, night and day. ♥ Blessed one, I will ask you a question, only one, tell Me, do you love Me with all your heart, with all your soul and with all your mind?

I love You my Lord and my God with all my heart, with all my soul and with all my mind but I know that my love is poor, miserable and insufficient for Your Bounty.

I will light a fire inside you then.

Come then and invade me! How am I to find the Way unless You fill my spirit with Your Light to guide my soul to the Truth and the Life?

Acknowledge your faults always and I shall help you surmount them. Come you who are Mine and My <u>property</u>, you are My property because you are poor and wretched. Misery attracts Me. I shall revive your strength and I shall encourage *you by lavishing My scents on you of blended incense. Never give up My child - never refuse Me a place in your heart. I am attracted by poverty, I seek poverty and misery. I have brought you to Me so that My Fire consumes you before the very eyes of all who see you. I am showing My Infinite Love through you to all mankind so that every man may see and learn that I am a God of Love, a consuming Fire.* ♥

My God, You rained a downpour of blessings on me, knowing that what You own and is Your "property" is wicked and imperfect, and that I would be unable to give You anything in return.

I blessed My property. Your candour delights Me. Listen, I raise the poor from the dust, I lift the wretched and place them in My Sacred Heart, then I show them to My angels. I teach them My precepts and I become their Master and they My pupils and their sins are forgiven by Me. Like frost in sunshine their sins melt away. Then I ask the saints to watch and pray over them and I fill them with My Spirit of Understanding to enable them to perceive the Truth and reach a deeper understanding of My Knowledge.

Lord, You who fostered me father-like after resurrecting me from the valley of death, and You who guided me in Your Light ever since and You who delivered me from evil, tell me, are we not all Your children?

Yes, you are.

Since we are all Your children I <u>implore</u> You then to let those who hear and hear again but do not seem to understand, to allow them to understand.

Have they repented?

Lord, I do not know if they repented but if You open their eyes and let them 'see', they will see Your Glory and then they will perceive Your Faithfulness and Your Beauty, they might then come to You and repent!

Child, even if I open their eyes they will not see Me! They will not see Me because they are surrounded by darkness, so how do you want them to see Me even though I am near them all the time? Their obscurity blinds them. So daughter, speak out and do not be afraid of them, do not be afraid to speak out the Truth, nor allow yourself to be silenced. I am with you My child, My daughter. No, do not be silent, set to work with your God. I have reared you and brought you up for this mission. Like a young man marrying a virgin, I have offered you My Heart and asked for yours. It is I Jesus who formed you and wed you and as the bridegroom rejoices in his bride, so am I rejoicing now in your poverty and your weakness. ♥
I pursued you like a lover pursues his maiden, I went in all directions seeking by

what means I could make you Mine and now that you are Mine I will keep you.
♥

I am frail and my persecutors are hounding me untiringly but my hope is in You. I live in this exile just for You, nothing delights me in this world any more and already my eyes are languishing for Your world of Peace. My heart and my soul are pining away with love for You, You are my Refuge and my Joy. I had asked You to accept me if it was possible and be to You less than a slave. Yes, an auxiliary-slave.

The poor and simple always praised My Name and always will. ♥

Jesus said these words as if He was talking to Himself.

This is why I thank the Father for hiding Wisdom from the learned and the clever and revealing them only to mere children. Happy you who are poor and miserable, yours is the kingdom of God. Alas for those who have their fill now, they shall go hungry; happy are <u>you</u> when people abuse you and persecute you and speak all kinds of calumny against you on My account, <u>rejoice</u> and be glad! for your reward will be great in heaven. This is how they persecuted the prophets before you. Daughter, do not weary, carry out the work I have given you. Imitate Me your Lord and follow Me with no trace of doubt. I shall humble you more. Stay poor and weak, docile and obedient. Be pleasing in My sight. ♥ *Love Me and bless Me.* ♥

I am Yours and under Your Eyes I have found true peace. I bless You.

RATIONALISM, THE WEAPON TO COMBAT MY DIVINITY

July 6th, 1990

Peace be with you. Here is My Message:

Peace be with you. I am your Redeemer who speaks to you, I am He who loves you most. ♥ *I have come to your nation to give sight to the blind and take away the sight from those who claim they see. I have come to you so that you listen to My Voice, the Voice of My Holy Spirit, the Constant Reminder of My Word and all that I have given you. Listen to Me inhabitants of the earth, how I love you! In spite of your awesome wickedness and your apathy towards Me, I your Jesus, love you.* ♥

Today, My beloved, I come and stand before you as your Shepherd to tell you My Kingdom is near and before this generation has passed away, all that has been foretold by My prophets of today will have taken place. ♥ *Pray for those whom I have given mouths to praise Me but use them only to defile My Holy Name; pray for those whom I have given eyes to see My Beauty, My Holiness and My Marvels but turned blind, with scales on their eyes from their sins; pray for those whom I have given ears to hear My Word and My Hymns of Love, but allowed their hearing to dull for fear of hearing and be converted; pray for those from whose mouths comes false evidence and are unconscious of it, their leaders will fall and they will have to face Justice; pray for those who never cease to throw venomous arrows at each other, they have to realize how they are harming My Body; pray the prayer your Holy Mother has given you in Her previous Message to relent and to draw back My Father's Justice, ask the Father to give your generation a hearing. Amend for those stubborn souls who never cease to do evil, pray for all these souls My little hearts, because you are the salt of the earth and I Jesus tell you: take courage little hearts for I am with you.*

I shall see that My Name is kept Holy even though My enemies brought this great apostasy in My Church and a disastrous abomination in the heart of My Sanctuary and still hold fast because of their pride. I tell you truly that My dwelling place shall be rebuilt on its <u>early bricks</u>, the Day is near when I shall come upon these wise men and destroy all their so-called wisdom and their hostility towards My Divinity. I shall pull them out by the roots so that they will not thrive any more. They have apostatised from Me, yes, they have accustomed their steps to walk with Apostasy and have as their guide and travelling companion, Rationalism, the <u>weapon</u> to combat <u>My Divinity</u>. If any man is thirsty for knowledge let him come to Me and drink and I shall give him living water, do not go and drink from a man's doctrine which is coming from his own rationality, that man is putting honour from men before the honour that comes from God. So for these I say: alas for you when the world speaks well of you!! The day will come when they will have to speak from the ground, but before their voice reaches Me they will be muffled by the dust and the thick layer of their sins. Justice will prevail. ♥

I tell you solemnly that in these coming days, Satan and all the foul spirits shall not work subtly as they did before. No, the time has come now when he and those foul spirits shall show themselves openly to every inhabitant of the earth. Satan shall send false prophets and he shall multiply them like sand, creating confusion among you, to deceive even the elect. So take care that no one deceives you, this sign is the sign of the eve of My Great Signs that are to come. The demon today is like a wild beast that is wounded, thus becoming more dangerous, but do not fear you who love Me, I will grant you the safety you sigh for. But alas for those who defiled My Sanctuary, bringing great apostasy in My Church, brimstone and fire shall rain upon them! I tell you truly, in the lairs where the jackals[1] live shall soon run a highway, undefiled, which shall be called "Sacred Way."[2] The impure shall not travel by it but the living will walk there, for they know how to worship Me and they will bend their knee and say to Me, "Amen. Amen." ♥ *Little children, never have grudges against each other, be united, be united, be one. It is I Jesus who asks this from you. I bless you all, leaving My Sigh of Love on your forehead, this Sigh that brands you as Mine.* ♥ ΙΧθΥΣ ⋌⋋⊃

WHAT GREATER GIFT THAN HIS LOVE?

Our Holy Mother's Message:

Peace be with you. Children of Mine, I would like you today to read and meditate on Luke 15:4-7. Yes, Jesus does not want to lose any of you, this is why He is in constant search of your heart. Pray My little children as never before, keep God's Name Holy and remember that anyone who seeks the Lord will find Him. Anyone who knocks will always have the door opened to him. ♥ Work for your salvation, pray for every thing you need. ♥ I want you <u>happy and peaceful</u> in the Lord because the Lord has given you the Gift of His Love, so what greater Gift than His Love? Find Peace in the Lord, this peace that is missing from many of you. Penetrate into God's Love and He will purify your soul. Praise the Lord for He is good and patient. Do not come to Him just for your interests, do not come to Him unconsciously just out of duty, come to the Lord to praise Him and Love Him. Consider the blessings God is giving you daily; contemplate on the blessings He is giving you daily and offer Him your hearts, thanking Him. Beloved ones, show Him your gratitude too. ♥ Jesus is <u>Love</u>, Jesus is <u>Hope</u> and Jesus means He-Who-Saves, so do not doubt of the Greatness of His Love. Have <u>Faith</u> in Him, He comes to rescue even the least among you. Testify to the nations of this Great Love and spread His Messages to the four corners of the earth. ♥ I, your Holy Mother, am always near you. My children, I bless you. May the Peace of My Son reign in your hearts. ♥

---

[1]Here Jesus is alluding to the freemasons in His Sanctuary.
[2]Jesus means that He will overthrow free-masonry.

DO NOT HARDEN YOUR HEART, DOUBTING
A PRAYER FOR RUSSIA

July 8th, 1990

Message for the prayer group:

Peace be with you all. I, Jesus, bless you all. Feel My Presence at this very minute among you. Feel Me in your hearts. Do not harden your heart, doubting. Open your heart so that you may understand fully My Message of Love. I descend, I who am King and Sovereign, all the way to you to remind you of the Love I have for you and of My Sacrifice. I come to remind you to whom you belong. I have redeemed you all with My Sacrifice and you belong to Me.

If today My Spirit of Grace is being poured out on you so lavishly it is because the fig tree is almost ripe and very soon you shall be eating from it. ♥ *You cannot say any more "where is My God?" The pastures of the heath I shall turn green again so that you find your rest in them. My Vineyards I shall keep multiplying and My fruit-trees will yield abundantly, you will eat to your heart's content from My Heavenly Stores. Hear Me, your Heavenly Father, has He not opened His Celestial Stores in Heaven to feed a starving nation with manna? Your Heavenly Father rained down bread upon His people and from the rock at Horeb He let water flow from it so that they may drink and I, have I not multiplied the loaves and fish to feed thousands? O men of little faith, how is it then that you cannot tell the times? Why do you now doubt that My Holy Spirit of Grace[1] is being poured out so manifestedly upon you? Have you not understood that My Holy Spirit is filling you in your wilderness? I said, "I am going to water My orchard, I intend to irrigate My flower beds"[2]; "I shall pour out teaching like prophecy, as a legacy to all future generations."[3] Do not be afraid, it is I, your Lord, your Saviour. Had you penetrated into the mystery of the manna and the mystery of the multiplication of the loaves and fishes, you would have understood today fully the outpouring of My Spirit, you would have understood My Miraculous Feedings from your ancestors' times.... flower,*

(here Jesus interrupts me, it is 16.23 hours)

---

[1]Jesus in this whole passage mentions the Father, Himself as the Son and the Holy Spirit showing the action and the presence of the Holy Trinity in times of wilderness.
[2]Ecc 24:31.
[3]Ecc 24:33.

pray now for Russia with Me:

> O God make her follow You,
> O Lord save her soul and raise
> her as You have risen Lazarus.
> Embellish Your daughter so beloved
> in Your Eyes and place her in
> Your Divine Heart, so that
> her image reflects Your Divinity.
> Raise her so that she walks
> by Your side.
> Parade her near You and free her
> from her captivity.
> Wed her and make her
> entirely Yours.   Amen.

Say it to Me. ♥

I did.

Write, My Vassula[1], to this day's feedings.   Realize and understand My transcendence and fidelity to My Promise of salvation. I will hide none of the secrets from you generation, because I will trace out soon an open highway, undefiled and I shall call it "Sacred Way", leading you to an open Tabernacle. No more lairs for jackals![2] No more hidden works by night! No more prowlings in the dark! I the Lord shall bring everything to light. It will never be night again, because My Light shall shine on you forever. Yes, I will set out My knowledge in this open highway and I shall raise landmarks to lead you to it, I shall mark the road well. I shall then give you a spirit of fervour to worship Me your God and those who are My prodigal sons and daughters I shall take back with great love in My Arms and they will live in My Light. Then all Heaven shall celebrate their return, no man will say, "where is Our Lord?" for I shall engrave My Law deeply on your heart, this Promise is inscribed in front of Me. I will set up Jerusalem on its early bricks.

I had hoped on My Return to find <u>holiness</u>, but I find a fallacious people gnawing on My Body. <u>Love</u>, but I hear only a cry of hatred coming out from their desolation, where is the glory and the beauty I had once given them? Where is the Spirit with which I endowed them? These Cains have substituted darkness for light and light for darkness, they have turned unspiritual and My Law that commands

---

[1]Continuation of His message.
[2]Jackals here means free masons.

and is Sacred, they ignore all of it and trample it under their feet. This era is opposing My Law, contradicting every iota of it. Have I not said explicitly that anybody who received My Commandments and <u>keeps them</u> will be one who loves Me?

In your era many claim to be doctors of the Law but they understood neither the arguments they are using nor the opinions they are upholding. Oh how they weary Me with their talk! They weary Me because they do not safeguard My Knowledge nor My Law. I do not come through these Messages to condemn, I come to warn you out of Love and wake you up from your lethargy. I also come to encourage the remnant, from priests to laity, who love Me and remain faithful to Me and reflect My Image. You, who show your love, for your sake I will lay an open highway blessed; and on its sides I shall plant fruitful trees[1]. Your soil will nourish many and no one will be able to destroy the fruits of your soil nor make you barren. You will be all called "Faithful" and you will be all that is not pride, fallaciousness and rationalism. Your fruit will feed starved nations, nations that have collapsed into atheism. ♥ I intend to clothe you all in My garments of old[2] and rebuild My Church on its old foundation. I shall adorn My Bride in her early Jewels and from your mouths you will exult Me and praise Me without ceasing.

Beloved ones, I am the Light of the world and before you I am walking. Still, I am telling you this: there are other sheep I have that are not of your fold, I will lead all these as well under My Renovated Church so that there will be one flock and one Shepherd. Go out to the nations and teach them to pray to the Father this prayer:

Father all Merciful,
let those who hear and hear again
yet never understand
hear Your Voice this time and
understand that it is You
the Holy of Holies.
Open the eyes of those who see and see,
yet never perceive,
to see with their eyes this time
Your Holy Face and Your Glory.
Place Your Finger on their heart
so that their heart may open
and understand Your Faithfulness.
I pray and ask you all these

---

[1] The priests of the new era.
[2] The Early Church.

things Righteous Father
so that all the nations be
converted and be healed through
the Wounds of Your Beloved Son
Jesus Christ. Amen. ♥

Understand then that with this prayer you are asking the salvation of the world. Courage brothers, My pupils, courage. I am with you every day. Preach and defend My Word without any fear, proclaim My Name with zeal. Remind the world that I am Holy, teach them to live holy. Be gentle like I am gentle, have My patience and My Love. Only a little while now, a very little while and the One you are waiting for will have come. I will come as Love, yes, Love shall return as Love in this wilderness. I shall fulfil the Promise soon, but remember My dear friends, what My prophets told you to expect at the end of Times, they told you that there are going to be great tribulations before this Coming and that the foundations of the earth will shake and a great tremor is to come. The sky will appear to you as though it is of an eternal darkness, never fear though for I will be by your side. I have marked your forehead with My Seal of Love. I bless you all leaving My Sigh of Love on your forehead. ♥ Jesus Christ is My Name and I tell you:

I love you eternally. ♥

Be one. ΙΧθΥΣ ⋉⊃

I AM WITH YOU TO BIND YOU ALL TOGETHER IN LOVE

July 19th, 1990

My God! My God! Come and light up my darkness! Come quickly and help me! Visit me. My soul thirsts for You my God. When will I see Your Holy Face? My soul melts within me. Why do my persecutors persist in condemning me? O God, where have I wronged them? Lord, where are You? At least let those who persecute me say what crime they found me guilty of. O God, how I miss You.

Beloved, I have not spoken in secret, I am confirming My Word and they know it. ♥ You have not seen Me face to face but I am near you. I may be absent in body[1], but in Spirit I am always with you.[2] I am with you to bind you all

---

[1] Flesh and bone.
[2] Jesus very sweetly tried to console me.

together in love and to stir your minds so that your understanding may come to full development until you really know My secrets in which all the jewels of Wisdom and Knowledge are hidden[1]. Blessed one, I want you to have a visible image of My Divinity, meaning by loving Me fervently, by obeying scrupulously My Law, and little by little, therefore, I shall correct those who offend Me and persecute you. I shall remind them of how they have apostatised; I shall give them the chance to repent. Courage! I am telling you this daughter, whoever will listen let him listen, whoever will not, let him not. IXθΥΣ ✕◁▷

ANNIHILATE ALL THAT IS YOU BE ABSORBING ALL THAT IS ME

July 20th, 1990

O Lord, let Your Spirit rest upon me and <u>invade</u> me.

Let Me bless you. ♥ I give you My Peace. Let My Spirit rest on you, I the Lord will grant you the safety you sigh for. Keep firm in your faith because I am faithful to My Promise. I will put My Love Law into the hearts of your nations and I shall never call their sins to mind, I shall remind them of My Sacrifice, I shall remind them of My Cross, I shall remind them that I am God. And you, you whom I sought and found, offer Me your heart and I shall receive it as blended incense. Stay loyal to Me and yearn all that is Me to efface all that is you. Annihilate all that is you by absorbing all that is <u>Me</u>. ♥ Pray for the conversion of souls, pray for peace, love and unity. Remember, My Love is Infinite, a Love no man can understand fully on earth. ♥ I bless you. Turn to Me and bless Me. ♥

---

[1] Col 2:2.

THE TREMOR

July 21st, 1990

I saw in a vision that I was looking from outside a window. It was daylight; suddenly the earth started to shake violently under my feet, the ground was going up and down, the earthquake was of point eight, it was not stopping. I looked from the window at the sky because it was loosing its luminosity, I was staring up at the heavens while they were becoming darker by the second until they reached to become full night. Then I saw the stars falling, or rather as though they were speeding away from the eastern horizon to the western horizon, it seemed they were leaving the heavens. Then the tremor stopped and there was a menacing darkness. I saw that I had a faint light in my room. I looked out of the window, but there were about 3 or 4 houses which had a light in the whole town.

I AM SENT BY HIM TO PREPARE THE ROAD FOR HIS RETURN

July 22nd, 1990

Message from Our Holy Mother:

Peace be with you, beloved children. I am your Holy Mother speaking and I already thank you for coming here to hear Us. Open your hearts and understand every Word We are telling you. ♥ Jesus gives you His Love and His Peace, He guides you to Salvation and I am sent by Him to prepare the road for His Return; I come to open the way again for Him. ♥ Do not be surprised little ones, I know it is hard to live in wilderness but I come to you in many nations to prepare you. I am schooling you in rules of righteousness to set you free. ♥ Ask the Lord to guide your steps in the path of His Commandments, let your love comfort Him, let you love console Him, be His Balm. Feel loved by Me, feel loved by My Son.

Today I am calling the sick telling them: My child, do not be depressed, I, your Holy Mother love you but pray to the Lord and He will heal you. ♥ Cleanse your heart from all impurities by repenting, then open your hearts to God and He will shower you with His Love. Pray without ceasing, do not slumber. Pray with your heart and be like roses in the days of spring, like a bouquet offered to the Most High. Let your prayers be like blended incense reaching His

Throne. Let Me remind you what the Most High is longing for: your heart. ♥
Offer Him your heart and allow Him to be your Guide on the road I am
preparing for you. My children, Love is at your doors, praise the Lord and love
Him. ♥ God is love.

I bless you all, I also bless all those who are confined in a prison; towards them
I send flowing peace like a river in their heart. ♥

Vassula, be patient, My Son, Jesus, loves you to tears of affection. Never doubt,
feel His love. End your day always by praising Him. Have My Peace. ♥ We,
us?

Yes, Holy Mother. We, us.

PRAISE ME FOR MY NAME IS HOLY

July 27th, 1990

Rhodes

Explain to me my Jesus how to respect and follow Your Law and how to observe
Your Commandments. Guide me in the path of Your Commandments, I mean to
meditate on Your precepts. Forgive my faults and sins.

Peace be with you. ♥ *Before you uttered a word I have already forgiven you[1].*
♥ *If it was not for My Infinite Mercy, beloved, you would have already felt My
Justice upon you, since all that you have is wickedness and misery. Come, do not
watch Me from a distance. Come to Me, closer. I cherish you like the pupils of
My Eyes. Praise Me, My beloved, praise Me for My Name is Holy.* ♥

---

[1]Jesus understood my intentions.

SHED YOUR TEARS NOT ON ME

July 27th, 1990

Rhodes

One of the monks I met was shedding tears when I explained to him how Jesus suffers.

Come and place your ear on My Breast, My son, and hear My Heartbeats, every Heartbeat is a call for a soul, a supplication for a smile, a thought. Shed your tears not on Me My son but on your brothers, your sisters, who are dead and decomposing, not on Me My son, not on Me. Pray for them that My Father sends them My Spirit of Understanding, how else are they to convert?

Vassula, give them the prayer your Holy Mother has given you and I ask them to pray this prayer daily. Come, Scriptures are being fulfilled. I, the Lord, am building incense altars, on altars that were to be, but have lain waste because there was no one to handle them or light them. ♥

YOU ARE POOR BUT I CAN PROVIDE YOU

July 28th, 1990

Rhodes

Jesus, I am caught in a cloud of lethargy and I do not seem to come out of this lethargy. I am a poor wretch.

I know, but why do you not <u>ask</u> for My help? and why do you look elsewhere? If you turn your eyes towards Me you will see My Light and I will grant you the things you ask for. ♥ *You are poor but I can provide you. I suffice to say: grow! flourish! and within your desert I can make rivers flow. Child, do I ever abandon you?*

No, my Lord, never.

Then why was it that you failed to believe in My Presence[1]? Do you not realize that I have been in constant search of your eyes? I have made you My bride have I not?

Yes, You have my Lord.

Then look at Me now and then, this is your due! Listen Vassula, I do not need you, as you know I suffice by Myself. I have told you several times that I am Omnipotent but I love weakness because My Power then is at its best. Little one, I am with you every day, every hour and every second of your life. I am always among you. Remember, I am with My Mother.

Yes, my Lord.

Repeat after Me again: we, us, forever and ever. IXθYΣ ✕⬤

WHY DOES THIS NATION FEAR TO DRINK ME AND EAT ME?

July 30th, 1990

Rhodes - Monastery of St Nectario

I stayed at this monastery five days. Five days of fasting and not speaking. Just praying and meditating.

Lord?

I Am. Never doubt My Peace I give you. Enter into My Heart. ♥

When the Lord said: "My Peace I give you", I saw Heaven open and I was welcomed into His Heart.

Time is pressing, the hours are fleeing. Come near Me and listen to what I want to tell the church in Rhodos.

Look at the Palms of My Hands, My Side and My Feet, feel My Wounds. Those

---

[1]When I had seen Him with the eye of my soul, that afternoon.

who will not drink from My Wounds shall waste away, they shall pine away and dry. I Am your Salvation, so why does this nation fear to drink Me and eat Me? They cry for help but then no one comes to drink Me and eat Me and get healed. Have I not said that through My Wounds you shall be healed? Pick then your steps over this endless desert and let Me hear the sound of your step. ♥ *Come and receive Me. This nation fails to understand the Call of My Love. I look down from Heaven anxious to save you all, I pour out My Heart to you. I am sending you Wisdom all the way to your doorstep to teach you that My Theme is LOVE, but has anybody any ears to hear? I have made a New Song of Love for you, and for the sake of My Holy Name little ones I descend all the way to you. I, your Christ, come to ravish your heart with My Song of Love and delight My Heart. Do not say, "I sought Him, but I did not find Him; I called to Him, but He did not answer, I waited for Him, but He did not come." Seek Me beloved ones, in simplicity of heart and you <u>will</u> find Me. Call Me from the core of your heart and I <u>shall</u> answer you, open your <u>ears</u> and your <u>heart</u> and you shall hear My footsteps of My Return.* ♥ *The fig tree has ripened and soon you shall eat its fruit. Come, since many of you have wandered from the rightful path and fear to receive Me, keeping your sins secret in your breast. <u>Liberate yourselves</u> by going to confession, repent truly and fast so that you receive Me in purity and in holiness.* ♥ *My door is always opened to all of you, beloved. I am known not to be insensitive to the poor and to the sick man's needs, <u>so do not put your God to the test and do not doubt of My Infinite Mercy</u>. Yes, the instruments I use to transmit My words to you are poor, unworthy and common. Those whom the world think <u>common and contemptible</u> are the ones that I choose, those who are nothing at all to show up those who are everything[1]. Wisdom is given to mere children and not to those that call themselves wise. Hear Me, <u>Wisdom shall remain a riddle to those who boast and call themselves virtuous and holy</u>. I shall indeed destroy the wisdom of the wise and the more severe will be the sentence they will receive. I intend to leave in their midst a humble and lowly people who will be able to say to Me, "Alleluia, alleluia" day and night, night and day, joining the hymn of My angels, "Holy, Holy, Holy is the Lord God, the Almighty. He was, He is and He is to come"[2], with no one to disturb them because I shall remove all those proud boasters from their midst. I am telling you therefore, before My hour comes upon you, <u>seek humility, seek poverty</u>. You who obey My Commandments and teach others to obey them, <u>humble yourselves</u>, do not judge and you will not be judged.* ♥ *Do not condemn so that I too will not condemn you. Repent, and I will make up to you for those years you spent suppressing My Spirit. I intend in these last days to lead this wicked era with reins of kindness, with leading-strings of love, stooping down to all of you to give you My Food. I shall always be a Refuge to the poor and needy. Come, lean all of you on My Breast, like John My disciple, and hear My*

---

[1] 1 Corinthians 1:28.
[2] Apocalypse 4:8.

Heartbeats. These Heartbeats will bring you all the way to My Feet below My Cross. ♥ I, the Lord, am among you and I bless you all leaving the Sigh of My Love on your forehead. Remember all that I have given you today and show Me your love by following Me. My Eyes are upon you. Be one. ΙΧθΥΣ ><>

DO NOT BE IMPATIENT IN PRAYER

July 31st, 1990

Monastery of St Nectario

My Lord, revive me as Your Word guaranteed. Take away this spirit of lethargy that lies on me. For how long will I have this spirit? Instil a constant spirit of fervour in me, do not deprive me of Your Holy Spirit.

Vassula, I am only waiting to be gracious to you, raise you and place you in My Sacred Heart. ♥ If only you were alert to My Precepts your spirit would have been in constancy with My Spirit. You complain, you groan, yet My Sacred Heart overflows with Love and Pity for you soul! Put in action all that I have given you! <u>Remember My Presence.</u> Make an effort! Keep your distance from all that is not Me, keep your eyes fixed on Me and Me only. A vessel of My Word you are, but do not drift away with the first current! I have called you and wed you, making you Mine. Should you pass through these currents, I am with you, or through hurricanes, these will not uproot you. Should you walk in a nest of vipers, you will not be bitten. I have made your path easy, I will lift you every time you come upon thorns and briars. I realize your weakness and your astounding incapacity, this is why My forbearance is great upon you. So do not venture to say, "where is Your Spirit?" My Spirit is always with you My child. Listen, do not be impatient in prayer. Do not say, "God will consider My weakness, He is All-Merciful", then go on sinning. Open your ears instead and listen willingly to all My discourses and I shall give you My Light to understand even shrewd proverbs, for I am with you to save you.

Make my heart ready dear Lord, to praise You in constancy. I am surrounded by temptations that make me forget Your Presence.

See now? Now you are coming back to your senses. You are beginning to realize in what a wretched state your soul is in. ♥ A light has shone in you, rejoice soul! Rejoice! For if I was not standing by you, you would not be standing at all. ♥ Pay attention from now on and never let your heart sink, always come to Me for help. This, My Vassula, is not your last fall, I the Lord will lift you every time you fall with greater compassion and love every time. Bless Me now and love Me. ♥

I bless You Lord, You who fostered me father-like. If my feet wander away from Your Rightful path again, come quickly to my rescue.

Rely on My massive Strength, rely on My Love. Come more than once to Me today, Love is near you. I bless you. ♥

Later on, the same day, I commented about something, it sounded like bragging.

Daughter, consider My Work upon you, do not claim to know. Man does not know what love is unless I give it to him, not even a sage can discover it, though he might claim to know. I give an order from above and My Word flashes to earth, I send My Word to bring the thaw and warmth on icy hearts. Elevate your spirit and seek My Spirit of Discernment, I shall, in spite of your faults, stand by you to enable you to proclaim this whole message for everyone to hear. ♥ IXθYΣ
⤚◁▷

August, 1990

Monastery of St Nectario

My Lord, Holy Spirit of Truth, I know it is not by coincidence I am here. Holy Spirit of Truth, You who guided me and guide me, what am I to say to these two nuns who live here, what am I to do for them? Please speak to me from Scriptures first. I know You shall not fail me. (I open then the bible at random and my eyes fall on Romans 16:1-2.)

I commend to you our sister, a deaconess of My church, give her and her companion, in union with Me, <u>a welcome</u> worthy of saints and help her with anything she needs. She has looked (with her companion, by their prayers, their praises to Me, their penitences, mortifications and sacrifices) <u>after a great many souls</u>.[1] I have worked and laboured, often without sleep; I have been hungry and thirsty and often starving for lack of love; I have been in the cold for lack of love, so you who read Me, will you look after Me? After My lambs? Do not say, "do not bother me, I cannot go out there and give it to You!"

---

[1] Then Jesus turned His Head away looking in space and as though talking alone, as if He was talking in place of the two nuns. He said:

Then Jesus again continued like in the beginning of this message.

Today I am telling <u>you</u> who read Me, that My blessing are given to anyone that meets with the needs of this House. For all that you do, even the least, you are doing it to Me. Be blessed then you who will hear Me and do My Father's Will. Anyone therefore that will meet with the needs of this house shall be greatly rewarded by My Father in Heaven, be on your guard though from these that will encourage any difficulties and trouble, avoid them. Do everything in constancy with the Peace I am giving you. ♥ *Do everything in love for the sake of Love.* ♥ *All I ask is Love, remember always this.* ΙΧθΥΣ ⋊⃝▷

YOU SHOULD BE AWAKE AND PRAYING - PRAY!

August 1990

Lord?

I Am. ♥ *My Vassula, are you happy to be with Me in this way?*

O yes Lord, praised be Your Name.

<u>Pray more</u>, this is My advice. ♥ *I am in constant wait for your prayers. I am blessing you incessantly.*

Jesus then asked me to open the Holy Bible at random and write what He will show me. When I opened His Word, I read out:

<u>You should be awake and praying not to be put to the test.</u> (This was from Matthew 26:41)

I need Your massive Strength.

Hear Me. <u>Pray</u>, do not sleep. ♥

Can I look in meditation on You?

<u>Pray!</u>

I prayed.

Pray once again to Me.

Synchronise my spirit with Your Spirit. Amen.

Jesus quickly gave me the start of my prayer, the prayer He wanted. I think He dictated it to me.

My child, My beloved, what will I not do for you? I have reared you and realize to whom you belong to now, be happy!

I am more than happy.

Then show it! I shall open your mouth and you will speak. ♥[1]

Catch the foxes for us, those that make havoc of Your Vineyards that are flowering now.

A Glorious Throne is descending now very soon. I will lay their[2] hiding places bare and their race shall be annihilated, extinguished. The time of reckoning is soon over, just wait and see. I intend to refresh the earth with rich food and have My remnant full of My good things. I love you with an everlasting love and I am constant in My affection for you. Allow Me, you who read Me, to discipline you and if you accept My discipline I will bring you back to Me, I shall adopt you and teach you My Law. Like a child comforted by his mother will I comfort you. Love desires love. ♥ *Vassula, please Me and pray the Credo, looking at Me.*

Yes, my Lord.

I am listening.

I prayed.

Good! Come, we, us?

Yes Lord, we, us.

---

[1] I suddenly blurted out the following words.
[2] The foxes: freemasons. Freemasonry encourages all sort of sects e.g. New Age.

PROPHECY

August 4th, 1990

Rhodes

Flower, peace be with you. Fire, Justice, is soon to descend. Ecclesia shall revive.
♥ *The earth shall be set aflame.* ΙΧθΥΣ ⤫⊃

THE TEN COMMANDMENTS

August 5th-29th, 1990

Rhodes

Lord?

I Am. ♥ *Lean on Me, think of My Love. I have walked on the Way to the Cross alone, of the men of My people not one was with Me. They hated Me for no reason at all. By force and by law I was taken, suffering and humiliation was the prize of My victory. I have taken your faults on Myself and I allowed those very hands that I created to strike Me and disfigure Me, but through these Wounds you are healed. So bless those who persecute you, do not judge them, bless them and pray for them.* ♥ *Today I am telling you this with tears in My Eyes, there are many who are behaving as enemies to Me and to My Cross. Of all those who preach My Gospel, very few actually are working with Me and for My Kingdom.* ♥ *My whole Law is summarized in a single command:*

LOVE. ♥

Had they followed My Law and examined their conduct daily they would have discovered that they are not living according to My Commandments; and if they tell Me 'how is it that we are not following Your Commandments? How are we then to follow Your Commandments? Can we teach Your Commandments if You say we do not follow them?' Yet you <u>are not</u> following them because <u>love</u> is missing within you. <u>The Crown of My Commandments is Love</u>, to love is to live according to My Commandments. Do not be like Cain who had no love for Me and simply out of spiritual jealousy cut his brother's throat.

When I understood what God's intention was: to comment on His Ten Commandments, I feared to be unable to take everything down.

O God, I will never be able to do it alone!

Who told you that you are going to do this work alone? You shall write down every word I am going to tell you. Do not hurry, I can dictate to you in sessions if you wish.

Lord, go according to my capacity!!

You forget My Capacity that can fill your capacity. Come, share My Work to gain souls, do you understand My thirst? I am thirsty for souls, thirsty for your sanctity, thirsty for your reconciliation. I am thirsty, My dear children, for all that is Me and My reflection. I am thirsty to give you back your divinity; I am thirsty for a return of love; I am thirsty to renew your original source and alliance in My Holy Name - your original source that sprouts out of My Sublime Love; I am thirsty for adoration but behold what have you become and what have you done! O era! You have stopped adoring Me and <u>you have instead multiplied your false gods</u>. You are not obeying My Commandments, no, you are not observing My Law. Era of wretchedness, what have you become! You rarely invoke Me to adore Me, you do not call Me out of love <u>nor honour Me any more, offering Me your services</u>. I have been calling you all the days of your life to remind you who your Heavenly Father is and to whom you are to turn to, but your heart is not set for Me nor is your mind willing because you preferred to cut off the navel-string that unites us and makes us one, to make out your own law and call yourself, "godless." Taken by Vanity you want to consider yourself equal to Me. You are now saying "I am equal to God and I am sitting on His Throne, because my wisdom has amassed great luxury and great authority over the world." Your skill in trading is such that a multitude of nations follow your example. Yes, you followed indeed the primeval serpent's advice who so cunningly made your ancestors eat the forbidden fruit, assuring them that they will be like gods.[1] You thought then you would open your eyes but in reality you turned blind and to this day you are struggling to cut off this Cord that gives you Life and Sanctity, thinking you will find your freedom, but what you find is Death. ♥ *O era of wretchedness! <u>You are serving Folly instead of Wisdom</u>; you are serving the dragon instead of your Holy One. You are not obeying My Commandments, no you are not observing My Law I laid down to you. You are incessantly putting Me to the test.* ♥ *Your era, My child, is guilty of grave blasphemies because it is not keeping My Law, they are unmindful of My Commandments in which they can find Life if they observe them.* ♥ *Nation after nation has deviated in all ten of My*

---

[1] Genesis 3:5.

Commandments adding blasphemy to rebellion; with the empire of the dragon, the black beast[1] set up together with the second beast, alias the false prophet, blasphemous poles for themselves, on every high hill and under every spreading tree, to conquer the world and blow out the little light that is left in it. On each one of its seven heads the beast made idols representing its own gods, these idols are placed, with the power of the dragon, into high places. <u>Then they appointed priests out of their own number for the high places who officiate today in the heart of My Sanctuary</u> and they are not worshipping Me, they pretend to do so. They go out masqueraded as high priests[2], worshipping and serving the beast itself and its <u>production</u>, which is conformed to the world. They are worshipping alien and lifeless gods, just as their fathers once behaved in the past. They flout piety and repudiate My Commandments My child, they go out to teach all nations to worship the <u>image of mortal man[3]</u>, a worthless imitation, instead of My Eternal Glory. Ah! How they[4] lie heavily on Me! With the power[5] given to them by the dragon, they summit their implacable hatred and spirit of revenge by making war against the saints and all those who are not in their clan, and who refuse to worship the statue[6] of the beast. So I tell you, blessed are those who believe in Me and worship Me; blessed are those who follow Me; blessed are those who believe that My Promise is on its way to be fulfilled, for on these My Sigh of Love will be branded on their foreheads. I tell you truly, if a man serves Me, he must follow Me.[7] O era, do not be afraid to come back to Me, come back to Me while there is still time, for My Day is near and how will you face it?

It is said, you shall have no gods except Me. ♥ *Do not follow other gods, gods of peoples round you, but men have transgressed My Father's first Commandment declaring <u>their freedom openly</u> by means and encouragements of the black beasts, upon whose heads will lie the blood of many.*

<u>"Do not call My Name in vain"</u> is the following Commandment. Now, arrogant nations are attacking My Holy Name, people whom I mean nothing to, with mouths full of blasphemous talk and ready with flattery for others when they see some hideous advantage in it, they curse My Holy Name when engaged in arguments. They blaspheme against My Deity and My Holiness and those who officiate today in My Church, (but are revolving around the beast's power, boasting about their knowledge of My Law), are <u>those very ones</u> who are calling My Name in vain. They are those who shut up the kingdom of Heaven in men's faces,

---

[1]Apocalypse 13. (The black beast represents the free masons. The second beast represents the ecclesiastical free masonry.)
[2]Read message of 30.1.88.
[3]A false Christ. The New Age goes out to teach a false religion. Satan apes God.
[4]God gave me their name.
[5]Black masses.
[6]A false Christ.
[7]To follow Christ is to be crucified too.

neither going in themselves nor allowing others to go in who want to. They preach against stealing, yet they steal souls from Me. They "forbid" adultery, yet they commit adultery themselves since they follow the black beast and are faithful to him. They pretend to despise idols, yet they rob My Sanctuary. So if this generation blasphemes My Holy Name and uses It idly, it is because of the permissiveness, satiated in vice, given to them freely by these very ones garbed in black cloaks.[1] To destroy the roots of holiness and justice is their aim, and bring lawlessness at its zenith. ♥ Generation, in My Return, would I have to say: "there is not a good man left, there is not one who understands, no one, who looks for Me?" I have asked you to remember to keep holy the Sabbath Day, yet you have reversed It with impurity and sullied It with filthy enjoyments and the practices with which you dishonour your own bodies and minds since you have given up divine Truth for a lie and worship and serve creatures instead of serving Me. You have made Sodom and Gomorrah appear almost faultless and pure compared to your impurities. I tell you truly on that Day it will not go as hard with Sodom and Gomorrah as with you now, most of you do not observe the Sabbath Day, no you are not, you are not observing My Law.

Scripture say: "with all your heart honour your father. Never forget the birth pangs of your mother. Remember that you owe your birth to them, how can you repay them for what they have done for you?" (Ecc 7:27-30) and you are to follow this Commandment: "honour your father and your mother." Why are so many of you surprised that so few follow this Commandment? Foolish and wicked notions led these children astray into worshipping empty productions, filling their spirit from early childhood with a spirit of sluggishness. Many parents have not given their children that everflowing Source of My Spirit. Wisdom was calling them day and night, but this generation barred Her out, and every day that passed, your children strayed further and further from the Path leading to Me. If any one, young or old, acknowledges Me as their God, they would reflect My Image, and out of love, would obey and honour their parents as they would be obeying and honouring Me. But all things that are conformed to the world have depraved these children from coming to Me, love is missing. Many parents are complaining of their children's disobedience while they are doing exactly the same thing to Me. Why? Can they really claim to have abundant goodness, patience and toleration? Had they really all these virtues, their children too would have the virtue of obedience and would honour them both, but I tell you, this generation's minds are empty and so Darkness came and filled them up, for the image of becoming a philosopher is more important in their eyes than My Eternal Glory. Then, their lack of holiness is consumed by passion and from early youth go out and dishonour their own bodies. Your generation has flouted My Commandments and replaced Them with blasphemous imitations, and to this day out of the beast's mouth come

---

[1] Sect of freemasonry.

out evil productions to darken your children's minds and draw them as victims right into the lion's mouth, conquering their young mind to worship the first beast and serve man-made gods, giving <u>them</u> the honour and respect that was meant for Me and thus reflect this virtue, on their parents. ♥ I am telling you truly: for the unsubmissive who refused to take My Commandments for their guide and took depravity instead, <u>there will be fire</u> in the end for them. O happy the submissive in heart, they shall attain perfection. ♥ So I tell you: do not be unsubmissive to the Fear of the Lord. ♥

You know <u>I have forbidden you to kill, generation!</u> If you call yourself Mine and call yourself part of My Church and you preach against killing, how is it you kill? Do you presume to maintain that you are in the right and insist of your innocence before Me in the day of Judgement when you heap up crimes of unborn children? From Heaven I watch frightful sights. Ah! How I suffer to see how the womb that shapes this child, rejects him and sends him to his death without a name and without regret, the womb that shaped him recalls him no longer. For these I say: "you may sharpen your sword, but the weapon you prepared will kill you. Now you are not pregnant with child but with iniquity, you are going to conceive Spite and you will give birth to Mishap. You have dug a pit, hollowed it out, only to fall into your own trap! Your spite will recoil on your head and your brutality will fall back on your head."[1] And <u>you</u>[2], you who are reputed to be faithful to Me and hold firmly to My Name, I know all about you, yes, you are reputed to be alive and thriving and yet you are not, you are dead and decomposing. ♥ Repent! I had entrusted you with souls beyond number, but the devil traded with you to exchange them for his gold and silver. Yes, indeed! I know how you live now, you live like jackals[3] in hidden lairs[4], these lairs upon which I shall run an open highway[5]. I shall come suddenly upon you and expose your nakedness and when the day comes I shall not allow you to eat from the tree of Life. Listen carefully: you preach against killing, yet you kill My Spirit. You boast about the Law then disobey it because you have not understood the mystery of My hidden manna. No, you have not yet understood My miraculous feedings, nor the mystery of My Transfiguration. ♥ I have promised you to keep you alive in the end of Times with My Celestial Manna. I said to My church in Pergammun:[6] "to those who prove victorious I will give the hidden manna and a white stone, a stone with a New Name written on it, known only to man who receives it." ♥ I am today offering you this manna reserved for <u>your</u> times, a Celestial food, a nourishment of My Spirit for your starved spirit. I pour out My Spirit in its fullness to fill up

---

[1]Psalm 7:12-16.
[2]Here Jesus calls out to the false prophet with a lamb's mask.
[3]The once faithful ones "sold" themselves to Satan and follow the beast.
[4]The lodges of freemasons.
[5]That is: God will overthrow these lodges.
[6]Apocalypse 2:3,17.

...ior desert and I am offering you My celestial manna free, _for this is the_ _..ne poor_... But you have not understood, so you refuse to eat it and forbid others from eating it. I have already inscribed My New Name on the "white stone" which will be known _only to the poor_. You claim to be humble and poor yet you are neither humble nor poor. Your spirit is enthroned in the riches of Satan. ♥

I am the Ruler of the kings of the earth and _I have asked you not to commit any_ _impure acts or adultery._ Adultery has been refined in such a way by Satan, that it lost its meaning both in ecclesiastical orders and in laity. ♥ My endurance in your sin has come now at its end. For those[1] who sought Satan's blasphemous powers and erected them as banners to efface My Divinity and My Holiness, and My Holy Sacrifice, I tell you: it is your fault that My Name is being blasphemed among the godless. ♥ You have sullied My Sanctuary by ordaining perverted men with degrading passions, tainted all alike they do not fear Me. So if the godless today commit adultery and find it natural it is because of the _great permissiveness_ in My Church given under the instructions of the beast whose aim is to falsify the Truth. How is it you forget so easily that your bodies are members of My Body? I would like to see you free from perversion since your bodies are the temple of My Holy Spirit. ♥ I, your God, would like to see you live holy since I am Holy. ♥ Creation! By Acknowledging Me as your God you will be able to acknowledge My Law, and thus follow it, but many of you failed and now your corpses litter this desert. I have not commanded you to sin, so why use your freedom in a way that proves a pitfall for your soul? Pray to Me so that I may forgive you, otherwise you would be a loser. ♥ Marriage is to be honoured and kept holy. I am the Lord and I have called you to a life of devotion, of peace, love and holiness. I have called you to Myself forever. I called you to betroth you with My Tenderness and My Love and not until you understand that you are Mine and My betrothed, you will stop sinning and committing adultery towards Me. I will not cease, for the sake of My Holy Name, to take all means to bring you back to your senses, even if I must drag you out into the wilderness and expose you there My Sacred Heart and Its Fathomless Riches to make you understand the nakedness and wretchedness of your soul. Then like a scroll, I shall unroll to you all My Knowledge so that you renounce your sin. _I have the power to cure you_, so come and repent!

My Holy Spirit asks you not to steal. If you call yourself Mine and if you know My Law and claim to be in the Truth, then why not teach yourself, you who ordained yourself as priest as well as others, _not to steal?_ But you have allowed yourself to be bought and follow subtly the beast[2], who taught you to set banners of lawlessness. You are of the world and I have much to condemn you for. Your tongue proudly claims that you do great things, good things, honest things,

---

[1] Jesus is again referring those who worship the beast.
[2] Follower of the beast: the false prophet.

deceiving even the elect with your lamb's mask. But I tell you: you do not deceive Me, because I know that behind your lamb's mask, you hid a hideous catastrophe for mankind such as the world has never seen before. Your aim is to <u>abolish My Sacrifice</u>[1] and replace It by Iniquity and with <u>a Lie</u>. <u>You profess to be a Prophet to disown My own prophets</u>. Have you no fear to have your name blotted out of the Book of Life, since all you do is steal millions of souls from Me leading them to their death? Your miracles impress many today and even more the day you will rid off My prophets overcoming them[2] by your sword. ♥ Now you have armoured yourself to the teeth to make war on them because their witnessing disturbs your ears, and their obedience to My Commandments even more. They have not followed you nor the beast. They are the ones who have kept faithful to Me and have never allowed a lie to pass their lips[3], they are My Abels. In the eyes of the world you will appear to have overcome them, but your joy will be only for a very short time because like thunderbolt I shall let My Justice overpower you. I shall descend to breathe again life in them[4], raising them before your very eyes as columns of light in My Sanctuary, and then Heaven will open and you will see Me. And if you will ask Me: why are your rich garments stained with crimson? Why are your garments red, your clothes as if you had trodden the winepress?[5] I shall tell you: I have trodden the winepress alone. Of the men of My people not one was with Me. I have trampled upon My enemies in My wrath, they never ceased defying Me and provoking Me. I have come to efface from the surface of this earth all human doctrines and regulations which were poison food to all of you and forced by the sword upon you to defile My Divinity and My Holiness. This shall be the first battle of the end. <u>I Am the Majestic Rider</u>[6], <u>I Am the Word</u>. ♥

If this earth mourns, pining away and its trees have no produce and their leaves are withering, it is because you are not obeying My Law. Have I not said: <u>you shall not give false witness or testimony</u>? Yet from the core of My Sanctuary where lies the lance's blade[7] where among My Abels are the Cains too this Commandment is not obeyed too. Cain's appointed priests are sent out now to the four corners of the earth, not to bear witness on Me as the Resurrected, nor on My Sacrifice, but to condemn My Word by aping Scriptures[8], and to teach all nations a False Christ, under a <u>false ecumenism,</u> giving the world a portion of Rationalism and Naturism, a defiled food, <u>A Lie</u>. I tell you, they shall not prove victorious nor will they rule forever. Justice will prevail! I shall not leave you prosper forever since I know all about you and how by the power of the dragon you are appointing

---

[1]Daniel 12:11. (That is, the Holy Communion.)
[2]Apocalypse 11:8.
[3]Apocalypse 14:5.
[4]Apocalypse 11:11.
[5]Isaiah 63:2.
[6]Apocalypse 19:11.
[7]The false prophet.
[8]New Age sect apes scripture.

your own priests placing them into high seats to crush and overcome My own priests. I tell you: the time is almost over. I will drag you from your high seat to fall at the feet of My own priests, My saints and My angels and make you admit that you are the slave of the beast... Soon, very soon, I shall come to you like a thief, unexpected, and overthrow, the Lie, your False Christ, and place back The Truth. I shall soon come to shatter this false image you are making out of Me, compelling every nation to honour it.[1] No, victorious you shall not be! Daughters and sons of Mine, you who err aimlessly in this desert, return to Me, repent! Sin no more. I know you have many a times testified wrongly for lack of love, but you were not under your shepherd's protection to be taught My precepts because of your hostility towards Me. Yet, in spite of your arrogance and your hostility towards Me, I cry out to you, I love you! And My forgiveness has been granted to you already. Come back to Me as you are and I shall dress you with My Divinity, I shall give you back your divinity for the sake of My Holy Name. You want to testify? Testify on My great Love and Mercy. You want to bear witness? Bear witness in My Name, Jesus Christ, Beloved Son of God and Saviour. ♥ *Love one another as I love you. Rejoice you who have been given My hidden manna and have already received the Seal of My Love on your forehead.* ♥*

From Heaven I have commanded you not to covet your neighbour's goods nor your neighbour's wife, from laity to priests this Commandment has not been kept either. I have revealed My Love for every creature on earth with My Sacrifice and through this Sacrifice gave you eternal life and My Message of Love. Many of you preach love, forgiveness, humility, tolerance, holiness, over and over again, yet to this day many of you are ready to kill because you do not get what you want. You keep on throwing venomous arrows on each other because you do not have what I have given your neighbour. ♥ *From the time of My Abel to this day this sin is constantly repeated. The first man to covet his brother's goods was Cain, but how many more Cains are there today? and how many more Esaus? Motivated by convenience and nothing else he gave up his birthright, falling into apostasy. Why not follow Abel's example and be holy? To love is to live holy and according to My Commandments. If you who praise Me night and day yet covet your neighbours goods, I ask you to repent! If you ask Me: "how am I coveting My neighbour's goods, I, who consecrated My goods to You, my life and everything, how am I coveting his goods?" I will tell you: your spirit is coveting your neighbour's spirit, and those very gifts that I have given his spirit. The devil has set a trap for your soul, do not fall! Where do these wars and battles between yourselves first start in My House, if they are not mainly from spiritual jealousy? Cain wanted something and he did not get it, so he killed Abel. Esau wanted something and he gave up his birthright to get it.* ♥ *You have an ambition you cannot satisfy, so either you ignore your neighbour's happiness to dissatisfy him, or you go out and are ready*

---

[1]Apocalypse 13:16. (The root of the sect New Age is Freemasonry.)

to kill. I tell you truly if at heart you have the bitterness of jealousy, or a self-seeking ambition, never make any claims for yourself or cover up the Truth with lies for wherever you find jealousy and ambition, you find disharmony, hypocrisy and tepidness. Do not go on sinning, repent! and do not get influenced by those appointed by the false prophet and are members of Satan's dwelling. Do not listen to them. I shall soon descend with My Throne among you, so come and repent while there is still time. Come you who waver and hesitate between good and evil and who insinuate yourself into your neighbour's house in order to get influence over silly women who are obsessed with their sins and follow one craze after another in the attempt to educate themselves, but can never come to knowledge of the Truth.[1] Realize how pitiable you are to look at and do not misunderstand My reproofs, realize how I love you. ♥ Work for My Glory and do not look to your left nor to your right for if you look to your left you will behold ravenous wolves ready to pounce on you and tear you to pieces, and if you look to your right you will see a pit, dug up for you to fall into. Be happy then generation with what I have given you and share as I share with you. My Fire is imminent and, ah, so many of you will be unprepared because your era does not believe, they do not adore Me, they do not hope or love Me. Your generation has replaced The Truth and My Commandments by blasphemies. Love is missing among you. You do not live a life of love, nor have you understood what "the Fear of the Lord is the Beginning of Wisdom" means. If you fear Me, you are blessed; if you fear Me you can attain perfection; if you fear Me I will intoxicate you with My sweet Wine and fill you with My produce; if you fear Me you will live in Peace; if you fear Me Wisdom will come all the way to your doorstep; if you fear Me you will obey fervently My Commandments not changing one stroke from Them. So I recommend you all not to live with a double heart. Infuse your soul with My Divine Grace now that there is still time; repent while there is still time; come back to Me while there is still time. Do not heap your sin on sin. Alas! for those stubborn souls who shut their ears on these last warnings, what will you do on My Return? I am known to be Faithful and True[2] and I tell you, Justice shall prevail. ♥ Do not be bewildered, My child. Do not stand mystified with what I have given you to write for it has been foretold that in your days My Church would be betrayed by one who was My very own, just like Juda, and Her apostasy would come from within Her. I would be betrayed by those who shared My Meals, who had bonds with Me, who drank and ate with Me. But very soon now, everything that is covered will be uncovered and what I have said in parables and in metaphors will be made clear. I shall unveil My proverbs and parables to the poor. Before this generation has passed away, with My Power and My Glory, I shall overthrow the False Prophet. All that Scripture say must be fulfilled to the iota, this is why I have written everything down so that after the examination of these

---

[1] 2 Timothy 3:6-8.
[2] Apocalypse 19:12.

Messages, you will understand the mark of genuineness in every letter and that these are My Own Words given by My Grace to you all. I have come to revive this flickering flame of love before the false Prophet blows it away altogether. (Jesus wept) *I weep, I do. He is lodging in My House and instead of offering Me fragrant offerings and sacrifices, he is replacing these by all sorts of evil forms offered to him by the evil one: impurity, promiscuity, injustice, disobedience to My Law, debauchery and drunkenness with the blood of My prophets, My very Own. Without ceasing his mouth sends his boasts and blasphemies to the four corners of the earth, false blessings and true curses come out of this same mouth.* ♥ *I know all about him, I know him inside out and I tell you, he shall never reach the place of rest. I, the Lord, shall give you My child visions of he who carries on himself the blood of many, and of those who worship him. Stay awake, praying at all times for strength to stand with confidence by Me. Hear Me: this Rebel's sins have reached up all the way to Heaven and aroused My entire Justice, followed by an Infinite Grief in My Soul to have to condemn him and his entire stock. My Father created them with delight and great Love and I have loved them and sacrificed Myself to redeem not only the just but the unjust too. I laid down My Life for them but he and his clan instead turned against Me with full conscience to wreck his faith* (Jesus wept again) *and break My Covenant forever and ever. His aim is to distort the Scripture from beginning to end and make out of My Word, Truths, Wisdom and the language of My Cross a cymbal clashing, a rational theory, a philosopher's theory, aping Wisdom, and with these empty teaching nourish a multitude and lead them to their death. Out of his boastful mouth he apes the Good News, he apes My Resurrection and My entire Divinity. Ah! The time of your trading is soon over, the merchants that traded with you and supplied you with the best quality of merchandise will be sunk and all people will be horrified at your fate. Daughter, read Ezekiel 28:* ♥ *"being swollen with pride, you have said, "I am god; I am sitting on the throne of God, surrounded by the seas." Though you are a man and not a god, you consider yourself the equal of God; you are wiser now than Daniel; there is no sage as wise as you. By your wisdom and your intelligence you have amassed great wealth, you have piles of gold and silver inside your treasure-houses. Such is your skill in trading, your wealth has continued to increase and with this your heart has grown more arrogant. Since you consider yourself the equal of God, very well, I am going to bring foreigners against you, the most barbarous of the nations. They will draw sword against your fine wisdom, they will defile your glory, they will throw you down into the pit and you will die a violent death surrounded by the seas. Are you still going to parade as the High Priest clad in silver and gold? Are you still going to say: "I am a god, a Prophet," when your murderers confront you? No, you are a man and not a god in the clutches of your murderers! and you will die like the godless at the hand of the foreigners. You were once an exemplar of perfection full of wisdom, perfect in beauty. You were in Eden, in the garden of God, in the Core of My Sanctuary but your busy trading has filled you with violence and sin. You have corrupted your wisdom owing to your splendour. By the immense number of your sins, by the dishonesty of your trading, you have defiled My Sanctuary." Then read Apocalypse 18.* ♥ *Now sentence is being passed on this world. Now <u>the prince</u> of this world is soon to be overthrown, the second beast alias the False Prophet, the 'high priest', the Lance, the jackals, are all one and the same. He is the one who armoured himself to the teeth to make war on <u>My Law</u>[1] and on <u>My</u> <u>prophets</u>[2]. He and his clan are the jackals I have mentioned to you in My previous Messages. I have grown weary of him and his whole clan and I take no pleasure in punishing. I wanted to redeem them adopting them as sons of Mine but they allowed themselves to be bought by rich merchants who will fall with them. Feel My sorrow, feel My grief, feel My pain, they are idolaters of money.*

My God, come and <u>rest</u> in the hearts of Your Abels, those who really love You. Maybe they are few and not many but they are Your saints who endure trials, they are the people who love You, they are those who have constancy and faith, they are Your companions, they are Your first-fruits who never allowed a lie to pass their lips. I offer You these so that You may rest in them.

♥ *I will rest My Head in the hearts of My devout children, (the saints of your era). Come, love Me, console My Heart and amend for those who are depriving entire nations from My Love by building a wall between Me and My children. I have never deprived a soul from My Love. Pray My Vassula without ceasing. Many will be cleansed by prayers; many will be purged by sacrifices and fasting. Do not linger, time is pressing.* ♥ *Bless Me more, efface the world's iniquity by giving Me and showing Me more love. Ah Vassula, My daughter, please Me and tell Me these words:*

> *Jesus, teach me to love you tenderly.*
> *Give this grace to those who do*
> *not love You and do not*
> *know the Consuming Fire of*
> *Your Sacred Heart. Amen.*

---

[1]Alias Moses.
[2]Alias Elijah.

I DO NOT NEED PHILOSOPHERS AND SAGES

August 17th, 1990

I come to You my Yahweh to ask You to forgive my sins. Lord, listen to my pleading, I know You do forgive us and overlook all our sins.

I forgive you, I forgive you rather than let My wrath strike you. Desolate and uninhabited you were; you were famous for your desert; you were like a garden without water and I, like a watercourse running into a garden came to you to irrigate your soil, I saved you from the clutches of My enemy. The lion has left you and your land is a garden now thanks to My Infinite Love and Mercy. I am your Saviour and Jesus is My Name. Allow Me to write the following message for.. ♥[1] I, the Lord, am before him and I am setting fire and water in front of him. I have given him the liberty to choose, he can put out his hand to whichever he prefers. I note every one of his actions; I note down his conscious and direct sincerity towards Me and his conscious and direct insincerity towards Me. ♥ "Hurry up and come to Me and I will revive your flame. What little flame is left in you is dying fast! I love you with an eternal Love and My Mercy is Fathomless. You enjoy My favour." ♥ Many of you today say: let us drink, let us eat today, tomorrow we shall be dead. Do not lie to yourselves. Come back to your senses and face Me your God. To obey My Law is to love Me and anyone who lives in love lives in Me. I do not need philosophers and sages of your age, neither masters, I need weakness... poverty... simplicity... see? The days are coming where I will put My Law on your hearts. I come in these days of Mercy to prepare the nations and remind them that I can purify your inner self from vile and dead actions which can lead you into eternal fires. But this generation's heart has grown coarse and although I am talking openly to the nations they will still not listen to Me. Come, take your cross and follow Me. I shall bless each step you take. ♥ ΙΧθΥΣ ⊱⊙⊰

Later on, to the little prayer group:

I have invited many to My banquet but very few are willing to come[2], so I tell you: go to the poor now! Go to the blind! Some you will find dead but do not worry, I shall raise them. I have lifted you all and I shall lift many more, so go out to the poor and the sick and make sure to fill My House! Let those who were first

---

[1] A Rhodian.
[2] The little prayer group attempted many times to invite priests and archimandrites, even monks, but each one had an excuse and showed no interest at all for the Lord's messages. They were polite.

invited to My banquet, yet refused to come, be astonished to see the blind with their sight and the poor, <u>rich</u> with My Knowledge! and the dead, <u>raised back</u> to life! ♥ *<u>Thrive</u> in My Riches and do not fade away! Be constant and work for My Glory. Children, efface your egoism. My Kingdom is very near you. Be zealous and follow My Word. Keep yourselves pure and learn to efface yourselves so that My Spirit breathes in you.* ♥ *I have chosen you My angels not because you are worthy but because you are poor and wretched. Glorify My Name again by meeting to serve Me, be active in all good works. I am with you all the time.*
ΙΧθΥΣ ⊱⊰Ð

A VISION

September 3rd, 1990

I went to meet a priest. He is of a certain order and I recognize what the garments of that order of priest should look like. When the door opened and I saw him I was taken by surprise to look straight at someone who seemed to wear some fancy-masquerade garment! He had on him a light-colour purple long garment like satin, I could see the interior of his long and large sleeves were light olive colour and around his waist he wore a fancy belt of gold and silver. Around his neck he wore a thick gold chain. There was no sign of a cross on him. He looked like an ancient King. At first I thought that maybe because he is so special they dressed him up this way. Then when he greeted me I looked at his face forgetting what he was wearing. I was together with 'X', another priest of the same order and he did not react. I thought everything was normal and so I left this as it was without thinking of it much until I remembered the message of the Lord when a week before this incident He said: I, the Lord, shall give you visions of they who follow the beast; and He had said that these who follow the beast in His Church are dressed up, like High-Priests, masqueraded in gold and silver. They will deceive many, even the elect. That afternoon I had not seen a regular priest, I saw someone dressed as a "king", in fancy clothes.

Vassula, I have told you that I shall point out to you with My Finger all the thorns of My Body.[1] A man who does a thing like that ought to have been expelled from the community. (1 Corinthians 5:2)

---

[1] I open at random the Holy Bible for a prophecy.

THE LANGUAGE OF MY CROSS IS LOVE

September 10th, 1990

Yahweh Sabaoth, bring us back, let Your Face smile on us and we shall be safe. (Psalm 80:3)

Peace be with you. Lean on Me. I have not formed you for nothing, I have not commenced this Work with you to leave it unfinished. I have blessed My Work so that it glorifies Me, and you, you who are nothing and with no gifts at all to offer Me, I have given your shoulders My Yoke to confuse the wise and disperse them and show them that as long as they maintain their stand I, the Lord, will not reveal Myself to them. And you daughter, yes, stagger with bewilderment at My choice, for what man can say: "I have cleansed my heart, I am purified of my sin?" Yet your persecutors, deaf to My Teachings, hope for something to use against you. I tell you solemnly, of all the children born of women, a lesser than you has never been seen. The wound on you daughter, wounds Me too.

Yes, all of this generation is adulteress, but I mean to save your generation like I saved you, even if I have to drag her out to the desert and do unto her as I have done to you.[1] I shall expose her nakedness in her eyes, and at the first sound of repentance, I shall come flying to her as I came flying to you. Then in the presence of My angels I shall sing to her My Song of Love. I shall turn her away from the path of delusion and grant her the grace of My Law. Then I shall take her hand into My Hand to guide her back into My House, where I shall show to her all the Riches of My Sacred Heart, these Treasures My Heart kept for the end of Times, to enliven this flickering flame about to extinguish into a Consuming Fire, to give light to those who live in darkness and the shadow of death.

Vassula, My daughter, your persecutors will try to strip off you the garments I have given you and rob you of My Jewels! but I promise you to take away each hand that will approach you. I mean to end their debauchery and their misguidings. I mean to display a notice that will stand firm and forever, King of kings, the Lamb of God, the First and the Last, the Word of God, the Resurrected, the Christ, the Redeemer, to abolish and end their conspiracy against My Church and their false teachings of My Word and of My Image. I am not speaking in metaphors now, I am telling you in plain words that they are conferring a title that does not belong to Me and is not Me, a false Christ, a lifeless image, a false god, subtly hidden under a false ecumenism. But I promise you My child, that I shall prevail in the end. I will overpower these false teachers of your era and I will give

---

[1] A purification like in purgatory. When I saw my sins with God's eyes.

you the hidden treasures of My Sacred Heart, putting on your tongue the <u>language</u> <u>of My Cross</u> which is Love, with all Its Mysteries and Miracles and Wonders! Then I shall remind My shepherds the words "leadership and service."   I will command them that they should not be like great men making their authority felt among the poor.   No, anyone who would want to be great among the poor must be their servant, and anyone who would want to be first among them must be least, just as I came on earth not to be served but to serve and to give My Life as a ransom for many.   And you, little child, do not fear Me[1], I shall keep My Light inside you forever and ever! Pray for the salvation and the conversion of your era. I bless you, bless Me and love Me. ♥ IXθYΣ >⟨D

IT IS LOVE SPEAKING TO A HOSTILE WORLD

September 12th, 1990

Jesus?

I Am. Peace be with you flower. ♥ *Write down My Message for all parts of the world.* ♥ *Peace be with you.   Children of My Heart, realize how Heaven is opening every day to you, with My Grace, to give you calls for conversions, Reminders of My Word, instructions to teach you to follow My Commandments. Heaven is opening Its Doors daily in several places of the world to bring you Peace and Love; and Wisdom with all Her Glory descends on a Throne right in the middle of you all to open the eyes of the blind, to open the ears of the deaf and to resurrect the dead who litter this desert.   No, Wisdom will not show Herself to a crafty soul, She will come to instruct only the poor and the simple and pour out all Her Works on them, for these very souls know how to fear <u>Me</u>, the Lord and cherish My Word.   What greater gift then, than bringing Her all the way to your doorstep?   What greater joy than Her smile on you?   What greater delight than hear Her sing to you Her New Song of Love?   <u>Rejoice then creation!</u> for <u>I Am</u> at your very doors..   This Joy had been reserved for your times generation, when Satan and all his empire together with his worldwide authority are escalating at the peak of their power in My Church and in all nations, together with the false prophet of whose footsteps you hear clearer and clearer every day and everywhere. They are armed to the teeth to make war against My Church and all those who obey My Commandments.   I have reserved, beloved children, for your times, this Celestial Manna given by My Spirit.   It is this hidden manna[2] I had reserved for*

---

[1] I was afraid Jesus was upset with me.
[2] See Apocalypse 2: Pergamum, v.17.

times of wilderness and iniquity; it is the food of the poor and those who are starved, and I promise you they will receive as much as they want to eat and to them I shall confer My New Name; it is this Heavenly Food I am pouring from Heaven; it is <u>the outpouring of My Holy Spirit, filling your interior desert</u>; it is Love speaking to a hostile world; it is Love knocking on every locked door; it is Love calling from the other side of the Wall separating us, built up by My enemies; it is Love pleading as a beggar for a return of Love... a smile... a regret... a sigh. <u>It is I,</u>

<u>the Sacred Heart.</u>

I come once more to revive this dying flame in your heart into a Consuming Fire of Tenderness and Love. I descend to outpour lavishly all the Treasures of My Heart on <u>you</u> humanity and give light to those who live in darkness and the shadow of death. I come to break in splinters the doors of your dungeons and with My Flame melt your chains of sin. I come to free you from your captivity and your iniquity and end up your debaucheries. I mean to save you generation, even if I must drag you all the way to the desert and speak to you, showing you your aridity and how your whole body is filled up with darkness. I shall do it to save you. Ah, creation! <u>What will I not do for you?</u> My Spirit is upon you and It will rest on your forever and ever, so open up your hearts and let Me fill you with My Grace. Come and draw your strength from Me, strengthen your roots in Me, for what will you do then on the day of tribulation if your roots are frail? You will sway in the wind and be torn away with the violence of the storm and your branches will snap off like thin glass. No, you will be unable to survive. ♥ Come to Me then and thrive in My Riches so you do not fade away. Come to Me as you are, do not wait to be saints to come to Me. Come to Me as you are and I shall forgive your sins and purify your soul, I shall then dress you with My Divinity for the sake of My Holy Name to prepare you for our spiritual Wedding. I, the Lord, intend to wed you in My Glory and make you generation entirely Mine. I mean to make you find the Way and guide your feet away from tortuous paths. I will prepare you to be Mine forever and for all eternity.

Today I am bending from Heaven all the way to you out of Love and Mercy, but at the same time My Soul is sorrowful and in sheer grief to find My lambs and My sheep, some of them scattered, others lost, and others devoured by wolves hiding under lamb skins. So do not be surprised of My visit to you because every day that passes you will see Me more and more until you will meet Me face to face. I will come in flaming fire to sweep away all who do not acknowledge Me as their God and I am telling you, time is pressing, the hours are fleeing and the Day of My Glory is soon with you. Do not be one of those who say: "well, where is this Coming?", "where is this Promise?" My Coming is soon and My Promise is on its way to be fulfilled and your waiting will be shortened for the sake of My Mother's prayers together with all My saints. So then My beloved, while you are waiting, reconcile and live holy so that I will find you at peace. ♥ I shall be coming very soon now as Love, everything soon comes to and end, and one day you will all have to answer Me and give Me your accounts. So what will happen to the wicked and to the sinner? and what will happen to those who continue to offend Me? I am _Faithful and True_ and My Promise will come true. I shall not delay. For as much as you hear the footsteps of the false prophet and his clan on the surface of this earth, all the more will I make you hear My Own Footsteps to wipe off with My Blood the traces of venom they leave on their path for you as bait. This Rebel and his clan are thriving now, concealed in robes of High Priest, concealed as lamb, concealed as the Truth, to deceive many and lead them all to their death. I am not speaking in parables now but in direct words. The Times are here, those Times foretold in Scripture, when My enemies will be conferring a title that does not belong to Me and is not Me, a false Christ, a lifeless image, a false god, an idol - _subtly hidden under a false ecumenism_ - _the Lance's Blade which lies deep in My Sacred Heart_ and causes so much bleeding. By sword they will force you to eat their defiled food: a portion of Rationalism one day and a portion of Naturalism the other day and so on, aping the Truth, My Word, Wisdom and the language of My Cross. But fire will come on them from Heaven and consume him and his clan, this is sure and will come true. I am telling you all these things, beloved ones, so as to warn you from these false teachers and human doctrines and to tell you that in these coming days of tribulations My Sacred Heart which is on Fire will continue to pursue you. As the beggar hoping for alms, I too will be hoping to win your heart before the coming of darkness befalls you. ♥ I bless each one of you, leaving My Sigh of Love sealed on your forehead. I, Jesus Christ, Beloved Son of God and Saviour leave you with My Peace wholeheartedly. I love you Infinitely. ♥ Be one. ΙΧθΥΣ ⤚◁▷

BOOK IV

TABLE OF CONTENTS
BOOK IV

MY KINGDOM WILL BE GIVEN TO A POOR PEOPLE

September 18th, 1990

My Lord, You who guard me from evil and surround my soul with Your love Songs, let Your Holy Face smile on all who love You. Teach the youth of today to follow You and imitate You. Show them the Treasures of Your Sacred Heart and teach those who still do not understand and waver undecidedly before this Holy Name You have chosen: Sacred Heart, to learn that it is You, the Christ. Let those who keep on differentiating themselves because of theological terminology, yet are under Your Holy Name, come back to their senses and realize how they encourage this division in Christianity, and how they are not doing Your Will, but are granting Satan one more foothold to keep us apart, thus weakening Your Church. You are Jesus Christ, the Beloved Son of God and Saviour, The Sacred Heart, The Word, The Alpha and the Omega, The Light, The Redeemer, The Panto-Crator. You are <u>ONE</u> Christ. <u>You are not parcelled out!</u> So I pray to You, who want us to be united to unite us again in love, in heart, in our belief and practice.

This My child is what you are to teach them to believe and persuade them to do, but, My child, there will be those who will not listen because of their self-conceit. These people lie heavily on My Heart, they lack humility and true Wisdom, they are only full of antagonistic beliefs of the knowledge which is not knowledge at all. When it comes to judge, condemn, <u>and argue about words</u>, raising without ceasing questions, yet never realizing that they are a prey to the Tempter. Oh My child bear those hardships for My Sake, all these are not in vain. One day you will see the Light face to face. Come and feast now in My Love and My Tenderness. Repose your head on My Heart and listen to the calls of Love, rejoice in Me. Rejoice in My Splendour and My Riches.

I have stored this Wealth for you generation to lead you to Me with chains of Love, and if you ask: "how long until this Wonder takes place?" I will tell you: it is already taking place. My Footsteps have been heard by some of you. The Lord whom you are seeking will suddenly come upon you. The One whom you are longing for is coming. So I tell you, do not resist My Holy Spirit who will come now in full force to unwrap the death shroud which covers your nations, prohibiting you to see the Light. I will descend in full force with My Spirit, to unmask the deceivers and drive out the traders who infiltrated into My Sanctuary.
♥ *Turn your eyes to Me generation and see the Joy that is coming to you soon. My Holy Spirit will descend in its fullness not only to save the wretches but I will descend also for judgement, to give sight to the blind and take away the sight of those who say they see. And from those who call themselves wise and instructed I will confuse to the point that they would not know who they are and where they*

come from. I tell you solemnly, I will instruct the unworthy and those whom you call foolish and contemptible, I will raise and instruct them with My Knowledge turning them to devout pupils of the Truth, to shame those who hold back My Kingdom from them. ♥ *I tell you: "the dead will be making their way into My Kingdom before you;[1] My Spirit of Grace came to you at your doors but you did not want to believe in My Marvels nor in My Miracles and yet the ones you call contemptible and who are the rejects of your society, believed with humility, with fervour and with love. This is why I will bring back the sinners and raise the dead as columns of light; but to My sheer grief, even after you will see these great marvels, you will still refuse to think better of it and believe in My present Divine Works. So I am telling you:*

> *"My Kingdom will be taken away*
> *from you to be given to a poor*
> *people, a people who could not tell*
> *their right hand from their left*
> *and it will be to these wretches*
> *<u>I shall confer My New Name</u>.* ♥ *"*

ΙΧθΥΣ

VASSULA OF MY SACRED HEART

September 18th, 1990

Vassula of My Sacred Heart[2], do not allow anyone to take away from you the Gift I have given you. ♥

Lord! Forbid them to do this to me. By myself I cannot do anything and I am limited as You know!

Do not fear Vassula, My daughter. My enemies who are also your enemies, I shall overpower and My Teachings shall convert many more, see? How many times have I rescued you from the lion's mouth? and how many times have I enlightened you My child? and how many times have I shown you the Way? <u>Ah My Sweet</u>

---

[1] The "wise."
[2] Here, I was just thinking that probably I am the first Orthodox called: "Vassula of the Sacred Heart."

227

pupil![1] Have confidence in Me, rely on Me, ask and it shall be given to you. ♥ Come, evangelize with love for Love. Earn souls for Me. Desire Me, love Me, and trust Me. ♥ ΙΧΘΥΣ

Ecclesia shall revive!

September 19th, 1990

Lord, take my soul and my heart and place them in the middle of Your Sacred Heart.

Ah My child, how I longed to hear you say again these words to Me! How I long to hear these words from everyone's heart! ♥

MY CHILD, WELCOME INTO YOUR FATHER'S HOUSE

September 20th, 1990

Lord?

I Am. Come and console Me, come and comfort Me, rest Me. I have created you so that I may be the One and only in your heart; I have created you to remove My thorns that penetrated My Body; I have created you to be the victim of My Heart. I love you to passion, accept My Love, accept My Knowledge, accept the trials with patience and do not look on them with disdain. I have accepted My Cross with great Love, with obedience and I drank My Cup to its last drop out of Love and to please the Father in Heaven. ♥ I am only disciplining you in moderation.

My daughter, if you listen to Me you will learn. My Eyes are constantly watching you, guarding you and blessing you. I am He who loves you most, so do not fear My daughter, Vassula, do not dread My discipline which will orient you in My direction, showing you the magnificence of My Works, their Splendour and the Riches of My Heart and the Consuming Fire of My Love. ♥ Have I ever failed you? Have I ever resisted your calls when you needed Me?

---

[1]Jesus was so full of joy as He cried out loud these words!

Blessed nations, blessed people, blessed creation! Then how is it you resist My Love and have gone astray to become an easy prey for Satan allowing yourselves to call My Name in vain? <u>The spirit who is in you, generation, is a rebellious spirit</u>, ruling you all to live a sensual life, an aimless life, a godless life, thus interchanging holiness with perversion. ♥ Oh generation! Where is the Sign between Me and you? What have you done with It? Where is your faith in Me? How have you allowed to bring yourselves to give Me up? Have you not heard before that the nearer you come to Me, the nearer I will come to you? Keep your eyes fastened on Me without looking to your left nor to your right. Let Me one day say: "My child, welcome into your Father's House. You have been an appeasing fragrance to Me; you have kept My Law and lived holy; you have been fruitful and you have nourished the poor. <u>Come</u> then, My child, thrust yourself into your Father's Arms and live forever and ever in My Heart." ♥ ΙΧθΥΣ ⊃

THERE IS A DIVISION IN MY CHURCH, LIKE CAIN AND ABEL

September 21st, 1990

My beloved Yahweh, make us once more divine. Renew us. Fashion us into Your Divine Image, this Holy Image we lost.

My Vassula, I shall hear your pleas and like I have rained down on you My Blessings, I shall cover this earth to with splendid vestments, clothing her in glorious perfection and make her people fall on their faces to the ground in adoration to Me. But first I must descend My Purifying Fire upon this generation, I must descend to pull out the foxes from their lairs that make havoc of every new vineyard. I have told you this now before it happens, so that when it happens you may believe.

Like rousing a corpse from death, I shall resurrect this earth's decaying body into a glorious body, transfiguring you from priest to layman into a divine people. Today your generation lacks faith and refuses to believe in Me and every day that passes, more and more of My shepherds are being taken by the world and the lure of riches, they are aping Wisdom and when Grace comes to them at their feet they refuse this Grace, they do not want to receive Grace in return for grace. There is a division in My Church, like Cain and Abel. Brothers, yet divided. One blood, yet different. Abel was competent but Cain, incompetent; one was sincere, the other not; one was well-disposed and pleasing, the other one was ill-disposed and displeasing Me. And today My Abels who officiate in My Church, suffer. They suffer because they see that their own brothers are betraying Me, this is the plague that weighs heavily on My shepherds and makes this brotherhood broken and divided. ♥ Happy the man who keeps My Commandments for he shall feel My appeasing Love; happy the peacemakers when they work for peace, they shall be called sons of Mine. Soon Love shall be with you, this is why there must be constancy in My Abels who keep My Commandments and keep their faith in Me. ♥

My Vassula, I shall give you the rest[1] later on. Be persevering in your prayers and be thankful. Delight your Father who is in Heaven, do not fear. I am with you. Love's Eyes are on you. Jesus is My Name. ♥ ΙΧθΥΣ ⊃⊂⊃

Alleluia!

CARESS ME WITH SIMPLE WORDS

September 24th, 1990

Peace be with you. ♥ Vassula, I shall never fail you. Probing your prayers to Me, this pleases My Heart, say:

> *Jesus, You who saved Me,*
> *be blessed.*
> *Jesus, You who feed Me,*
> *be blessed.*
> *Jesus, I love You.*
> *Teach Me how to love you more. Amen ♥*

Caress Me with simple words, yet coming from your heart. Ah My beloved! Bless Me without cease. Rest in My Heart and console Me as I console you, this My Vassula is what I need now. ♥

---

[1]The rest of a certain passage of the Bible He wanted to teach me.

GOD WANTS EVERYONE TO BE SAVED

September 25th, 1990

Our Holy Mother's Message to us all:

Peace be with you, beloved children. Allow Me to remind you that the Lord knows each heart, the Lord is in search of your heart. Come to Him with a pure heart and He shall teach you, the Lord shall comfort your soul. He shall lead you in His Path and in the Truth. I beg you, you who still waver, do not shut your hearts to reason. Return to the Lord and He will return to you. A Joy from Heaven will now descend among you, a Light will shine in the midst of you. Be prepared to receive this Light, be prepared to meet the Lord. ♥

Today, whose hands are clean? and who can say truly his heart is pure? Whose soul is in perfect harmony with the Lord? Beloved ones! My own! My children, the road to the Lord is in the midst of you, it is found in the land of the living. Stretch out then your hands towards His Sanctuary and the Lord, from Heaven, will reach to pull you to Him. Stretch out your hands towards Him and He, full of Compassion, will lean down to you. Come to the Lord without delay. Lift your eyes to Heaven and look to no one else but Him, the Lord your God. Delight in no one else but Him, your Saviour. Seek, seek no one else but the Lord your Redeemer. Sing, sing to no one but to the Holy One.

Am I to remind you that the Lord is Tenderness and Compassion, slow to anger and rich in Graciousness? Jesus was the Stone rejected by the builders that became the keystone. I tell you truly that the Kingdom of God is among you and His Holy Spirit of Grace is blowing sweetly now on your nations to revive you, so come and see the Wedding of the Holy Spirit who will wed your lands. Do not reject the Holy Spirit that so manifestly is poured upon you, do not be like the "builders" who rejected the stone that turned to be the cornerstone. ♥ God wants everyone to be saved. And now this is My solemn warning to all who hear the prophecies of this book:

do not suppress the Spirit

the Spirit that now blows on you in the middle and in the peak of your apostasy. Do not say later on, on Judgement Day, "I had never heard, I had not known." Jesus and I are revealing things beforehand, before they happen, so that you cannot say when you meet God face to face, "I was unaware." The citadel of the proud shall fall and the devils shall be cast out from within her womb. ♥

May you be blessed; may you all be blessed for hearing Me. I am your beloved Mother, the Theotokos who loves you all. ♥

MY MESSAGES ARE PRAYERS

September 28th, 1990

Jesus?

I Am. ♥ *Lean on Me. Lean on My Shoulder as I came to you and lifted you from the pit and carried you to My House where I healed you, so will I continue to help your feet to be in the Righteous Path. Let your hands clutch on Me. I know you to be faint-hearted[1] but I shall make you strong to oppose evil.*

Ah creation! <u>*Mercy now descends before Judgement.*</u> *Welcome My Mercy* <u>*now*</u> *and My Spirit shall rest on you.* ♥ *Approach Me, you who desire Me, and take your fill from My Inexhaustible Wells of Life, for they who eat Me will hunger for More and they who drink Me will thirst for more[2], and I, like Manna, will replenish your soul and like a potter shall form you into what you have lost,* <u>*My Divinity.*</u> *Then I shall show you My Kingdom and I will send you Wisdom to teach you My Knowledge of My Holy things and I shall make you Mine forever and ever. You will be My sons and daughters glorifying Me together with My Assembly in Heaven. Then I shall send you out like mist to display like one displays a banner:* <u>*My Knowledge you received from Wisdom Herself*</u> *to teach others to grow upright in purpose and learning so that generation after generation My Holy Name may be kept Holy. Your descendants would have a rich inheritance born of you and thanks to My Infinite Mercy so will your children's children; and in the future the nations will know the meaning of* <u>*the Fear of the Lord.*</u> ♥ *My favours are not all past, My favours are inexhaustible, filling every valley, and My Tenderness is renewed* <u>*every day*</u> *upon you. I am pouring out continuously from My Heart My Love like flowing rivers to water your desert and revive you.*

<u>*It is not I*</u> *who forced you to dwell in darkness, it is not My wish to watch from above how you wall yourselves in and imprison your souls in the darkest dungeons. My desire is to bring you Home in peace; My desire is to make out of your deserts and parched lands, green pastures, to fill you.* ♥ *Vassula, all My Messages are prayers, read and write down Romans 8:26-27.*

---

[1] Jesus was smiling.
[2] Ecclesiasticus 24:21.

The Spirit too comes to help us in our weakness. For when we cannot choose words in order to pray properly, the Spirit himself expresses our plea in a way that could never be put to words, and God who knows everything in our hearts knows perfectly well what he means, and that the pleas of the saints expressed by the Spirit are according to the mind of God.

Meditate upon this. I love you, repeat after Me this:

> *Jesus, neither death, nor life, no angel, no prince, nothing that exists, nothing still to come[1], not any power or height or depth, nor any created thing, will ever come to separate me from You. I vow to remain faithful to You, this is my solemn vow. Help me keep this vow forever and ever. Amen.*

I repeated what Jesus gave me.

YOUR JESUS, I AM

September 28th, 1990

Soul, pray, this means, <u>speak</u> to Me! Do not ignore My Omnipresence just because the tempter keeps tempting you. Hear Me, resist, resist him. Come now, I shall manifest Myself again through you, if you submit to Me humbly and allow My Spirit to rest on you in My hours of My Passion. IXθΥΣ ⳉ

Your Jesus I Am. ♥

---

[1]Romans 8:38-39

I HAVE WED YOU TO SHARE MY CROSS

October 1st, 1990

My Vassula, it is I, the Lord. Feel Me, I am near you, discern Me.[1] I am sharing My Cross with you, My Crown of Thorns and My Nails. I have chosen you out of the land of the dead and revived you in My Heart to make you the victim of My Insatiable Love and make you an atonement for many souls who prefer to remain divided and differenciate themselves under My Sacred Name. I am sharing My sufferings and My grief with you daughter. Console Me and I will console you. Vassula, My child, I have raised you to appease My Justice, I have raised you to delight My Soul. Do not fear then My child, My Father has found favour in you for all that you are not. You have no merits, none at all, but I favoured you in spite of your wretchedness for My Loyalty and My Gentleness are without measure. Sacrifice more My child. Incense and myrrh of Mine! How I love you! I shall make you zealous for Me, your God, and loyal to My Commandments. I shall anoint you with My oil. O property of Mine, live in Me and allow Me to live in you! I am He whom you should never resist, never fail, never deny! I am He who breathes in you Life! Allow Me to invade you entirely, show no resistance to Me, am I not overwhelming you with favours? Am I not consuming you entirely with My Flaming Fire of My Heart? Have I not shown you to My angels and to the Holy ones living in My Assembly? Have I ever deprived you from suffering, soul? Hence, it is your due to Me now to love Me, it is your due, soul to prostrate yourself to Me and adore Me; it is your due now to delight My Soul and receive Me in My Holy Sacrifice. ♥ Come... come... Approach Me, allow Me to whisper now and then in your ear My Love for you; allow Me to caress you with My Tenderness; allow Me to caress you with My Blessings. Come and lean your head on My Heart, you are not just My tablet, soul, you are also My beloved bride whom My Heart loves and desires to sing to you. My Voice is sweet and My Heart a Blazing Furnace of Love, and My Fragrance attractive and delicate. See how I come flying to you before you even open your lips and have the word in your mouth for Me? As a flower among the thistles I have you now, as a net cast into the sea I have thrown you to catch souls for Me your King. If you do not know this Vassula, My daughter, I tell you now: follow the marks of My Blood and take the Cross I have entrusted you with. Follow the marks of My Blood, these marks you sought from your youth[2], they will lead you to Me, into My Arms and into My Heart. O Vassula! I shall guard you like the Pupil of My Eye. I have lifted you from the pit to give you a place together with My predilected

---

[1] There, Jesus touched my arm.
[2] When I was a child, I had visions of following Jesus on the way to Golgotha and being near Him under the Cross.

234

souls of My Heart, I have wed you to share My Cross as our matrimonial bed and henceforth made you Mine for eternity. Lower now your eyes before your King and Spouse; lower your eyes and allow My Hand to rest on your head to bless you and breathe on you My sweet Sigh of Love on your forehead, the Breath of My Tenderness. ♥ My child, I would like to see you free from all worry. I am only waiting to be gracious to you, I am only waiting to hide you in My Sacred Heart forever, where you will find True Peace.

LET MY IMPERIAL COURT PREPARE FOR ME MY WAY
I AM SENDING YOU BEFORE ME MY MOTHER

October 10th, 1990

Peace be with you child. Allow Me to use your hand, it is I, your Jesus, it is Love who speaks to you and asks you...

O come and invade me!

Ah My Vassula, I shall then fill you... hear Me and write My message for the entire world.

Please be with you. Love is speaking, love is offering, Love is healing, even injuries that appeared to be beyond healing. Love is consoling those who are not cared for, My Love for you is eternal and I am known to be constant in My affection Approach... come close to Me, by praying with your heart, I am offering you a place in My school, I am offering you Wisdom to teach you My Knowledge. Blessed are they who humbly accept My Instructions and lay My Words to heart.

Hear Me, My beloved: Scripture says, "the language of My Cross may be illogical to those who are not on the way to salvation, but those of you who are on the way see it as God's power to save"[1] and it is this language I am coming to teach you. It is this language of Love you will hear in My school, and you, you who are willing to learn, be blessed, be strong and happy. Though obstacles are bound to come, do not fear, rely on Me, but alas for the one who provides them, he shall have to answer Me in the Day of Judgement!

---

[1] 1 Corinthians 1:18.

My Return is imminent and I am giving you constant signs to prepare you. Love is on the path of return, I am on My way back to you. Tell Me, when a king enters into a city, will there be no preparations to receive him? The whole city will be in turmoil and the king will send before him his elect and his imperial court to prepare a way for him and make his paths straight. He will send his messengers to announce his coming; he will ask them to shout with a loud voice: "here is your King, your King is coming with His Heart in His Hand to offer It to you! Mercy now leans down from heaven and from His Throne, He has taken pity on you." This is why, before My Return, I am sending you before Me, the Arch of Alliance, I am sending you the Woman of the Apocalypse, the second Eve, who will crush the serpent's head with her heel; I am sending you before Me My Mother, to open a broad highway and level it in this desert; I am sending you the Queen of Heaven, the Door to Heaven to prepare you and to school all you who still lie in the dust, to come forward and make your peace with Me, your King, before My Great Return; I am sending you the Queen of Peace to thresh from one corner of the earth to the other and gather you one by one; I am sending you before My Great Return, My servants the prophets to remind you of My Law and to turn you back from your evil ways and live holy and announce to you events before they take place; I am sending you My angels to remind you of My Holiness, My Magnificence and My Splendour. I am sending you My mouthpieces to shout and proclaim on the rooftops of your houses the Wedding of My Holy Spirit. I will not grow weary of calling you to wed Me, I will not get discouraged by your hostility nor by your aridity. I will be in pursuit of your heart and like a young man marrying a virgin, the One whom you wounded all along will wed you. And I, in My Love, shall make you replace the Thorns encircling My Heart, by a flowered Wreath and like a bridegroom wearing his wedding wreath I too shall wear it, because this wreath will be My Wreath of Victory, this will be the Prize of My Mercy... Generation, I shall make you Mine, I shall lift you up and carry you as a bridegroom carries his bride into his rooms and in My everlasting Love I shall carry you into My Sacred Heart and make you Mine for eternity. Soon, very soon now I shall tear the heavens open and come down in full force! If you were to understand fully what I mean, you would not spend your time being lethargic, you would be in constant prayer to Me, for suddenly and as quick as thunderbolt I shall descend in flame of devouring fire and unveil all that has been hidden from you. I shall with My Finger point out to you all those that honoured Me with lip-service, never serving Me with the language I had taught them, the language of My Cross, the Language of Love, the Language that teaches you things beyond human understanding. I shall reveal to you the Cains whose language is not My Language but this one of rich merchants and trade. Pray for these Cains, do not judge them; spend your time with prayers for them, do not allow your tongue to slip. ♥

Do not be one of these who say to My seers, "see no visions" and to My prophets "do not prophecy." Let My Imperial Court prepare for Me My Way, no prophecy ever came from man's initiative. When My seers and prophets speak for Me, it is by Grace that they do and by My Holy Spirit that fills them, moves them and opens their mouth to repeat My Words. And I shall continue recalling you the Truth, by my mouthpieces even if you know the truth; I shall keep revealing My plans to My servants the prophets and show My Magnificence in visions to My seers. Leave My elect and My predilected souls free to prepare the Way for Me your King, let them complete their witnessing. I am sending you My Celestial Court to prophesy for these end of Times in the wilderness of your era to convert you before My Great Day comes. Realize that I do not descend only for Mercy but also for Judgement, I do not tell My messengers to call only the just, I tell them to call also the unjust, the poor, the lame, the rejects of your society, and everyone they meet in the streets to come and fill up My school. I want to call all those who never sought Me nor ever knew Me, to come and prosper in My House, for these are the Times of Mercy and of Grace. ♥ Then let all those who see you, gaze and stare at your transfiguration, let it show on your faces and by the glow of your heart that you have been attending My School and that you are My pupils and I, your Master. Let them see in your eyes the reflection of everything you have witnessed, let them see on your body the marks of My Wounds, and if anyone asks you how you received them, tell them that you received them in the House of your Master's friends where He at first received them... Then lift up your cross and follow Me. I, Jesus Christ, Beloved Son of God and Saviour blow My Breath on you and bless you all, leaving the Sigh of My Love on your foreheads. Go in peace and be one in My Name. ♥ IXθΥΣ ⤜⬤▷

Message of Our Blessed Mother:

Peace be with you. Incense of God, take courage for I am with you. I am with you and with My innumerable angels I surround you, to protect you. I come down with the saints to guide you, I am the Queen of Heaven; I am the Queen of Peace; I am the Mother of your Saviour; I am the One who precedes the Lord's coming; I am the One who opened a broad highway for your Redeemer to descend on earth and today again, the Most High is sending Me to make smooth and level a Path for His Return. Although Satan uses men to delay My Work and put obstacles in its midst, do not fear, the Lord is Almighty and in the end Our Hearts will prevail. Rely on His massive Strength for He can uproot mountains and melt the rocks, nothing can stop His Powerful Hand.

What do you see above you? Look above your heads what the Lord is raising, the Lord is raising over you the Banner of His Great Love and Mercy. He is coming to restore you with His caresses and feed you with delights; He is coming to fragrance you with His delicate perfume of Myrrh; He is coming to soothe your wounds with His balm of Tenderness; He is coming down to pour out His oil on you generation and anoint you. The King will bring you into His Rooms to console you and wipe away your tears. Like the pupil of His Eye He is watching over you, and you, would you in your turn return His Love? Offer Him your heart and your will.

Many of you have forgotten God's ways, you have been drifted away, like taken by a current in a lake, into a pool of lethargy. Polluted with materialism your course changed direction and from holiness and the rightful Path you have been led right into the devil's nets and into the lion's mouth! You have not followed the marks of Precious Blood Jesus left behind Him as a signpost for you to follow, no, you have followed the polluted directions Satan put up for you, directions leading all to the desert where there would be no one to care for your sores and no one to console you, and where you would die.

<u>Your generation failed to appreciate God's great Love</u>, this is why your lands are set aflame by egoism, by godlessness and by the fury of Satan and still to this day his hand is raised to strike you and set aflame all the nations. Because of your atheism and your perversity you have wrapped yourselves in the shroud of death, you have wrapped your beloved ones in a cloud of flint. I call in agony from above, to you all to make peace with God, to reconcile with your families.

When you come and pray in pilgrimages do you come with a clean heart? Have you ceased to do evil? Are you in peace with your neighbour? Have you confessed and repented truly of your sins? Have you blessed your enemies and forgiven them? Have you repaid evil with love? Are you indeed ready to meet the Lord with your hands full of good works? Bless those who persecute you, and pray for them, do not judge them. Keep on praying. For what use are your offerings when your heart is unforgiving, holding grudges? Where is your holiness then? Purify yourselves and live in the Light of God and in the Love of God. Be a true witness of the Gospel by the warmth and glow of light in your heart; be a witness for Jesus by bearing His Cross with Him; be a witness for the Church by being constant in your faith and by being united with Christ's Vicar. Never allow your tongues to slip, be perfect as the Lord <u>is</u> perfect. Let it show that you are indeed the first-fruits of God's great Love; let every eye witness your good behaviour and know that it is because you are children of the Most High; let the marks of His Five Wounds be noticed on your body too, let these be the Sign to show you are His pupils and He your Divine Master. Live Our Messages and be like grains to spread them, let your cry of love go out through all the earth and to the ends of the world. I bless each one of you and I thank you for giving Me your time. ♥ Go in peace. ♥

THE TERRORS OF THE NIGHT WILL SOON BE OVER

October 17th, 1990

Jesus, you have told us in these books many things before they happen, so that when they do happen we may believe You have told us how you will resurrect my sister Russia and how You will make an end of her atheism. And look! On the 14th, St Basil's Church on the Red Square opened her doors for You! and I, her sister rushed to her that day to rejoie her feast! But what I got from her was a slap on my face... Your servant and brother of mine whom I love, struck me[1]. Your servant refused to bless me, because he said, I was going to our brothers the Catholics and receiving from their hand Holy Communion. Am I to feel ashamed, before You my Lord? This would have been an affliction I could bear had it not been for worse to come. He said "this means excommunication." You had given me a sign before this happened, making me feel Your sorrow by turning my mouth, just before, dryer than wood and my lips dryer than parchment. How long will the Christians be divided? Come, and set our hearts right, give us back our innocence. Come and make a dawn of darkness. I thank You my Lord for giving me an occasion to be struck and humiliated, and giving me the courage to line up with the others in spite of my injury to go back to him again and kiss the cross he held and the hand that just struck me.

Vassula, your pain is nothing compared to Mine. Even though he drew a sword on you My daughter, do not despair, there is hope for reconciliation. Soon, I shall overwhelm you with a great Miracle[2]. Very soon now I, the Lord, shall adorn My Bride with Her glorious perfection of Her youth, hence a covenant of peace will be sealed between brothers. Like the Morning Star My Church shall rise, the ban will be lifted... Like an olive tree loaded with fruit She shall stand solidly before Me. Like a vine putting out graceful shoots, Her blossoms will bear fruit of glory and splendour... and there will be only one flock and one Shepherd... I am the Resurrection... daughter?[3] Let not your hope be void, you need not fear. The terrors of the night will soon be over.[4] Remember, by your side I Am. I do not leave My Eyes too long on their misconduct lest My wrath flares up My Justice, so I let My Mercy take over. ♥ I am curing all your diseases and wiping away with My Blood all the traces of venom, to redeem you all from the Pit. I am Love and Love in all His Tenderness is forgiving the strikers, the mockers, the unjust and in My Holy Compassion I shall lift you all in My Heart. Do not despair Vassula My daughter, there is still hope for reconciliation and a revival.. there is still

---

[1] I am speaking symbolicly.
[2] I saw suddenly in an interior vision, someone dressed up like a bride, in dazzling white-silvery clothes and all glittery.
[3] Jesus turned and looked at me, His Eyes full of compassion.
[4] Jesus was consoling me, His Words were like a balm of caresses healing my wounds.

hope...[1] "Do not be afraid of those who kill the body but cannot kill the soul, fear him rather who can destroy both body and soul in hell." (Matthew 10:28) I will come to bring peacefulness to the brothers and remind them of My Tenderness of My Love and Mercy so that they too in their turn may imitate Me. Do not hurry away.[2] Come, Ecclesia shall revive. Ecclesia shall revive, wait and you shall see.

IXθYΣ ⳨

THE PARABLE OF THE WEDDING FEAST
I AM WHO I AM

October 20th, 1990

Jesus?

I Am. All I ask from you is love, this is My Theme. I need every drop of love in your heart, I want all the love you have to redeem those who are heading for the eternal fires. When I say, "revive My Church" or "embellish My Church", or "unite My Church", I mean you to pray, pray, pray without ceasing. Pray from your heart. Love Me fervently and with your expiations which will join these of My martyr saints, you will glorify Me. Yes daughter, with your expiations and your fervent prayers offered to Me with love you can alter coming disasters. You can alter natural disasters, you can extinguish the flaring wrath of My Father, you can relent Him, you can relent Him. You can embellish My Church; you can bring together My People under My Name to celebrate mass around one altar; you can repair their shepherd's staff, this staff they broke first in half then into splinters. For men this unity appears impossible, but for Me everything is possible. So pray and expiate for your brothers. I need victim souls, I need generous souls to repay evil with love, to repay evil with self-sacrifice. So offer Me your will and I shall make you My instruments of Peace and Love; I shall make you My instruments of Reconciliation and Unity. ♥

Lord, our own apostasies are rebuking us. Forgive us and help us to make reparations. Bring us back in the love of our bridal days, the early days, and remind us the affection we once had in our youth for You. Do not allow anymore any evil to overcome us.

---

[1] Jesus was once more trying to console me. It looked like the one who was wounded more was trying to console the other one whose wounds were less grave.
[2] I thought it was over and I was getting ready to leave.

Yes, offer Me your prayers and I shall restore My House which is your House too.
Be loyal and this special favour will be granted to you. Like in the transfiguration,
I shall transfigure My Church to have all the radiant glory of Her youth, in Her
bridal days. I will do all these things for the sake of My Holy Name. I shall unite
you to demonstrate My Power.

Lord, there are other things too, I asked You this before but I would like to ask You
again and I do not know how to say it!

I shall open your mouth and you shall speak![1]

Lord have You not said that the Advocate, the Holy Spirit, will teach us everything
and remind us of all You have said to us? Then doesn't Scripture say... "in the
Church God has given the first place to apostles, the second to prophets..".[2] and
doesn't Scripture say... "there is a remnant, chosen by grace. By grace, you notice,
nothing therefore to do with good deeds, or grace would not be grace at all!..."[3] and
last doesn't Scripture say... "at all your meetings let everyone be ready with a psalm
or a sermon, or a revelation..."[4] So why Lord nowadays most of the prophetic or
private revelations are looked upon by some priests with contempt? With one eye
instead of the two? and why are some priests and bishops even, attacking with
contempt Your messages?

In reality, My child, they are wrestling against Me because they are suppressing
the Advocate. Daughter, these people are not objecting to you. No, My angel,
they are not, they are objecting to Me, not to you. If they ignore you My flower
it is because you have grown in the middle of their desert, they will not water you
so that you wither and fade away. They keep forgetting though that I Am your
Devout Keeper.

Vassula, I shall remind you of the parable of the wedding feast.[5] ♥ Daughter,
many are called but few are chosen. To believe is a grace given by Me, to have
faith is also a grace given by Me. These are the Times of Grace and Mercy; these
are the Times in which My Holy Spirit is poured out upon you; these are the Times
when My Holy Spirit shall lift you out of your great apostasy, to wed you. Your
era's wretchedness shall peel off your generation, because with My Own Hand I
shall unwrap your death shroud to clothe you in the garments of your wedding.
Feel My delight My Vassula! Feel how I already rejoice at this coming event! My
Holy Spirit will come to bring Fire to the earth, and how I wish it were blazing

---

[1]Suddenly a flow of words came out of me.
[2]1 Corinthians 12:28.
[3]Romans 11:5-6.
[4]1 Corinthians 14:26.
[5]Matthew 22:1-14.

already! These are the Times of the Wedding of My Holy Spirit; these are the Times your King of Peace is sending His servants, His angels, His prophets and His Celestial Court to go out to the four corners of the earth and invite His friends to His Banquet and into His Kingdom and offer them His Celestial Manna. ♥ *I have been sending My messengers in true righteousness all the way to your doorstep to announce My Return, but many of you did not believe them and treated them as imposters. Others would not come because they put honour from men before the honour that comes from Me. Since I have invited you and you have refused Me, since I have beckoned and you do not want to take notice, since you have ignored all My supplications and rejected Love's offer, I shall fill up My House and give My Kingdom to the rejects of your society to confuse you all. I shall give them back their sight and heal them, I shall open the Doors of My House wide open to let them in. My messengers will call aloud in the streets, and in the public squares. They will be sent by Me to invite the corpses they meet at each street corner, and those who have never been told about Me will see Me, and those who have never heard about Me will listen and understand. I shall be found by those who did not seek Me. Like I have revealed My Holy Face to you, daughter, I shall reveal Myself likewise to those who did not consult Me. Of My Spirit you do not want! neither of My Heart offered to you in My Hand! I tell you this now, before it happens, so that when it <u>does</u> happen you may believe that <u>I Am who I Am</u>:*

My Kingdom will be taken away from you and it will be given to a people you call contemptible and foolish, the rejects of your society and My House will be rebuilt and risen by those you call simple minds. They, with their love, shall restore the ruins of My House and all that has lain waste, and it is My Holy Spirit who shall shepherd them and console them... The citadel of the proud shall soon fall into a heap of dust. Justice shall prevail. Pray for these shepherds, pray for their conversion. Be blessed, My child. I shall not be long, soon you shall see Me face to face. I Am.

α ☧ ω

FOLLOW THE MARKS OF MY BLOOD
THE TRUTH IS LOVE

October 22nd, 1990

Vassula, beloved, I am the Holy One in your room. It is I Jesus. Are you happy of My Visit?

Very! I bless You. Very much Lord!

Hold fast to all the teachings I am giving you. Let no one deceive you. Reap progressively My harvest of kindness and tenderness. I will increase your visions so you may testify in My Name. I shall provide you with words to be able to testify. My daughter, remind the world of My Great Love, this will be the message for all times. Peace be with you. I am Jesus your Redeemer, I am the Holy of Holies who speaks to you. I tell you truly, I shall pour special graces on those who accepted this testimony because by having accepted this testimony of Love they are attesting the truthfulness and the Infinite Love of the Most High, since all that is written comes from Me. Beloved ones, I give My Spirit <u>without reserve</u>, I give My Spirit to remind the world over and over again of My affection and the great love I have for you. I give My Spirit without reserve to remind you all of My Five Wounds and of My Passion.

My child, you who read or hear Me, look around you, Dawn is soon with you.. and you will not have to consult the shadows of the night that whisper and mutter, nor will you have to walk in distress and darkness, for your wizards who blasphemed My Holy Name and substituted darkness for light will be wiped away. Beloved ones, Dawn is soon with you and as soon as it is light your seedlings shall blossom. The traders who infiltrated My Church will be dismayed and all the buyers dejected, every merchant grown rich shall swoon. Dazzled by My Glory and by My Light they will remain baffled and stunned before Me. The signal is being hoisted on the roofs of your houses, My ambassadors are sent at their post now to wait for My signal. My Return is imminent, so you who are My messengers, swiften your step, go on every hill and announce that judgement shall soon fall on those traders, for they have become an <u>abomination</u> in My Sight! Have you not read before to stay awake and watch so that when you see the <u>disastrous abomination</u>, of which the prophet Daniel spoke, erected in My Sanctuary, you would know that this is the sign spoken of by the prophet for the end of Times? How is it that you cannot read the Times? The bricks of My Sanctuary have fallen down and you are living in the middle of this great apostasy of your era. My oppressors think now they have the upper hand, and the traders believe they will continue trading in My Sanctuary but I tell them, "you who have corrupted your wisdom by trading My Image for a lifeless statue, a false god, an idol. You who struggle to erect this disastrous abomination and abolish My Perpetual Sacrifice, you will drink the full winecup of My Justice." The figure daubed with assorted colours, this figure these traders are trying to make you revere to and follow <u>is not me</u>, it is an invention of perverted human skill to degrade the concept of My Holiness and My Divinity, it is a false ecumenism, <u>it is a defiance of all that is holy</u>. I suffer because of the sins of these traders. Pray for these priests who became traders, their sin is grave. Pray that I may put My Spirit of Truth in them and make them keep My Laws and sincerely respect My Divinity. ♥ Beloved ones, you whom I marked as Mine on your foreheads, do not allow these traders to *compel you to follow this false image, be on your guard. I am telling you all this before because I want you to feel confident in Me your God when the times of great distress are upon you. I mean to visit you. Already the hour is coming of My Great Return, and woe to these merchants who are struggling to erect their disastrous abomination in My Sanctuary and abolish My Perpetual Sacrifice by forcing you to eat their defiled food! Woe to these traders who conspire to ruin My Word by rationalizing it! Woe to the blasphemers who blasphemed ten times My Holy Name! Woe to the followers of the Beast who carved images[1] blaspheming against My seven Spirits! Their citadel will become a heap of dust by the Breath of My Mouth! and you My child who read Me or hear Me, you whom I visited your grave and made My Breath enter you, I tell you: follow the marks of My Blood I leave behind for you as a sign and if you are stopped and interrogated on your way by a passer-by, tell him that you are my pupil and I your Master and that you are on your way to witness a crucified Christ, a resurrected Christ. And if you will be stopped by a trader beware of his dishonesty, beware that he does not exchange the Cross I have given you for a corrupt so-called wisdom. Without a sound, without a word, embrace more fervently than ever the bar across your shoulders and follow the marks of My Blood and they will lead you to Me; and if anyone of these start proceeding against you, do not cover your face against insult or strike, offer your backs too so that they know you from your wounds. Let them be a perfect imitation of My Wounds for they will be given to you by the very same ones who stroke Me, your Master, and then the Sign of the Son of Man will appear in the skies. A great light shall be seen in your darkness, for I, the Holy One, mean to save you for the sake of My Name.*

Come, My child, you who hear Me or read Me, I have shown My Love for you again in this testimony. Do not say that I am too far away to love, for at this very instant My Eyes are upon you with a special tenderness and an affection you can never understand fully. Had I to return just for your sake alone to redeem you, without the slightest hesitation I would come and repeat My Passion, for your sake alone! Now do you believe Me when I tell you that a man can have no greater love than to lay down his life for his friends? I am telling you all this so that you may find your peace in My Sacred Heart, so that you may find True Life in Me, so that you may find true love and rest in Me your God. I know that you are weak My child, but your weakness attracts My Omnipotence. Can you take in what I say? I say, peace be with you! I am the Victim of Love who speaks to you, I am He who gave you this testimony of Love as a reminder of My Love. Absorb Me and allow Me to invade you. ♥ Feel how My Heart yearns for a return of love! Do not resist Me. Come to Me as you are, come and drink the flow of My Heart and you shall thirst for more. Oh, so many of you wandered away from the Truth and went this way and that, the Truth is LOVE. I am the Truth. Be witnesses for

---

[1]False Christ. False teachings. Rational and naturalism teachings.

244

the Truth, receive the Holy Spirit of Truth, receive the Holy Spirit of Grace. ♥
*I bless you all, leaving My Sigh of Love on your foreheads. Be one under My
Holy Name.* ♥ IXθΥΣ ⇒◁▷

TAKE MY CUP AND DRINK FROM IT

October 23rd, 1990

Lord, I am daily facing marvels beyond me and my poor knowledge, to meet You
every day in this way is quite beyond my mind!

Peace be with you. Realize what joy you give Me little one.

How I wish to be now up with You. Do You know that?

*My child, yes I know that but you have to wait. You must accomplish first your
mission, it is your due now.* ♥ *Fertilize these arid lands with all that I have given
you, nourish the lands. I love you to folly, never doubt of the greatness of My
Love. Alone you are not, never, I am wherever you go. I am your Holy
Companion.*

Fountain! that turn arid lands into fertile gardens! Well of Living Water! Give us
flowing streams so that we may live. Allow me to share with You Your Cup.

*Then take My Cup and drink from it, and if you feel faint from its bitterness come
and lean on Me, come and rest in Me. Vassula, My property, I your King, hold
you captive of My Love and I shall be guarding you like a sentinel is guarding a
gate. I have given you the gift of My Love, espousing you to Me, so I shall make
sure that no intruder trespasses upon My property, My property now I have turned
into a garden, where I can go to and rest.* ♥ *Allow Me to breathe in you, allow
Me to accomplish My Works in you, be docile and accept Me your Master and
King. Love is My Name.* ♥ *Come to Me to eat from My Hand.[1] I shall feed you
till the end.* IXθΥΣ ⇒◁▷

---

[1]Jesus means in this manner with writing which feeds my soul.

THROUGH YOUR NOTHINGNESS
I HAVE REVEALED MY GREATNESS

October 24th, 1990

My heart wants to serve Your Greatness but I am needy and in misery and unable to lift my finger without You.

True, for if I was not standing by your side you would not be standing at all. Soul! Enwrapped in My Light, are you willing to obey My precepts?

I am willing to obey Your precepts.

Come and share My cloak then, let Me be your Guide and I shall continue to reveal to you the secrets of My Sacred Heart. I shall continue to unfold to you the depths of Heaven, I shall not fail you soul. Remain poor, needy and fervent for My food. Yes, hunger for My Food and desire it, do not be like the rich who do not hunger nor seek My Food. Seek the Riches of My Heart. Through your nothingness I have revealed My Greatness, through your misery I showed My Mercy, and through your frailty, My Strength. I have shown the world now the ardent Flame of the Burning Desires of My Heart, all I want from you now is a return of love. Daughter? I tell you truly, you who wish to serve Me your God, every time you will open your mouth to witness for the Truth, I shall bless you. Each time you speak of Me I shall light a fire in you. Pray and ask and I shall give more than you have asked, I shall remind you always My Instructions so that you may repeat My Words. I shall not leave you. I am known to be the All-Faithful. So My Vassula, allow Me to use you until I come and fetch you. Blessed one![1] *Remnant of Mine! Flower, come to Me in the right spirit and trust Me, will you kiss My Feet? Come, take your Master's Hand and follow Me.* ♥

---

[1] A thought passed my mind, to what will the Lord do with me after He fetches me; it was not an intelligent thought. That's why Jesus surprised said, "blessed one!"

THE DEVIL HATES YOU

October 30th, 1990

Vassula, puny little creature, do you know how many thorns you plucked out of My Heart?

No Lord.

Sufficient to rest Me, sufficient to rest Me My child. The purpose of your creation was also to rest Me, I have created you and even though you are dust and ashes I find in you a profound rest. Accept Me, accept My Cross on you, be grateful to me now. Child look at My Lips and listen to Me carefully, faith, have faith in Me and trust Me. I know your ineffable weakness and that without Me you cannot raise your little finger, this is why I have chosen you. I have chosen weakness to show the world My Power, I have a reason why I have chosen you in your state. Trust Me and draw your strength from Me, I shall remind you how the devil hates you and today you felt his claws on you. Yes, if I had left him he would have torn you to pieces, but you are under My Divine protection. Every single minute of his is aimed on you and all My other chosen souls. I tell you, because of your nothingness and because of your poverty, puny creature of Mine, you are undoing Satan's patterns, you are undoing stitch after stitch his embroideries, he called you worm when he knew you are My chosen one. Yes, be like a worm and eat up and ravage his designs, see? I can use for My Works even worms... Yes, eat up like a worm his patterns. I have allowed you to feel his hatred, he hates you because the Father Himself loves you for loving Me. This infuriates him beyond one's imagination. Happy is the man who does not lose faith in Me. Delight My Soul and fill Me with joy by remaining nothing. ♥

GOD IS A MOST TENDER FATHER

November 3rd, 1990

Our Holy Mother's Message:

Peace be with you, little children. Like a mother feeding and consoling her little children so am I too feeding your souls, by giving you the Word of God. Like a mother consoling her children in times of distress so am I too leaning towards you to console you. I am looking after your soul with My prayers, the Lord is

not slow to carry out His promises, but is waiting patiently that everyone will have the grace to see the Light and be converted. The New Heavens and the New Earth promised are ever so near you now. In the meantime while you are waiting sanctify, I beg you, your lives and live holy. I want to see in you dear children, a real conversion! Anyone who has escaped the vices of the world but then allows himself to be led by principles not coming from Wisdom but from Folly are certain to fall. <u>God is Love</u>, He is forgiving and slow to anger. God is a most Tender Father, examine your soul now and then to know whether you are standing in His Light or not. Be like a garden for the Lord where He could enjoy His rest in you, where He can delight His Soul in its delightful essences and where He could rest His Head on its green grass. <u>Let Me transform your heart into a beautiful garden for the Lord</u> so that when the King of kings comes to visit you, He would not turn away His Eyes from you but would offer you to become a victim of His Soul, a captive of His Heart. Lose no time therefore for His Eyes keep watch on each one of your steps. The Prince of Peace exhorts you to pray for peace and I, the Queen of Peace, beg you to pray for peace. Satan is now like a mad bull and My Heart is sick at what I see coming, though out of Mercy the Father has not shown Me everything. I roam all around the earth to look for generous souls but I cannot find enough generosity to offer Jesus and appease the Father's Justice. Tremendous amendments are to be done still. Jesus needs generous souls who are willing to expiate for others, this is why I weep. My Eyes dissolve in tears of Blood at these terrible sights I see coming. Today, if I tell you all this, it is not just to impress you or frighten you but to ask you to pray for Peace. It is God for His Own loving purpose who sends Me all around the world and in every house to gather you one by one and convert you before His Day. Beloved children, do not come in these gatherings to look only for signs, if I come all the way from Heaven to your doorstep it is to bring you the Peace of the Lord and My Peace. ♥ Allow Me therefore to transform your hearts into a beautiful garden for the Holy One so that He may find within your depths a spirit of holiness, love, peace, purity, obedience, humility and faithfulness. Then your King will use all these virtues and combat the powers of evil, rise up from your sleep children and change your hearts. I am happy to see so many of you fast on bread and water and today I ask these generous souls to add something more to their days of fasting, I ask you to repent and confess. Dear children, watch your lips from judging one another, do not, with all your fasting, allow your lips be the cause of your condemnation. Love one another, live our Messages, your King is addressing to you His Peace. I will keep patrolling the world to bring to the Lord those who are far away from Him, I need your generous prayers, children of Mine. I bless you all, I bless your families, your friends and even those you carry heavily in your hearts. Yes, all are children of God. ♥

YOU MUST TRUST ME FULLY

November 7th, 1990

Lord, let everything founded in the Truth remain, and everything founded in Falsehood be extirpated and thrown into the fire. Lord, I feel you far, yet I know You are not, have I been insensible to Your Presence?

My child, do your best and I shall do the rest. Even though I may seem far from you, do not fear, I am not far. I, the Lord, keep a vigilant eye on you. Pray soul! Pray that Justice relents and does not come suddenly upon your nations like a thunderclap. Vassula[1], I have prayed for you to the Father and asked Him to hasten His Step.[2] Read Jeremiah 44:7-9. ♥ Allow Me to use your little hand.

Use it Lord and use all of me as an atonement for Your Sacred Intentions.

I am happy[3] and I like it when you repose entirely your confidence in Me, for you are speaking to Me your God, not a man. You are reposing your confidence in Me and you must trust Me fully. So when you come to Me to offer me your will, look at Me full in the Face. I delight to hear you abandoning yourselves, reposing thus your confidence in Me. I rejoice to hear this adoration, for adoration it is if you offer Me your whole being, heart, soul and mind. Vassula, little soul how could I resist your pleadings? To know that these come from such a vulnerable soul, a soul that I resurrected only yesterday! How could My Heart, little soul, resist your calls? Draw from My Heart, little soul and cling to Me and pray for your brothers, for those who still lie as corpses under a thick layer of dust. Pray that My Breath sweeps away this dust and My Finger touches their heart so that they too turn to Me, for they have deserted Me in favour of leisures and not to say more than that.
♥ Be blessed My child. ♥ Bless Me. ΙΧθΥΣ ⊃⊂▷

---

[1] Jesus changed tone here.
[2] Diffusing the messages.
[3] Jesus was smiling.

JUDA

November 11th, 1990

Lord?

I Am. Rest in Me. All Heaven is full of joy, this is what you call the beatitude in its plenitude. Daughter, if souls only knew how wonderful it is to live in God no one would be lost so easily, unless they chose to be lost like Juda, he chose the way to perdition. Not that My Heart did not melt with sorrow every time I saw him take one further step away from Me; not that I had not prayed for him; not that I had not cried My Eyes out for him. I had opened so many ways for him to take, all leading to Me, but no sooner had he started one than he came out of it when he would realize I had laid it for him, for to sin he added rebellion, heaping abuses in his heart for Me his God. When he realized that My Kingdom was not an earthly kingdom in earthly glory he shut his heart and cut out our bonds and estranged himself <u>immediately</u> from Me. His senses of what is righteous or not was darkened and obeyed the ruler who governs the air. Today I am asking the sick like I asked the sick man at the pool of Bethzatha[1], "do you want to be well again?" I can heal you instantly and all Heaven shall rejoice and celebrate! My gift is free, so come to Me as you are. I shall heal you soul, so that you can share My Kingdom and live in Me your God. ♥ IXθΥΣ ⟩⟨⟩

THE THEOLOGIANS AND PHILOSOPHERS HAVE NOT YET FOUND THE KEY TO UNITY

November 15th, 1990

"I will celebrate Your Love for ever, Yahweh, age after age my words shall proclaim Your Faithfulness for I claim that love is built to last for ever and Your Faithfulness founded firmly in the Heavens."[2] But now a Greek Orthodox theologian is attacking me and hounding Your messages. O Lord show them that You are my help and consolation and that only through Your great Love You have saved me and others.

---

[1] John 5:1-9.
[2] Psalm 89:1-2.

Vassula of My Sacred Heart[1], My Holy Spirit has been your guide so do not pay attention to the theologian's conclusions. Pray that she too may receive the Spirit to understand that human reckonings and human doctrines made a devastating desert out of My Church.

Lord, she is shocked to have read in Your messages that You are like a beggar begging for our love.

Has she not read, "happy those servants whom the Master finds <u>awake</u> when He comes. I tell you solemnly, He will put on an apron, sit them down at table and wait on them."[2] ♥ I am known not only as Omnipotent, Majestic and a God of Justice but as a most Tender Father and only those moved by My Spirit will call Me Abba. ♥ I am a God full of pity and My Mercy is boundless.

Lord, she is profoundly disturbed about this intimacy I have with You. She calls it sweet and sentimental!

She has not penetrated My Wounds to understand, had she penetrated My Wounds she would have understood that these Wounds were given to Me out of Love for her. A man can have no greater love than to lay down his life for his friends, <u>and you are,</u> <u>all</u> of you, My friends. I have lain down My life out of love, but daughter this is the Cross I have charged you with. Remember, I am bearing It together with you, to unite you.[3] Justice will have to intervene. My Vassula, I am with you always to the end, do not be afraid then and disconsolate. I knew, My angel, all along that these people would hound you. Like hunters each one would pull out his weapon and pursue you because I am sending you <u>to a people not your</u> <u>own</u>. The leaders of your nation shall persecute you and deject you and treat you as they please because what I have given you to carry in your hand is not a man's teachings but Mine, and since My Language and My Teachings do not penetrate them, they would disagree and they will treat you as an imposter. I have told you already that the world will condemn you, but even when they are condemning you declare to the world what you have learnt from Me. Daughter, if My Language cannot be understood by the world it is because their doctrine is not grounded in the Truth which is Love. I have deported you from Egypt to a people not your own, to unite My Church but no one yet knows the whole way to unity and no one yet has grasped the outsetting of My Plan, they have not yet recognized the paths I am preparing for them to tread. The theologians and the philosophers have not yet found the key to Unity that Wisdom holds. I speak but they do not take in what I say, only My Own take in what I say, I know them and they know Me. So, My

---

[1] Jesus made it a point to call me in this way because the Name, Sacred Heart, is not Greek Orthodox.
[2] Luke 12:37.
[3] The Churches.

Vassula, do your work before the appointed time. I have entrusted you with My Cross, bear It with love. Soon there is going to be a time of great distress unlikened to any other, but soon after that a fountain will spring from My House to water this desert. So courage daughter, bear this bar across your shoulders with love and nothing will go in vain. If clay[1] washes away with the first drops of rain, your soul remains forever, so death is swallowed up in victory. ♥ Love is near you to guide you, so beware of these philosophers and theologians, the more severe will be the sentence they receive! Bless Me and love Me as I taught you to love Me, intimately, but never forgetting that I am Holy. ♥

I HAVE GIVEN YOU SPIRIT-ANOINTED MESSAGES

November 23rd, 1990

Peace be with you. Daughter, do you wish to progress?

Yes Lord, I do.

Then My child, I shall help you progress, this is My wish too. Do not fall asleep, be awake of the dangers surrounding you. Flower, even though My enemies tear upon you and pluck out your petals, I shall always replace them, should they leave you crumpled up, do not fear. I shall pour from the heavens My Dew and revive you. Beautiful you should look and beautiful I shall make you and keep you, you are My envoy and you have nothing to fear of men. If they accuse you because you call Me Father it is because they have not understood that the Spirit of Love you received and speaks through you, brings you peace and love to cry out, "Abba!" My Spirit is united to you My child. I have given you Spirit-anointed Messages for your era to revive you. Every word I have given you is Spirit and it is Life. The sheep that belong to Me recognize My Voice from far. Soon I shall send My Light far and wide, from one horizon to the other. Yes, I shall make discipline shine out. Have My Peace, this is My Blessing. Love Me as I love you and remember, I am your King, so give your King the love He deserves! Be blessed. I Am. ♥

---

[1] In other words, "if you, who are but dust and ashes die, your soul is immortal."

I SHALL SING TO YOU MY SONG OF LOVE

November 27th, 1990

Dearest soul, peace be with you, are you happy to be with Me?

Yes Lord, very. Praised be the Lord.

Daughter, when you strain working for Me I use your efforts and your fatigue to heal other souls. Yes, learn that everything you do with a spirit of sacrifice I make good use of it... I am the Teacher of mankind. Remain near Me so that I whisper in your ear My intentions, stay My beloved near your God. It is He who loves you most. Stay near Me My child and allow Me to feed you My Bread. Come near Me My daughter and with Me you will find no brutality, I will only watch over you and be your adviser. I shall sing to you My Song of Love, a Song that will save you and all mankind. Clay you are, but does it matter? I have given you an immortal soul, a soul that shall shortly return to Me. You are without majesty and without beauty unless you reflect My Divine Majesty and Beauty through the purity of your soul and this, My child, can manifest itself only if you imitate Me. To imitate Me is within your power, so approach Me, My child, and offer Me your will and I shall not delay. I shall come flying to you with chains of love, to bind you to Me and teach you how to praise Me and how to worship Me day and night. I shall teach you the hymns of My angels; I shall show you My Glory and My Strength; I shall teach you how to cling to Life; I shall teach you how to prostrate before Me and worship Me, so come near Me and I shall watch over your soul.

But Lord, what do You like in me, the sinner?

Your nothingness and your misery... when the coldness of the world becomes unbearable for you, come quickly into the Furnace of My Heart. I am your Refuge and I shall shelter you. Your Father in Heaven knows that you do not belong to the world yet He is sending you into the world to show the world the Heart of your God and that I Am who I Am, sent you. Come now and rest in Me and allow Me to rest in you. ♥ ΙΧθΥΣ ⤝⚬⤟

YOUR MOTHER IS CARING FOR YOU MY CHILD

December 4th, 1990

Lord, You are All, and I am nothing. You are stupendously Great, so what are my praises for You the Holy of Holies? No man can glorify You enough, yet my heart calls incessantly Your Name because You have set my heart on You.

Your praises and your calls are not in vain, love Me and praise Me without ceasing, for as long as they come from your heart, they are acceptable to Me. ♥

Lord, You have opened the doors of heaven for me and from the Stores of heaven You fed me the Manna You reserved for my soul, You gave me the Bread of heaven!

All the words I have spoken to you are Spirit and they are Life, grow in My Spirit so that you become a perfect witness to My Holy Name. And now I ask you not to give way to distress[1], see My Vassula, My Cross is heavy and, ah! I need to rest now and then. I said, "who is generous enough to bear My Cross for Me?" and you answered "take me, purify me and use me as You please." The Cross of Peace and Love to unite you all is at your charge now... but pupil! since all eternity I had predestinated you this Cross, you belong to Me and for this reason you must reflect My Divine Image. I am He who provides your soul from My Infinite Resources, I shall not abandon you soul. I shall fill you like an incense bowl so that your love reaches up in Heaven like a column of perfumed smoke. ♥ Therefore, do not weary of writing, do not weary of blessing your persecutors, do not weary of giving your back to the strikers. You may be sorrowful to the point of death, but the Queen is always nursing you back to joy and life. The Queen provides you with courage and comes and dresses your wounds with Her Maternal Love and Affection. Your Mother is caring for you My child, like She has cared for Me. In your misery and distress She comes flying to you and takes you into Her Room[2], that same Room of Her who conceived Me. ♥ So do not hold back your tears, because while you are shedding them in this exile because of the walls My people built in all directions in My House, dividing themselves, I too shed Tears of Blood to blend them in yours, so that when the Father sees your tears blended in Mine, He would not refuse your pleadings to lift the ban, for they will be no longer your tears but Mine. ♥ Shout pupil, that the whole earth, from end to end, will repent and come back to Me under My Holy Name as one. ♥ Vassula, bear

---

[1] I was sad because of more persecutions.
[2] Her Heart.

My Cross with love and not with consternation, be happy.

December 6th, 1990

Message for a consecrated soul:

My lips have uttered:

> *Come, come to Me*
> *and I shall shepherd you,*
> *I shall never fail you*
> *nor will I ever forget to pasture you,*
> *with Me you will never*
> *hunger or thirst.* ♥

IΧθΥΣ ⊃

YOU SHALL FROM NOW ON BE THE SLAVE OF MY LOVE

December 10th, 1990

God! How You make me suffer from Your Love! How You make me suffer for thirst of You!

Daughter, how would you like to live in My Wounds?

I would like anything You like me to have.

Then I shall robe you in holiness, I shall make you strong in your love for Me to last forever. Although you are still far from being perfect I can make you perfect. I have formed you in this particular way to witness for the Truth and glorify Me. I have sent you to a people not your own to proclaim My Love, those who want to hear let them hear and those who do not want to hear let them not hear. Tire not of meditating and writing, bereft you must not feel. I am with you, by your side, in this exile. Love Me, adore Me and live for Me, your Lord. Allow Me and leave Me free to envelop you into My Infinite Love. Ah... how I delight when you desire

Me and thirst for Me! Born-again! Worship Me! Surely you will not make the Bridegroom wait too long? Come quickly to your Holy One and He will place your head on His Sacred Heart, and when you will listen to His Heart-Beats you will no longer resist Him ♥ , you would only desire to glorify Him. And He will pour out His Spirit on you to invade your spirit and annihilate all that is you, never again shall you be "you"; your "you" shall be no more. I shall invade you little one completely so that your motives will be My Motives, your desires shall be My Desires, your words shall be My Words, your thoughts My thoughts, and I shall hide you in the deepest place of My Sacred Heart. I shall efface your "you" altogether, if you allow Me. From now on after your consecration[1] to My Sacred Heart, you will worship Me from the depths of your heart and serve Me with a Fire inside you, you will serve Me in fidelity and more fervently than ever before. Weak you are, but My Strength shall sustain you. I will not allow you to lose sight of Me nor will I allow your heart to flutter elsewhere, your heart will look for Me alone and desire Me alone without ceasing. I shall make you dislike all that is contrary to My Holiness and to My Will. I shall sift you through to make sure that not one rival remains within you. From today, the bonds I have enlaced you with shall be tightened even more now by Me, I shall make your soul thirst for Me and your heart sick with love for Me your God. I am only waiting now to consume your whole being with the Flames of My Heart and My Love. Whatever you do from now on will be done merely for My Interests and My Glory and nothing for you. You shall from now on, in other words, be the slave of My Love, the victim of My Heart and the benefit of My pleasures, the toy of My Soul. I shall make your traits resemble Mine, from the sorrows when you see the deafness of souls and the agony to see them fall. My Vassula, I shall give your soul its fill. No, I shall not spare you from My Cross, like the Father had not spared Me. How can I? My Affection for you is unmeasurable, besides, everything comes out of My Generosity and my Infinite Love. I shall arrest your eyes, your thoughts, your desires to become captives of My Heart. Love is seeking love. Unworthy you are, and you deserve nothing, but your frailty, your misery, your total incapacity and your nothingness beseiged My Affection and retracted My Wrath. Look at Me in the Eyes.

I looked into My Saviour's Eyes.

See? You have seen Fidelity and Truth face to face. Henceforth, your consecration must be loyal, invoking My Name day and night, night and day. I shall make your spirit repulse all that is not Me. Like a thirsty traveller you will thirst for all that is Holy but I shall be always ready to offer you water from the Springs of Life and Blood from My Divine Heart. Your soul shall bear more than

---

[1] I had an act of consecration to the Sacred Heart that I intend to do this evening.

ever before <u>the Marks of My Body</u>, for the conversion of many souls. This is why you shall voluntarily take the road to Calvary. I shall develop your zeal to please Me furthermore and observe My Law, so that you build up and plant all that I have given you. ♥ *Rise now and restore My House, do not stop loving Me, otherwise you will wither as quick as grass and fade away. And remember one major thing,* ♥ *Love loves you.* ♥ IXθΥΣ ⊱⊙⊰

Praised be the Lord! Glory be to God!

Like clay in the hands of a potter I shall mould you as I please since you have given Me the liberty to do so, <u>and</u> your will.

Praised be the Lord! You have asked me to be the slave of Your Love. Since I am not worthy to be Your salve, the slave of God, lead me into Your purifying Fire and refine me, my King, as gold is refined so that I am able to glorify You, for I am only committing sin after sin. Out of pity Lord, allow Your Light to shine in my darkness. Teach me to be the victim of Your Heart, and embrace Your Cross ardently and not with consternation, while on the road to Calvary, this road that leads to happiness since its The Path of Holiness and in which You, as the Perfect Victim, first tread on It. I am constantly sinning, yet You do not punish me, as my sin deserves. You are sparing me without ceasing, and You allow Your Light to be in me, this is why I know that <u>God is on my side</u>. Now I must fulfil the vows I made You in the consecration to Your Sacred Heart. Allow me to stay in Your Tent forever, allow me to cling on You and gaze on Your Holy Face and I will bless You all my life, and my soul will feast in Your Love and in Your Presence.

Pupil! Rejoice then in My Tent, and worship Me. Remember I have given you something very precious, guard it and embrace it with love. My Cross will guide you into holiness little soul. ♥ *I give you My Peace.*

I bless You Jesus.

The One who loves you most, blesses you. IXθΥΣ ⊱⊙⊰

FATHER, TAKE ALL I HAVE

December 18th, 1990

I feel in me that I am entering another phase of my life in God. Like a student, going to a higher class which will require harder work.

Lord?

I Am. ♥ *Take My Hand and say with Me this prayer:*

Father, take all I have. Amen.

Offer the Father everything and you shall be saved, do not fear Him. Abandon yourself to Him. ♥ *Vassula, allow Me to breathe in you, be confident for I am with you.* ♥ *IXθYΣ* >⃝ *Read Isaiah 55.* ♥ *Vassula, add these lines to My Message given for the meeting.* ♥

I am coming to you today to tell you how complete My joy is. Since I am the One you are looking for and you have come from far to hear Me, I tell you My very beloved ones, I your God am smiling on you. Remain in My Love. Pray for Peace and be witnesses of the Truth. I God, am with you and bless you. ♥

THE NEW HEAVENS AND THE NEW EARTH

December 19th, 1990

My Lord!

I Am.

If only my people[1] would listen.

The ban would be lifted and they will listen, so courage little one. I am with you. Love is near you. Oh Vassula, beloved, I am so close to you![2] I Am and I watch every step you take. Rise and kiss Me, I am near you. Kiss the Sacred Heart in front of you. (I kissed His Sacred Heart.) *Yes, please Me now and write.* ♥ (I looked on His Holy Face and my heart leaped with joy.)

Peace be with you. It is I, beloved children, the Sacred Heart. It is I, your Saviour, who pursue you to gain your heart and make it entirely Mine. Today I have assembled you as in a school, to be together and learn directly from Wisdom. ♥ *I intend to give sight to the blind so that they may see My Splendour, and instruct the unlearned to grow in My Spirit and know how to tell sin from virtue.*

---

[1] The Orthodoxy.
[2] Jesus meant by my little writing table.

I intend to gain every heart, even those who turned into granite and are unyielding as millstones. Like a man who invites his friends to share his property, I too invite you to share My Property.

My assemblies are similar to a school, they are to progress you into your spiritual life and remind each one of you the contents of My Word. In My School I prepare your spirit for My Great Return and by My Grace I discourse to you now and then of future things to let you know their outcome ♥ *If you do not learn from Wisdom how then will you be able to live according to My Law? Besides, many of you did not know Me, no more than the one I have sent you, but I am the Resurrection. See how former predictions have come true? I raised her from her grave and have taken her by the hand and formed her to court her.* ♥ *Yes, <u>I am the Resurrection and the Light</u>, have I not done the same to you too? Have I not taken pity on you? and those who were far away from My Heart, have I not sought and found? and have I not with everlasting Love taken you back to Me? and have I, your Lord, not been courting you all these years to win your heart? I have roused up My Mercy to suppress My Fury and I poured out My Love instead of My Justice; and My Peace was offered to you followed by Grace and My Compassion leaned down from heaven granting you the requests of your prayers. I have never ceased blessing you. "Like a watercourse running into a garden," I said, "I am going to water My orchard. I intend to irrigate My flower beds, and see My watercourse has grown into a river and My river will grow into a sea[1]."*

Today I tell you, your Shepherd shall soon live among you and shall pasture His flock in the gardens of His City. No-o you are not yet one flock, but I shall fetch you one by one out of the desert. Therefore My little flock, when from far you see your Shepherd coming up from the desert, know that I shall have with Me the rest of My lambs, and all the things I have done to you, daughter, I shall do to your brothers too. I shall save you. I shall unite you to your other brothers and Wisdom shall be your Holy Companion to instruct you without ceasing. I shall soon lift the ban and your great apostasy will come to its end and the prayer I have given you shall be accomplished. My Will shall be done on earth as it is in Heaven, and under My Hallowed Name many nations shall come from far away, from all the ends of the earth to dwell close to My Holy Name, extolling My greatness by the divinity I would give you back. And My Kingdom shall come, because My Throne shall descend from above into My Holy City and I shall reign among the remnant left, who will see Me face to face. Love shall return as Love ♥ *and My Will shall be done on earth as it is in Heaven because <u>you will be one</u>, worshipping Me around one Tabernacle with love in your heart and a Fire burning inside you. I shall accomplish My priestly prayer* ♥ *on earth as in Heaven. Your souls shall be rooted in Me, in Love, in Unity and filled up with the utter fullness*

---

[1]Ecclesiasticus 24:30-31.

of My Spirit. Yes, My beloved ones, I shall not only give you your daily bread but also a hidden Treasure out of My Heart, <u>The Celestial Manna</u>[1] that transfigures, uplifts your spirit into a copy of My Spirit. You shall be transfigured with the outpouring of My Spirit ♥ to know how to forgive fully those who trespassed against you. I shall put inside you a Spirit of Understanding and Mercy to make you understand what "the fear of the Lord means." Yes, beloved ones, and once you do, I shall give you Wisdom to be your travelling Companion and guide, to lead you into sanctity, this sanctity which will paralyse Satan, obstructing him from coming between us and between you and My Love.

So when you will see the sky dissolve into flames and the elements melt in the heat, know that this is the sign of the beginning of My Promise, and of the New Heavens and the New Earth, the Renewal of My Church, the Revival of My Church,

<u>*the Revival of your hearts.*</u> ♥

And <u>you</u>, you who are consecrated souls to Me, you who represent Me, I tell you this, do you remember how I heard Elijah's complaint to Me about Israel's behaviour? and how he believed that they had killed all My prophets and broken down all My altars? Do you remember what My answer was to that? I said, "I have kept for Myself seven thousand men who have not bent the knee to Baal. ♥ And today I am telling you beloved brothers: I have kept for Myself a remnant, chosen and transformed by My Grace <u>to remain faithful to Me</u>. This remnant I am raising up to rebuild the altars that once were and reconstruct My Sanctuary, they are the builders of My New Church. So while the wicked are continuing their evil deeds - persecuting you, My prophets and My saints of the end of Times, and while the proud are struggling for worldwide authority, I, your Redeemer, am raising up and training these builders in My Sacred Heart, to be the pillars of My Church. Brothers, I shall never abandon you, never... come... lift up your cross and follow Me and when you feel weary on the way, lean on Me, lean on My Heart and My Heartbeats will give you the courage you need and the strength to proceed on your way to Calvary. Be blessed. ♥ I have told you all this today so that you may find peace and hope in Me, I have spoken to you today in plain words. ♥ Beloved ones, stay vigilant and awake and you will hear My Footsteps. The Word now is very near you and on His way of Return. I bless you all, leaving the Sigh of My Love on your foreheads, this sigh that marks you as Mine. Be one under My Holy Name. ΙΧθΥΣ ⤳⊃

---

[1] That is: The Holy Spirit.

YOU WERE WRESTLING WITH ME

December 22nd, 1990

My Jesus?

I Am. I treat you very gently so that you, as My flower, grow. I want you strong and believe Me I shall make it possible, you shall be strong daughter, since you carry My Word. In front of you, I Am, to break all barriers that come up while you are witnessing. I am the Most High and I tell you daughter that I shall see to it that no power from beneath stops you from proclaiming My Message. I have taken you out of the land of Egypt to respond to Me in a foreign land and witness to a people not your own so although your behaviour was appalling and your senses blemished, unabling you to see the Light, Mercy[1] and Compassion was seized by your astounding misery, guilt and wretchedness and came to your rescue. No-o Vassula, you have not deserved any of My Gifts. Why, I had servants in My Hand who honoured Me, never uttering but My Name in holiness, who blessed Me without ceasing, who praised the Holy Trinity wholeheartedly, but yet, My Heart an Abyss of Love, cried out for you. You had accumulated sorrow upon sorrow in My Heart, treason upon treason. You were wrestling with Me, puny little creature... but I knew that your heart is not a divided heart and that once I conquer your heart, it would become entirely Mine. An object of your era, you were wrestling with Me, but I have thrown you down in the struggle and dragged you in the dust and into the desert where I left you there all alone. I had provided you with a guardian angel since the beginning of your existence to guard you, console you and guide you, but My Wisdom ordered your guardian angel to leave you and to let you face the desert on your own. I said: "you are to live in spite of your nakedness!"[2] because no man is able to survive alone.[3] Satan would have taken over completely and would have killed you. My order was given to him too, I forbade him to touch you. ♥ *Then, in your terror you remembered Me and looked up in Heaven searching desperately for Me. Your laments and your supplications suddenly broke the deathly stillness surrounding you and your terrified cries pierced through the heavens reaching the Holy Trinity's Ears... "My child!" The Father's Voice, full of joy resounded through all Heaven, "Ah... I shall now make her penetrate My Wounds[4] and let her eat My Body and drink My Blood. I shall espouse her to Me and she will be Mine for eternity.* ♥ *I shall show her the Love I have for her and her lips from thereon shall thirst for Me and*

---

[1] Mercy and Compassion = The Lord
[2] I became "naked" as soon as my guardian angel and all Heaven had turned their back to me.
[3] Abandoned by Heaven.
[4] The Son then spoke.

her heart shall be My Head-rest. She shall eagerly submit daily to My Righteousness. I shall make her an altar of My Love and of My Passion. I, and I only shall be her only Love and Passion and I shall send her with My Message to the ends of the world to conquer an irreligious people, and to a people who are not even her own. And voluntarily she will carry My Cross of Peace and Love taking the road to Calvary." ♥ "And I, the Holy Spirit, shall descend upon her to reveal to her the Truth <u>and the depths of Us</u>.[1] I shall remind the world, through her, that the greatest of all the gifts is LOVE." ♥ "Let Us[2] then celebrate! Let all Heaven celebrate!"...I have taken you by the hand and formed you to become a <u>living sign</u> of My Great Love, a witness of My Sacred Heart and of the renewal of My Church.

The Father, then the Son, then the Holy Spirit had spoken.

I am the Resurrection ♥

ΙΧθΥΣ ><□▷

(For further explanation of this message see 25 December 1990.)

YAHWEH IS WITH YOU

December 23rd, 1990

O Father, like thirsty land I yearn for You. Rest me for a while on Your Knees now and console me. Let me feel enveloped by Your consoling Heart. I need Your warmth.

Repose your head on My Heart, rest and feel consoled. ♥ *Your Abba is caring for you, your Abba is happy to have you near Him. Repose your head on My Heart, My child, and listen to the Desires of My Heart. My Heart is still seeking, longing, pleading for the rest of My children's love... (a few seconds pause). Child?[3] What would you give to console your Abba?*

O Lord, anything you want, My love, my will, my heart and my soul.

And what more?

---

[1]The Holy Trinity.
[2]The Holy Trinity spoke.
[3]Suddenly the Father's Head turned and looked at me.

262

My life, as an atonement to Your Desires.

Descend then from My Knees and go and bear witness in My Name, go and tell the nations of My Great Love. Remind them that My Promise is very near to its accomplishment and that My Return is imminent, the New Jerusalem[1] is at hand. I am going to renew My Church and My people. So, My child, descend from My Knees and go out into the world for My Sake... and make My Love known to the world. Let the world realize how I love My children. As it is, you have not sought Me, it is I who found you and have chosen you to go out to the world before My Great Day. It is I who formed you and although you were aloof to Me, I have chosen you and revealed My Holy Face to you. So when you have accomplished all the work I have commissioned you for, My child, I shall take you up to Me and you may then rest on My Knees. I shall in the meantime, while you are in the world, protect you from your oppressors. I want you for your part to look up in Heaven constantly for Me and talk to Me. "Yahweh is with you", have always these words engraved on your mind and on your heart, for I-Am-With-You. Now let your heart treasure all that I have told you and remember, offer Me prayers to reach Me like incense, for the conversion of souls and the revival of My Church.

TODAY A CHILD IS BORN

Christmas Day
December 25th, 1990

I shall announce Your Name to my brothers[2] and praise You in full assembly[3] whether they[4] like it or not.

Daughter, although many of you do not know the way to Peace and the way to unity, do not despair, hope in Me. I shall come to comfort you soon and you My child, your pleadings[5] have been heard in Heaven by everyone. I shall come to unite you, My Word has been given and My Will shall be carried out. In the meantime summon a nation you never knew and give them the instructions I have

---

[1]Church.
[2]The Greek Orthodox.
[3]Psalm 22:22.
[4]The Greek Orthodox.
[5]For unity.

given you, and if a "sage" now and then accuses you of calling Me Father, remind him that today a Child is born and His Name is Wonder-Counsellor, Mighty-God, <u>Eternal-Father</u> and Prince of Peace[1]. Pray for those who call themselves doctors of the Law, that their spirit becomes a humble and poor spirit. Pray that all nations come to My Light and that the vengeance eating their hearts be ripped off so that I may wrap their hearts in My Peace. Pray that east makes peace with the west and the north with the south. Pray that this excessive pride and haughtiness that seized certain shepherds of Mine be replaced by humility. Pray that they understand what I have meant by "anyone who wants to be great among you must be your servant and anyone who wants to be first among you must be your slave. Yes, just as the Son of Man came not to be served but to serve and to give His life as a ransom for many."[2] <u>Imitate Me your Lord and you shall live</u>.

IXθΥΣ ⤙⬭

Explanation of message of December 12th, 1990

In the beginning when I was suddenly approached by my guardian angel to open the way for the Lord, I, as a "professional" sinner, had no love for God even when my angel was telling me things about Heaven, I was just satisfied to be together with my angel. I was not looking for more. When God approached me, replacing my angel, I was somewhat disappointed. I felt Him as a stranger whereas having already been acquainted with my angel my surprised feelings had turned to love feelings. And then I could not understand why God wanted to take my angel's place. I even went as far as to believe that God was jealous from the love I was giving to my guardian angel and I had felt sorry for my angel. Later on, after a very painful purification given to me by my angel, God approached again for the second time to take my angel's place. He stayed with me for a few days, opening my heart slowly, and with Wisdom, so as not to frighten me away. When I've just about started to open for Him He ran away and hid. I turned around to look for my angel and I could not find him either. I felt a few souls[3] approach me, begging me for prayers and blessings. I prayed for them and blessed them. Then they asked me to bless them with holy water. I ran quickly to the church to fetch holy water for them and I blessed them, sprinkling on them holy water. I took the opportunity to ask them whether they had seen where my angel was and The One whom my heart already begun to love but I did not get an answer. Every day that went by seemed like a year. I was looking for Peace and I could find none. I was surrounded by many people and many

---

[1] Isaiah 9:5.
[2] Matthew 20:26-28.
[3] From purgatory.

friends, but I never ever before felt more lonely and abandoned as those days. I was as though I was going through hell. Many a times I cried out for my angel to come back to me, but no, he had turned his back and was gone! "My soul failed at his flight. I sought him but I did not find him, I called to him but he did not answer." (Song of Songs 5:6) I roamed for three whole weeks in the desert all by myself until I could not bear it anymore, then out of my distress I cried out to Yahweh, searching Heaven: "Father! O God, take me and use me as You wish, purify me so that You are able to use me!" With this cry coming from the depths of my heart suddenly Heaven opened and like Thunder the Father's Voice full of emotion cried back to me, "I God love you!" Instantly I felt as though I dropped out of a tornado into a beautiful peaceful world. My angel re-appeared and with great tenderness started to dress my wounds, those wounds I received while in the desert. This happened during Easter 1986.

December 30th, 1990

Lord and Saviour?

I Am. Delight Me and work for Me, pray to Me and remember Me. ♥ *Come.*

I CAN BE YOUR OASIS IN YOUR WILDERNESS

January 6th, 1991
Epiphany

While in the Orthodox Church I said to Jesus, "I wish I could have had a voice to have been able to sing to You in the church choir." Jesus answered, "sing to Me with your heart, I rejoice much more to hear your heart sing to Me."

Later on my eyes were wandering all over the icons and the frescos on the walls. I was thinking, "Wow! Look at all this great Holy Family and that one day we will make part of it, angels, saints, our Holy Mother, and the Holy Trinity. What a wonderful Holy Family!" And my soul longed to be with them already, to be part of the family and be in constant adoration to the Holy Trinity.

O God! Let me be part of this Celestial Family! So pray for me Holy Angels, pray for me to be with you in Heaven one day and join you together with the saints, in a constant adoration to the Holy One.

Pray for me, saints of the Most High, to learn to love God to perfection.

O sweet Holy Mother intercede for me and teach me to be submissive to my Father and obedient, that I may do His Will.

O Holy Trinity, Source of Sublime Love, Fountain of Inexhaustible Tenderness, come and teach me to be intimate with You, uniting me in Your Spirit of Love. O make me ready for this Hour because the night is almost over and the real Light is soon to come.

> Holy Father, I pray not only for myself, but for all mankind too. Since we are all Your children, I pray and ask You to look upon us with Mercy. Eternal Father, teach us to love one another so that we may do Your Holy Will and be rightfully called Your children. Amen.

Beloved child, I Am who I Am. It is with full Compassion and with great Force that My Kindness and My Love are now being revealed to you all. I am revealing you My Holy Face without reserve to purify a people who cannot tell their right hand from their left, and who live in profound darkness and wickedness. ♥ *Your Abba is calling you without ceasing. I am Love, if only you would listen to Me today.*

> Lord Jesus Christ, Beloved Son
> of God,
> Sacred Heart,
> Blessed be Your Name.
> Sacred Heart, help us to
> carry our crosses in this world
> and be submissive to the Father
> as You were submissive and
> obedient to the Father till the end.
> Amen.

I, the Lord Jesus, bless you. I am the Word and the Word was given to you and made His Home in you, so sanctify yourselves that the Word may come and live in you. ♥

O Holy Spirit of Truth
descend upon us and be our
Guide and Holy Companion.
Holy Spirit of Love
come upon us and teach us
to be in the real Love of God.
Remind us the True Knowledge
this knowledge the
Father had given us but
that we lost because of our sins.
Holy Spirit of Peace, give
us Your Peace -
a Peace the world cannot give.
Make out of each one of us
vessels of Light and
"peacemakers so that when we
work for Peace we will be
able to sow seeds which will
bear fruit in holiness. "[1]
Amen.

Beloved, I tell you solemnly that I the Holy Spirit of Truth, provide you day and night, night and day, with considerable graces to help you all on your way to perfection. Since I am your Life, allow Me to direct you and be your Guide in this exile you are living in. I can be your Oasis in your wilderness, O how little do you know Me. Creation! You spend your whole lifetime, creation, seeking your happiness in futile things, when I, Omnipresent, offer you Love, Joy, Peace and Freedom to free you from the dungeons of evil. My Graces are multiple yet you are unaware of My Presence and of how many graces your spirit can obtain from Me. I ask from My faithful ones, prayers, for the salvation of souls. All will vanish one day, all will wear out like a garment, but your soul remains forever. The Harvest is ready and soon the Reaper shall come and reap His Harvest. ♥
Be prepared for the Reaper. ♥

---

[1]James 3:18.

OH HOW LITTLE DO YOU KNOW THE HOLY TRINITY

January 8th, 1991

Our Holy Mother's Message for the prayer group for January 19th:

Peace be with you my beloved children. I am inviting you all today to pray for Unity. To unite you must love, to unite you must be humble and obedient. Do not let anyone lead you astray by other doctrines, remain faithful and you shall not stumble. Today their lands do not yield happiness nor virtue, because your generation has deserted the Lord, the outcoming of this is sin. Happy the man who has been sheltered from it. Had your generation walked in the way of God you would have lived in peace.

O children! I am calling to you. My cries go out to all nations. The dead[1] cannot hear nor praise the Lord but you, you who are attentive to My calls, praise the Lord, glorify the Lord with your love, with your faith and with your hope. ♥ Heaven belongs to you My child, so I beg you, you who have a mouth, speak to the Lord and bless Him. You who have eyes, look at His Beauty, take more of your time to contemplate His Wounds, the Wounds which were given Him for your salvation. You who have ears, hear Our supplications. You who have a heart, love the Lord, adore Him, and offer your heart to Him. No, the dead[2] cannot speak nor see, they cannot hear, nor feel.

Beloved, He who has created you is stooping to you, with His Heart in His Hand, offering It to you. As a bridegroom offers his bride a ring as a sign of alliance, so is the Holy One offering you His Sacred Heart as a Sign of His Love, to wed you. Like a bride adorned in her jewels, the Lord, the King of kings, shall adorn you with His Jewels.[3] Do not sleep but stay awake.

You have been bought and paid for with His Precious Blood, drift not away with the first current. Let His Fire consume you into a living torch in His Church; let Him mould you into a living torch in His Church; let Him mould you into an Image of Himself to be faithful and sturdy and He will use you to be the pillars of His New Church. O children! Do not be afraid, for God has always done great things, have confidence in Him. A mission of angels is being sent to you to spread the Heavenly grains everywhere in the world and bring a message of Peace and Love in your great tribulations. These grains will be welcomed as

---

[1] Spiritually dead.
[2] Spiritually dead.
[3] His Thorned Crown, His Nails and His Cross.

rain on a thirsty soil, have you not noticed how God has opened the Doors of Heaven to rain down His Celestial Manna? Yes, His Holy Spirit of Grace? The Almighty has taken pity on you and said, "let My people eat. Let them eat the Bread of Heaven." His order was given from above. Like in the times of Moses, the Father fed His people with manna in the desert, more than they could eat, and Jesus, His Son, has He not multiplied the loaves and fishes? Have the crowds not eaten as much as they wanted? And today, why are some of you surprised that the Holy Spirit descends with full force on you to feed your nations with this Celestial Manna? Oh how little do you know the Holy Trinity! Distressed and starved you shall not be left, never, nor shall you be abandoned to wander, starving in this desert.

The blackness of your era shall not last forever, your sins shall soon be purged and the Beast will be paralysed soon. Together with His clan they will grovel in the dust because a Light shall soon appear in the horizon, this shall be the Great Sign. So if your feet still waver between good and evil, pray that they will not lead you into temptation. If your heart still refuses to sing to the Lord a Love Song, pray that the Evil one may not deceive you. If your eyes avoid to look up in Heaven, seeking heavenly things, pray that your room in Heaven shall receive you one day. If your soul still belongs to the world, pray that the vices of the world will not coil in you, for you would be nestling a Serpent within you. Pray with your heart. Sacrifice with joy. Let your labour be worthwhile and I promise you that your lamp will not go out at night, be thirsty for God! I am watching over you all and at this very minute I stoop to you to bless you all. ♥

THE PERFECT FRUIT OF DEVOTION

January 8th, 1991

Blessed be our Lord, who performs constant marvels of love for us. You hear our supplications and our petitions when we call to You for help. Blessed be our Holy Mother, who offers me a Church for my birthday present where we[1] could unite and pray. You are our protector and our hope.

Flower, be with Me. Ten more days to come, then it is your birthday, the day I called you and planted you flower. Ah! Look at Me, it pleases Me. My property, My own, how I the Lord love you! How I delight in you! Spiritually you were dead, but now I have risen you to come and live in My world. Feel happy! for

---

[1]The prayer group and the monthly meetings.

look at what I have given you! Look at the treasure I have given you, your meditation is worth a lot. This dialogue between us is a treasure sought by many but I brought it to you and offered it to you. I came down from Heaven all the way to your room to give it to you as a gift. My treasure is sought by many but few can have it. Vassula, Vassula, be in union with Me, desiring Me at the same time, for this is the perfect fruit of devotion. How I delight to take this fruit! Offer Me your time, offer Me your hand, be My tablet. Have I not sanctified you in My Holiness? So offer Me in your turn your self, your will, your energy. Allow Me to use you little one, allow My Love to cover you My dove. Love Me. ♥

THERE IS A BIG PRICE TO PAY FOR PEACE

January 9th, 1991

I wept for all the false accusations said about me by 'X' and that damage so much.

Flower, this is My Cross too ♥ *but allow Me to treat you as I please. Your love reaches Me as incense. When a sudden deadly scourge descends on you, My child, offer it to Me, I shall make good use of it. Nations[1] are at the verge of war, do you understand?! Little one, offer Me your sufferings because there is an anger ready to flame... Have My Peace... Have confidence in Me. My Vassula, remember, I shall comfort you. Then there is your angel by your side to console you and dress your wounds, but for the time being allow Me to leave My Cross on you. Courage, daughter! My Cross is heavy and weighing on you but I know that you will be willing to carry It till the end. I the Lord bless you, I shall reward you in heaven.* ♥

Daniel, my angel:

Your Jesus loves you, it is I, Daniel. Remember, the Lord has rested you, but now, would you not want to rest Him too? Vassula, satisfy Him then and allow Him to crush you with sufferings. There is a big price to pay for Peace, there are many lives at stake. How often does the Lord crush you with such a weight?

Not often.

---

[1] The Gulf War.

No, not many times, so the few times He does, accept them and do not be vehement about it. Vassula, all these sacrifices are not going in vain, they fortify you as well. Remain in God's Love.

> *Eager He is, to purify you,*
> *Eager be, to glorify Him. ♥*
> *Daniel, your angel. ♥ d.*

I smiled. Somehow my angel always manages to make me smile. I smiled at the prose he has written. That is typical of my angel.

IN YOUR POVERTY, I AM KING
I HAVE COME TO EDUCATE YOU AND MILLIONS
OF OTHERS THROUGH THESE MESSAGES

January 16th, 1991

O Lord! Where are You again? Like thirsty ground I yearn for you, reach down from above and visit me. My lamp is running short of its oil. Come as usual to fill my lamp.

Have My Peace. Upon My Shoulders I am carrying you, like a shepherd carrying His weak lamb. I carry you, because I know you are weak, miserable and unable to walk by yourself. I, the Lord, am pouring on you grace after grace for your survival. I overlook all that you do not do in My favour. Daughter, have confidence, I have rescued you from Death to walk by My side. I have rescued you, flower, so that you walk in My Presence.

But Jesus...

Talk little, shsh... listen to Me. [1] *Listen... how many have I raised up in this particular way and educated little by little?*

Not many my Lord.

Then trust Me. [2] *I shall bring you to fulfil every vow that rose to your lips in your*

---

[1] Jesus said these words like a soft melody, whispering them. I could have died from His Tenderness.
[2] Jesus again whispered softly.

act of consecration. Listen... who was more determined than I and My Mother for your salvation?

No one.

No, no one, in spite of your childish insolence, I offered you My Sacred Heart to become your dwelling place. Why Vassula, I have taken you by the hand across the desert and have shown you Heaven, and your eyes saw thousands of myriads of angels surrounding Me. ♥ Daughter, I granted you many favours and all this from the Love I have for you.[1] Listen to Me[2]... I have come to educate you and millions of others through these Messages. I have not come for you alone, I have not come to raise you up alone but to raise through these writings nation after nation to glorify Me. And as I have taken you to My Banquet Hall, I intend to take soul after soul in My Banquet Hall too. Do not stand mystified at My Beauty.. I Am Perfect... Listen to Me... Do not let your eyes turn away from Me, praise Me, and I shall, if you allow Me, hold them captive. I shall hold your gaze on My Perfection to arouse in you a desire for your own perfection. ♥ I want you beautiful, blessed and holy, so allow Me to lead you step by step into Heaven. It is true that I have lifted you to be a sign of unity and to go out and witness but am I not providing you for your mission with everything that your soul needs? You were uninhabited, a desert. Hear Me then, to fulfil My purpose, I came into your wilderness to pitch My Tent in you to prosper you and make out of you My Property and My Dwelling. ♥ Now you belong to Me and you are My Own and My Temple, for this reason I guard you like the core of My Eyes from the Slanderer, who without ceasing endeavours in various methods to invade and ravage your land and make a desolation out of you. ♥ Like a watchman I watch over you day and night. Like a sentinel I guard you from all intruders. Aha! No-o, no one will be allowed to enter into My Property. ♥ O beloved, blessed of My Soul, allow Me to whisper in you My Desires so that they be written and read by a multitude of souls and that out of these lines they may hear

My Voice -

Love's Voice.

I have not spoken to you only, I am speaking to every soul. So come to Me, you who are needy, I shall lift you out of your misery and press you to My Heart. Come to Me you who are desolate and I shall make rivers flow out of you. Oh come to Me, you who are weary and place your head on Me, rest in Me, soul. Your hardships, your worries, I shall bear, give them to Me, offer them to Me and

---

[1] I was trying to interrupt.
[2] Jesus was whispering tenderly again.

272

I shall relieve you. Rejoice! For in your nothingness I Am Everything, in your poverty, I am King, and in your abandonment to Me I can do My Will! Righteousness and Justice are observing you, so do not fail Me, soul. Salvation is at your door. ♥

Vassula, let My Love cover you, be attentive and do not neglect Me. Remember, I am your Spouse. I, the Lord, bless you. Keep Me locked in your mind, this pleases Me so much. I love you infinitely. Come. ♥

I SHALL HAVE YOU EXPOSED AS A SIGN OF REJECTION, THE REJECTION FOR UNITY

January 18th, 1991

Message for my birthday:

Peace be with you. ♥ *My Divine Heart shall encourage you to proceed without fear and the Father is generous. Have confidence in Me, trust Me little child. I shall fill you with consolation.[1] I have tested you, allow Me to assess you now and then Vassula. Even when everything may appear to you as lost, do not get discouraged, I shall smoothen your way but at the same time I shall have you exposed as a sign of rejection, the rejection for Unity.* ♥ *Sincerity is missing among them, so how can they make up the differences between them?*

But Lord, do You mean that they shall reject Your messages in the end?

No, My Messages shall follow their course without you, ♥ *but you shall be tossed around. I shall permit your persecutors' defiled hands to strike you and mistreat you openly. I shall allow them to contradict you... and like crows ravaging the crop they will attack you. You will appear in their eyes as the loser because the wounds they will inflict on you will be impressive, these wounds, My child, shall be given to you from within My House and by My Own, they will be given to you from Cain's clan. I will allow them to strike an innocent child, but their gladness shall turn into mourning. Yes, you will appear as the loser My Vassula, but have I not appeared as the loser too? I appeared to have failed My Mission, I appeared in the world's eyes as the greatest loser ever. You are a sign given to them to arise questions that will be controversial. I do not mean to discourage you, Vassula.*

---

[1]For the past days I neither felt God near me nor "saw" Him. I felt as though He deserted me, and I was melancholic.

Even when some of them try to stop My Messages from spreading any further among the people, be firm, My Vassula, be firm as a rock.

Lord, if they "brake" me as You seem to make me understand, wound my soul near to death, how would I be able to be firm and standing?

Lacerated you shall be, but I, the Lord, shall be standing by your side <u>and your strength shall be My Strength</u>. Come, fear not, bear witness for Me.

ST. MICHAEL'S MESSAGE

January 19th, 1991

Message for the prayer group:

Peace be with you. I, Saint Michael, ask you to consecrate your days and nights to petitions, fasting and prayer. Soon, all things that have been hidden to you shall be revealed, may it be the Lord's Will that you shall find His Mercy in His Day. If only you who have hardened your heart would listen to Him today, if you would only open your heart to hear His Voice... open your hearts, not your minds... Everything goes in accordance with the Scriptures. Soon many will start bending their knee to God and many tongues have not uttered a prayer shall start praying. Be united, you who are God's people, in your convictions and in your love, be united in prayer. I bless you all, in the Name of Father and of the Son and of the Holy Spirit. ♥ Rest in the Lord's Heart, Vassula, be the sign of His Love. Have My Peace. Saint Michael.

January 21st, 1991

"You, who have seen my wretchedness, and known the miseries of my soul," (Psalm 31:8) take pity on me, take pity on all of us.

Daughter, when this time of Grace is over, so will be My Mercy, then your era shall have to face My Justice. I bless you for lending Me your ear, your time and your hand. I bless you and your companions. ♥ Take My Hand, I shall offer you Joy and Peace. Love is near you. Have My Peace. IXθΥΣ ⤜◗

THE SPIRIT IS ACTIVE AND ALIVE

January 24th, 1991

My Lord?

I Am. I give you My Peace. Write:

Message for the prayer groups:

Peace be with you. Beloved, you whom My Heart seeks to attract without ceasing, you whom My Heart loves to folly, you whom I created out of My Sublime Love, you whom I made out of your body, My Temple, live holy... And you who sin constantly, offending Me, My Heart has forgiven you. Rejoice! Be joyful! For your Master is not far away, your Lord is on His way of Return. Come and praise Me, come... Even the pebbles and the rocks will soon cry out on My Return: "blessings on the King who comes!" Whoever comes to Me, even in his or her state of sin and is repentant, I shall not turn away. Yet to this day there are some who do not believe in My Mercy nor in My Love, not only do they not believe but it is they who betray Me. Today I am telling you as I had once said, "no one could come to Me, unless the Father allows him."[1] This is why I am telling you to pray that all may receive through the Father's Mercy, Grace. ♥ Grace to be converted, yes, to "come" to Me. It is necessary that one be brought by Grace given to him from above, I shall never reject anyone who accepts this Grace. So do not waste your time seeking objections to object My Spirit's Works, if I call and you do not respond, you are not responding to Grace. Beloved ones, I ask you to pray that everyone receives this Grace to believe and be converted.

The Words I am giving you are Spirit, they uplift, they revive and they give Light in your inner darkness. I have, children of Mine, given you many signs to believe that the Spirit is active and alive, so do not wait for material signs. My Spirit comes with full force in these days to help you now when night is yawning its darkness all around you. How My Heart pities you to watch your little hands grope their way through this night! I am giving you many signs that you may believe that these are the days when My Spirit is being poured out on all mankind as never before. So you who still waver, distrustful and doubtful, asking Me to give you a sign to show you that these Messages, among others, spread in the world are from Me, I tell you again most solemnly: it was not Moses who gave your ancestors bread from Heaven but My Father. It is He who gave them bread

---

[1] John 6:66.

from Heaven, it is My Father who feeds you, for the Bread of God[1] is that which comes down from Heaven and <u>gives life to the world</u>. Your ancestors ate manna in the desert and I have given the multitudes already a forerunner of My Eucharist. I had multiplied the loaves to feed them, as I feed you My Body, to give you Life. I had multiplied the fishes too, a symbol of My Name, a symbol of He-Who-Feeds-You, a symbolic sign of My Name, ΙΧθΥΣ which means Jesus Christ, God's Son and Saviour. ♥ So I tell you most solemnly today that the Messages My Spirit is outpouring on every nation, are not merely words, they are Spirit and they are Life. Have you not read what Scripture says, "He gave them bread from Heaven to eat." (Exodus 16:4) Are these signs not enough to convince you? Today I am feeding your interior desert with a Celestial Bread, still another miraculous food, ♥ a Miraculous Food that does not perish but enlivens your spirit. For as the earth makes fresh things grow, as a garden makes seeds spring up, so does My Glorious Food reactivate in you <u>Life</u>, ardour and devotion. Like a spark that can give fire so does My Holy Spirit come down on you to reanimate this flickering flame inside you into a consuming Fire of Love. Scripture says, "an unspiritual person is one who does not accept anything of the Spirit of God, he sees it all as nonsense. It is beyond his understanding because it can only be understood by means of the spirit." (1 Corinthians 2:14) The New Heavens and the New Earth are right at your doors now, yet many of you have not understood and see it all as nonsense. These unspiritual people prefer to take all of My Signs in a superficial way and scorn My Celestial Messages but Scripture are being fulfilled, for they had indeed announced that during the last days there will be people who will make fun of My Promise. Since I knew that men have an infinite capacity for sinning and that the Enemy would be enthroned in the end of times into My Sanctuary, I have, for this reason, kept for Myself a remnant to be the builders of My New Sanctuary, the First-Fruits of My Spirit. As I had once kept for Myself seven thousand men who had not bent the knee to Baal in those days of Elijah, today too I have by My Grace kept for Myself this remnant, a hundred and forty-four thousand people[2], all with My Name and My Father's Name written on their foreheads.[3] These are the ones who never allow a lie to pass their lips[4], these are My first-fruits of the New Heavens and the New Earth. These will be the trees[5] of life which would bear twelve[6] crops of fruit in a year, one in each month, and the leaves of which are the cure for the pagans.[7] To refresh your memories, I shall explain to you once more what the book of Ezekiel the prophet[8]

---

[1] Jesus now means the Holy Spirit.
[2] Symbolic number: from all around the world, a perfect people. (Apocalypse 14:1).
[3] Apocalypse 14:1.
[4] Apocalypse 14:5.
[5] Trees of life = the new-born = the first-fruits.
[6] Symbolic number : The New Church. The People of God.
[7] Apocalypse 22:2. The new disciples who by means of the Spirit will go out to convert godless people.
[8] Ezekiel 47:12.

says: "along the river, on either bank will grow <u>every kind of fruit tree</u>", this means: Spirit-anointed priests to laymen. "With leaves that never wither and fruit that never fails, they will bear fruit every month because this water[1] comes from the Sanctuary"[2] since this water will come and rise from the throne of God and of the Lamb and flowing crystal-clear, down the middle of the city street[3]. "And their fruit will be good to eat and the leaves medicinal." Like a tree you shall be, renewed by My Holy Spirit that never fails you and your leaves shall be medicinal. Yes, your witnessing shall cure the sick, converting nation after nation, but not on your own, it will not be you speaking, but My Holy Spirit who lives in you. And like builders, I shall send you from the ends of the world with a cane in your hand like a measuring rod[4] to reconstruct My Sanctuary and the altars that lie in ruin and have become the haunt of the devils.[5] Pray My beloved ones, that everyone may have time to convert. Pray that Grace comes upon them so that they recognize and acknowledge the Truth. Pray for those who have turned to myths rather than the Truth; pray for the conversion of the world; pray that I inhabit every soul and that I make her My Property; pray that I may flow in these souls like a river down the middle of a city street.[6] Sacrifice for these conversions. Little children, stay near Me for a leopard[7] is lurking very near by. Stay near Me in constant prayer, an infinite prayer ♥ Allow Me to leave My Sigh of Love on your foreheads blessing you all. ♥ Be one under My Holy Name. ΙΧθΥΣ ⊃⊂ There My Vassula, this will feed many. I love you My child. ♥ Love blesses you. Bless Me.

Lord, I bless You. Maranatha.

GOD IS CALLING YOU TO HIMSELF

January 31st, 1991

Our Holy Mother's Message for 23rd February:

Praised be the Lord and peace to you all. <u>God is calling you to Himself</u>, meditate upon this. God has been calling you since you were born, born for

---

[1] Water coming out of Christ's Heart.
[2] Water coming from Christ's Heart.
[3] Apocalypse 22:1-2.
[4] Apocalypse 11:1.
[5] Apocalypse 18:2.
[6] Apocalypse 22:2.
[7] Apocalypse 13:2. Deuteronomy 7:4-6. Hos 7:4-6.

Him, born to love Him, born to please Him, born to return to Him, <u>respond to</u> <u>His Call</u>. I have been trying through My Messages here and in other parts of the world to bring you back with love, to the <u>true Life in God</u> for your salvation. Little ones, yes, I call you little, because the Lord has revealed His Face to you and not to the learned nor to the clever. Realize too that it was not flesh and blood that revealed to you the truths, the imminence and the grace of these Messages of your era for your salvation and made you believe them, but the Father Himself by His Grace upon you. So if your neighbour has not yet been stamped with the seal of the Holy Spirit of Grace, pray that He too receives this Grace for his conversion and enters into the Kingdom of God. ♥ <u>God is</u> <u>calling everyone to Himself</u>. Try to understand God's Call <u>of Peace</u>. I exhort you to pray <u>for Peace</u>, be zealous <u>for Peace</u>. Blessed children <u>let Me tell you</u> <u>once more that I need your prayers of Peace</u> for I take them all and offer them as a bouquet of spring flowers to the Almighty. ♥ Your prayers do not go in vain, they are a real glory to God, they are a proof of your love. ♥

Satan is very powerful and his fierce anger is pursuing all the first-fruits of the Lord, those who bear witness for Jesus. Jesus, in His earlier Messages had made you understand how Satan is trying to extinguish the small flame that is left in this world and leave you without light, without happiness, without mercy. He is blaspheming all God's Powers. Indeed the earth, without your fervent prayers of Peace, will feel Satan's vomit[1] pour out to blow away the little light that is left in you. I am melancholic beyond words. I have prayed for you all, I will always. Children, please meditate on Our Messages, live to the word Our Messages. I, your Blessed Mother, bless you. ♥

TELL ME THAT YOUR HOPE IS IN ME

February 4th, 1991

Daughter, have My Peace.

Take pity on me Lord, I seek and do not seem to find You. I call and I do not seem to hear Your Voice. I do not know where I am walking, my persecutors are hounding me. If Your Strength will not uphold me I shall surely be crushed. O for the wings of a dove to fly up to You! God, how I love You!

Peace daughter! Come, I want you to look for higher things, I am constantly

---

[1]Apocalypse 12:15.

helping you to reach a higher level of prayer. I remain always near you. ♥ *Be strong. I love you to passion and My Love shall remain. Dearest soul, be patient, I shall unfold everything in its own time, yes, everything has its own time.* ♥ *My Spirit has come down to rest on you so let nothing disturb you. The prince[1] of this world has great power and this was given to him to accomplish the Scripture. I have told you this so that you understand... never doubt of My Presence.* ♥ *I am with you to guide your feet into the way of perfection but My Vassula no one reaches perfection unless they go through My Cross. Learn that self-abnegation will lead you into the path of perfection, I will be glorified and you purified.* ♥ *I know with what reluctancy[2] and difficulty your spirit accepts this special way I have given you, but this is one more reason why I have chosen you. I desired to have in My Hands a simple and weak instrument, a nothing, to shame the wise and the learned. I wanted someone without any knowledge. I have chosen you and not you, Me. I am the Holy One who came to pitch My Tent in you. I have come upon you suddenly like a sweet breeze and like the wind, no one knows from where it comes from. Lean on Me now, I shall guide your step. I shall never abandon you ever, you are living under My Light. You have, soul, inherited My Love. So: Hope, daughter, tell Me that your hope is in Me.* ♥

My Lord Yahweh, my Hope is in You.

Faith, daughter, tell Me that you have put your faith in Me in all its fullness and I will tell you that your soul shall be rewarded. Have faith and exult Me by offering it to Me.

My Lord Yahweh, I believe and I have faith in You and Your Promise. I trust You.

Love, daughter, tell Me that you love Me with all your heart, your soul and with all your mind. Show Me that your love is pure, beloved; show Me that you love your neighbour as yourself.

Teach me my Lord Yahweh how to love You and love my neighbour as myself.

I Am. Pupil?

Yes Lord?

Have faith in Me, love Me and reach perfection. You are not alone even in your sleep, beside you I Am. Learn that Heaven is rejoicing for I have, through your pains,[3] saved a soul. ♥ *I have, with the love you have for Me, warmed a heart.*

---

[1] Satan.
[2] For fear I am wrong.
[3] Physical back pains and interior suffering.

♥ *Do not fear, Vassula My daughter, have My Peace and honour Me by remaining faithful to Me. Despise all that is not holy, thirst for all that is Me. I have cultivated your soil to yield a harvest and through your perseverance, (do not take this on yourself) I have worked and toiled in you. I have lifted your soul to Me. I tell you, My Mercy is great! Oh if you only knew and realized fully what I have offered you... I am like a mother to you. I am Protective. Like an over-sensitive mother who cares for her child, I Am. I have in these past years revealed My Face to you, have I not?*

Yes, You have my Lord.

I, the Light[1], have come in you and have given you Light in your darkness. Are you happy to have been with Me all these years?

Yes my Lord, as happy as in Paradise.

Wait and you shall see how happy you shall be in Paradise. ♥ *I have prayed to the Father for you that He may overlook your astounding weakness, My Vassula, and that He maintains your strength by giving you His Strength. I have guaranteed to you that you will glorify Me in the end. Pray My child that peace may come in this world.* ♥ *Love Me, be blessed.*

A LIGHT HAS SHONE IN YOU

February 5th, 1991

Where are You again my Lord? Why are You hiding? or am I in the dark again and cannot see You? Are you withholding Your favours? Yet I know You cannot be far. "If my feet have wandered from the rightful path, or if my eyes have led my heart astray, or if my hands are smirched with any stain" (Job 31:7) forgive me.

My child, be blessed! Peace be with you. Adjust Vassula to Me and stop listening to the Tempter. I tell you: approach Me, approach Me My child. I am He who provides you with real Knowledge. O Vassula! a Light has shone in you, so how could you doubt? It is I, the Lord, who saved you. I had said through My prophets that I shall give My Spirit even on the least and the most wretched of all, but My child this is only the beginning of My Promise. ♥ *I Am the All-Faithful. O My child rejoice! Rejoice! because soon I shall bestow My Spirit to all mankind.*

---

[1]Here Jesus is speaking.

I will make crystal-clear waters[1] flow out of every living creature. Vassula, I hid My face from you for just a few days so that you look for Me, forsaken you are not.

I was horrified Lord!

O no, do not be dismayed, how else would I revive in you a spirit of concern? Concern to finally raise your head and search Heaven looking for Me, the Holy One? You are from below and I Am from above, you are living in a place where your spirit fails to satisfy you because you are surrounded by all that is not Me and I Am to be found where your spirit, your soul ought to be languishing and yearning to be. Blessed of My Soul, until you learn to constantly seek Me and desire Me, I will continue to put you to the test now and then. It is My pleasure to drench you with My Spirit today and not yesterday, tomorrow and maybe not the day after. See?

Yes, Lord. I finally think I understand now.

Bathed in My Light, search for Heavenly things, keeping My Principles. ♥ *Without Me you are alone and you cannot do a thing, you could not even master your thoughts so I tell you: give your eyes no sleep. I do not mean to discourage you Vassula, but from My Lips come Teachings and Wisdom. I mean to make you walk by My Side and in the way of virtue, I mean to enrich your spirit so that I display My Knowledge through you so that you may glorify Me. Lift your eyes then in Heaven and look at Me, daughter, and when you see again My Holy Face, you will grow once more, radiant and your heart will throb again with delight. See? You heart will be arrayed majestically and in holiness once your eyes meet My Magnificence. Lean on Me, I had only examined you My child.* ♥ *I bless you. Bless Me, Love Me.* ΙΧθΥΣ ⤜⊃

THE MORE MEN WILL TRY TO EFFACE MY VOICE, THE MORE WILL I BE HEARD

February 6th, 1991

My Lord, guard me from all these evil attacks. Defend me, who else will? Satan is putting people to plot against Your messages and against me, will You allow things

---

[1]Apocalypse 22:1.

to go out of hand my God? We are with Your help constructing and they are destructing, how am I to go on? I am no one and if You will not stand by my side I can be "massacred" interiorly.

Flower, have My Peace, do not be distressed. Beside you I Am and I know, oh, how I know everything that goes on inside men's hearts... Nevertheless, realize that in spite of everything, I, the Lord, shall augment. Yes, I mean that I shall make My Voice be heard through these Messages more and more; and the more men will abuse you and try to efface My Voice, the more will I be heard. ♥ Daughter, no one will stop Me from proceeding. I the Lord Jesus shall help you, My Vassula, let this be always in your mind.

I wept.

Weep not. Beloved, weep not... Come. ♥ Trust Me. ♥

I AM THE HOPE THE WORLD IS LOOKING FOR
YOU HAVE INDUSTRIALISED MY HOUSE

February 7th, 1991

Message for the world:

Peace be with you. ♥ I Am Jesus. I am the Hope the world is looking for, this Hope they are looking for is within their reach. They have but to stretch their hands towards Heaven and search Heavenly things, they could seek Me and I shall respond to them. I am not hiding My Face, nor am I turning My Eyes away from them, My Eyes observe you all and survey all your steps. ♥

My Spirit indeed fills the whole world to brighten this darkness and give Hope to those who grope their way in this endless night. Beloved, with Heaven your homeland and earth your pilgrimage all the more reason to rejoice and to hope. ♥ O creation, am I to unveil your death shroud and not bring you to life? or I, who bring to life, am I to send you back to death? I am Mercy, I am Love. Look up in Heaven and see the Signs of the Times, I am coming to gather nation after nation and show My Holy Face to each one of you and remind you of My Love. But look, the beginning of sorrows have started, the beginning of your birth pangs too. You are witnesses since you became believers, that what you read in Scriptures is coming to reality. The outpouring of My Spirit in these last days of darkness is being poured out lavishly upon mankind, you are witnesses to things

282

which were in riddles and said in parables before. *You are witnesses of Satan's cruelty, but I promise you little children that soon after your sorrows (which will aggravate) will come Joy, and after your birth pangs Love will be born among you! But today I look with dismay from above on this generation's crimes which now have outdone the sins of Sodom and Gomorrah. Because your hopes are built on a false Christ. This generation is vile, rebellious and polluted with blood, and living under Satan's shadow. O era! your fine and so-called wisdom has indeed walled Me out because your hearts, pompous and filled with arrogance, consider to be the equal of Me your God. "Are you still going to say, I am a god, when your murderers confront you?"[1] Already blood is flowing in your streets. In your wickedness you build up your hopes in all that is not Me. You have put your hopes on men and not on Me, on riches that do not save you, disregarding the Treasure I offer you in Heaven. You are building your expectations on mankind, based on a Lie, because you believe you can accomplish everything in your own human strength. Indeed, you[2] have amassed great wealth in your busy trading, but tomorrow you shall die. ♥ Few are those who ask: "why is it that the Lord and His Mother descend suddenly upon us?" and only a remnant of My sacerdotal souls are concerned about Our regular manifestations. I have said that I am going to send My Messenger to prepare a way for Me[3] and this is exactly what My Mother who is your Mother too is doing. Scripture are being fulfilled and I tell you solemnly that the One whom My Abels and My Jacobs were longing for, will suddenly come, entering His Temple to extirpate the Cains and the Esaus who made havoc and ruin out of My Church. ♥ You have industrialized My House, this House which should have been a House of prayer! You have indeed turned My House into a den of thieves! If I am as you[4] say: "the Holy One" then where is the honour you owe Me? If I am indeed your Master, where is My respect? If I am your God, where is My adoration and My incense? Where is My devotion? How is it that you cannot read the Signs of the Times? How is it that you cannot understand Heavenly things? How is it that you do not believe anymore in My Marvels? Why are you persecuting My Abels and My Jacobs? if not openly, in secret? I appear as well as your Holy Mother and We manifest Ourselves through souls in many nations, but Our manifestations weary you, and even anger you. "How tiresome it all is" you say[5], for to this day you have not understood the Heavenly things like My Abels and Jacobs. No, you have neither understood My Love nor the devotion you owe My Mother. You call to faith and rely on your strength, your authority and your reasoning, My Voice calling out today for repentance to the sinners disturbs your ears. When Righteousness suddenly shines out with healing in its rays, you refuse My Gift which is offered today in your dark*

---

[1]Ezekiel 28:9.
[2]God is referring this passage to the Freemasonry thinking.
[3]Ml 3:1.
[4]The Cains and Esaus.
[5]Ml 1:13.

era. Am I to accept your persecutions over and over again? Am I to sacrifice year after year My Abels and My Jacobs who are the incense of My altars and the sturdy pillars of My Church? You have closed your ears to My Voice to listen only to your own. You have deprived many of eating the fruits of My New Vineyards because Satan has entered you and ambushed your spirit, and lo, others are atoning for your crimes.[1] Others are atoning for your vanity and your folly, to save you. Everyday these generous souls offer their cheek to you, to be struck, to be abused and afflicted, for your sake. These generous souls expiate with their own blood to save you. I am waiting to hear you, but you are not saying what you ought to. You do not repent but you go astray as you pursue your course, dragging millions behind you. You go for seats and authority but not for conquering and saving souls, but you shall fall... and this continuous apostasy shall cease... and in you My Abels and My Jacobs I shall rebuild My altars that once were, but that now lie in ruin. I shall make crystal-clear rivers flow out of you and your witnessing shall be fruitful because these waters will be coming out of My Source and like trees of life growing by this Holy river, My children shall prosper from your witnessing. Children, courage, I have not abandoned you, nor have I forgotten you. Anyone who lives in Me will feel My Love, anyone who feeds from Me shall not be cut off to die. He who remains in Me shall live. I, the Bridegroom, descend to wed you in My Peace and Love and remind you that from the Beginning you were Mine. I, the Lord, bless you, leaving the Sigh of My Love on your foreheads. Be one, under My Holy Name. ΙΧθΥΣ ⋈

WHERE ARE YOUR OFFERINGS YOU OWE ME?
I COME TO YOU ALL WITH MY HEART IN MY HAND
THE LIGHT OF YOUR BODY IS YOUR EYE

February 14th, 1991

Peace be with you. Flower, love Me, sanctity does not come in one day. Abandon yourself entirely to Me, adore Me and love Me and I shall do the rest. Do not sleep. Soul, your sins are numerous, and so are the wounds you give Me. Each time you sin it comes on Me, as a stroke, or a scourge, or a hole in My Body by a nail, why Vassula? Why? I, who revealed to you My Holy Face, have I revealed to you My Face to be struck? and have I shown you the Wound of My Heart so you would pierce It more? On earth there is no one to be found more wretched than you are! O what a wretch! Do not go now, sit and hear what I have to say.
♥ *Had it not been for My Infinite Mercy, the Father's Justice would have struck*

---

[1] Suddenly Jesus' Voice became tender and sad.

you and you would have withered instantly. Have I taught you to sin? Where are the offerings you owe Me? Where are the sacrifices you promised Me soul? Why have you been neglecting Me? Lent is here, lent will bring My Passion back to you, yet you are neither ready nor prepared. I filled you with Celestial food to grow in My Light and become a vessel of light. I made you Mine and with everlasting Love I have risen you from the pit to become My bride in My Presence and the presence of My angels for ever, yet your eyelids heavy with sleep took the best out of you. ♥ O My Vassula! If only you knew how I the Lord love you! I am thirsty for love. I know dear child that the times you are living in are evil but have I not made you discern good from evil? and now My territory's soil is growing coarse again. Tell Me, was it by your efforts you saw the Light? No, I toiled[1] in you to maintain you in My Light, I poured on you grace after grace. I treated you not as your sins deserved, I treated you as I never ever treated a soul before. I gave Love for apathy, tenderness for unholiness, mercy for wretchedness. Yes, I showed My Holy Face to sin, I treated you as I treat the jewels[2] of My Heart. I prayed for you to the Father, Vassula, so that He remembers My Sacrifice and thus spares you. ♥

O God, I did not want to hurt You nor anger You!

I am constant in My affection, flower, and My Love for you is everlasting. Learn from Me, be <u>constant</u>. Come, I want you in My Presence perfect! I want your soul to be like a watered garden filled with My Dew and exhaling a delicate fragrance so that My Soul delights in you. Vassula, are you willing to do My Will?

I am willing to do Your Will, but I only seem to be doing the opposite, Lord...

I shall help you carry on My work, leave everything in My Hands. O My child, subject to sin you are but come to Me, shed those scales from your eyes and behold who is standing in front of you... I Am is face to face with you! speaking and offering you in His Hand, His Heart. Do you want this Heart of your God? Take It, I am offering It to you, soul. Stretch out your hands to receive My Heart.

I'm not worthy of Your Love Lord.

I know, but no one is worthy of My Love and this is how I come to you all today. I come to you all with My Heart in My Hand. Do not say, I have sinned and refuse It. I tell you, My Great Mercy has forgiven you, so come, come and take this Heart which loves you. Have you not heard that My forbearance is long? My Compassion is great. Come, do not put Me off day after day, from now on,

---

[1]God means, he worked in me.
[2]Jewels: perfect souls.

daughter, I want you to be faithful in your convictions and sincere towards Me. Concentrate on My Holy Presence, I am never absent. It is you who dim the light in your eyes from the accumulation of your sins and the impurities of your soul absorbs every day to the point that you turn blind. The light of your body is your eye, when your eye is sound, your whole body too is filled with light, but when it is diseased your body too will be all darkness[1] and in your darkness, with the light of your eyes dimmed, you cannot see Me, but I̲, I am never absent. Vassula, today I have spoken to you plainly, out of Love. Since you are more apt to rebellion and to sin, than what is holy, I shall allow Myself to speak to you plainly in My jealous Love. Do not imagine that My jealous Love can be easily put aside, oh no, when I open My Mouth, it is for your salvation that I speak, not for your condemnation. Allow Me to reprove you out of My Love, now and then. ♥ ΙΧθΥΣ ⤸

February 24th, 1991

Before my journey to England, Scotland and Ireland.

My Vassula, take this passage as an introduction for each of these countries.

Jesus showed me John 10:14-16.

Tell them that it is I, the Lord, who sends you to them. ♥ *The sheep that belong to Me will listen to My Voice, I am coming to them to lead many on what was an unknown Path to them back to the Truth. I am coming with a blazing Fire of Love to guide you, beloved ones, back Home. My Sacred Heart is your resting Place.* ♥ *For you creation... O what will I not do! I am your Holy One, but your era has re-crucified Me. I am He who loves you most, yet the One who receives unmerciful lashes from the apathy of this era. I am the Light of the world, who comes in this dark era to give you the Light of Life, have My Peace, My little children. I offer you My Peace, I offer you the gift of My Love. Come to Me as you are, do not wait to be saints to come to Me. Come to Me as you are, do not fear Me. I am the most Tender Father, I can be your Holy Companion. I and you, you and I, and I shall reveal to you My Holy Face. I shall reveal to you the Holy Face of your God, your eyes shall see Love face to face and when this happens, angered demons shall take flight and you will then understand, beloved one, that from the beginning you were Mine and I was yours for all eternity. Be one with Me, Love is at your door. I, Jesus Christ, bless you.* ♥ ΙΧθΥΣ ⤸

---

[1]Luke 11:34.

YOU ARE MOST IMPERFECT AS AN INSTRUMENT

February 25th, 1991

Love seeks a return of love. ♥

I suddenly was thinking of the spelling and grammar mistakes now and then in these texts, and what He had said about it to another mystic who is dead now, when she had the same problem.

Yes, you are obliging Me to reduce Myself to your level of grammar to reach you, and your limited knowledge of words. Oh yes! You are most imperfect as an instrument (Jesus was smiling) but I can use you even in your imperfection. Little one, your Jesus has blessed you over and over again, and one day, Vassula, one day, I shall appear to you in My Light and absorb you into My Light... but now I and you will continue as it is. ♥

Praised be the Lord! (Satan said 'finally', as it had taken me some time to write those praising words. Immediately Jesus' Voice resounded telling him, "silence!" Satan wanted me to think it was Jesus telling me 'finally.')

WEALTH IS TO BE CONVERTED

February 26th, 1991

Today I was thinking, if I could get a message from St Paul, or St Peter, I wanted to penetrate into mysteries and I asked the Lord for His response.

Lord?

I Am. Listen flower, today My concern is your redemption. Why seek into My mysteries which I am not willing to give you? Sanctity is My concern for you, repentance is what I seek from you. Daughter, understand what My Interests are - understand what My concern is. Even when Lazarus had departed for four days into My mysteries and had seen and understood these mysteries, I had requested him on his return to keep silent and keep those secrets for himself. I did not want him to give away My Riches to souls who would not make sense out of them. Wealth is to be converted, wealth is to admit you are a sinner and come to Me humbly, repenting, and lead a holy life, following My Precepts. Wealth is not to *try and decipher My mysteries, and if you try this will only lead you through winding ways leading nowhere. So come to Me as a child and allow My Hand to cultivate and enrich you in <u>this</u> kind of knowledge. Let your wealth be Me, let your knowledge come through My Word; let your interests be My Interests,*

<u>your perfection</u>

I love you. Come, do not be impatient in prayer. Love is near you.

We, us Lord?

Flower, yes! ♥

February 28th, 1991

Lord You have been our Refuge age after age. (Psalm 90:1). Lord?

I Am. Lean on Me, beloved. Rest in Me, absorb Me. I am <u>All</u> you need. Come, we shall pray the Rosary. ♥

HAPPY THE MAN WHO KEEPS HOUSE WITH ME

March 1st, 1991

London

Before the conference and prayer meeting with one day.

O Yahweh, You are my God, blessed be Your Name. You have carried out Your Plan and brought me here, in this land, to witness and give You Glory. Open my mouth in Your Assembly to only glorify You.

I shall. I the Lord bless you. Listen to Me: prophesy to them. ♥ *Rely on My massive Strength, every achievement comes from Me and not from you. I set fire and water before every soul and I let them choose. I shall never violate man's liberty, never... I allow man to chose and I want them to know how I delight when they choose what is right. Nevertheless, I shall always pursue the sinner to give up sinning. I shall always go in all directions to conquer him and every time he falls I shall be there to lift him. I shall not push him away or reprove him, his enemies might rejoice, but I, I will only have tears in My Eyes and I will ask him to thrust himself into My Arms, and if he does I will then ask him if he would allow Me to inhabit him. If he accepts, I shall then make out of his soul My Possession and in this Territory I shall pitch My Tent (in him) and from thereon I shall encircle My Property with My Love to make sure that no intruders will trespass into what I have just made Mine and forever. ♥ Happy the man who keeps house with Me, he shall gain Knowledge and enter into everlasting Life. ♥*

DO NOT FEAR LITTLE MESSENGER

March 2nd, 1991

Church of Holy Ghost - Balham, London

Just before leaving for my first big meeting at Holy Ghost Church.

Lord?

I Am. Serve Me now My beloved. I shall be with you. Victorious I shall be, do not fear little messenger. Proclaim My Word in My Assembly, I am He who says to My souls, "come and eat this Celestial Food." Let your interior desert bloom. I will bring back the exiles into their house, My Sacred Heart. ♥

I AM WILL RETURN

March 4th, 1991

York

At All Saints Lower School. I was invited by Father Ian Petit.

I Am. Love is near you, Love is generous. Remember My Presence and you shall not falter. Daughter, come and pray with Me to the Father:

Father,
though night still covers this earth,
I know that above me,
Yahweh,
who sees His children in darkness
will take pity on them.
With Power and Glory
He shall descend to dissipate this
menacing night into a bright day.
Peace and Love shall fill us,
and our soul will be filled with His Light.
I Am, will be back.
I Am, will return.
I Am, will be with us.
Glory be to the Highest!
Amen.

Later on, I came to the Lord wondering if I really <u>had</u> to be sent out, like now, travelling to witness. Travelling every day by car, trains or by planes in different places was not easy, but quite exhausting.

My Lord?

I Am. Little one, every time you call Me My Heart leaps with joy, if only you understood this My child... You have asked Me if you had to go out and witness like you do now. Yes, it is necessary, not that I need you, but Vassula, going out and witnessing in My Name glorifies Me and at the same time purifies you. Flower, I shall give you the strength you need, the words you need. Treat Me now as a King deserves; treat Me as your Holy One has to be treated, I Am is with you. Come My Child-Saved-by-Me, come, your step must follow My Step, your foot where I had My Foot till the end of your mission. ♥ *We, us?*

Yes, forever linked.

So come to Me as often as you can and I shall fill you every time you come to Me. Lend Me your ear My child so that I may train your ear to hear My Voice. Satisfy Me My child and you will prosper in Me, Love is with you and blesses you:

Later on again I went to the Lord.

Ah yes! You are back with Me. I shall elaborate your talk tonight. I am He who shall clarify many things. Repeat after Me these words:

Jesus, touch My heart,
You are my Delight.
Speak to me,
lead me,
and humble me. Amen.

Delight Me and praise Me all the time. I love you and because of that I shall leave My Cross on you. I Am He Who bore It till the end, honour Me and glorify Me by bearing My Cross now and then to rest Me. Come. ♥ ΙΧθΥΣ ⌖

EVERY DROP OF MY BLOOD MADE YOU MINE

March 8th, 1991

Daughter, be in peace. I am Love. Little one, I am with you to help you sanctify your life, I speak to every soul through these Messages and through you. ♥ *I have fed you My Bread, I have fostered you and made you Mine. Have I, in all this time, ever been harsh with you? Have I been punishing you? So, never doubt of My Love. Lean your head on Me and rest, rest your mind on Me. Think of no one else but Me, I am He who loves you most. All I ask from you is Love. Love Me, adore Me, think of Me, allow Me to be ever present in your heart and mind. I awakened you from your sleep so that you see My Beauty and that you live with Me. Every drop of My Blood made you Mine. I paid for your soul by pouring out My Precious Blood for your salvation. Every agony I suffered was with Love, knowing that My Sacrifice would save you. Everything I did was for your salvation. My daughter, let all this be clear to you, I am Love and Love continues to save. I have not stopped just there (on My Cross), I continue to call for your salvation. I continue to pursue the sinner. Be prepared, therefore, because I shall soon come to fetch you, I the Lord love all of you to distraction. Love Me, praise Me and be holy. Feel Me so that you may remember My Presence. Come.* ♥

DO NOT FEAR ME MY CHILD WHEN I DECREASE YOU

March 9th, 1991

Scotland

I've been discussing with Father McGinnity which prayer is the most pleasing to the Lord. We were saying that silence in contemplation was best.

Lord?

I Am. Lean on Me, I am your support and strength. Yes indeed, My Vassula, silence is the most efficacious prayer of all. Meet Me in My Silence, let your spirit be drawn towards Me and be absorbed in Me, in My Silene. Allow Me to invade you My child, allow Me to envelop your soul in My Love. Open up to Me and let your God invade His Property, I Am owns this Property. Let I Am free to increase, let I Am multiply His Virtues in you. Do not fear Me My child when I decrease you, I Am is here to look after His Property and shine in you. Allow Me soul to encircle you with My Tenderness, you will be overwhelmed by My Beauty. Do not look at your nakedness soul and refuse Me, come to Me in Silence as you are. Abandon yourself to Me in Silence and you shall live. Be blessed, be blessed soul. Let nothing become My rival.

Lord, let <u>nothing</u> become or be Your rival!

Fast then on Fridays, this is your due now to Me. ♥ Come.

I had stopped fasting on Fridays because of my schedules and travelling. I realized that in spirit of my travelling I could easily fast but I had wanted it more 'easy' on me, by pure laziness and weakness.

BRIGID'S - MY HOLY SPIRIT SHALL BE PRESENT

March 10th, 1991

Belfast

Just before the meeting at St Brigids' Parish Hall:

My Vassula, treat Me now as a King and glorify Me by serving Me. My Own will recognize My Voice, I will call them and they shall come.

Lord, my strength, my Stronghold, my Refuge, my Light and Life, here I am. I'm coming to obey Your Will. Lord, I ask You to give me Your Strength to glorify Your Name again. Be PRESENT among us and open their hearts to receive Your Holy Spirit.

I shall be very PRESENT daughter, My Holy Spirit shall be PRESENT. Justice will prevail in this country. I the Lord shall place My Hand on this country and I shall make them feel My Presence[1], those that have ears let them hear. Go now My beloved, beside you I Am. ♥

PRAY AS NEVER BEFORE

March 12th, 1991

Dublin

For the priests and nuns of Blackrock College:

My Lord, my Delight, my Everything, I love You to death. Lord?

I Am. Lean on Me My child. I am the One who loves you most. Ah Vassula! Child of Mine, allow Me to use your hand again to convey My Message to My children, a Message which I held in My Sacred Heart for them.[2] ♥ *Peace be with you. I have come to your very doors, it is I, the Sacred Heart who speaks to you. I come to offer you My Heart, today I am coming to you in this special way to*

---

[1] I saw in an interior vision, the Lord's Hand blessing all Ireland.
[2] It seemed as if Jesus was waiting for this hour for quite some time.

remind you of My Ways. I am coming to you because you are poor
you do not have much, you still have your sight for the Grace of y
Heaven is upon you. ♥ [1] *But My Soul is grieving beyond your und*
see from above dissensions like never before in the Heart of My S
Body is bleeding and My Heart is one big Wound. The shepherd's staff which I
had given them whole, lies now broken in splinters but I mean to visit you soon to
put together the shepherd's staff I had left behind Me. Therefore, beloved ones,
you who have received this Grace, pray for those who still do not know their left
hand from their right, pray as never before that they too may receive this Grace
before the day of Purification. I am telling you that soon, very soon, Love shall
be with you as Love, pray that all may be ready and converted so that no one will
be drawn in darkness and the shadow of death for all eternity. Mindful of My
Mercy I come to warn your generation and out of Love I come to call you by the
Power of My Holy Spirit of Grace back to your senses. Love is seeking a return
of Love, this is My Theme. ♥

DIE TO YOURSELVES SO THAT GOD MAY LIVE IN YOU
NEVER STOP PRAYING YOUR ROSARY

March 18th, 1991

Message of our Holy Mother:

My Vassula, here is My Message: ♥ **have My Peace. Children of My Heart, God is in your midst and His Kingdom is near you, if you have eyes you will see it. Dearest children, listen to God's Voice in these days of lent, listen to God's Voice by diminishing yourselves so that God can augment in you. Efface yourselves so that His Spirit would be seen in you; die to yourselves so that God may live in you, be nothing so that He may be Everything. Allow Him in this way to take full possession of you and make out of you His Property. So I am telling you, children of My Heart, so long as you struggle to become something, the Spirit of Holiness that wants to live in you is choked by your rivalry. Do not let your spirit become a rival to God; diminish so that He augments; allow His Spirit to form you in this way into the way of Sanctity. Bear in your minds that humility, docility and self-effacement are the key virtues pleasing God and with these you become poor in spirit and thus blameless.**

Dearest children, Jesus was humble even to accept death. Never be the one who

---
[1]Then Jesus speaks to them of His Church.

...ays, "I have everything and I know everything and I do not need anyone's advice." Stay poor, be poor, so that in your poverty God may reign in you and be King, allow no conceit to overtake you. My prayers are that your holiness augments in Him who created you and that your love for each other increases and overflows to purify this world of its wickedness and its apostasy. Never stop praying your rosary, come with joy to pray the rosary. The rich man will not reply but the poor man will come to Me with his rosary and in his poverty I shall listen to him while he prays this simple prayer for all that is poor and simple is deadly to Satan, who is Vanity Itself. This is one of the main reasons why Satan hates the rosary. Satan is powerful and today he is sifting you <u>all</u> like wheat because this is his hour, this is the reign of darkness. Remain faithful to the House of God and keep the Traditions that have been taught to you and listen to My beloved and blessed Vicar of My Son.

Every priest has been given the grace by God to act and represent My Son and so I pray for those who are not yet submitting humbly to the Vicar of the Church to submit and be willing. Jesus is Faithful and True. Imitate your God, He who is Perfection. ♥ Be perfect by imitating Him in His Humility, His Submissiveness, His Obedience, His Docility, so that you too may receive the greater gifts of Suffering and Mortification, all of which will lead you to sanctity and into His Sacred Heart, <u>your Abode</u>. ♥

My priests, be like a field that has been well watered by frequent rains so that Jesus' lambs are attracted by its green pastures and may have something to feed upon. No lamb is attracted to graze on thistles and brambles, allow Me to rebuild your temples and make them pleasing to God. Happy the ears that hear and understand what I say, for I tell you not everyone's name has been written down in the book of Life of the Sacrificial Lamb. ♥ So pray for those who do not seem to understand nor are willing to open, that they too may be given God's Grace to hear with their ears, understand with their heart and thus be converted and see God's Glory. ♥ I bless you My dearest children, every one of you. ♥ I love you.

ALAS FOR THOSE WHO SHED INNOCENT BLOOD OF UNBORN INFANTS!

March 20th, 1991

I, Yahweh, am your Father. Come, you will accomplish your work by My side, daughter. I shall reinforce you every day because this will be necessary for My

Work that will go over the whole world. I have lit your lamp so that you see, My child. I have chosen you to teach you from My Hall. From My Own Mouth you have received My Word, keep My Teachings as the apple of your eye.

Yes my Lord and God.

Even now in your nothingness, I who am Everything shall expand and like mist that creeps everywhere I intend to envelope all My creation in Me, from the stranger to My best friend, for My Jealousy[1] has bypassed Me wanting to check it. I have created you for one purpose: I have created you out of Love to love Me. When body and flesh are going to be consumed and wear out, he who was pleasing to Me shall be drawn into My Soul for ever and ever; but alas for him who did not fear Me! Alas for him who never saw wickedness as folly and foolishness as madness! Alas for the heart who believed that he could reach the zenith of his strength by his own efforts and without Me! Alas for him who has not obeyed My Commandments! Alas for whose heart is filled with malice! Alas for the jackal that plotted by night! Alas for him who judged his brother and caused him to live in terror! Alas for the lips that bore false-witness! Alas for those who shed innocent blood of unborn infants! Your compensation shall be hell! Alas for the impure who receive My Son's Flesh and Blood in a state of sin, how abhorrent you are to Me! Alas for him who offend Me by refusing confession and absolution and come to receive My Son, guilty! Repent! Repent for your sins! What good is your offering to Me when you have a serpent coiled inside you? If you ask Me: "what must we do then to gain eternal Life?" I tell you: repent! Follow My Commandments, produce the appropriate fruits, and I, in the presence of My angels I shall offer you the room I have reserved for you. Watch and be on your guard against all these things. Allow Me in your wilderness to manifest My Spirit as I please and when I please and upon whom I please to save you. ♥

Correct us Yahweh, all loving Father, gently and with mercy but rapidly too!

Love Me, adore Me and place Me as first and above all.

Teach us to love You without anymore offending You. I am desperate without You O Abba!

My Eyes are upon you My child constantly and My Spirit shall invade you more than ever to leave nothing of you. I Am All and I can fill you with My Light. Ah creation! I am Loyal and Gentle, leave Me free O creation and with most loving affection I shall fill your spirit with divinity out of My Spirit. Leave Me free to annihilate your lethargy which led you into this great apostasy and the ruin of your

---

[1] Jealous love.

soul, allow Me to fill you with My Fire to become loyal and fervent servants of Mine. Let Me transform you to become the delight of My Soul, I Am whom I Am is with you. ♥ *Be blessed and have My Peace, you who read Me.*

I WILL SOW LOVE EVERYWHERE

March 24th, 1991

Let every creature do Your Will, my Lord.

Daughter, the thing I want most out of you is love. I want you to love Me, love Me, love Me, praise Me and feel My Presence, this is what I request of you My Vassula.

Lord, teach us to love You as You want. Teach us to love one another. We need Your help because we cannot love by ourselves unless You give us the grace to love.

I shall teach you by Grace,[1] I shall teach you as I am teaching you the Knowledge of your fathers. I shall supply you all with what you need most: spiritual food. I shall infuse in you all, love and holiness, I shall not delay My Promise. Soon all that I have been telling you is going to happen and he[2] who crushed you all these years will lose his grip. ♥ *I will sow love everywhere! There will be no more stumbling in the night. Come, daughter. We, us?*

Yes my Lord.

So love Me, do not fear Me. Love Me, do not neglect Me. Love Me, do not forget Me, this is all I ask from you soul. ♥ ΙΧθΥΣ ⟩⊂⟩

---

[1] Jesus smiled showing His dimples.
[2] Satan.

MY HOLY SPIRIT SHALL BE POURED
ON THE PAGANS TOO
MY GRACES UPON YOU WILL BE MULTIPLYING

March 25th, 1991

Lord, this week is the Holy Easter week for the Roman Catholics and next week is the Holy Easter week for the Orthodox. I feel it is not right to have different dates and to be differentiating ourselves in You to the point that one hears remarks as: their Jesus is not our Jesus!

I love you all the same but many of you do not seem to understand this. ♥ *Wretched you are all, sinners you are all. Frail you are all but all of you are My offspring, see Vassula? Have I made any difference? I have come to you and showed you My Sacred Heart.[1] I went in all directions seeking by what means I could make you Mine. I showered blessing upon blessing on you to raise you from death and form you since you lacked Wisdom. I courted you and in My Tenderness I Myself have chosen you to become a witness to a people not your own and of whom many are far from understanding why Wisdom has chosen a foreigner among them.* ♥ *I, the Sacred Heart, am determined to show them that I have taken you, a foreigner to them, to share the Riches of My Sacred Heart and share My delights and sorrows. Yes, I have come to teach foreigners too of My Sacred Heart's Riches, today I have made a new song for them for I am one and the same! So pupil, continue not to differentiate yourself under My Name, even if you are whirled away by the breath of My enemies I shall not leave you defenceless. I shall always come to your rescue My child. If they challenge[2] you do not respond, I shall respond in your place.* ♥ *Scripture says: God does not have favourites, but that anybody of any nationality who fears God and does what is right is acceptable to Him. (Acts 10:34-35) But men have divided themselves, they have segregated themselves under My Holiness; but wait and you shall see, My Holy Spirit (to the great astonishment of many) shall be poured on the pagans too. I tell you solemnly, these things shall take place before this generation shall pass away. So courage My child, do not be afraid. I shall unite you all in the end... and the viper shall not be allowed to throw his venom in your food anymore. Generation, your food shall be whole and pure, sorrow and lament will be ended. I love you and My people shall bear My Holy Name[3] in one in this unity.*

---

[1] Jesus means that He has come to a Greek Orthodox and not to a Catholic and speaks to me in Catholic terminology.
[2] From laity to priests and bishops (Roman Catholic). Some say I should change to prove myself as authentic by becoming a Roman Catholic.
[3] Just christians, under Christ.

Oh that You would tear the Heavens open and come down! At Your Presence not only the mountains would melt as the prophet Isaiah said[1] but the three iron bars You made me draw, representing the Roman Catholics, the Orthodox and the Protestants.

I promise you: I shall not leave My Church divided for long. I Myself shall come upon Her with full force and rebuild Her, have confidence in Me, My beloved one. I shall not put up with this faithless generation anymore, after all the Father's wrath cannot be withheld any longer; this is why My Graces upon you will be multiplying, to save you. ♥ *Vassula, the earth has not yet enjoyed My Peace fully, like a dry soil it thirsts for this Peace I bequeathed to all of you and I, like a watercourse running into a garden, I shall come down to irrigate you and you My child, rejoice! for I have taken root in you and made My Home in you and in you I shall grow, if you allow Me. Pray now with Me, My child, to the Father. Repeat after Me this prayer:*

> *Father,*
> *blessed be Your Name*
> *since Your Beloved Son Jesus Christ*
> *came to the world*
> *not to condemn it,*
> *but to save the world,*
> *Have Mercy upon us,*
> *look at Your Son's Holy Wounds,*
> *that are wide open now and*
> *remember the price He has paid for us*
> *to redeem all of us.*
> *Remember His Sacred Wounds*
> *and the two Hearts*
> *You Yourself united in Love*
> *and who suffered together,*
> *this One of the Immaculate Conception*
> *and Your Beloved Son.*
> *O Father,*
> *remember His Promise now*
> *and send us the Advocate*
> *in full force,*
> *the Holy Spirit of Truth, to remind*
> *the world of the Truth*
> *and of Your Son's docility,*
> *humbleness, obedience and great Love.*

---

[1] Isaiah 63:19.

Father,
the time has come,
when the reign of division cries out
for Peace and Unity.
The time has come
that Your Son's wounded Body
cries out for Righteousness,
that of which the world has not
known yet,
but through the Immaculate Heart
of Mary
and the Sacred Heart of Jesus,
give us
Precious Father
this Peace in our hearts
and fulfil the Scriptures
by fulfilling
Your Beloved Son's Prayer to You
that we may all be one,
one in the Divine Holy Trinity
so that we worship and praise You
all, around one single Tabernacle. ♥
Amen.

My daughter, love Me as I love you. Love one another as I love you. ♥ *Be blessed, come.* ♥

A PRAYER FOR UNITY

April 8th, 1991

My Lord?

I Am. Little one, Peace be with you. Love Me and cling to Me for your have not seen the last of Me.[1]

I'm pleased and relieved!

----

[1] Jesus means in this way, interiorly, and hearing Him in locutions.

I shall not allow your strength to crumble, I shall give you My Food as I always did. Flower, My Message this time is a prayer for all nations a prayer for unity. Come, write:

> *Praised be the Lord, for the Celestial Food[1] you are giving us and this is to fulfil Scriptures and to complete Your Work. You have given Your knowledge to mere children and not to the learned, for this is what pleases You Lord.*
>
> *Praised be the Lord to have laid open roads so that your people walk in them and come to You and fill Your House, for though You have sent Your Son into the world and the world plainly saw the Light, they have not all accepted the Light but turned instead towards darkness, falling in apostasy. The world has apostatized because they have refused the Truth and preferred to live under a Lie. Yes Lord, You so much love the world that You are today, in spite of our wickedness, sending us without reserve Your Holy Spirit to enliven us and revive the world, renewing every creature, so that everyone sees Your Glory and believes and thus be converted.*
>
> *Praised be the Lord for opening the doors of Heaven to pour out from Your Reserves this Hidden Manna[2] reserved for our Times. No, it was not Moses who gave bread from Heaven, it was You, Father, who fed the true bread, and as Your Son Jesus Christ is the Bread of Life, the Holy Spirit too nourishes us, for all Bread that descends from Heaven is Life. It is written in Scriptures: they will all be taught by God[3] and flesh and blood cannot reveal the Truth unless the Truth is given by the very One who established the Truth and imprinted It into our hearts. ♥ Father, may Your Name be praised always and glorified again. Let the world pass from Darkness to Light, from Lie to the complete Truth, from Lethargy to Fervour. Father, Creator of Heaven and Earth, the hour has come to show us the New Heavens and the New Earth where Your Holy Spirit will make His Home in us. Most Tender Father, as You glorified Your Son and Your Son glorified You, let Your Holy Spirit of Truth glorify again Your Son. In a short time, Father, according to Scriptures, the first heaven and the first earth shall disappear soon, to prove to the world that Your Word is something alive and*

---

[1]Spiritual food.
[2]Apocalypse 2:17.
[3]Isaiah 54:13.

active and that Jesus has indeed conquered the world. ♥ *When that day comes, Your Son's prayer to You will be also fulfilled, for we shall all be one in You as the Holy Trinity is One and the same. We shall not differentiate ourselves under Your Name anymore.*

Praised be the Lord and Glory to the Highest for sending us, in our great apostasy, Our Holy Mother whose Heart You Yourself united in love with Jesus' and who suffered together. And it is together again that the two Sacred Hearts will renew us and bring us back to Life; and in You lost sheep will be found, wandering lambs shall be reminded of their true fold and their True Shepherd, this Shepherd who neither deserts his flock nor abandons the lost but heals the wounded and supports the weary.

Praised be the Lord in Whose Holy Spirit we receive baptism. Indeed, fountains of living water flow out and are given to the man who is thirsty since they flow out freely from Your Holy Sanctuary,[1] this Sanctuary which You raised in three days and from Your fullness we are receiving in these last days the Grace of Your Holy Spirit to revive us, for this is Your Manna from Heaven, the Spiritual Food coming from the Spirit. Let your people, Father, realize that the ban soon will be lifted and that the Lamb's and Your Throne will soon be in Its place and among us. Prepare us, therefore, Righteous Father, for this Glorious Day when we can praise You and glorify You all around one Holy Tabernacle. ♥ *Father, I thank You for hearing my prayer and for having given me Your Words to indicate to the world the Riches of Your Sacred Heart.* ♥ *Amen.*

Come now, daughter. Come now, little friend, do not stop loving Me. Words of encouragement you will always hear from Me, so be confident and trust Me.

---

[1] Jesus' Chest (Body).

I NEED THEIR HEART TO REBUILD INSIDE IT
MY CHURCH INTO ONE

April 13th, 1991

Lord, our division (and I am now only talking the division between Orthodox and Catholics), is a real scandal! How is it possible that we, Christians, continue to be divided and not only a temporary division but a division that lasts, with deep roots, founded on conflicts that are so absurd! Each one being a rival to the other and some of us still holding anger and hatred. How is it possible to speak with integrity when an old quarrel is still unresolved in our hearts? Can we really face You and say that we are reconciled with our brothers and we can come to You with good conscience to offer You our offerings on Your altar? No, we cannot as long as we live under Your Holy Name and are not reconciled. We cannot claim to come to You with a clear conscience, yet, we all know that Your greatest wish, dear Christ, is UNITY and yet we hold firmly on the barriers that separate us and we do not seem honest enough to say: "we are not inclined to bend since it is we who hold the real Faith and the Truth." Have we not understood how much more Beautiful Your Bride would look if we unite? How much more Powerful the Church can become? How much more progress She can make? How many more Fruits She could produce? Now She's like stagnant. Can we honestly say She's progressing and earning souls in Her when we see daily in front of our eyes, soul after soul leaving Your Bride for a second-rate philosophy, yes, esoteric sects, like New Age, Jehovah's Witnesses and others. Yet these people, I feel, are in search of You, so help them to find You.

Ah, My dove, I have not been teaching you in vain... they have not yet understood that I need their heart to unite them. I need their heart to rebuild inside it My Church into One. Unity will be by the heart. Look, I have commissioned you to bear witness to a people not your own, but many of your own have not yet understood why Wisdom sent you to foreigners. Your people believe that you have been yielding to foreigners, they have not realized that it is I, the Lord, who united your heart to theirs. Double indeed is your cross on you My child, since you are whirled away too by some of the foreigners who challenge you without cease to become one of them. By remaining as you are I am teaching to both of them a lesson of how you should unite and what unity will be like. Unity is not to differentiate yourselves under My Holy Name, unity is to share Holy Communion and believe in My real Presence, in the Holy Eucharist. ♥ Unity, My child, is to give to each other your riches.

"Lord, teach us, when we judge, to reflect on Your kindness and when we are judged to look for mercy." Wisdom 12:22.

Ah, my child, your race is not finished yet but remember, in front of you I Am and at your side, your Mother, to encourage you, and at your heels, your guardian angel, to protect you. Hear Me, among brothers the leader of them deserves honour, so honour My Peter. This is only a reminder of the Most High. ♥

Now I know that I shall never be deserted, You have directed my soul towards You. I have stretched out my hands to Heaven and You have lifted me. My soul rejoices in You, oh that You do to my brothers too what You have done to me!

Not only will I lift into My Heart your brothers, daughter, but even people who do not know Me, I will lift into My Heart. Hence Mercy and Grace shall come even to the heathens, for they too are part of My creation. ♥ *Daughter, I am known to help the poor and the wretched... come now and caress Me again with your gentle words that come out from your heart. Repeat them to Me.* ♥

> Lord Jesus, use me to dry Your Tears.
> Lord Jesus, use me to wipe Your Tears.
> Sacred Heart, use me to console Your Heart.
> Sacred Heart, use me to pluck the thorns
>   encircling Your Head and Your Heart.
> Lord Jesus, use me as Your Head-rest.
> Sweet and Gentle Jesus, use me in every way
>   to please You and console You.
> My desire is to bring to Your Lips a smile.

Then I shall use you if you offer Me your will too. ♥

I offer You, Jesus, my will, my heart, my soul, my spirit, my body, everything.

Love then shall do His Will in you and My Peace shall reign in your heart, and My Image shall reflect in your soul, and your spirit shall worship Me in accordance with My Spirit and your body will reject all that is not holy since I shall transfigure it and perfect it into My Glorious Body, to become an altar for Me, your God. You shall share My sufferings but also My joy. I shall continue teaching you so that you will bear witness not only to a crucified Christ but also to a resurrected and victorious Christ. ♥ *I shall remind everyone that wonders, miracles and signs are also part of Me.* ♥ *Come, then.* ♥

α ✠ ω

DO NOT LET SATAN FIND YOU SLEEPING

April 10th, 1991

Love loves you, love Me. Without trials you will not grow. My affection for you is manifest, this is why Satan hates you all the more. Even if you feel you are under a constant threat from My enemy, I am near you to support you. Realize that I have made you to be a threat to him. Anyone who snatches souls from him is a threat to him, this is one of the reasons why he never loses any occasion to aim at you. Very often he uses people for his purpose, out of nothing at all he can produce an act of accusation to utterly ruin the one he wants to strike; but this is not all. One of his most malicious acts is to <u>suggest</u> in the sleeping soul all sorts of ideas that lead the soul into an agitation and a total unrest, wrenching out all peace within that soul, this is why you must stay awake. Do not let him find you sleeping. ♥

TWELVE BEATITUDES

April 14th, 1991

"Blessed be Yahweh, who performs marvels of love for me." Psalm 31:21.

Peace be with you. Now, tell Me pupil: are you happy to have Me as your Spiritual Director?

Yes Lord, more than happy. I am learning many things directly from Your Mouth, and others too!

Would you like to write?

I am ready to serve You my God, make me ready and open my ear to hear only Your Voice.

Hear Me then:

Blessed are those who work for Peace, they shall prosper in My Peace and radiate My Light forever and ever.
Blessed are the compassionate, they shall see Mercy in the Day of Judgement.
Blessed are the generous souls who share My Cup, they will be called heirs of My

Salvation.

Blessed are those who espouse themselves to Me, this same joy I feel as a Bridegroom they too shall feel, the day they meet Me face to face.

Blessed are you who have not accepted any other testimony but the One and only Truth I Myself have given you.   I tell you: Come! come into My Kingdom and share everything I have, with Me.

Blessed are those who do not differentiate themselves under My Holy Name, but show their unity through their humility and love, they shall be called Pillars and Foundation of God's Sanctuary.

Blessed are you who believe without seeing, rejoice, for the Grace you received from My Father and pray for those who have not yet received this Grace.

Blessed are you who accept to be scourged, humiliated and nailed with Me to the Cross, and who bear the marks of My Body on yours, your room in Heaven will be opened to receive you and your compensation will be great.

Blessed are those who keep My Name Holy, when they call and ask in My Name, I shall listen.

Blessed are the small ones who praise and adore Me, in them I shall do great things.

Blessed are the faithful, who observe My Commandments and from Scriptures do not change one stroke from what has been written, theirs is the Kingdom of Heaven.

Blessed are you My lambs who are chased like game, for My sake, by ravenous wolves, because I shared your meal side by side with you.   I tell you, all your sufferings are not in vain, the Father sees all this and takes accounts of everyone's deeds.   It will not go as hard on Sodom and Gomorrah as it will go on them for having persecuted My Holy Spirit.   So stay awake because no one knows the Day nor the Hour of My coming; your King will be coming soon.   The One you have been waiting for so long shall suddenly come upon you, so courage, beloved ones.

Indeed, the devil's smoke has penetrated into My Sanctuary but what smoke lasts forever? I shall, with the Breath of My Holy Spirit, dissipate and blow away this smoke and no authority nor any power from beneath will be able to intervene. ♥ I am coming to bring Fire to the earth and purify nation after nation. ♥   Be blessed. ΙΧθΥΣ ⤜⤙

THE INNER POWER OF MY CHURCH IS MY HOLY SPIRIT

April 15th, 1991

Lord, come to us in full force with Your Holy Spirit. For, most tender Abba, as You glorified Your Son and Your Son glorified You, the hour has come that Your Holy Spirit of Truth glorifies Your Son. Prove to the world that Your Word is something alive and active and not just printed words on paper. Let Your Holy Spirit "turn the hearts of fathers towards their children and the hearts of children towards their fathers." Ml 3:24.

Peace be with you Vassula. Scriptures never lie. It has been said that in the last days to come, people will keep up the outward appearance of religion but will have rejected the inner power of it[1] Ah! My beloved, will there be any faith left on My Return?

The inner power of My Church is My Holy Spirit in it, alive and active, like a heart in a body, My Holy Spirit is the Heart of My Body, which is the Church.
The inner power of My Church is My Holy Spirit who gives freely and distributes its gifts and its graces so that the Church gets some benefit.
The inner power of My Church is My Holy Spirit, the Reminder of My Word, revealing nothing new but the same instructions given by the same Spirit.
The inner power of My Church is My Holy Spirit, that transfigures, uplifts and turns you into real copies of Myself.
The inner power of My Church is My Holy Spirit, this Fire which enlivens you, purifies you and makes out of your spirit columns of fire, ardent braziers of love, living torches of lights, to proclaim without fear My Word, becoming witnesses of the Most High and teaching others to look only for Heavenly things. ♥
The inner power of My Church is My Holy Spirit, the Life and the Breath that keeps you alive and makes your spirit desire Me, calling Me 'Abba.' If you refuse, My child, and suppress the gifts of My Holy Spirit, what services will you be able to do and offer Me? Do not be like corpses that keep up the outward appearance of religion but reject the inner power of it, with futile speculations thus limiting Me in My Divinity. Do not stop those who come as children to Me, living a life of devotion to the Holy Spirit, it is I who calls them to the wedding of My Holy Spirit. The secret of holiness is: devotion to Me your God and you can do nothing of yourselves, unless My Spirit living in you guides you and teaches you Heavenly things. I tell you truly, whoever fears Me will accept My correction - so do not sleep now, for these are the Times when one should be awake and vigilant more than ever. These are the Times to open your ears and listen to My Spirit and not

---

[1] 2 Timothy 3:5.

disregard it, do not play the sage at the wrong moment by pushing the Breath of My Holy Spirit aside and suppressing the inner power that activates My Church. You want to be prudent? Open your eyes then. You want to be prudent? Open your heart and your ears, My friend, not your mind. A prudent person never scorns a warning from the Spirit, only the proud do not know anything about fear. The fear of the Lord is the beginning of Wisdom. You want to be prudent? Look for the Truth that desperately leans over your misery to save you! Look Who is bending towards your wretchedness and your wickedness to pull you to Him and lift you from your graves to breathe Life into you again! O come! Do not misunderstand Me, <u>I am not forcing you nor am I trying to violate your liberty!</u> I have taken pity on you generation. Do not say that all I had to say has been said. Why limit Me as yourself?

I am the <u>Reminder of My Word</u>, yes, <u>the inner power of My Church</u> and I am <u>free</u> to send you new portents and do fresh wonders. I am free to raise you generation and pour healing ointment on you from the Riches of My Sacred Heart, when I wish and on whom I wish. I am building, yes, re-building My Church that lies now in ruin. So do not let Me face you generation in the Day of Judgement and be obliged to tell you: you, you were one of My persecutors who pulled down while I used to build. Mercy is at your doors now and My Compassion knocks on your doors in your times of tribulations.

You say yourselves holy? Prove yourselves holy by showing Me your adoration to Me. Prove yourselves holy by showing Me the souls you are converting and bringing to Me, for My Kingdom consists not in spoken words, nor of <u>an outward appearance of religion</u>, but an Inner Power that only <u>I</u> can give you through My Holy Spirit, if you seek it. Feel My Presence and My Love I have for each one of you. I, Jesus Christ, am present and bless you all out of the depths of My Sacred Heart, leaving My Sigh of Love on your forehead. Be one. Ecclesia shall revive.

♥
ΙΧθΥΣ

STAY SILENT AND IN THIS SILENCE
I SHALL FIND MY REPOSE

April 20th, 1991

Lord, I thank You for making me Your Property and Your bride, teach those who do not understand that You do allow Your persecutors to attack me, because You can also be glorified in this way too. And You made it very clear that You will never allow them to hurt or touch my soul. Make them understand the difference, for a difference there is.

Flower, My Cup tastes bitter, but do you still want to share It with Me?

I want to share Your Cup with You.

Yes, Prove your love for Me by offering your will, be eager to glorify Me, your God, by embracing My Cross. You have become My Property in which I draw My delights out of you, you have entrusted your life into My Hands. Daughter, listen: stay weak, for in your weakness I can do great things. Be nothing, for in your nothingness I can be Everything. Stay silent and in this silence I shall find My repose. Stay pliant so that I may shape you into a copy of My crucifix. Stay limited, so that My Power will be seen in you. Become a model of Myself by being docile, patient, pure, obedient, humble, faithful and in constant prayer, like I was with the Father. Never sleep. Never cut the bonds you have with the Father. My life on earth was an incessant prayer with the Father, at favourable and unfavourable times. Listen to the Father and do His Will. Your food is given by Me, your Redeemer, all that you eat comes from Me to teach you to live the only True Life in Me your God. I tell you truly, do not be afraid of those who kill the body but cannot kill the soul, fear him rather who can destroy both body and soul in hell.[1] Remain in Me and I in you, I shall allow your mortal nature to be put to the test so that you grow in your trials, but your soul shall not be touched. Flesh and blood cannot inherit My Kingdom, so do not fear, through your trials I am glorified too. ♥ *Abandoned you shall never be.* ♥ ΙΧθΥΣ ⌖

FOR CANADA, ST GEORGES

April 23rd, 1991

I come in your country to leave you a sign of My Great Love. I come, I your King, like a beggar in rags and bare-foot, to ask you to make peace with Me and ask you a little bit of your love. Out of My Boundless Mercy, I bend all the way to you to take you out of your lethargy and your darkness so that you may taste My Great Love for you. ♥

---

[1]Matthew 10:28.

CHATEAUGUAY, CANADA

April 24th, 1991

Please Me daughter and glorify Me.

Help me Lord to proclaim Your Message of Love.

I shall take over completely, so do not worry. I will be standing by you, so come.
♥

LOVE IS THE ROOT OF MY LAW

April 25th, 1991

Before the meeting I prayed again for the Lord to help me.

My Vassula, can I ever demand from you something beyond your capacity? Daughter, the fulfilment of My Law is Love, Love is the Root of My Law and the other commandments cannot stand if Love is not there. Created you are to glorify Me. Listen: My Spirit shall invade you.[1] Give to Me the families of this nation. Give Me, flower, the glory due to Me now, tell them,[2] I am your Redeemer and I come not to condemn anyone but to save with saving justice. So call on My Name, beloved children, Jesus means He Who Saves. I am at your very doors beloved ones, I bless all of you. ♥

---

[1] For the meeting.
[2] The Canadians of Chateauguay.

IN YOUR HEARTS I SHALL REBUILD THE UNITY
OF MY CHURCH

May 2nd, 1991

Message to someone:

Peace be with you. The coming of My reign on earth is at hand and My Will shall be done on earth as it is in Heaven[1] and in your hearts I shall rebuild the unity of My Church. I shall not wait any longer for human approval, and My Bride shall once more be vested in glittering Glory, the ban of division shall be lifted and the Woman clothed in splendour in the sun, whom I am sending before Me to educate you, will encourage you. I have given Her the power over every race and every land to open a broad pathway for Me. ♥

The smoke that penetrated into the heart of My Sanctuary, staining Chalice, Tabernacle and all that is holy shall dissipate with one blow of My Breath. The nations then shall speak one language and all of them shall worship Me around One Single Tabernacle, this One of the Sacrificial Lamb, this One of the Perpetual Sacrifice that My enemies are trying to abolish and replace by their disastrous abomination.

Very soon now, My friend, I shall be with you all again and My priestly prayer to the Father shall be fulfilled. You shall be one like Us, in the Holy Trinity. I still have hidden in My Sacred Heart many things to divulge to you and show you, for the Treasures I have within Me are innumerable, but they would be too much for you to take now.[2] Your soul will not be able to take in everything, but little by little I shall unfold to you the Treasures of My Sacred Heart and step by step I shall guide you into what looks like a Light-House, a Mystery of Unfathomable Riches that have been hidden for generations and centuries. I shall reveal to you, My friend, the rich glory of <u>Hope, Wisdom</u> and <u>Knowledge</u>. Be rooted in Me and you shall bear fruit; remain in Me and you shall live. I have told you My friend all this so that when trials come, you may not falter. Love is by your side. ♥
Love Me. ♥

---

[1]Jesus in saying this was looking up in Heaven. He said it very majestically.
[2]Jesus was speaking with humour.

RESTORE MY HOUSE
I SHALL MAKE MYSELF A THRONE IN YOU

May 3rd, 1991

Lord, drench me with Your Holy Spirit, come and invade me with Your Holy Spirit, so that the enemy finds no space within me. Let Your Holy Spirit subside in the very depths of my soul to water it and lead it with riches, these of which are not of the world. Blessed be God.

I Am is with you, have My Peace. I went down into your room and befriended you, I was then a stranger to you, but see? My Teachings lifted you in My Heart and today I have turned your aridity into a fertile soil. My dove, I delight in you; My little one, I live in you. My head-rest, I repose in you. Glorify Me now and restore My House; glorify your Father who is in Heaven by treating Him as a King.

Ah, My daughter, My Mouth is dry for lack of love, I thirst for lack of love. Dress My Wounds with your love, pluck My thorns and console Me, praise Me all the time from your heart, speak to Me and do not wait until tomorrow. Delight Me and stay small. Allow Me, My Vassula, to use your little hand, offer Me your time and I shall saturate you with My Fountain, and the Treasures I shall give you can never be assessed, no man can fathom their magnificence. I, the Lord, shall make Myself a Throne in you to govern you and I shall allow Myself, since you have given Me your consent, to follow the passions of My Heart. I am in My Domain and I have full authority over you now. Praise Me often and bless Me. Love is with you. IXθYΣ ⤜●

APOSTASY CHALLENGED MY MERCY
THE WOMAN CLOTHED WITH THE SUN

May 6th, 1991

Lord, my God, who could bring us salvation, but You? Who could bring us back home, but You? Who could bring us happiness but You? Then: Maranatha!

Daughter, the dead cannot praise Me, this is why I shall descend with full force upon you and raise you all to remind you of My greatness, My splendour and My sovereignty. Come, write My Vassula:

Peace be with you My sons and daughters. ♥ *I have counted My sheep and My Heart is crushed with sorrow, only a remnant are left today who have not been raided by Apostasy; only a handful have not lost their faith; only a few are left who survived the perils of Rationalism, and I, from above have strained My Eyes waiting for you to offer Me your heart and your abandonment, but this generation's heart is gross with foolishness. Yet, even if you have not observed My Law of Love but have turned away your hearts and made your own law and statutes, I shall not stand by and see you stray more and more from My Commandments. I mean to rescue you generation, I mean to school you back to your senses and guide you with great love back into the path of Righteousness. I shall teach you to invoke My Name; I shall teach you to walk in My Presence; I shall teach you to live a life of prayer, My child; I shall teach you to love Me with all your soul; I shall unbind your death's cords that bind your soul to all that My Soul abhors, if you give Me your will, My child.*

Look, look around you, My Holy Spirit comes to meet you and revive you all. Dressed as a beggar, with Tears of Blood streaming down My Cheeks, I descend from My Throne, leaning all the way to you, to save your soul from disaster and from famine. For the sake of My Holy Name I shall demonstrate Myself through these very things you do not believe anymore, I shall demonstrate My Holy Spirit through marvels, through miracles. I shall demonstrate My Power through weakness and wretchedness as never before. I shall come with thousands of myriads of angels to pour on you, generation, My Celestial Manna, this hidden Manna[1], and fill your mouth with My Food so that your mouth proclaims My Glory. Apostasy challenged My Mercy, and Rationalism, this plague of your era, challenged My Power. I am sending before Me, to educate you, the Woman clothed with the Sun, the second Eve, to school you and lead you step by step into Heaven. I am sending you My Holy Spirit in this Night to be your Companion and Consoler and remind you of My Word. I am sending you a mission of angels of hope to expel your fears. Come and listen all you who are starved. Happy the man I invite to the Wedding of My Holy Spirit, he shall be filled with My Celestial Food and though their faults overpower them, My Holy Spirit shall blot them out in His rest in them. ♥ *Understand, My beloved, that My visit on earth is not to condemn you, but to save you. Who is going to see Me? Who will take notice? Who will recognize the Throne descending from the Heavens among you? Do not resist My Holy Spirit of Grace, I am with you always.*

Pray fervently for the conversion of your era, open your hearts and speak to Me. Will you offer Me your will? O House of Mine! Come, come to Me and walk in My Light. Yet, when I come in My Great Return, will I find any faith on earth? Today I am speaking in plain words, My little children, in a short time Love will

---

[1] Apocalypse 2:17.

return as love. I will come back to you and I tell you truly, if you recognized My Holy Spirit and have seen Him, it is because you belong to Me, since the world can neither acknowledge Him, see Him, nor receive Him. ♥ *Ah My little ones what will I not do for you! I am longing to see you strengthened with the gifts I am pouring on you.[1]*

Receive your strength
in prayer
a constant prayer to Me.

I bless each one of you; and you[2] who came because your cross is crushing you, lean on Me beloved and offer Me your distress and your hardship. I love you, I shall come to your help. Glorify Me by praising My Name, receive the Breath of My Holy Spirit on your foreheads and be one under My Holy Name.

ΙΧθΥΣ ⋈⟶

APOCALYPSE 21 EXPLAINED

May 13th, 1991

My child, allow Me to speak to My children by giving Me your consent to use your hand and your time. ♥

I am bound to You out of love. Lord, am I not Your Property? So use me fully and as You please My Lord, for this is my delight. Come Holy Spirit and invade me.

City![3] Whom I came to visit to proclaim My Love through you to all of you and to heal your sick inhabitants, I shall not let you perish in guilt nor will I wait to see you decay, I shall triumph over you. I am your King, I am the Perfect One. Hear Me, I intend to model you, generation, into a reflection of My Divinity. The sinner's brood I shall consume by a roaring Fire. Your generation will have her wedding with My Holy Spirit[4] and I shall, with My consuming Fire, change the surface of this earth into a divine, prosperous and new Earth, and the world of today will be gone. I shall turn you all with My consuming Flame as pure as gold

---

[1] Jesus had paused there. Then, majestically, straightening then not moving, said these words.
[2] Jesus speaks specifically to one person in the group.
[3] God suddenly and unexpectedly changed tone and His Voice with great force cried out to me calling me City.
[4] Apocalypse 21:2.

314

and transparent as glass[1] because your hearts will be Mine and in Mine. I and My Father will be your Abode[2] and you too will be Our abode. I intend to give you back your divinity, creation, so that My radiant glory will be like a lighted torch[3] inside you. Then like a sentinel guarding a gate, I shall guard you too from anything unclean which may want to come inside you.[4] I shall make out of each one of you a radiant city, I shall renew you entirely for this is the way I shall have you ready to wed My Holy Spirit. My Holy Spirit will make His Home in you, transfiguring you to become His Holy City,[5] His Domain and His Property. The world of the present shall be gone and My Will on earth shall be done as it is in Heaven. Love shall descend as love and I, the unseen God, will become visible inside your heart, the hour is coming when you shall no longer grope your way in the dark, since your heart will be lit by My radiant glory.[6] My glory will become visible in your hearts. ♥ Come, My child, hear My Mother now. Remain near Me. We, us?

Yes my Lord. I am seduced by You, seduce others too.

Intercede for them ♥ and I shall come and seek out and save what was lost.[7] Read Isaiah 41:17-20. Love loves you. IXθYΣ ⋊⊃

LET YOUR TOLERANCE BE YOUR WITNESS DISCIPLINE ALSO YOUR LIPS

Our Holy Mother's Message for prayer groups:

Children, I am calling each one of you today to examine your hearts. ♥ Let your tolerance be your witness. I implore you to re-examine your hearts. God's Message to you all is the proof of His Fidelity, God does not demonstrate Himself to judge you, God demonstrates Himself to show His Fidelity in your lack of fidelity. God is seeking your reconciliation, He is coming to take you out of the Power of Darkness and show His Reign on earth. The unseen God will become visible in His Glory in your hearts and the Heavenly things will become visible in your hearts and the pale reflections of what you have taken as shadows

---

[1] Apocalypse 21:21.
[2] Alluding to God Almighty and the Lamb were themselves the temple - Apocalypse. (Inside us, the 'city.')
[3] Apocalypse 21:23.
[4] Apocalypse 21:27.
[5] Read Apocalypse 21:1-3.
[6] Apocalypse 21:24.
[7] Luke 19:10.

before shall prove their reality. The Reign of God's Kingdom on earth is very near you now, I implore you therefore to be ready for this Day. If you say you have died to yourselves and the principles of this world, prohibit then your hearts from fluttering into the world, live for God and place Him as first. Have no more to do with quarrels, disputes and accusations, do not allow your lips to condemn you. Fear the Lord and Wisdom shall soon come upon you like dawn, the Lord seeks and desires an undivided heart. I had asked you and am asking you again to pray, pray, pray with your heart, a simple conversation with your Father who is in Heaven, because if I request from you today to offer God an undivided heart, it is to teach you to keep faithful to the principles I have been teaching you. What is valuable to God is the heart which honours Him by keeping itself exempt from all temptations that lead to sin. If you have disciplined your bodies by fasting, I request from you to discipline also your lips to pronounce only prayers and praises to the Lord, do not allow your lips to condemn you. Set your heart, your mind, your eyes and your lips on Jesus and be whole and undivided. I invite you, dear children, to put all these things into practice, nevertheless without leaving the other values of the Law undone, and remember that the Heart of the Law is Love. ♥ I bless you all.

REALISE THE URGENCY, THE GRAVENESS AND THE IMPORTANCE OF MY CALL

May 18th, 1991

Toulouse - France

Jesus?

I Am. Be in peace little one. There will be more than one that I shall bring back to Me. I have indeed called you here[1] because this is where they need Me. I love you to passion. Always remember this, I draw to Life. I do not repel anyone, sinner or unjust, all of you are My children. My Message is a Message of Love, a call to your real foundations, a reminder of My Word and of My Existence. Do not fear Me, fear only the one who pretends he does not exist and draws you ever so maliciously to Death. I am the Light. Come, tell them that this Message is not given to them to draw sensation but to make them realize the urgency, the graveness and the importance of My Call. The urgency of their conversion, the graveness of the condition of their soul, the importance to change their life and live

---

[1]Jesus wanted me to go to Toulouse instead of Montpelier.

holy. The importance of My Messages which are spiritual food, a nourishing supplement to their spirituality, a medicinal ointment to their wounds inflicted on them in this darkness by the evil one. I want My children to listen very carefully to all that I have to say: let My Spirit of Truth guide you back to the Truth; let My Spirit of Knowledge remind you of the One and Only True Knowledge I Myself have given you. I, your Lord and Saviour bless each one of you. ΙΧθΥΣ ⤬⟨⟩

VASSULA OF MY SACRED HEART

May 23rd, 1992

Yahweh, my God, You are lavishing Your scents on me, praised be my Yahweh. You are mine and I am Yours. Give me Your Shoulder to lean upon, unworthy as I am, a puff of wind that passes unnoticed and does not return, a speck of dust washed away with the first drops of rain, allow me to be in the Presence of Your Splendour. Lead me through this wilderness with a sensitive hand Beloved.

Vassula, even in your wretchedness, I shall speak to the nations through you, to make your generation proclaim their praises to Me.

Generation, I am going to pasture you. Daughter, I descend every time you call Me from My Throne to come all the way to you in your room and meet you. Subject to misery, you have captured My Infinite Love, rejoice! Rejoice that your King hears you every time you open your mouth and call My Holy Spirit to come and assist you. Invoke My Name, My child and Love shall overshadow you entirely and keep you company. ♥ *Delight your King now and let Him hear from His Poverty-Stricken child, her vows once more.* ♥

I got up and repeated my vows to the Sacred-Heart of Jesus.

Vassula of My Sacred Heart, I accept your consecration, your offerings pleased My Heart. Honour Me, your Lord, by staying devout and loyal to Me, I, who am your Rewarder. ♥

BRING BACK MY PEOPLE TO THE REAL
FAITH BASED ON LOVE

May 25th, 1992

Jesus, I have been charmed by Your Perfection, I have been seduced by Your Beauty. Your Consuming Love beseiged my frailty to consent and become the victim of Your Love, but how was I to retract upon seeing so much Beauty all at once? Your Graciousness mesmerizes me all day long. What spells lie in Your Love?

Beloved of My Soul, your eyes have seen My glorious Majesty, your ears have heard My Song of Love and I Myself have put My Own Light in you to make you forever Mine. My Nails and My Thorned Crown I have given to you to show My closeness to you. Your Spouse I have become, making you My bride to share My Cross as our matrimonial bed. My Passion will seize you to become a copy of Me your Spouse, I am your Comforter in days of sorrow. I have chosen you and not you Me, to show you My inexhaustible Riches.

Lord, what do You want me to do for You?

Bring back My people to the real Faith based on love. Pray that My Church be one, exempt from all evils. Expiate, daughter, expiate for the sins and iniquities of the world that so much offend My Sacred Heart... My daughter and bride, look into your Saviour's Heart, look inside this Heart that saved you. Take My Heart, console it by loving Me. I, Jesus, kiss you on your forehead. IXθYΣ ⊃

LET ME PREACH TO YOU

June 1st, 1991

Daughter, let Me preach to you, it is I who have given you the Knowledge. Pray that My Kingdom on earth becomes as it is in Heaven.

318

Here Jesus deciphers <u>chapter 21 of the Apocalypse</u> part of <u>chapter 22</u> and <u>Daniel chapter 11:31-39</u>. Ezebiel 48.

My Lord?

I Am. Peace be with you. Soon, very soon now I shall strip off your old behaviour and your old self creation, to vest you with My Divinity[1] and remind you of the True Knowledge. So listen, My beloved ones, to My Holy Spirit, allow Me to prepare you all so that you may be ready to receive My Kingdom. I the Lord invite <u>everyone</u> to share with Me and see My Glory. My Heart is sick with love for you generation... alas! for those who would still be carrying their sin, coiled inside them as with child when My Day comes![2] Pray that everyone may be ready when that day comes. Ail for your brothers who still live in darkness and <u>have flung My Glory for a worthless imitation</u>, this very one that the prophet Daniel speaks of.[3]

I shall speak to you in plain words considering the state of your soul and your lack of Knowledge. I do not come by force upon you with My Holy Spirit to violate your liberty, nor do I come to condemn you, I come to you out of Mercy to give you freely the fullest Knowledge of My Will. Through My Perfect Wisdom I come to augment in you the Knowledge I Myself have given you. <u>I do not come to add new things into that which has been given you already</u> but I come to place My Kingdom in the middle of your hearts. ♥

Citadels![4] Have you not yet understood? Have you not yet understood that I, the Lord, live in you? Have you not understood that <u>you are My sanctuaries</u>? When I speak to you about Heavenly things are you ready to receive them? Listen: Scripture says: "zeal for Your house will devour Me." Indeed, today <u>again</u> My zeal has reached its zenith and from above Fire shall come down and devour My sanctuaries[5], I shall transform you, Citadels[6], into a state of Grace in which you will no longer apprehend to desire My Glory nor fear to admit My Divinity.[7] The

---

[1]Allusion to New Heavens and New Earth, Apocalypse 21:1.
[2]Allusion to Matthew chapter 24:19.
[3]To the unbelievers who do not believe anymore in the Perpetual Sacrifice: Holy Communion. The Resurrection.
[4]We are God's house, a citadel for God. God called out to us calling us "Citadels", Daniel 11:31-39.
[5]Us.
[6]That is: us.
[7]Here God means that the unconverted and the unbelievers who refuse the Holy Eucharist and deny the Real Presence of Christ in the Eucharist, God shall change with Grace.

Plunderer[1] infiltrated like smoke in you, <u>you</u> who are the sanctuary of My Holy Spirit, the sanctuary citadel of My Divinity. Satan's smoke penetrated through hinges and holes, invading you in your sleep, because you had not acknowledged Me in My Divinity but rather followed your own irrational ideas. I tell you this: I shall <u>fill</u> your darkness with My Light because I intend to wed you, generation, with My Holy Spirit.[2]

It has been said that by force the Rebel will feed you one day a portion of Rationalism and the other day a portion of Naturalism with the intention to abolish and extinguish the little light that is left in you, <u>you</u> who are My temple. The Invader[3] has invaded many of My Citadels,[4] forcing his disastrous abomination[5] inside you and <u>abolishing My Perpetual Sacrifice[6]</u> from within you[7] to erect in its place a worthless imitation[8], an image of mortal man, which is an abomination in My Holiness.[9] ♥ You are My Holy City[10] and <u>you</u>, you who allowed My Holy Spirit to flow in you like a River,[11] you are My New Jerusalem[12], the First-Fruits,[13] those very ones who had constancy and faith[14]. And like dew coming from My Mouth, like raindrops on the grass, you shall put Hope in many arid hearts because all the radiant Glory of My Heart shall reflect in you, making you glitter like some precious jewel of crystal clear diamond.[15] I tell you solemnly, many of you who are not born of the Spirit shall receive from above, by My Grace, the <u>Spirit of Truth</u>. The Spirit of Truth shall descend in all His radiant Glory out of Heaven and make His Home in you. My Holy Spirit shall wed you to become His bride,[16] embellishing you by His Holiness, and suddenly the Heavenly things will become visible in your hearts and My Kingdom unseen yet to the heart shall become visible and crystal-clear in all its Glory. Beloved of My Soul, Citadels, blessed are you that will be found blameless.[17] (This[18] is My way of teaching you Heavenly things, it is not without labour, My child, but be reassured, all that I

---

[1]Satan.
[2]Apocalypse 21:2. Apocalypse 21:9-11.
[3]Satan.
[4]Us. Allusion to Daniel 11:31 - 'forces of his will come and profane the sanctuary citadel.'
[5]Sects like New Age etc... Materialism, rationalism that lead to atheism.
[6]Once these people fall into these sects, or into atheism, they also stop receiving the Perpetual Sacrifice which is the Holy Eucharist. Dn 11:31.
[7]Read Daniel 11:31-39 and Apocalypse 13:14-18 and Apocalypse 21:1-27.
[8]Sects: aping the Word of God.
[9]Jesus was weeping.
[10]Jesus said this very majestically. Apocalypse 21:2.
[11]Read Ezekiel 47:1-12. Apocalypse 22:1-2.
[12]Apocalypse 21:2.
[13]Apocalypse 14:4.
[14]Apocalypse 13:10.
[15]Apocalypse 21:11.
[16]Apocalypse 21:2. Apocalypse 21:9.
[17]Allusion to Mt 24:19-20.
[18]Jesus speaks to me now.

have to say shall be written and read, this is Wisdom teaching you, My Vassula.
I love you and My love for you is everlasting. ♥)

I shall let everyone marvel at My first-fruits, and little by little the old world will
vanish[1] and wear out like garment.[2] Only a little while now and all that had been
covered shall be uncovered and all that had been hidden shall be unveiled in front
of your very eyes. My New Jerusalems! You, who are the first-fruits of My Love,
you whom My Holy Spirit seduced by My New Hymn of Love, you whom I wed,
go out to the nations and sing to them My New Hymn of Love.[3] Work for Peace,
sow the seeds I have given you. Be like trees growing by the banks of the River
of Life[4], let your leaves be a medicinal[5] balm for the wretched and let your
branches bear fruit in holiness. ♥ Be My breech-menders[6], restorers of My
ruined sanctuaries. Give to those who fell into Satan's impious nets and were fed
portions of Rationalism and Naturalism. And My healing Water from My Breast,
this stream that flows out of My Sanctuary[7], will fill you and make you
wholesome. No man shall be able to arrest this rivulet. The stream will keep on
flowing profusely out of My Heart; it shall flow everywhere, breaking into several
parts, separating into other and several rivulets going into all directions and
wherever this healing Water flows, EVERYONE, sick, lame, blind, will be healed.
Even the dead shall come back to life again. No one will be able to stop Me from
purifying you. Ah! Beloved ones, from rebels, I shall raise levitical priests; from
dishonouring Me I shall turn you into pearls, radiant cities of light to honour Me
♥ and I shall live in you because you shall be vested in My Own Holiness. I, the
Lord, will be in the land of the living. And those who stifle My Holy Spirit and
see everything as nonsense, I tell you: I have things that go beyond your minds,
I shall demonstrate the power of My Spirit and make your lips open and your heart
cry out to Me:

Abba!

Love shall perfect you. Wisdom shall teach you to acknowledge My Holy Spirit
and I shall make you join the saints too. I bless each one of you, leaving My Sigh
of Love on your forehead. Be one under My Holy Name ♥ ΙΧθΥΣ ⤳ and
you, who are My chosen instrument to bring My Love before pagans and rebels,
continue your journey with Me. Allow Me to call you when I wish. I Am is with
you and loves you. Come. ♥

---

[1]Apocalypse 21:4.
[2]Hebrew 1:11.
[3]Apocalypse 14:3.
[4]Apocalypse 22:1.
[5]Apocalypse 22:2. Ezekiel 47:12.
[6]Isaiah 58:12.
[7]Christ's Body (Heart) Ezekiel 47:12.

I SHALL NOT ALLOW MY CHURCH TO PINE AWAY
THE SPIRIT OF REBELLION

June 6th, 1991

When my spirit becomes cold and I fall in a kind of lethargy, Lord, and when I become so ill-disposed to dialogue with You and meet You in this special way, do I, like a leaf wither and dry slowly before Your very Eyes?

I have been waiting for you. I had been speaking to you soul but all I heard from you was silence. Give Me your attention soul, I have so much to say to you and arouse your interest. Lethargy? Then cry out to Me! I shall breathe on you and the ice will melt.

Lord, there are times when the Light You have given me seems to vanish behind obscure smoke.

Child, your voice can carry as far as Heaven and all the way to My Throne, so <u>cry out</u> to Me and like a flash in the clouds I shall answer: "here We[1] are. We shall hear your petition."

Then come <u>now</u> and rescue me. Fill my lamp with oil, breathe on me to revive me, imbue me with Your fragrance of myrrh, perfect me in Your Presence, show Your kindness on me.

Do not withhold your question, speak child![2]

What You do to me with so much Love, Faithfulness and Mercy, will You not do it to <u>everyone</u> of Your children, who are in the same need as I am?

Be blessed![3] *I God shall come and rescue each one of you. I shall not allow My Church[4] to pine away. Generation, I mean to save you, but not by menace or disaster, anger or blame. I mean to save you generation, by enveloping My Love and Mercy around you to cover your nakedness. I am sending you My Holy Spirit lavishly upon you so that your spirit filled with My Spirit cries out to Me:*

"Abba!"

---

[1] The Holy Trinity.
[2] Jesus seemed eager to hear the rest of my sentence, which I knew He already knew.
[3] Jesus seemed very happy.
[4] We are the Church.

Today tears of Blood flood My Eyes from the <u>deafness</u> of My creation. A most obstinate spirit has penetrated into My Domain[1], their soul is fainting within them. I look into what was once My <u>Faithful City</u>[2] to see her today become a harlot's!

Lord! Your Reign, has it not yet begun?

Write this: "happy are those who are invited to the wedding feast of the Lamb." (Apocalypse 19:9) My Reign <u>has</u> begun in many hearts already. I have espoused these souls to Me making them new[3] and I tell you: My Spirit of Truth will continue to swarm over My whole creation and beseige City after City[4] and the obscenities, the iniquities, and all the impurities to be found within them, <u>I</u>, <u>with My Own Hand</u> shall extirpate. I shall extirpate all that had been planted by Folly with the Fire I will send from Heaven. ♥ Daughter, the first Heaven and the first earth shall disappear. (Apocalypse 21:1) and each one of you shall be renewed by the Love of My Holy Spirit. I shall change the face of this world.

Is this what You mean by the renewal of Your Church, the renewal of ourselves, because <u>we</u> are the Church? The New Jerusalem?

Pupil, you have said well, <u>you</u> are all My Church, My Sanctuary citadel[5], My Domain, My City, My Property, My Jerusalem. ♥ I shall renew City after City[6] with My Fire of Love. I mean to gather you from the four corners of the earth and cure you. I mean to burn with My Fire the <u>disastrous abomination</u>[7] installed inside My Temple[8], the disastrous abomination is <u>the spirit of Rebellion</u> that claims to be My equal. It is the spirit of Evil that enthroned itself in My sanctuary[9] taking the place of My Perpetual Sacrifice,[10] turning your generation Godless. It is the spirit of Rationalism and of Naturalism that led most of you into atheism, this is the spirit that makes you believe you are self-sufficient and that you can achieve <u>everything</u> by your own efforts and by your own strength. This disastrous abomination turned you into a waterless country of drought, a desert. My Perpetual Sacrifice you have abolished from within you because you have lost your faith generation. How many of you are thirsty for Me? Very few come to drink Me and yet you can drink Me without money. <u>Who</u> is hungry for Me? You can have Me free, at no cost at all, yet almost no one is hungry to eat Me. Evil has

---

[1]God means our soul. His Domain where He abides is to be found in the <u>core</u> of our soul, which belongs to God.
[2]God means <u>us</u> here. He calls us "city."
[3]Allusion to Apocalypse 21:5 - 'Now I am making the whole of creation new.'
[4]God means, soul after soul.
[5]Deuteronomy 11:31.
[6]Us.
[7]Deuteronomy 11:31. Deuteronomy 12:11. Mt 24:15.
[8]The Temple is <u>us</u>.
[9]Sanctuary is <u>us</u>.
[10]The Holy Eucharist, Holy Communion.

warped your understanding, fascinating your spirit to absorb all that is not Me. Instead of absorbing My Light, Satan made you absorb his darkness; instead of becoming radiant and beautiful, you dulled, pining away, and like a withered branch you are now ready to be cut off and thrown on the fire to be burnt. Do not be afraid of Me, <u>I am the River of Life</u>. ♥ I am the Way to Heaven, I am the only Truth that leads you to share My Glory for Eternity. ♥ Temple of God! Daughter of Mine, walk with Me. ♥ ΙΧθΥΣ ⤜⊃

YOUR KING WILL ABANDON NO ONE

June 12th, 1991

Lord, You pursue my persecutors and overtake them and they cannot touch me. Foreigners[1] come wooing my favour but yet.. when I go to my own[2] like poverty at their elbow, like a beggar in want, to tell them of Your Wonders, it seems like their ears are sealed, so that they would not hear Your New Hymn of Love. Am I to tread the winepress alone and have not one of the men of my people with me?

Is My Own Arm not enough for you? Are My Own Eyes that watch over you day and night not sufficient for you? Daughter, soon I shall show My Holy Face to them, I will inundate your country[3] with My Spirit, and Rivers shall flow over, pour out. I shall not hide My Face from them... hope My Vassula, hope... your King will abandon no one. ♥ *He shall come with healing ointment in His Hand and cure you one by one. Rejoice, My daughter, rejoice. I shall unseal their ears for My Glory.* ♥ *Come, the mysteries of the kingdom of heaven are revealed to you, pray that they may be revealed to them too.* ♥ ΙΧθΥΣ ⤜⊃

---

[1]The Roman Catholics.
[2]The Orthodoxy.
[3]Greece.

OUR TWO HEARTS ARE UNITED

June 13th, 1991

Message of Our Holy Mother:

Vassula? Will you write down My Words to assuage this desert?

Yes, Holy Mother, Mother of God.

Write, My daughter: blessed of My Soul, beloved of My Heart, today I ask each one of you to apply your heart to walk with God. ♥ God is your Strength, your Life and your Happiness, no man can live without God. Jesus is the True Vine and you the branches. A branch cut off from the Vine dries and withers immediately, it is then of no use but to be thrown on the fire. ♥ Walk with the Light and do not be afraid in abandoning yourselves entirely to Him, give yourselves to God and your hearts shall be filled with Joy. Understand beloved children that God in these days is coming to save you and untangle you from Satan's nets and bring you back to His Sacred Heart. Our Two Hearts are united in spite of the arguments and the denials of the world for this Truth, for they have not all accepted this Truth but use this Truth instead to combat one another. Our Two Hearts are united and thirst together for your salvation, children. Come and hear Us this time: make Peace with God, be reconciled. Lift your face to God and ask Him to fill your heart with His Light. Learn to love God as your Father, He who loves you more than anyone can imagine ♥ and without ceasing sends you from His Heart His flowing Peace, like a River to assuage the interior desert of your soul. Do not live out of words only, act and live every word given to you in the Gospels. Do not be dead at the letter of the Law, live it. ♥ Do not be afraid if anybody mocks you or refuses to believe in the Wonders God is giving you today, for I tell you: if anyone reduces you to silence, the stones will cry out[1] all the harder. Only God can give you Peace and Happiness. I am praying for you without ceasing so that from hard stones this generation's heart can turn to God and be like a watered garden; from an uninhabited desert, a Holy City full of God's Light, a Light coming from God, and not by sun or moon.[2] After the storm will be over and gone, flowers[3] will spring up, changing the surface of this earth. I, your Holy Mother, bless each one of you. ♥

---

[1] Images of Jesus and Mary that pour out Tears of Blood are a Divine Manifestation when men try to suffocate the Holy Spirit. (Luke 19:40).
[2] Apocalypse 21:23.
[3] Flowers: the first-fruits, the newly converted. Allusion to Apocalypse 21:1-3.

MY GARDEN, I FIND NEGLECTED

June 17th, 1991

Message for Pistoia in Italy (near Florence):

Peace be with you. I have come all the way to you to tell you:

I am here.

Beloved, My Sacred Heart is on Fire, this is why I descend from My Throne to come all the way to you and offer you My Peace and My Love. Mercy is at your doors. If there were two knees to receive you with great love at your birth and two arms to hug you with affection, I tell you, I have done more than that, I have laid down My Life for you. I am the Source of Love. Come, renounce all that stains your soul and follow Me. Do not say, "my way of life is faultless." You are without beauty and without majesty so long as your soul is stained and imperfect. Come, I can perfect your soul since I am offering you free and at no cost My Blood and My Flesh. Surrender yourself to Me, I am the Life. Today I suddenly descend upon you, I look around Me and My Heart is filled with grief. I had once cultivated this earth and turned it into a Garden, with the subtlest odours from its flowers. I left behind Me "levitical priests" to keep it, I entrusted them with My Interests, but My garden I find neglected, My flower-beds dry. I am surrounded by an endless desert, devastated, even the jackals have difficulties of surviving it. Scorpions and vipers are the inhabitants which prosper in its treacherous dryness and if only a remnant of My lambs are alive it is because I had been sending you without ceasing My angels to snatch away My lambs from the viper's fangs and the scorpion's sting. I had been told that I would find all My sheepfold secure and untouched in My Return and My garden kept and watered but hardly had I gone, scarcely had I turned My back than they turned My garden into a haunt of the lizard and the spider.

O come! You who err still in this wilderness saying: "I have sought My Redeemer but have not found Him." Find Me, My beloved, in purity of heart, by loving Me without self-interest. Find Me in holiness, in the abandonment I desire of you. Find Me by observing My Commandments. Find Me by replacing evil with love. Find Me in simplicity of heart. Sin no more; cease in doing evil; learn to do good; search for justice; help the oppressed. Let this wilderness and this aridity exult; let your tepidness inflame into an ardent flame. Relinquish your apathy and replace it by fervour, do all these things so that you may be able to say, "I have sought My Redeemer and I have found Him. He was near Me all the time but in My darkness I failed to see Him. O Glory be to God! Blessed be our Lord! How could I have been so blind?" I shall then remind you to keep and treasure My Principles <u>so that you may live</u>. ♥ I shall come like a lightening, as a flash in the clouds with My Holy Spirit to wipe away the tears from every cheek, so courage My beloved, Love shall return as love. I, the Sacred Heart, bless you all leaving My Sigh of Love on your forehead. Be one under My Holy Name. ♥ IXθΥΣ ⊃<⊃

THE THORN

June 18th, 1991

Sacred Heart, You are the Theme of my life. You are on my side and ever ready to help me. Now You have made me Your Property and Your Own Arms are my enclosure, what more can I ask? You have swept my accusers in a twinkling of an eye and the fire that was surrounding me is not there anymore!

Lord You have given me a vision now again of Your Sacred Heart, I could hardly recognize that it was a heart at all! Your Heart looked one big wound... Scarcely had I lifted my head from my oppressors than I found that another fire has been lit, yet another wound on Your Heart, another big thorn in Your Head my Jesus... this time I am going to bargain with You, if You allow me, here is what I propose: take this big thorn off You and put it in me instead. I shall keep it until the Father gives this persecutor the Grace and the Light he needs to be able to understand his mistake, and that I belong to You.

Vassula, let it be so, let it be as you ask. I accept your sacrifice My child, be blessed. I am not alone to swallow My Tears, your Holy Mother is weeping too. Come to Us in this way by sharing, this storm too shall be calmed. ♥ The Father sees everything, My child. I shall overturn entire valleys and uproot mountains were these too, to become a menace for My Love Verses, Love Verses which are a Call for your conversion. My Love Messages shall proceed. Satan's grip is getting loose now and I shall soon put a muzzle on his mouth. ♥ Love is near you all the time and He peers inside His room[1] now and then to check that all is well, this room where He takes His rest. ♥

I am Yahweh. Flower, Saint Bede is by your side.

Who is he?

Yahweh loves you.

---

[1] Room: my heart, God's resting place.

PRAY FOR YOUR BROTHERS

June 22nd, 1991

Ah, how Mercy and Love incessantly cover me and bless me! Wisdom is my personal Teacher and She is instructing me and others. Your Holy Presence ever so constant by my side reassures me and gives me hope and courage. Ah, Yahweh my Father, I long for You, how I long for You! Yahweh my Abba, You have seduced me to the marrow.

I preached to you My Knowledge. ♥ *Learn from My Mouth. Free! you will one day, commit your spirit into My Hands.*

Lord, as You have by Grace mesmerized me, by Grace too, mesmerize the rest of the world, for instance the pagans, the godless, and especially those who claim to be gods because of their wisdom, and who claim to be Your equal.

I shall come to their help, now they lie helpless, trapped in Satan's nets, but you have to pray for your brothers so that I may reveal My Holy Face to them too. ♥

THE REBEL AND THE GREAT APOSTASY

June 27th, 1991

Come, let us work, put your faith in Me. ♥ *It has been said that before My Great Return there would be signs given to you, you are to watch these signs preluding My Day of Glory. One can, by reading the Scriptures carefully, discover all these truths, how is it that your minds are not opened to understand the Scriptures? Come now and understand. Hear Me now My child: your generation is thriving in its rebellion, how they have apostatized! For My part, I increased My calls, My warnings. I beckoned to you day after day, I increased My Blessings but I got no response. I said: "would I find anyone when I come?" Why did no one answer when I called? but instead of a response to My supplication you turned your backs to Me, "who does He think His Message is for?" is all I heard. How they rebel and how they blaspheme against My Divinity! but no man is able to push away the Appointed Time, nor the Hour. They shall come upon them as sudden as a thunderclap. Today daughter, the Antichrist is the spirit of Rebellion given by*

Satan, as Scriptures define him: <u>the Rebel</u>[1] who is the disastrous abomination set up in My Temple of which the prophet Daniel spoke of. Each one of you is My Temple... the one Scriptures call Rebel and is defined as the disastrous abomination is one of the two preceding signs of the end of Times. The other sign is <u>your great apostasy</u>. ♥ Your era, My child, has defected from giving Me the adoration which is your due to Me but also your Life. Satan's plan was to conquer this era and make you believe you can do without Me. So, <u>the spirit of Rebellion</u>, which is the Antichrist, entered into My Dwelling[2], that is the spirit of Lawlessness, not to say more, and it has installed itself today in the very core of My Sanctuary.[3] This spirit of Rebellion is the one that makes those ones who have it cry out: "I am a god!"[4] Men have defected and in their defections Satan's way was opened to step inside them and lead all of these to a violent death. <u>This spirit of Rebellion</u> which devastates one's soul, one's mind and one's heart, is <u>the Enemy</u> of which the apostle Paul spoke of, the one who claims to be so much greater than all that men call 'god', so much greater than anything that is worshipped[5], the one who says: "I will rival The Authority."[6] So these men enthrone themselves in My place[7] and promulgate their own law to make war on My Law and anything that comes from My Spirit. Day after day, hour after hour they keep grieving Me and offending My Holy Spirit. O dust and ashes, you who removed My Perpetual Sacrifice from within you, do you want to die? Why do you rival Me? Why do you deny My Holy Spirit of Grace? <u>Anyone who denies Me is the Antichrist</u>, for he is denying the Father, the Son and the Holy Spirit who are one and the same because <u>all three of Us agree</u>[8].

Today many of you are denying the outpouring of My Holy Spirit. The graces and the gifts My Holy Spirit is giving you out of My Infinite Generosity are ignored and suppressed. These peoples deny and reject all the gifts of My Spirit. Many go around keeping the outward appearance of religion but are rejecting the <u>inner power</u> of My Church, the inner power which is <u>My Holy Spirit</u>. They say, "I have kept My faith, all there is to come now is the trophy of My Righteousness." I ask you: have you done <u>everything</u> you can to present yourself in front of Me? I have been trying to awaken you and tell you that you are like a dried-up river, and that all you say is hollow and while the sinner is being converted by My Holy Spirit, no sooner does he enter My House, no sooner does he discover the Treasures of My Heart reserved for all of you, than you come upon him like a gale to tempt him back into godlessness. ♥ He who has just escaped from rebellion, you tempt him

---

[1]Read 2 Thessalonians 2:1-12.
[2]In our souls.
[3]The core of our hearts.
[4]Ezekiel 28:2. Isaiah 14:14. 2 Thessalonians 2:4.
[5]2 Thessalonians 2:4.
[6]Allusion to Isaiah 14:14, "I will rival the Most High."
[7]Allusion to Ezekiel 28:2, "I am sitting on the throne of God."
[8]1 John 5:8.

back to rebel. In the Day of Judgement I shall tell you: you have not believed Me, but made Me out to be a liar because you have not trusted the testimony I have given you about the Advocate, the Reminder of My Word, yes, <u>My Holy Spirit of Truth</u>, this very One you never ceased to <u>ignore</u> and persecute, never ceased to deny and suppress. Instead of joining the saints who acclaim and praise with blessings and shouts of joy My Holy Spirit, you hound them and persecute them unceasingly, clinging to your illusion of piety. You are provoking Me with your constant denials. How can I then not let the stones manifest My grief? You prohibit My first-fruits to acclaim My Holy Spirit, this is why I tell you: if these keep silence the stones will cry out[1] My grief.[2] What I once said to Jerusalem I tell it to you now with sorrow: "if you in your turn had only understood the Splendour of My Message of Peace! but, alas, it is hidden from your eyes!" If you in your turn had only grasped the Splendour of My Holy Spirit, bestowing blessing upon blessing on all of you... but alas, you neither see nor hear the Advocate, the Holy Spirit, whom the Father sends in My Name, teaching you and reminding you of all the truths I have given you ♥, because the prince of this world is using your freedom for your own downfall.

Lord, show Your Mercy to these too, and like You made me hear You, let them hear too; and like You showed Your Beauty to me, leaving me dazzled, show them Your Perfection too.

They are not listening, they are listening only to their voice. Even while My Tears flow before them there is no reply. I have gone in all directions to find a way of breaking through their deafness and tell them to come to Me and base their strength on Me, so that I in My turn lead them to holiness and allow them to inherit My Light. I am the Holy One they are so wickedly betraying and I am the first to forgive them, had they one moment of regret... but as long as they maintain their stand of self-sufficiency they shall <u>not</u> hear Me nor will they be able to see how today I am revealing entirely and as never before My Holy Face to all the world.[3] I, the Lord, shall keep on shining on you creation and I shall spread across the face of this earth My Light, the sun that has darkened and the moon that lost its brightness[4] in your era, leading you in your darkness to apostatize. Soon, your distress shall be over. I intend to turn your marshlands[5] into a garden, the night into day, your cities[6], which are only a rubble now, into cities of Light. Your broken altars[7] will be rebuilt and of your temples[8] I, with My Own

---

[1]Luke 19:39.
[2]Divine manifestations of images and statues of Jesus and Mary shedding tears.
[3]Allusion to Joel 3:1.
[4]Allusion to Matthew 24:29.
[5]Us.
[6]Us.
[7]Us.
[8]Us.

Hand shall lay the foundation. ♥ *I shall make the whole creation new.[1]* <u>*I shall*</u> <u>*renew you all with My Holy Spirit*</u>. *Come, Vassula, My lamb, all shall be written and as I want everything to be written. Love is by your side.* ΙΧθΥΣ ⟩⟨⟩

I, YOUR SAVIOR, AM CLAD IN RAGS MADE OUT OF SACKCLOTH

July 6th, 1991

Lord, heal me.

If you listen carefully and bring no objections to Me, no rivals and no doubts, if you come and admit you are a sinner and show no hesitation to repentance, I shall heal you. You belong to Me and I have given you My Heart, this is why I want you to crucify all that is you. Let the only marks on your body be those I have on Mine. If you see footprints that do not belong to Me, do not follow them. My Footprints are stained with Blood and perfumed with myrrh. Were you to hear something from someone clothed in splendid robes, let it die with him and give no heed to what he says. I, your Saviour, am clad in rags made out of sackcloth[2] and walk barefoot. My cloak is soaked in Blood and My Heart is covered with flames of Fire, My Lips are parched for lack of Love.

Lord, heal everyone, everyone!

Fill My Heart with joy and pray for all those whose hearts are shut to reason and to My Wisdom.

For this reason Lord, draw us close to You, we are so weary walking in this exile.

My Dew from My Mouth will relieve your heart, I shall deliver you from your sorrow. My Eyes look down at the world, they scan each one of you. Should I descend now I would only find a handful with My Sign on their forehead. The Heavens I have opened with the price of My Life so that they are yours too. I ask you: what man clings on death and not to Life? Yet how much longer will you not reason? For ever? How much longer must you reject My Love, disown and offend your Anointed? Righteousness and Justice are sitting on the Throne that is coming among you from Heaven to tell you that the way to your room in Heaven, the

---

[1]Apocalypse 21:5.
[2]Apocalypse 11:3.

Home of the Light is through Me. If you abandon yourselves to Me, I shall show you the way Home; if you rely on My Love, I shall bring you to the Room of She who conceived Me, to nurse you back to health. I am not tying a rope round your liberty, I am only binding you with a wreath of Love. ♥ I love you with an everlasting Love and My Tenderness for you is an Inexhaustible Source. Listen daughter, tell this to the foreigners and to your own, tell them how My Heart aches for lack of love. ΙΧθΥΣ ⤬⟊

Jesus is sending me to a USA prison, to witness.

I GOD AM WITH YOU

July 8th, 1991

To be read for Kansas City Prison, to the prisoners:

Behold, it is I, Jesus of Nazareth, that come upon you speaking through this weak instrument. I tell you: the world has not yet fully known the Peace I bequeathed to you because the world rejected My Ways of Righteousness. I have said that in the world you will have trouble but you are not alone, NEVER. I am with you every minute of your life. I am ever so present, beloved of My Soul. Today I am sending you this instrument of Mine all the way to your doorstep. She has not come to you because she chose to, no, I chose to send her to you and therefore what she reads to you is what I say to you. My little children, My Return is imminent, I will come back to you. Love shall return as Love. I have told you this now before it happens so that when you see the evidence of My Words, you may believe. Come to Me as you are, do not wait to be saints to fall into your Saviour's Arms. Come to Me as you are and I shall forgive you your sins that bind your soul. Ah creation, Mercy bends all the way to you. Approach Me, do not fear Me. A man can have no greater love than to have given His Life for his friends, you are My friends. Do not say: "what can I say? How can I speak? From day to night and night to dawn I cry aloud, yet no one hears my supplications. Who will ever hear me?" But yet I tell you, I, I the living God heard you. It is I who come into your room to tell you with My Heart in My Hand: I love you My child and I bring to you My Blessings to flower in your heart. ♥ My son, take My Sacred Heart, it is all yours. Take this Heart that loves you, do not refuse It. I am He who loves you most. Look My child: when you see footprints that are not Mine, do not place your feet into them, for they will only lead you to your death. My Footprints, My child, are showing I am barefoot, they are stained with My Blood and perfumed with myrrh. My child, the Five Wounds on My Body are wide open again and My Cloak is soaked in Blood. I am clad in sackcloth and in rags because of the iniquities and the sins of this generation. My Lips are dryer than parchment for lack of love. Love is missing since this generation heap one betrayal on another and lead Me unceasingly back to the Cross to be re-crucified. It is you whom My Heart seeks; it is you who can console Me; it is you who can be a balm and soothe My Wounds; it is for you, My beloved, My Heart cries out to reach you. Come, I Jesus shall bear you on My Shoulders and lead you into My House which is your House too. Befriend Me, befriend Me and I shall become your Holy Companion every single day of your life. I, the Lord, shall deprive no one of My Mercy nor of My Graces. I bless you all from the core of my Sacred Heart. I God am with you. ♥ ΙΧθΥΣ ⊱⊱

I NEED VICTIM SOULS MORE THAN EVER

July 12th, 1991

My Lord?

I Am. Peace be with you. Let Me rejoice and let Me feel you have your ear opened for Me. Soul, feel My Presence. I Am is with you every minute of your life. Vassula tell Me, are you happy to be with Me in this way?

Yes, my Lord and I bless you.

Delight Me and try to follow My Lips when I speak to you. When I bend over you, when I look at you, do not pretend I am not there. Lift your head flower towards Me and absorb My Light. I will embellish you, I will revive your stem. Peace, My Peace I give to you. Allow Me to use you as My tablet for just a little while longer then... then I, your Saviour, shall pluck you and transplant you in My Garden forever and ever.

I your Redeemer shall resurrect many hearts to worship Me. Pray without ceasing, dialogue with Me. Bless Me often for all that I am giving you. Tested you shall always be, this, My beloved, is for your growth. I desire to stimulate your desire for Me, your thirst for Me and ah... what will I not do for your soul to perfect it! Had I to make you suffer a hundred scourges bringing you near to death for the perfection of your soul, I would do it without hesitation, to save you.

Lord, this might bring a soul perhaps close enough to give up everything!

Are you doubting of My Wisdom?

No, but maybe some souls might not be able to take all this.

I know each soul's capacity, so trust Me. Remember one more thing, you want to glorify Me?

Yes.

To glorify Me you must go through My Crucifixion. I need victim souls more than ever. Pray more often and bend to My requests, abandon yourself to Me and offer Me your will so that I accomplish My Divine Works in you. Carry My Cross when I am weary and console My Heart that aches for lack of love. Abba is near you all the time, delight Me and bless Me. ♥

SATAN HAS COVERED THE ENTIRE EARTH WITH HIS SMOKE

July 16th, 1991

My Lord?

I Am. Little one do not get discouraged in this exile. I am by your side to help you carry this burden. Come and rest in My Sacred Heart, make it your Oasis while you are crossing this desert. I shall not abandon you nor will I neglect you. I am your Hope and your toil does not go in vain. Dearest soul, I offer you My Patience. Saturated by My Love, oh what will I not do for you.... out of the path you were to tread on, I laid out for you a bed of roses. I shall not conceal how I, your Saviour, love you. I am today revealing to all humanity My Jealous Love. I am revealing you all My Holy Face to remind you to be holy and live holy. You belong to Me, created from the Source of My Sublime Love, meant to have eternal foundations in Me and be an image of My Divine Nature. Death was never meant for you but you have accepted the powers from below, generation. Daughter, I the Most High, had foreseen the betrayal of My Church and the inflictions My Body would receive. Today, the sun does not give you daylight nor does the moon shine on you. Satan has covered the entire earth with his smoke. You have apostatized.. you have made out of My Perpetual Sacrifice a mockery, a worthless imitation, a disastrous abomination. You are concealing the Truth with a Lie, you are guilty for blasphemy... My Holy Presence in My Tabernacle disturbs you so you made out your own law, forcing Me out of My Throne.[1] Have you asked My consent before doing so? but these are the signs of the Times, your great apostasy and the spirit of Rebellion, which is the Antichrist in your days and the abomination of the desolation. Ah Vassula, practise all that I have given you and share My child My agony, all I want is love, faithfulness and mercy. (Jesus' lips trembled holding back His Tears.) I feel betrayed as when Judas betrayed Me.

Come Lord and rest in the hearts that love You.

Flower, I tell you, I am revealing My Holy Spirit to mankind in this way to save you and to remind you of My Word. The Holy Spirit of Truth is My Witness, the Holy Spirit brings nothing new but gives you the fundamental truths that I Myself have given you. ♥

NEW YORK, MEETING WITH CONCHITA OF GARABANDAL

July 18th, 1991

Feast of Our Lady of Mount Carmel - 1.15am

My Lord, I thank You for all that You have done to me. I shall never be able to praise Your Holy Name enough!

Love is near you. Love rests on you. Love shall accomplish one thing after the other in its own time. Do not fear, your Saviour is like a watchman, guarding you without cease. ♥ *The Most High will not abandon you. Hear Me, long ago I prepared this, before you were even born I planned it and now I carry it out. See? I am sending you to My children so that you give them your news, and to encourage them thoroughly. Have faith in Me, trust Me. I know your hardships and your misery, but soon, very soon now I shall come and overturn the Rebel and reign in your hearts, generation. The Kingdom of God is soon with you.* ♥ *I bless My dear children of Garabandal. Learn that I Am is by your side.*

ΙΧθΥΣ ⤜⊃

Our Holy Mother asked me to read to everybody 2 Corinthians 1:10-11.

---

[1] Jesus here, means the new system of putting the Holy Tabernacle at the side of the Church or even in a side room with the pretext that Jesus is in a safer and more quiet place.

ALTOGETHER YOU ARE NOTHING

July 18th, 1991

Vassula, altogether you are nothing, but even a nothing give Me such delights to speak to you, to have Me as your Holy Companion gives Me so much happiness! I shall guard you and place you in My Heart. I Love you. Have My Peace.
IXθYΣ ⊱⊙

I HAVE LITTLE TIME LEFT NOW BEFORE MY FATHER'S HAND STRIKES THIS GENERATION

July 23rd, 1991

Greece - Rhodes

"For your Creator is your Husband, Yahweh Sabaoth is His Name." Isaiah 54:5.

Yahweh my Father whom I adore and long for, You who led me out of the countries underneath the earth and who lifted my soul entering it, consuming it with Your Fire and leaving me in total rapture for You. Yahweh, Your Majesty and King of kings, You who lead me by this marvellous road, keep me free from sin and from falling. I am a sinner and am more apt to sin than do good. Fortify your city.

Be in peace. I the Lord love you. Take My Hand and follow Me. Pray My Vassula for there is still a long way to go for your perfection. You are not exempt from sin nor from falling and falls you will have, but I am near you to help you up and press you on My Heart so that you may feel My Love and how I cherish you. Come, we shall pray together:

> *Father, come to our help*
> *and guide our steps to perfection.*
> *Bring back our divinity*
> *and make us the perfect*
> *dwelling of Your Holiness.*
> *Amen.* ♥

Jesus?

I Am. My Holy Spirit, My Vassula, shall go to the very ends of the earth and seek *even the least amongst you to save you from the disastrous abomination that dwells within many of you now... The Heavens soon shall deluge at My Coming upon you. I, the Lord, have done many wonders for you <u>and shall do more than these coming days</u>.[1] Pray My child, pray for those who offend My Holiness and blaspheme My Holy Spirit calling My Spirit foolish. Have I not said: "...everyone who says a word against the Son of man will be forgiven, but <u>no one</u> who blasphemes against the Holy Spirit will be forgiven." (Luke 12:10) for the Spirit is not opposed to the Son nor is the Father to the Spirit, since all three of Us agree[2]. Many of you are condemning My Celestial manifestations and persecuting those whom My Spirit speaks through them because you do not believe they come from Me. Daughter, look at the Wounds of My Body[3]... <u>I have little time left now before My Father's Hand strikes this generation</u>. Listen to your Father from whom you are sprung, listen to His Voice:*

I went all ways, seeking to gather you and remind you to live holy since I am Holy, but only a remnant of you pay attention when I speak. I have spoken through those you call contemptible. I have spoken through weakness and poverty, <u>but you have made a cult in persecuting My Holy Spirit that guides them, to the point of frenzy</u>!! I have been sending you through them the spirit of Elijah and the spirit of Moses, those two witnesses dressed in sackcloth[4] to prophesy and remind you of My Law, before My great Return. They are to speak to you in My Name and bring you back to the truth and back to your senses but over you spread a heavy darkness and your claims to your knowledge became a <u>battlefield to My Knowledge. The Lie was and is persecuting the Truth</u> but Scriptures never lie. It was said that "the beast[5] that comes out of the Abyss is going to make war on them and overcome them and kill them."[6] Indeed your battlefield is drenched now with <u>innocent blood</u> because My Holy Spirit of prophecy has become a <u>plague</u> to those who belong to the world.[7] Their frenzied persecutions and total <u>rejection</u> they have for My mouthpieces are similar to those of Sodom; their <u>stubbornness</u> to open their heart and comply, their refusal to open their ear and listen to My Voice today have gone <u>beyond</u> the stubbornness of Pharaoh in Egypt.[8] Today I am giving you "things that no eye has seen and no ear has heard," things beyond the mind of man.[9] All these things that lift your spirit to call Me: Abba. My Holy Spirit is

---

[1] The fall of Communism in Russia after the 3-day putsch.
[2] 1 John 5:8.
[3] Jesus' garment was soaked in His Own Blood, His ankles which I could see had blood with wounds like stripes.
[4] Apocalypse 11:3.
[5] In this context God made me understand that beast meant lie.
[6] Apocalypse 11:7.
[7] God is alluding to Apocalypse 11:10: '...because these two prophets have been a plague to the people of the world.'
[8] God is alluding to Apocalypse 11:8: ... their corpses will lie in the main street of the Great City known by the symbolic names Sodom and <u>Egypt</u>...
[9] 1 Corinthians 2:9.

calling you all to true devotion and to a better knowledge of God Himself, that is why I am continually repeating the same truths given to you. I shall continue calling you until I break through your deafness, generation. I shall not stop calling you in agony, not until I hear from you the word:

Abba!

The new heavens and new earth are soon upon you. ΙΧθΥΣ ⪢⪤

THE HUMAN RACE GRIEVES ME TO THE POINT OF DEATH

July 24th, 1991

Message for the Rhodes prayer group:

My eagerness to preach to them is beyond human understanding and that is why Wisdom is at the door of their heart. No one is worthy of My Wisdom, nevertheless, the Father out of His Infinite Graciousness is willing to give Wisdom to mere children. Ah... My beloved, you are all My offspring, wretched you have become and still are, yet, what Father would ignore his child in his misery and send him away to continue his immorality until Death overcomes him? Would he not intervene and quickly rescue him? Now that I have lifted you from the pit, lift your gaze on Me, your eyes shall behold Perfection. Allow Me to keep house with you, you shall not regret it... I the Lord bless each one of you. Be a vessel of light for the others who walk around like tainted vessels, unable to tell their left hand from their right and bring them to Me, I shall give you My Strength. Do not fear, the human race grieves Me to the point of death and My Heart lacerates to watch such iniquity and sin into the world. You, you have heard My laments because I came near you. You have heard My Voice, rejoice! Rejoice and be glad that I healed your eyes that were dim, your heart that was sick with lawlessness. I made you come back to Me through My Mercy and now allow Me to use you all for My Divine Plan, young and old alike. Pray and ask for My guidance, you are very precious to Me. Pray without ceasing for this shall be your nourishment. ♥
ΙΧθΥΣ ⪤⪢

LOVE AND PRAY

July 27th, 1991

Lord, perfect us in Your Beauty.

Little one, I give you My Peace, ask always and it shall be given unto you. Pray frequently, fervently, and while the sinner still continues his wickedness without remorse, you shall continue to sacrifice. Love and pray for all those who have turned their backs to Me. Lend Me an ear and I shall accomplish all that has to be accomplished. I, Jesus, will continue to help you and do all the work I have asked from you. My little pupil, stay near Me and love Me. I the Lord love you and bless you, have My Peace. Come, Love is by your side. ΙΧθΥΣ ⤐

SANCTIFY YOUR LIVES

July 29th, 1991

Rhodes

My Lord, Your Name is an oil poured out[1] like those the icons pour out. It is your signature, my Lord. "A spreading olive tree so fair, so sturdy, was Yahweh's Name for you..."

My daughter.

You <u>are</u> my Creator?

I Am...[2] *Ah My child, I came not only for you in this way but for all My other children too, to ask you to live holy and turn away from your evil ways of living. Let Me fill your hope. I intend to come and visit every kind of misery on this earth and break you free from sin. I Am is My Name and I am Holy so I want you to live holy. Sanctify your lives and turn into My Direction.* ♥ *The Evil one has no hold over those who stay awake and pray without ceasing. Open your hearts so that I enter in you and make My home in you. Have My Peace.* ♥

---

[1] Sg 1:3.
[2] I sighed filled with joy but languishly desiring to be with Him.

LET NOTHING STAND BETWEEN YOU AND ME

July 30th, 1991

My Vassula, let nothing stand between Me and you. Like the moon and the sun are steady and follow faithfully their course of nature and do not simply vanish from the sky, I too am steadfast and by your side. Yet even if these become unsteady, I shall never be unsteady. I am, I was, and will always be steadfast by your side. When I reveal Myself, in fact when I reveal My entire Self to you and tell you that I shall never abandon you nor withdraw My gift from you or strip you of My Jewels, believe Me, and do not have the slightest shadow of doubt. ♥ I have raised you up to be with Me and follow Me. So pupil of Mine, follow your Master, let your thoughts settle on Me. You were dead because you never knew Me but the Word came to your ear and with a blessing raised you and with the Breath of His Holy Spirit revived you and opened your eyes. Then, with a Kiss from His Mouth made you His bride:

- <u>I shall save you all in this way</u> -

Do not be afraid when I come with My Cross, My Thorned Crown and My Nails and offer them to you because these priceless Jewels that I will be offering you, are these very ones I embraced ardently with love, they are the Instruments of your Redemption. Allow Me to use you Vassula, so that through you in writing and orally I can pour out My Heart on this generation. ♥ Hope in Me, desire Me, do not feel downcast. I Am is ever so near you, am I not worthy for more joy!

O yes Lord! But let me feel You more!

Have I been with you all this time, and you still do not feel <u>or notice My Presence?</u> I have been <u>preaching</u> to you a considerable number of years and you still do not feel Me?

I want <u>more</u> of You. I want to be drenched completely and <u>literally invaded</u> by Your Holy Spirit.

Come to Me and eat Me... drink Me and at no cost at all! Eat Me and you will hunger for more, drink Me and you will thirst for more! Receive Me with joy and let Me rejoice. Learn how My Heart palpates and rejoices every time I and you become one, united in love. Come and get sanctified by eating My Body and drinking My Blood.

Yes, I thirst for You my Lord.

Hope in Me, thirst for Me and soon, very soon, your Holy One shall come and fetch you and take you to His Home which is your Home too. I bless you My daughter.

I bless You, my God. **IXθYΣ** ⊃○⊂

SET OUR TWO HEARTS LIKE A SEAL ON YOUR HEART

August 2nd, 1991

Rhodes

For the Greek prayer group:

Jesus, my Lord, blessed be Your Name. May Your Holy Name stand in Glory for ever and ever.

My Holy name stands and will always stand in all its Glory. ♥

May Your Hand guide us to the Truth and the only One Truth. Let nothing part me from this Truth You Yourself have given us.

You came empty to Me and departed full. I never stood in awe of greatness nor of strength. I Myself have filled your mouth with My Wisdom so that you may learn and not fall into error. ♥ I have given you My instructions so that you may find your defence in them. Listen now and understand:
<u>set Our Two Hearts like a Seal on your heart</u>
The Immaculate Heart of your Mother shall be your defence and My Own Sacred Heart your Home. With this Sign sealed on your heart, the foxes that make havoc of My Vineyards that are now in fruit, shall be caught. You, My little ones are:
<u>Our Vineyard[1] of Our Two Hearts.</u>

Come, My little children and listen: who among you delights in Eternal Life? Adore Me then in the splendour of My Holiness. Be constant with your prayers, Satan will be chained by the Rosary. Be constant in your confessions, little children, to be able to come and receive Me in the Holy Eucharist as often as you can. Fast on bread and water two days a week to make reparations and sacrifice. Do not look to your left nor to your right, look in front of you where I Am.

---

[1]The prayer group is being named, 'Prayer group of the Two Hearts.'

Wherever I go you shall go, wherever I live you shall live, these, My beloved, are My Principles. My Word should be taken in like your daily food, it is your Heavenly Bread, it is your Life. Come often to Me and consecrate yourselves to My Sacred Heart and I shall breathe on you and make you Mine to spread My Word to the four corners of this earth, and remember, let your thoughts be My Thoughts, your desires My Desires: imitate Me. Blessed are you who do not see Me and yet believe, I leave My Sigh of Love on your forehead. Bless Me and love Me.

Tell them My Vassula how I honour the Room¹ in which I was conceived.
ΙΧθΥΣ ✖◗

LET YOUR HEART BE LIKE A GARDEN

Our Blessed Mother's Message for the same group:

Blessed children, let your heart be like a garden, agreeable to the Lord, a resting place for your King. Allow Him to enter your heart so that even when He finds it arid and desolate, He would transform it into a garden of delights. Allow Him to breathe in your heart to revive it, His Breath is of the subtlest fragrance. Then, with His Blood, like morning dew, He will wash away your stains to perfect you, My little ones. Ah... how I love you... Come and listen to your God, His conversation is sweetness itself, compassion in its fullness. Pray, My beloved ones, pray without ceasing. Your answer to your problems can be found in a constant prayer, let this be your weapon. Pray with your heart, dialogue with God in this way, Satan flees every time you invoke God with love. So today, tomorrow and always, I will say to you: pray, pray, pray. My Love for you is great, do not allow Satan to tempt you to cut Me off from your sight. Be on your guard. I, your Holy Mother bless you all.

---

¹That is: Mary's Heart.

I AM AN INEXHAUSTIBLE FIRE

Yes my Jesus? (Jesus called me.)

Vassula, let your prayer groups be called: Prayer group of the Two Hearts ♥ ♥ since Our Hearts are united in love and one. I Am by your side, Love is near you.

Later on, late in the evening I asked Jesus to explain to me what happens to me when I'm living the Passion.

We are united as in one single body, then... I hold you, I seize you entirely, since you are My property, and I arrest your spirit. Like a kernel covered by the flesh of its fruit, I too cover you in a similar way, your spirit becomes embodied in My Spirit, in Me, your Christ. ♥ Love Me, adore Me and pray. I am inseparable from you. O come, come, let your love be an inexhaustible fire. I Am an Inexhaustible Fire that consumes souls. So imitate Me your God, this is My desire for everyone. Have My Peace. ♥

PRAY FOR THOSE WHO SPEAK OF UNITY BUT STRETCH A NET FOR THOSE WHO PRACTICE IT

August 4th, 1991

Rhodes

Lord, when the time comes for Your visitation will we be ready? No one knows the hidden things You have, yet, how many will continue to press their persecutions on Your message? They twist what You say; all they think of is how to prove to the world that these messages are diabolical, New Age (sect), or from an evil spirit but my Yahweh whom I adore, I intend, with Your Strength to "pay You my thank-offerings, for You have rescued me from Death to walk in Your presence..." Psalm 56:12-13.

Fragrance of Mine, lean on Me. Hear Me: shout! Shout to the nations without fear. Repent! for the Time of Mercy is almost over. Change your lives and live holy, sacrifice and amend your lives before the Coming of the Lord. Pray, pray for those who suppress My Spirit. Pray for those who speak of unity but stretch a net for those who practice it. I shall ask their accounts in the day of Judgement because I have called and no one would answer. I have spoken openly, yet no one listened. The House I am rebuilding with the price of My martyr saints' blood, they keep tearing down. Pray for the Peace of My House, peace between brothers, sincerity in the heart, lowliness and love, then... unity will blossom in each heart... and My Holy City, Jerusalem, will in one united whole, glorify Me. ♥

Ah, Vassula, nothing is in vain, My Work that keeps you up late at nights will not go in waste. My word shall reach the ends of this world. Be reassured My child. I, Jesus Christ, your Mother, the saints and your guardian angel are all beside you. Do not fear, your Abba is your Strength and your Shelter. You are very precious to Me, My child. α ω

CARESS ME WITH YOUR LOVE

August 5th, 1991

Rhodes

Lord, I feel like a boat without oars! My spirit is far from Yours, help me!

My wretched bride, who is taking care of you? Who is taking care of your needs?

You my Lord.

Say: You, My Spouse. I have spoken through your confessor's mouth, I am your Spouse. ♥ *Happy are you who received this grace, Heaven is your home.* ♥ *We, us?*

Yes Lord forever. My Lord and my God, I bless You, praised be Your Name. Glory be to God.

Come, rest your head on My Heart, feel this Love I have for you. Feel Heaven in you and rejoice, rejoice My little one for your Saviour is with you and it is He who guides you and it is He who forms you to resemble Him. ♥ *Ah.. be thirsty for Me and desire to drink from the Living Waters of Life. I, the Lord, shall provide your soul with this Water forever. Alone you are not, NEVER! Caress Me with your love, your thoughts, your heart, your good actions. Daughter and bride of Mine, I shall help you.* ΙΧθΥΣ ><D

DO YOU REMEMBER NINEVEH?

August 6th, 1991

Save us all, Jesus! Wait my Lord for all Your children to convert before Your Day comes! Your Throne is soon to descend among us, but are we all ready? Allow Your River whose streams refresh arid cities to flow in us Lord. Drench us, invade us, beseige us, and once You are in us, Your cities can never fall! Sanctify Your dwelling. Divinise us.

The Anointed One blesses you and urges you to pray. Do not despair[1], I am giving you enough time to reform, but will your generation understand? Will they be willing to change their lives? You have to take in consideration, My child, the daily offenses that are committed against Me. For how long must your Anointed One be offended? Have you got anything to tell Me, daughter? I hear nothing from you.

Grace! We need grace to come back to You, just like me. I did not know anything about You and of how much I offended You my Lord, not until You came by grace to me.

Keep praying for your brothers then. I said: it will not go as hard on Sodom as on this generation. Do you remember Nineveh? They were at the verge of a great disaster, but they listened to Jonah, My mouthpiece, and from the highest to the least... all fasted, repented and vowed to change their life and live holy. "Put yourselves on the ways of long ago. Enquire about the ancient paths.[2] Seek the Truth. Daughter, happy the man who will follow My advice. Let Me tell you one more thing: ♥ I, the Anointed One, will engulf you all with My Fire and consume you to give your soul a new life. I have little time left now, these Times of Mercy and Grace are almost over. I am not concealing My Plans, nor am I hiding My Face, I am revealing as never before My Face and you, My beloved ones, your duty is to go and spread these Messages of the Second Pentecost and what the Spirit teaches. ΙΧθΥΣ ⋉⊃

---

[1] I had felt that somehow my prayers would not be enough nor of those others who prayed, because we are so few.
[2] Jeremiah 6:16.

THE WAY TO MY CROSS IS MARKED WITH MY BLOOD

August 6th, 1991

Rhodes

My Spirit is with your spirit. I fill you. Ah, Vassula of My Sacred Heart, always remember these words:

The Way to My Cross is marked
with My Blood

and everyone who willingly takes this road, I bless and anoint. You are hounded for My Sake? Do not fear, I am near you and by your side to encourage you. You are condemned, but it is only by the world. For My Sake you are disgraced by human lip, rejoice! for I was too! Have I not said that no man is greater than His Master? You are the jest of your people[1] but so was I, your King. When they scourge you on the Way to Calvary, your blood will mingle with Mine. What better favour can I offer you than making out of you another live crucifix for My Glory? When I see your feet on the point of stumbling, I lift you and place you on My Shoulders, like a lamb. Come, with Me you will always be safe. ♥

Jesus, You are my Hope, My Strength, my Joy and my Song. I will always take refuge in Your Sacred Heart.

PRAY, PRAY, PRAY AND KEEP PRAYING

August 10th, 1991

Rhodes

I Am asks you to abandon yourselves daily to Me. Seek Me and you shall find Me. I and your Holy Mother tell you: pray, pray, pray and keep praying. Satan comes when you sleep, so do not give Satan a foothold. Pray, for prayer is your weapon against Satan. Love loves you. ΙΧθΥΣ ><)))°>

---

[1] Many Greek Orthodox theologians and monks mock me.

August 11th, 1991

To the young prayer group of Athens and Rhodes:

I have said, you are My children of Light and I shall add to this: and your Dwelling is My Sacred Heart. Remember, My Love for you all is Great, never, never ever forget this. IXθYΣ ⋈⬭

Jesus then asked us to read Colossians 3:5-17.

I LET MY HEART BE TOUCHED

August 12th, 1991

Rhodes

For the group:

My Lord and my God?

I Am. I shall speak freely to My lambs.

All I ask from you is love, love Me without restrain. I am the Source of Sublime Love. Come to Me and draw from Me and fill your hearts to be able to give this love to others. I am Present wherever you are, so never ever forget that where you are, I Am. I the Lord bless you. ♥ *Care for your brothers and sisters and lead them to Me, let them too see My Holy Face.* ♥ *I, My little children, have created you out of Love to love Me, to console Me, to praise Me.*

You want to Glorify Me? Then love Me and adore Me, the door to Heaven are your prayers to Me. I want prayers from your heart, so I tell you, pray, pray, pray. Remember that your Mother's Heart and Mine are united in Love; so you, you whom My Heart loves, come to both of Us and I shall offer you your rest in My Sacred Heart and protection will be offered in your Mother's Heart. I am the Resurrection and I shall resurrect many more of you as I resurrected you. I am Mercy and out of My Boundless Mercy I let My Heart be touched. Love and Mercy is at your very doors, now! IXθYΣ ⋈⬭

I AM AN ENDLESS OCEAN OF MERCY

August 13th, 1991

Rhodes

O Yahweh my God and Father, smile on us.

Lord?

I Am. It is I, Yahweh, your Abba.

O God, have mercy on our wretchedness.

Flower, I, Yahweh your God am most Merciful. I Am an endless Ocean of Mercy, Compassion and Tenderness. ♥ *I have given you My Law but it is not enough to say you know My Law, you have to practice My Law. It is not enough either to say you believe I Am. I desire you to love and adore Me. Even the demons believe that I Am, but they do not love Me nor do they adore Me. They listen to My Voice but they do not love Me. Be loyal to Me and you, you who are My seed, come to Me, your Abba and console Me. I Am weary and you are only a remnant who can console Me, you are the smallest of the flock and My Eyes are upon you. Your Abba, from His Throne, tells you: I love you all with an eternal Love. Be blessed.*

I CAN CHANGE STUBBORNNESS TO COMPLY

August 13th, 1991

Lord, forgive us, for we have really failed to appreciate Your Great Love, we failed to appreciate Your Great Sacrifice, we failed to love and stay united. We keep repeating our errors continuously. O Lord Jesus we need desperately Your help to come back to our senses. Come and rescue us. The garland of divinity has fallen from our heads. Look on us and see our wretchedness, our pitiful degradation, our atrophy to what is holy. Make us come back to You, by coming to visit each one of us, as You have visited me. Visit the rest of Your children and show them Your Heart.

I want My Vassula to hear from every lip:

> *Jesus, I love You. Save my soul and save the souls of others too.* ♥ *Amen*

So pray for the conversion of these poor souls. Pray novenas and <u>I shall</u> listen. I can change stubbornness to comply, so pray to My Sacred Heart and I shall do the rest. ♥

YOUR COTE IS MY SACRED HEART
PEACE

August 18th, 1991

O Lord, I am so troubled, to the point of death. It is my Gethsemane today. My soul is battered and distressed. Satan has definitely made me a target to dash me to pieces. Pitiless, he pierces me through and through. I am the butt of my persecutors, where then is my hope?

<u>In My Sacred Heart, My dove</u>. Your cote is My Sacred Heart, turn to Me and My Spirit will console you. Offer Me your troubles and I shall thrust them in My Heart, I shall make good use of them, I shall liberate souls from purgatory... Then forget your troubles of these days and rest in Me your God, I am an Ocean of Peace. Give Me, daughter, all your tribulations and My Peace shall annihilate them. Have My Peace, My lamb, <u>I</u> love you. <u>I</u> offer Peace. Rest in Me. Go now in Peace. ΙΧθΥΣ ><>

RATIONALISM BLURS THE SPIRIT, DULLS THE SENSE OF DISCERNMENT AND KILLS HUMILITY

August 19th, 1991

Lord, when peacemakers[1] work for Peace, sowing seeds which bear good fruit, guided by the Holy Spirit, why are they told to keep quiet? why are they hounded? why are they disbelieved?

Because they[2] are bought like expensive material by merchants. Rationalism blurs their spirit, dulls their sense of discernment and kills their humility. Like Sodom and Egypt they are rejecting all that comes from the inner part of the Church, the inner power which is:

My Holy Spirit

Nevertheless, I shall give you My Strength to proceed, for this is My Will.

THE RICHES OF MY SACRED HEART

August 20th, 1991

How delightful it will be for all Christians to live together like brothers. How much greater Your Glory would be to see us humble, around one single Tabernacle and Altar, praising You with one heart, one mind, and one voice... yet when I follow Your orders and I witness of unity, I am not understood nor believed. Like a millstone they smash me on the ground.

My child, the Anointed One is your Shepherd and He shepherds you by opening your path. Clothed in My Blessings all I ask from you is to pass on the Love I have given you to the nations. Allow Me to use you, little soul, Abba has you in His Arms. I Am is with you. Look at Me, what will I not do for you... and you, can you utter the same words?

---

[1]Peacemakers: those who evangelize the Word of God to bring the world back to God and reconcile with God.
[2]The disbelievers.

Yes Lord.

Arise then and continue to witness. Your race is not yet over, but do not lose heart, by your side I am to encourage your little heart. Your ankles are bonded to Mine, and My Lips are stuck to your ear to whisper to you and remind you that you are not greater than your Divine Master, you who are just My pupil. Will they not induce on you the same marks as your Master, the Prime Martyr? My daughter, love Me and I shall continue to pour out to you the Riches of My Sacred Heart, all this Wealth that had been reserved for your Times. ♥ I had once said, that from My Sacred Heart, I will perform at the End of Times works as never before, works that will marvel you, to show the radiant glory of My Sacred Heart. I had promised that I would expose My Sacred Heart entirely and wholeheartedly to entice hearts because My words are sweeter than honey. ♥ Everything shall be accomplished in time. Trust Me, let no one deceive you My child. My Gift has already proved Itself, I bless you. Wisdom shall continue Her Good Works with you. ♥

α ✕ ω

SILENCE IS THE BEST WEAPON AFTER PRAYER
RUSSIA SHALL OPENLY HOLD MY NAME HOLY

August 30th, 1991

My Lord and my Life.

I Am. Silence is the best weapon after prayer. I will trample on My enemy soon. ♥

Vassula, hear Me: your Holy One is resurrecting Russia to be a noble nation. Russia will be perfected in the Arms of her Spouse. ♥ I the Lord shall perfect her. Have I not said to you My child that I have My Hand on her cold heart warming it?[1] and the day My bride will open her eyes and see Me her Spouse standing beside her, she shall see and understand what My Hands have done in her midst, and from thereon, Russia My bride shall openly hold My Name Holy and all erring evil spirits within her will flee. I had told you all these things before they happen so that you may believe that it is I, the Almighty, who is guiding you. Hear Me: I shall not conceal My Plans. If men are tempted to conceal My Plans,

---

[1] See prophetic message on Russia of 11 March 1988.

I, with My Own Hand shall unveil everything to you all before they happen. ♥
The Holy One has been warning you. I had not been menacing anyone of you.
♥

*A Ray of Light from Heaven shall come in the midst of My Body[1] and change the
face of this earth and bring peace among brothers[2], this will be the reward of the
martyr saints' prayers, sacrifices, penances, constancy and faith. Do not be afraid
when the <u>hour of great distress</u> comes if you were constant and kept your faith, for
this <u>Hour</u> has to come to change the face of this earth, thus everything said at
Fatima will be accomplished. The Father loves you all and He judges no one.
Already The Reaper is at work.* ♥ *<u>The Father's Works will astonish you all</u>; and
to you, My child, look back into My Messages. Had I not said that I, the Lord,
have done many wonders for you and <u>shall do more these coming days</u>?[3] See how
My predictions come true? and now I am telling you that the Heavens soon shall
deluge with My Coming upon you. <u>My Fire shall be hurled on this earth to burn
up her crimes,</u> I will not restrain My Hand.* ♥ *My Holy Name is daily profaned
and my observances are scorned, this is to fulfil the words said in Scriptures.
(write) "Immediately, there was a violent earthquake and a tenth of the city
collapsed. Seven thousand persons[4] were killed in the earthquake and the
survivors, overcome with fear, could only praise the God of Heaven."[5] (Apocalypse
11:13) There is very little time left now. Forgive your neighbour while you have
still time. Make reparations, fast. If you are a sinner who sows trouble between
friends, repent. For the sake of My Holy Name return to Me. You are master of
your will but not of My Plans and I urge you to surrender quickly. Satan is
sending his adepts untiringly to all of you, so be on your guard more than ever, his
reign is near its end. This is why he will just for one last time vomit on this earth
hoping to sweep away as many souls as he could.* ♥ *This is why there <u>must</u> be
constancy and faith in you, because you can avoid and even stop Satan from
vomiting on this earth.* ♥

Courage, daughter, lift your head and lean on Me. I shall continue helping you.
IXθΥΣ ⊃

> Lord, all Merciful, let those who say: "We will go our <u>own</u> way,"
> return to You. And those Christians who say to the Pope: "we will
> go our <u>own</u> way," return and obey the Pope. Let their human
> pride lower its eyes and their arrogance humbled. Amen.

---

[1] Church.
[2] Here I understood that the Lord was alluding to the UNITY of the Churches.
[3] God refers to His Message of 23.7.91, that in the coming days He shall do more
wonders. Prediction alluding to the fall of communism in Russia.
[4] That is, a great number of all classes.
[5] Read also: Matthew 24:22 and Matthew 24:29-30.

RUSSIA REBELLED AGAINST ME

September 3rd, 1991

Lord, Father and Master of our lives, do not abandon us now nor in the days of distress. Lord, Father and Master of our lives, help Russia to grow in Your Spirit. You have pierced the Red Dragon through that had beseiged her.

Lord, Father and Master of our lives, rescue us from the Rebel that still remains among us.

Ah, My child, I shall teach you all by My Purifying Fire, wait and you shall see. ♥ *Hear Me now and write My child:*

Not long ago most of the nations of the world never believed that the enemy, the Red Dragon, would lose its power in Russia so suddenly. Vassula, if your sister Russia rebelled against Me, it came through the sins of the world and its crimes. Tyranny comes from below.

But how did her children feel, those martyrs who belonged to You?

How can I describe what her children suffered, to what can I compare them, daughter? All Heaven mourned for her children. Her sons laid helpless, but who was there around them to mourn for them? Was there anyone strong enough among them to pierce the Dragon through? not when their skins were shrunken against their bones. Her children went begging for bread, oppressed by the enemy, they collapsed under their burden. If they left in secrecy to take refuge in My Arms, they would be punished severely, they were not allowed to show their zeal for Me. Their pursuers were swifter than vipers eyeing each step they took and had they any suspicions that The Book of Life would be hidden under their mattress, My children would be harassed, tracked, then captured. Ah daughter, My Eyes wept ceaselessly to see this nation reduced to silence by the sword, priests and prophets were made prisoners and were forced to dwell in darkness. Many of them were slaughtered pitilessly before My very Eyes. This nation who at one time honoured Me and praised Me openly, radiant as a sapphire, a Citadel of delights, was reduced into a waterless country of drought by the sins and crimes of the world. I tell you, My daughter Russia, your sister, has not yet shown you what she will accomplish in My Name. ♥

*The Day of Festival has yet to
come and how I wish it were
here already!*

Pray, pray for this Glorious Day. ♥

September 9th, 1991

My Jesus?

*I Am. Love Me Vassula, it appeases the Father's wrath on this generation. I have
prayed for you My little one, to the Father, to liberate you of 'the thorn' you took
from Me.[1]*

Lord confirm please what I have come to hear from You by giving me a passage
from Scriptures. (I open at random the Holy Bible and my finger goes on to Luke
22:42) It reads:

> "Father", He said, "if you are willing take this
> cup away from me. Nevertheless, let Your will
> be done, not mine.

Be blessed, I shall guide you. IXθYΣ ⊂⊃

THE FOUNDATIONS OF THE EARTH WILL ROCK

September 11th, 1991

Lord, I look up at the heavens and search for heavenly things. I search Your Holy
Face to feel Peace and be able to rejoice. I search for your Holy Face to be able to
contemplate.

---

[1] I had offered Jesus to take upon me this 'thorn' from Him. (18.6.91) It meant
one thorn less on Jesus. 'The Thorn' that Jesus talks about is referred in a
message dated 18.6.91. This thorn was given to Jesus by a loved one who actively
persecutes the Message. Satan confused him and now uses him.

And I for My part My Eyes look down at the world of today, searching nation after nation, scanning soul after soul for some warmth, for some generosity and for some love but very very few enjoy My favour. Very few bother to live a holy life; and the days are fleeing and the hours are now counted before the great retribution. ♥ *My cities[1] have become a harlot's - Pitiless! They have become a citadel for the demons! All corrupt from within, eaten up by worm! A refuge for the viper and the scorpion! How can I not breathe on these renegades My Purifying Fire?*

Jesus suddenly changed tone and after waiting a few seconds, with a tone very grave that left me in awe said:

The earth will shiver and shake and every evil built into Towers[2] will collapse into a heap of rubble and be buried in the dust of sin! Above, the Heavens will shake and the foundations of the earth will rock! Pray that the Father's Hand will not come down in winter. The islands, the sea and the continents will be visited by Me unexpectedly with thunder and by Flame. Listen closely to My last words of warning, listen now that there is still time. Read Our Messages[3] and stop being scornful or deaf when Heaven speaks. Lower your voices and you will hear Ours. Think twice before you judge; think more than twice before you condemn the Works of the Holy Spirit. I shall not spare anyone who mocks the Holy Spirit, blaspheming Him outright. Justice will send them down to the underworld. ♥ *Lift all of you your faces and search the Heavens for My Holy Face to contemplate! Lift your eyes towards Heaven and you shall not perish. Repent! and ask the Father to relent. Soon, very soon now, the Heavens will open and I shall make you see*

The Judge.

---

[1] Cities here is used by God for the word 'souls.'
[2] Like the Tower of Babel.
[3] Jesus' and Mary's, those Two Witnesses.

THE PURIFICATION

September 15th, 1991

Lean on Me, blessed of My Soul. I give you My Peace. Write:

O Jerusalem!¹ Turn your eyes to the east and to the west. Turn your eyes to the north and to the south and I Am there! I tell you truly that once more My Spirit will be poured on you and My Image will be spread across the face of the world. What I have planned shall happen and what I have told you shall be fulfilled. Come close to Me and listen carefully: today I come all the way to your doorstep holding the banner of Peace. I am coming to save you Jerusalem. On it is written: <u>Faithful and True²</u>, <u>the King of kings and the Lord of lords.³</u> Will I hear from you Jerusalem: 'My King, it is You that I have to worship' or will you still be unaware of He who offers you His Peace... now? Will you in these last days before the Day of Retribution recognize My Holy Spirit who descended from above in all His Glory to make house with you? During your whole lifetime, generation, you flouted My Law and turned away, rebelling. Are you ever going to be prepared to meet Me, your God? I am soon going to pass through your City⁴ and it will be sooner than you think! These will be My last warnings. I solemnly tell you:

> *Wake up from your deep sleep!*
> *You are heading for your ruin.*
> *Shake off the dust that covers you*
> *and rise from the dead.*
> *The End of Times⁵*
> *is nearer than you think.*

1. Soon, very soon, I shall suddenly open My Sanctuary in Heaven and there, your eyes unveiled, you will perceive like a secret revelation myriads of Angels, Thrones, Dominations, Sovereignties, Powers, all prostrated around

The Ark of the Covenant.

Then, a Breath will slide over your face and the Powers of Heaven will shake. Flashes of lightening will be followed by peals of thunder. "Suddenly upon you

---

¹That is: O generation.
²Apocalypse 19:11.
³Apocalypse 19:16.
⁴That is, through <u>us</u>. We are cities.
⁵The End of Times is NOT the End of the world, it is the end of an epoch.

will come a time of great distress, unparalleled since nations first came to existence.[1] *For I will allow your soul to perceive all the events of your lifetime, I will unfold them one after the other. To the great dismay of your soul, you will realize how much innocent blood your sins shed from victim souls. I will then make your soul aware to see how you had* <u>never</u> *been following My Law. Like an unrolled scroll, I will open The Ark of The Covenant and make you conscious of your lawlessness.*

2. If you would still be alive and standing on your feet, the eyes of your soul will behold a dazzling Light, like the glitter of many precious stones, like the sparks of crystal-clear diamonds. A Light so pure and so bright that although myriads of angels would be standing nearby, in Silence, you will not see them completely because this Light will be covering them like a silverish golden dust. Your soul will only perceive their form, not their face. Then, in the midst of this dazzling Light, your soul will see what they had once seen in that fraction of a second, that very moment of your creation...

They will see: He who held
you first in His Hands, The Eyes
that saw you first.
They will see: The Hands of
He who shaped you and
blessed you... They will see
the Most Tender Father, your Creator,
all clothed in fearful splendour.
The First and the Last.
He who is, who was, and
is to come,
The Almighty.
The Alpha and the Omega,
<u>*The Ruler*</u>*.*

Shrivelled with your awakening, your eyes will be transfixed in Mine which will be like <u>*two Flames of Fire*</u>*.*[2] ♥ *Your heart then will look back on its sins and will be seized with remorse. You will, in great distress and agony suffer your lawlessness, realizing how you were constantly profaning My Holy Name and how you were rejecting Me, your Father... Panic-stricken, you will tremble and shudder when you will see yourself as a decaying corpse, devastated by worm and by vulture.*

---

[1] Deuteronomy 12:1.
[2] Apocalypse 19:12.

3. And if your legs will still be holding you up, I will show you what your soul, My Temple and My Dwelling was nursing all the years of your life. Instead of My Perpetual Sacrifice, you will see to your dismay that you were fondling The Viper and that you had erected this Disastrous Abomination of which the prophet Daniel spoke in the most profound domain of your soul:

The Blasphemy

the Blasphemy that cut off all your heavenly bonds linking you to Me and making a gulf between you and Me, your God. When this Day comes, the scales of your eyes will fall so that you may perceive how naked you are and how within you, you are a land of drought... Unhappy creature, your rebellion and your denial of The Most Holy Trinity turned you into a renegade and a persecutor of My Word. Your laments and your wailing will be heard only by you then. I tell you: you will mourn and you will weep but your laments will only be heard by your own ears. I can only judge as I am told to judge and My judging will be just. As it was in Noah's time, so will it be when I will open the Heavens and show you The Ark of the Covenant: "for in those days before the Flood, people were eating, drinking, taking wives, taking husbands, right up to the day Noah went into the ark, and they suspected nothing till the Flood came and swept all away."[1] This is how it will be in this Day too; and I tell you, if that time had not been shortened by the intercession of your Holy Mother, the martyr saints and the pool of blood shed on earth, from Abel the Holy to the blood of all My prophets, not one of you would have survived!

I, your God, am sending angel after angel to announce that My Time of Mercy is running short and that the Time of My Reign on earth is close at hand. I am sending My angels to witness of My Love "to all who live on earth, every nation, race, language and tribe."[2] I am sending them out as apostles of the last days to announce that "the Kingdom of the world would become like My Kingdom of above and that My Spirit will reign for ever and ever"[3] in your midst. I am sending My servants the prophets to cry out in this wilderness that you should:

*Fear Me and praise Me
because the Time has come
for Me to sit in
judgement![4]*

---

[1] Matthew 24:38-39.
[2] Apocalypse 14:6.
[3] Apocalypse 11:15.
[4] Apocalypse 14:7.

My Kingdom will come suddenly upon you, this is why you must have constancy and faith till the end.

My child, pray for the sinner who is unaware of his decay. Pray and ask the Father to forgive the crimes the world ceaselessly commit. Pray for the conversion of souls, pray for Peace. ♥ IXθΥΣ ✠

YOU WILL LEARN TO LIVE A TRUE LIFE IN GOD
THE DAY OF THE LORD IS AT HAND

September 19th, 1991

My Lord, You are my Cup and my very soul rejoices in You. Your great Tenderness upholds me to cross this desert, my side by Your Side, my hand in Your Hand. "It is for You I am putting up with insults that cover me with shame, and make me a stranger to my own brothers, an alien to my country's other sons; but zeal for Your House devours me!" Psalm 69:7-9.

Vassula, let Me whisper My Words in your ear that you may glorify Me. Do not listen, My lamb, to what the world says because from it comes nothing good. Listen to Me, I who am your Father, and by listening carefully, you will carry out the work I have confided you with. Trust Me, My child, and come to Me for advice. Come to Me for consolation. Come to Me when the fever of this world raises against you and burns you, come quickly to me, your Abba, and I will heal your blisters. I am He who loves you most tenderly and I will nurse you always back to health. I shall always soothe the wounds the world inflicts on you for the sake of My Holy Name and for witnessing on My Love. Remember: up in Heaven I Am watches over you and takes care of all your problems. Remember too that everything you do is not for your interests nor for your glory but for the Interests and the Glory of He who sent you. ♥ *Let My Spirit of Truth shine on you so that you, in your turn, reflect My Image, reminding the world of My True Face, since the world seems to have forgotten My True Image. In a short time all of you will learn how to live a*

True Life in God

and be one with Me as the Holy Trinity is One and the same, because all Three of Us agree. ♥ *My little children, I shall not be long, I am already on My Way of Return. I am telling you this before it happens, because when it does happen you may believe that this Voice you have been hearing all these years, came from Me. I am telling you this so that you may rejoice, because I too rejoice for this Day when Satan's head will be crushed by My Mother's heel. Hear Me: I shall pour out My Spirit on this evil generation to entice hearts and lead everyone back to the complete Truth, to live*

a Perfect Life in Me your God.

But be brave, because there will still be a Fire before My Day, so do not fear nor be sad, because without this Fire the world's face cannot change... and when it comes, it will show the world how wrong it was. It will show its godlessness, its rationalism, materialism, selfishness, pride, greed and its wickedness, in short, all those vices the world worships. No one can say that I have not been telling you the outset of My Plans. No one can say that I have been hiding My Plans from you.

I am The Truth

and The Truth will always open His Heart and expose to you His fervent Plans <u>as they are</u>. The Truth will always give you the choice of proving yourselves to Him. If I had not spoken to you, if I had not been opening <u>now</u> the Heavens to you, you would be excused, but I <u>have</u> been calling you day and night without ceasing. I <u>have</u> been sending you My angels to speak to you; I raised from nothing, wretched souls and formed them into fervent disciples to go and knock on your doors and repeat to you the Words I Myself have given them. No, they were not speaking as from themselves, but were only repeating the Knowledge that I Myself have instructed them with. ♥ They went to you in their poverty and barefoot to tell you of the things that are to come, not adding nor deducting anything from that which I have given them, all they said was taken from Wisdom Herself.

Now, I solemnly tell you, that when that Day of Purification comes, many will be sorrowful to the point of death for not having allowed My Holy Spirit of Truth to enter their house,[1] but have welcomed in His place the Viper, the Abomination of the desolation and shared their meal side by side with My enemy. They welcomed inside their house the one who apes the Holy One, they worshipped the Deceiver, who taught them to misconceive My Holy Spirit:

My Holy Spirit, the Giver of Life and
The Inner Power of their soul

---

[1]That is: their soul.

He who breathed an active soul into them and inspired a living spirit. ♥ *I tell you solemnly, My Fire will descend in this world quicker than you expect it to come, so that those without sight of their sins may suddenly see their guilt. It is in My Power to bring this Day forward and it is again within My Power to shorten this Hour, for this Hour will bring so much distress that many would curse the hour of their birth. They would want the valleys to open and swallow them, the mountains to fall on them and cover them, the vulture to devastate them quickly. They would want to dash themselves to pieces but no one will escape from this Hour, those that truly love Me will suffer only for not having done more for Me. They too will be cleansed. But woe to those who rejected Me and refused to recognize Me, they have their judge already. The Truth that was given to them will be their judge on that Day.*

You heard Me say many times from My mouthpieces that

"the Day of the Lord is at hand"

and that My Return is imminent. If you love Me you would be glad to know that My Holy Spirit will come upon you in all His force and in all His glory. If you love Me you will continue to pray for the conversion of all My children who are unaware and still live under Satan's power. If anyone loves Me as I love you all, he will listen to Me and will remain faithful up to the end of his ministry. My little children, if you loved Me, you would perform even greater works than those I performed while on earth but no one has performed anything greater yet because of the so little faith you have in Me and the ever so little love you have for one another. No one yet has loved Me as much as I love you, but on the Day of Purification you will understand how little you have done because I will show My Holy Face in you. You hear those Footsteps? They are Mine. You hear the sound of My Breath already? It is the sweet sound of My Holy Spirit blowing through your wilderness and your aridity. You felt a Breath slide over your face? Do not fear. Like the Dove's wings, My Holy Spirit touched you slightly while hovering above you. ♥ *O come! Come to Me and as Moses lifted up the serpent in the desert, I too will lift your soul up to Me and revive you! As I was lifted up in Heaven, you too will be lifted up to Me to be nursed on My Breast. O come to Me! Get thirsty again, thirst for My Everlasting Wells, thirst to be with Me, your God! I will without hesitation offer you to drink and turn My Water into a spring inside you, welling up to eternal life, for from My Breast flow fountains of living water, an inexhaustible Source. O come to Me! Hunger again for My Bread and you will not die! Today, as yesterday, I stand up and cry out:*

*"If any man is thirsty, let him come to Me! Let
the man come and drink who believes in Me!"[1]*

*My forbearance is great and although I know you are sinners and you have
polluted the earth with innocent blood[2], if you come to Me repentant, I will forgive
your guilt and your crime. I am an Abyss of Grace. Do not be afraid... do not
fear Me. Fear rather the Hour if it finds you unaware and asleep. This is the
Voice of your Father; this is the Voice of the Sublime Source of Love; this is the
Voice of He who once said:*

"Let there be light!"

*and there was light. Come to Me and I shall give you My Spirit without reserve.
Do not be like the soldiers who shared out My clothing and cast lots for them at
the foot of My Cross. Come to Me with John's spirit, <u>come to Me out of love</u>,
come to Me to console Me and be with Me. The Hour is coming when the world
will find itself only in distress and darkness, the blackness of anguish, and will see
nothing but night. Bewildered, they will call out to Me, but I shall not reply, I
shall not listen to their cry. Frenzied, they will blaspheme My Revelation, Wisdom
and the Truth. The whole world will be inundated by distress upon seeing the*

*Ark of the Covenant
My Law.*

*Many will fall and be broken, rocked and shaken because of their lawlessness.
When the heavens will tear open, like a curtain ripped in half, showing them how
they flung My Glory for a worthless imitation[3], like stars that fall from Heaven
they shall fall, realizing then how Folly led them astray, how by trying to climb up
to the summit and rival Me, was only folly! When that Day comes, I will show the
world how wicked it was, how they befriended the Rebel and dialogued with him
rather than with the Holy One. The hour has come when constancy and faith,
prayer and sacrifice are vital, they have become an URGENCY!*

My little children, you who are sad now will rejoice later on. Come, let us pray:

*Father all Merciful
raise me up to Your Breast,
allow me to drink from the
Running Streams of Eternal Life,
and by this I shall know that*

---

[1] John 7:37.
[2] There was a stress, that Jesus put in my mind, on abortions.
[3] Allusion to Daniel 8:11-12. That is, the Holy Communion.

I enjoy Your favour.
O come and rescue me before
the Hour comes upon me.
Cure me,
for I have sinned against You. ♥
Father,
Your Lips are moist with Grace,
Your Heart is a blazing Furnace of Love,
Your Eyes are Two Flames of consuming Fire.
O Father,
Your Beauty is Perfection in itself,
Your Majesty and Splendour leave even the
brightest of Your angels dazzled.
Wealthy in Virtue and Grace,
do not hide Your Holy Face from
me, when the Hour comes.
Come and anoint me with the oil of love.
God, hear my prayer,
listen to my supplicating voice!
I must fulfil the vows I made You
Eternal Father,
although the current is opposing me,
I trust,
I know,
I believe,
that Your Arm will be there
to lift me and pull me out of this current.
O how I long to gaze on
Your Sanctuary and see Your Glory
in the Ark of the Covenant!
O how my soul languishes to gaze
on the Rider of the Heavens
who carries the Name:
Faithful and True
He who will sweep away iniquity
from the world,
He who is Just.
O come and cover me with Your Cloak
since Your Love is known for its generosity.
O Father! Do not brush me off
like I deserve because of my sins,
but help me. Provide me with my
Daily Bread
and keep me safe and away

from the Viper's fangs.
Make me heiress of Your House,
make me Your child of Light,
make me a perfect copy of the
Supreme Martyr, to glorify You
for ever and ever. ♥
Amen.

Heaven belongs to you My child.[1] Live for Me, breathe for Me, have Me as First.
Love Me, My child and all that I have is yours. By your love and your faithfulness
My House will be your house too. Rely on Me your Abba, come close to Me and
take your place in My Sacred Heart. ♥

ALWAYS DEFEND TO DEATH THE TRUTH
THE KEYS TO UNITY ARE LOVE AND HUMILITY

September 23rd, 1991

All day long, I sigh for You my Yahweh, my own. Your love that You showed me I cannot forget, never. Your Kindness my Yahweh, my own, I shall remember as long as I live. I pine away with love for You my Yahweh, day after day and I no longer wish to associate myself in this world that wounds You, and to know that I am among the first who wound You... My soul wants to proclaim all Your wonders to the world and my feet want to run to the hill-tops and cry out to the world:

"Your Creator is Your Husband!
His Name, Yahweh Saboath.
Yes, like a forsaken wife, distressed in
spirit, Yahweh calls you back.
Does a man cast off the wife of his youth?
says your God." (Isaiah 54:5-6)

Yet I fear, O my Yahweh, my Abba and my own. My soul yearns and pines away for Your House and
all I long for now is to be with You.
So do not ask me why my
spirit is downcast,

---

[1]After having read the prayer God had dictated to me for Him, He was very touched and with emotion in His Voice told me what followed.

since my sighs are no secret for You and all that I sigh for is known to You.

> My soul awaits You, my Yahweh,
> come and invade me,
> come and consume me.

Vassula... do not hide My child[1]... Daughter of Egypt, I have appointed you as assayer of many nations and you are very precious to Me. Do not misunderstand Me, I do not need you and you are not indispensable for this work either; but having chosen you, a nothing, glorifies Me and purifies you. Then, everything I own I wish to share with you. Do not fear proclaiming My Messages, My Holy Spirit will fill you with My Words and you will boldly proclaim My Word. ♥ *So go now to those to whom I send you, I shall not abandon you nor will I leave you uninhabited. My Holy Spirit is your Guide and your Counsellor. I have only begun to reap My Harvest... reap with Me... You have not sown this Harvest. I did all the sowing in you and now I want it everywhere. Now that the Harvest is ready all I ask from you is to reap it with Me, My daughter. Offer your assistance as a sacrifice, I am not asking you much... What do you see, daughter?*

Your Son's Holy Face, smothered from pain, His Face is like on the Holy Shroud.

Is this not enough a reason for proceeding and sacrificing a little bit of your time and energy? Look again, daughter... what do you see now, Vassula?

I see something like a soft <u>red</u> cloud filling the sky, hovering above us and yet moving like mist and taking more of the sky, it moves gently but steadily.

Write: "like dawn there spreads across the mountains a vast and mighty host, such as has never been before, such as will never be again to the remotest ages." (Joel 2:2) Yes, it is near... and now what do you see, Vassula?

Live human torches.

See carefully those very souls I created... these shall never reach the Room I had prepared for them, these souls are under Satan's power and they will not share My Kingdom nor My Glory, they are heading for their damnation... Tell Me, have I deprived any soul of My Love, My Glory and My Kingdom?

No Lord.

---

[1] I was hoping that I need no longer go out to the nations and be present witnessing. I was hoping that my Father consents with my desires: to stay home, meditate, love Him, meet Him in writing, meet Jesus in the Holy Eucharist and thus avoid crowds.

But they have chosen not to love Me and willingly followed Satan. They cut off, by their own free will, the bonds of our union; and now look again Vassula, what do you see?

O Lord, a Woman, sitting on a white rock. I see Her from the back, She's wearing a long black dress and has Her Head also covered with a long black scarf. She appears to be in great distress and is doubled with Her pain. I see myself approach her, she lifts her face and I start to weep too with Her. It's Jesus' Mother, our Mother, Her Face is very pale and filled with tears. Upon seeing me She stretched Her left Hand and pressed it on my arm.

I am the Woman of Sorrows, familiar with misery. I am the one who will recover for you <u>Hope</u>. I am the one who will crush and trample with My heel the serpent's head. My Eyes weep ceaselessly these days without relief, My Eyes have grown sore over all My children. Vassula, My daughter, do not close your ear to God, do not close your ear to My request, you heard Me weeping. I have defended your cause and always will. When the Lord fastens you to Him, it is out of Love to pour out His Heart in your heart. Today[1] <u>to you in turn His Cup will be passed</u>, do not refuse to drink. Hesitant you must not be. Your streets are polluted with innocent blood and Our Hearts are sick, this is the reason for My Tears, this is the reason why the Lord will share His Cup with you.

<u>Treason barricades unity among brothers, insincerity of heart induces God's Cup to augment.</u> They wrenched the Body of My Son, divided It, mutilated It and paralysed It. I am reminding you all that through Him, <u>all of you</u> have in the One Spirit your way to come to the Father, yet you remain divided under My Son's Name. You speak of unity and peace <u>and yet stretch a net for those who practice it.</u> God cannot be deceived nor is He convinced by your arguments. The Kingdom of God is not just words on the lips, the Kingdom of God is love, peace, unity and faith in the heart. It is the Lord's Church united in One inside your heart. The Keys to Unity are: Love and Humility. Jesus never urged you to divide yourselves, this division in His Church was no desire of His. ♥ I implore My children to unite in heart and voice and rebuild My Son's primitive Church <u>in</u> their heart. I am saying My Son's primitive Church, since that Church was constructed on Love, Simplicity, Humility and Faith. I do not mean you to reconstruct a new edifice, I mean you to reconstruct an edifice <u>inside</u> your heart. I mean you to knock down the old bricks inside your heart, bricks of disunion, intolerance, unfaithfulness, unforgiveness, lack of love, and reconstruct My Son's Church by reconciling. You need intense poverty of the spirit and an overflow of wealth of generosity, and not until you understand

---

[1]Meaning, these coming days.

that you will have to bend, will you be able to unite. ♥ So, My Vassula, join Me in My prayer as you saw Me praying before. I am with you My child very much. Comply with Love's desires, Jesus will never abandon you, be united in your love with Him, for one purpose:

to glorify Him. ♥

Now, daughter,[1] do you understand why you should not give up reaping with Me? Keep on praying and bless those who persecute you, your hour has not yet come, My dove. I will be gentle with you and you will be all the more loved by Me - do not try to understand what is beyond your power. Drive in the sickle when you see Me driving in My Sickle. Do not delay your step, follow in time with My Pace. If I delay, delay too. Speak up when I give you the signal and keep silent when I look at you. Always defend to death The Truth. Scathed you shall be from time to time, but I shall allow it just enough to keep your soul pure and docile. Know that I am always by your side, reap when I reap, learn to be patient as I am Patient. Be very humble and effaced. I have entrusted you with My Interests[2] to work with Me at My side, and I have appointed others too to join their services in this work. ♥ Vassula, My child, a little longer, a very little and your soul will fly to Me, so there is no reason to feel downcast as you tell Me. You have only to lift your head and look Who comes all the way to your room, Who sups with you, Who shepherds you. Ask Me to forgive your sins so that you may receive My Peace and that you may have joy again. Tell My children that soon I will send My Holy Spirit in full force to shepherd you and lead you all back into the true Fold and live a

True Life in Me your God.

---

[1] The Father's Voice again came back.
[2] I also heard "Ministry."

I WILL POUR IN YOUR EYES MY TRANSCENDENT LIGHT

September 26th, 1991

My eyes are always on You, O my God. The close secret[1] to You is given to those who love You and fear You.

> You have lifted my soul from the pit
> to discover Your Sacred Heart's Wealth;
> I have discovered
> the Mercy Your prophets spoke of,
> I have discovered
> the Love and Meekness Your disciples tasted;
> I have discovered
> the Peace, You Yourself have given us.
> In Your Sacred Heart, You allowed my soul
> to discover
> that Suffering is Divine
> and Mortification agreeable in Your Eyes.

Then in my soul came a brilliant Light and like a tuneful noise of doves, I heard and felt a Breath slide over my face and You filled me with Your Mysteries.

Taste more of My Secrets, My child, by being obedient to My Law. Lower even more now your voice so you may hear only Mine. Lower your head so that Mine would be seen, lower yourself so that I can lift you up to Me. Many a times you inspect the Secrets of My Sacred Heart with your own light, you have only to ask Me, My child, and I will pour in your eyes My Transcendent Light and it will fill your entire soul. See to it then, My child, that the light inside you comes from Me, then, only then, My priest, will you understand that My Works are Sublime, Glorious and Majestic. Only then, pupil of Mine, will you understand as I desire you to understand why Humility allowed Himself to be disgraced, disfigured, despised and pierced and gave His Life as a ransom for many. I have come to stir your love and rouse it, see? So do not shield your flesh from pain nor from any mortification. Allow the Seal of your Saviour to be on your flesh as well as in your soul so that a complete transformation be done inside you. EVERYTHING then that your nature repelled, objected to and looked at with disdain, will appear to you Divine. ♥

---

[1]Meaning the intimacy.

Grant Lord that everything You say, be done. Lower my head, lower me and lower my voice. I do not want to appear empty handed in Your Presence. No, I do not want to end up in Your Presence with empty hands. And those human thoughts my nature finds natural, uproot them and burn each one of them.

Devote your soul entirely to Me and reflect on My Law before it comes upon you. Do not forget how your nature had reduced you to desert and desolation. I shall rid your human thoughts if you allow Me and replace them with My Thoughts to glorify Me. I will give you a courageous heart, My little one, to be able to face My opponents and resist their contradictions. I shall give you an eloquence of speech, an endurance and a resistance to the menaces of your persecutors, who are My persecutors too. I shall give you courage to stand with confidence.

You are My seed and because the Harvest is ready, and the crop ready to be reaped, I do not loose time as you have noticed. I reap without ceasing to feed many who are at the point of death. So, My beloved, "put your sickle in too and reap. Harvest time has come and the harvest of the earth is ripe."[1] Allow Me to widen the space of your heart, for now your Captor will fill you with His Knowledge and His Confidences. I am only waiting to be gracious to all of you and reveal to each one of you My Riches, My Generosity and My Love. I am telling you today all this so that My Word goes from this generation to the next; and you who are learning will, in your turn, teach your own children. ♥ If they listen and do as I say, their days will end up in happiness. So turn to Me and praise My Works. Meditate on My Wonders. ΙΧθΥΣ ⤜⫐

ST MICHAEL'S FEAST

September 29th, 1991

St Michael:

I love you child of God, trust Me. ♥

The Lord:

Rest in My Heart. I the Lord bless you. Come, My Heart is your rest. ♥

---

[1] Apocalypse 14:15.

I AM THE LORD OF PEACE, NOT OF DISSENSION

September 30th, 1991

I give thanks to Your Name for Your Love and Mercy; though I live in a place where I am surrounded by persecutors, false witnesses and abuses, You keep me alive and on my feet. You fill my table and like a most tender mother You feed me by Your own Hand. O Lord, pity me, sometimes I have trouble more than I could stand, and if I did not have You near me, I would be finished! I want a complete peace between brothers.

I say peace be with you! Stand up and call My servant![1] "I am the Lord of Peace not of dissension and I have offered you My Heart; let no one be deceived; those who linger over grudges for too long I shall withdraw from them My Heart and all the favours I so generously offered them; unless My servant collaborates with love and stops brooding over this sin, I tell you that I will withdraw all of My favours: never model your conduct on the One who divides; I am giving you a Treasure of Unity, ever so frail; learn to protect this Treasure. ♥ "

BLESS ME FOR THOSE WHO NEVER DO

September 30th, 1991

Jesus?

I Am. Little one, saturated by Me, you will not fail Me, at your side I Am and always will be. Bless Me for those who never do, reveal Me without fear, without doubt and hell shall not prevail. Caress Me. Yes, look in My Face and say: "Jesus I love You. You are my Life, my smile, my hope, my joy, my everything, be blessed." Come, rest in My Heart and allow Me to rest in yours. ♥

---

[1] Message for someone.

BLESSING ON HIM WHO COMES
IN THE NAME OF THE LORD

October 1st, 1991

To the Canadian pilgrims (140 laymen and 9 priests), at Lens, who came to spend a week with me.

Tell them that today like yesterday and always I bless them. Let every ear open and hear, every heart open to receive My Word. All I ask from them is love, fidelity and a continuous prayer. I shall be with you soon. Come. ♥

In the evening.

My Lord You have come and revived my soul and since then a new life trickles in me because this Stream flows from Your Own Sanctuary. Look at Your child, Lord? Alive again! You have redeemed me, You have redressed me and You showed me the fathoms of Your Love. Your fragrance mesmerized me and Your Beauty left me forever dazzled and hung on You. Your Tenderness and Graciousness set a spring in me, blessed be Your Name for ever and ever! In You every race shall be blessed and all nations will, in the end one day, united in one, cry out:

> "Blessings on him who comes in the Name of the
> Lord!"

For as the rain allows the earth to sprout, so will the River[1] from Your Sanctuary irrigate Your cities.[2]

MEDITATE ON IS. 54:5

October 2nd, 1991

To the Canadian pilgrims:

Peace be with you. Let this day be a day of joy! Soon My salvation will come, so be prepared to receive Me. Besides you whom I have already gathered under My

---

[1] Holy Spirit.
[2] Our souls.

Name, there are others I shall gather. Ask My children to meditate on (Isaiah 54:5)

> *For your Creator is your husband. Yahweh Sabaoth is His Name.* ♥

Let everyone today call Me,

Spouse

Pray for the peace of the world, pray for Our intentions. ♥ IXθYΣ ⊃

I HAVE SENT YOU MY FRIENDS

October 3rd, 1991

During Mass together with the Canadian pilgrims, Jesus said to me in a locution:

"I have sent you My friends."

WELCOME ME AS I WELCOME YOU

October 4th, 1991

For the Canadian pilgrims:

Lean on Me, give Me all your worries, thrust them all in My Heart and I shall annihilate them. Bless Me as I bless you, love Me as I love you. Creation! Realize that all I ask from you is a return of love! I confer on you everlasting blessings, so today and every day put your trust in Me. Draw from My Heart's Wells and I shall fill you, investing you with My splendour. I know your hardships and your extreme poverty so do not be afraid, to come to Me as you are:

- poverty infatuates Me -

Welcome Me as I welcome you. Go in Peace and be the witnesses of He who loves you more than any other man. Be witnesses of He who offered you His Sacred Heart. IXθYΣ ⊃

I AM SENDING YOU LIKE LAMBS AMONG WOLVES, BUT DO NOT FEAR

October 5th, 1991

To the Canadian pilgrims:

Peace be with you. Restore My House. I am sending you like lambs among wolves but do not fear, I Am is with you. Embellish My House by your devotion to My Sacred Heart and the Immaculate Heart of your Mother. ♥ *I bless you all, leaving the Sigh of My Love on your forehead.* ΙΧθΥΣ ⋈

UNITY MESSAGE
THEIR DIVISION HAVE SEPARATED MY HEART FROM THEIRS, BE THE DEFENDER OF THE TRUTH

October 7th, 1991

I want to put everything I have for Your Glory. I do not have much, in fact I have next to nothing because I am insufficient, poor, weak and most wretched, yet whatever I might have, take it my Lord.

My closeness[1] to you has lit a fire inside you and saved you and others. I want your free will, offer yourself to Me and I shall make rivers flow out of you. I need intense poverty to bring My Works out on the surface. I will supply your soul since you are my bride.

Vassula, your cities are filled with dead and their stench rises all the way to Heaven, they are decomposing by the millions. Pray, pray for peace, love, faith and unity. ♥ *The Holy One is tormented about that which has to come, saddened beyond description. I will have to let My Hand fall on this evil generation.*

Daughter, for My sake, take My Cross of Unity and carry It across the world. Go from country to country and tell those who speak of unity, yet never cease to think the contrary and continue to live the contrary, that their division has separated My Heart from theirs. Shout and eventually My Voice shall break through their

---

[1]His intimacy.

deafness. I am with you in this desolation so do not fear. ♥ I have entrusted you with My Cross, this Cross will sanctify you and save you and so carry It with love and humility. Invoke My Name without ceasing. Your Mission, My child, is to witness for Love and to demonstrate My Holiness in their lack of love and fidelity. Go forward without fear and be My Echo. ♥ Witness with joy, with fervour, witness with love for Love. ♥ Whenever My enemies pierce you, rejoice! and offer all your wounds to Me and I shall soothe you immediately. Every time you lift your eyes looking for Me, My Heart rich in Mercy will not resist you. You are My child whom I adopted, raised and fed, so do not fear men, they cannot destroy you. Soon I shall set you free. In the meantime, go around with My Cross of Unity and glorify Me.

Be the defender of the Truth

and of the One Church I Myself have established. Go to every nation and present yourself to them. ♥ Tell them that I want Peace and One Church under My Holy Name - tell them that he who maintains to be just, yet remains divided, will eat from the fruit he has sown and will perish. ♥ Tell them also how I abhor insincere hearts, their solemnities and their discourses weary Me. Tell them how I turn away from their loftiness and their rigidity. Their judgement appears indeed great and impressive to men but not to Me, I cannot congratulate a dying Church nearing putrefaction. Tell those who want to hear that:

unless they lower their voices, they will never hear mine

Should they lower their voices then they will begin to hear Mine and thus do My Will. I am One, yet each one of them made a Christ of their own. I am The Head of My Body, yet all I see are their heads, not Mine. Tell them to lower their heads and they will see Mine, tell them to lower themselves so that I may be able to lift them to Me.

Do not let them terrify you, My child, be patient as I am patient. Be prudent by remaining by My side. You will wear My Jewels¹ so that you remain faithful to Me. They will keep reminding you of Me. Pray, My bride, pray to your Spouse and I shall in the end reward you. Glorify Me and I tell you: toil, sacrifice and nothing will go in vain. ♥

Tell everyone that I shall establish My Kingdom in the midst of

poverty

---

¹His Cross, Nails and Thorned Crown.

those very ones who have time to hear My Spirit, adore Me and do My Will - in these My Soul rejoices!

Daughter, I love you in spite of your misery. Allow Me to continue My Works in you. Adjust to Me as I adjust to you and through you My Presence will be felt, and in you I shall draw this generation to unity. Be confident because I am with you. My Seal is on your forehead and with this Seal and with My Grace, My Kingdom on earth will be established as I want. Have My Peace. Remember: I am with you all the time. Come, enter into My Wounds. ΙΧθΥΣ ⋈

UNITY MESSAGE

I INTEND TO REBUILD MY CHURCH ON THE VIRTUES
YOU HAVE MENTIONED
UNITY WILL NOT BE OF THE LETTER
BUT OF THE SPIRIT

October 13th, 1991

There is no one, my Lord, in my heart but You. Little by little You correct me. You have won my heart showering blessing upon blessing on me. But am I doing Your Will now? Am I near You following You? Am I coming to my neighbour's help as far as I can? Am I following Your Commandments? Am I enjoying Your favour still?

Learn to lean on Me. Daughter, are you willing to continue carrying the Cross I have predestinated for you?

I am willing, so long as I do not lose You and am with You, united and one.

Do you know what this means and what it requires?

Sacrifice, abasement, humility, effacement, <u>love</u>, <u>faith</u>, <u>hope</u>, docility, self-abnegation, prayer, prayer, prayer, patience, penance, mortification, suffering, fasting, and trust in You? and a spirit of forgiveness.

You have said well, but it is not just to know these things. You want to remain in My favour? Then you must put everything you mentioned into practice. ♥ *The Kingdom of Heaven is like a trophy, he who wins it will cherish it. Again, the*

Kingdom of Heaven will be given to those who come with their hands full of good fruit ♥ *and so My Vassula, I intend to rebuild My Church on the virtues you have mentioned. If you walk with Me you will not be lost. Do not be tempted to look to your left or to your right, as I had said to My disciples "salute no one on the road."[1] You want to serve Me as you say, you must follow Me then with My Cross of Peace, Love and Unity to glorify Me. Do not look with consternation on the other crosses I lay on your way, since they all come from Me. Glorify Me. Your table is always full and your cup brimming over, so do not complain for nothing, I shall probe you and test your love for Me now and then to build you spiritually.* ♥ *Do not drag your feet behind Me, follow My pace light-heartedly. Rest in Me when you are weary and allow Me to rest in you when I feel weary. Listen now to your Holy One, do not be taken away by every wind that comes your way. Be rooted in Me and you will not be uprooted. Daughter, enrich My Church with all the Knowledge I have given you and tell them that the Heart of the Lord is an Abyss of Love, yet no man is fully aware of its depths nor of its riches. I know you are frail daughter, yet have you lacked resources? Trust Me, trust Me, and be the reflection of what Unity will be like. Do not be like those who persist in differentiating themselves under My Holy Name. Do not be like those who pretend that Unity is appealing to them and remain dead to their word, achieving nothing but a resentment from the Father. Both the Father and I abhor their arguments, contrary to what they think.* ♥ *Yet nothing retains Me from crying out to these men of power:*

"Descend! Descend from your thrones and may these scales on your eyes fall to see what a desolation you have made out of My House! You have robbed My Sanctuary and all that was within it! You shattered the Shepherd's staff not only in half but in splinters! but today, open your eyes and see! Keep your eyes open and you will get to know poverty, sackcloth and barefootedness[2], keep your eyes open and with one look get to know My Heart."

I could utter only one word in their assemblies and with that single word unite My Church but the glory of Heaven will be given to Me by Poverty, Wretchedness and by those they call contemptible. I will have My House rebuilt by strangers, for in them I will place a spirit of zeal, a spirit of fidelity, then your stores will be filled again and your vats overflowing with My new wine. ♥ *If you say you love Me and call yourself under My Name, then for the sake of My Holy Name and the sake of My Love:*

unify My churches

---

[1] Luke 10:4.
[2] Poverty, sackcloth and barefootedness symbolizes Jesus' Heart.

The real Christian is the one who is <u>inwardly</u> a Christian, and the real Unity is and will be <u>in</u> the heart. Unity will not be of the letter but of the spirit.

If you love Me daughter, as you say, embrace the Cross I have given you, your feet then will not stumble. Nothing in this world is Its equal. Let your gaze never leave My Gaze. Pupil? Come, follow Me... ΙΧθΥΣ ⤲◗

MESSAGE FOR THE PRISONERS

October 13th, 1991

Strangeway Prison, England

Vassula, I prayed for you to the Father, it is I, Jesus. Concentrate on what has been assigned you. Now write:[1] peace be with you. I heard you call Me 'Father!'

<u>Here I Am</u>.

Do you wish to come back? I shall frown on you no more since I am Infinite Mercy, I shall not pronounce sentence on you either. <u>Your heart is what I am seeking</u>. ♥ I need love, I am thirsty for love. My Lips are parched for lack of love. I have decided not to look on your past, only at the present. The Queen of Heaven[2] is by My side and of all women She persistently prayed for you, more than all Sovereignties, Dominations, Thrones, Powers and Angels, more than any created thing. So welcome Her in your prayers, honour Her as I honour Her. You are all baptised in Me and there should not be any distinction between brothers. If you only knew what I am offering you today you would not hesitate to offer Me your heart and your abandonment. Come back to Me and do not fear, the One who speaks to you now is your Holy Companion, He who loves you most. Believe in My Love, consider and meditate on <u>My Passion</u>. Offer Me your heart and I shall turn it into a garden with the subtlest odours, where I, your King, can take My rest. ♥ Allow Me to make it My Property and you shall live, do not turn your heart away from Me. Do not keep Me at a distance, speak to Me freely, <u>I am</u> listening. I invite you all to meditate on these words:

<u>- repay evil with love -</u>
<u>- imitate Me -</u>

---

[1]Message for the prisoners.
[2]Our Lady.

and remember, I am with you all the time, never, ever forget this. I bless each one of you, leaving the Sigh of My Love on Your forehead.

ΙΧθΥΣ ⤬◯Þ   Jesus Christ Beloved Son of God and Saviour.

UNITY MESSAGE
I DO NOT WANT ADMINISTRATORS IN MY HOUSE
UNIFY, FOR MY SAKE, THE FEAST OF EASTER

October 14th, 1991

Lord?

I Am. Evangelize with love for Love. Be rooted in Me, My child. Hand over everything to Me and allow Me to be your Spiritual Director, directing you and giving you My directives for the unification of My Churches. You are to be a sign for them and they will learn that since I Am is One, you too will be one as We are One. Scriptures will be fulfilled because My Sacerdotal Prayer to the Father will be accomplished. ♥ I am in you so do not fear.

This is very promising Lord!

Your mission, little one, is to bring My people under one Name, My Name, and break bread together. ♥ There is no need to worry, do your best and I will do the rest. I need humility to accomplish My Works in you and thus bring everything on the surface.

Your faithless generation, that sheds so much Blood from Me, will rebuff you, but My Vassula, I shall hold you on your feet in spite of the impressive wounds you will receive from this evil generation, help will be given to you from above. I have preached to you and to others. Do not stop there, forward the Teachings I have given you both in public and in your homes. ♥ I know how frail you are but I also know what I have chosen. ♥

Lord, I feel content to know that we will be united, although no one yet really knows how. The problems are apparently great and the schisms greater still. As You say "the staff of the Shepherd has been broken not only in half, but in splinters. And Your Body has been mutilated, wrenched and paralysed." You ask us all to <u>bend</u>. How? What is to be done? Which is the first step? I am a Greek Orthodox and I am sharing with my Roman Catholic brothers everything, and I do not differentiate myself under Your Name when I am with them, nor do they treat me any different from their own. I also know that many of them go to the Greek or Russian Orthodox churches...

Speak up child!

Give me the right words Lord.

Say... and they are not allowed to share Your Body.

No. They are not allowed, although our Sacraments are the same. Yet we Orthodox are allowed to share Your Body. I was even told I was excommunicated because I go to the Roman Catholics not to say more. I am also persecuted from both sides because my confessor is a Roman Catholic! And You do witness all this my Lord Jesus!

Yet, the day will come when they will break bread together on one altar ♥ and no one will stop My children from coming to Me. No one will ask them "are you an Orthodox?"[1] This fortress they have built to divide you is already condemned by Me. You are all brothers in Me, this is what you are to teach them to believe and persuade them to do. As for those who remain divided in body and spirit, differentiating themselves under My Holy Name I tell them as I have told the church in Sardis:[2] "you are reputed to be alive in the eyes of the world but not in your Maker's Eyes. Revive what little you have left, it is dying fast and wherever the corpse is, there will the vultures gather." Unite! Assemble! Invoke My Name together! Consecrate My Body and My Blood together! Do not persecute the Way! Humble yourselves and bend to be able to unite and glorify Me. You speak of the Spirit but do not act in the Spirit. ♥ You speak of the Way but you rank first to obstruct It! How little do you know Me... You call out My Name, yet you murder My children between the sanctuary and the altar. I tell you solemnly, all of this will be brought to you in the Day of Judgement. ♥ Can you face Me and truly say "I am reconciled with My brothers." Can you truly say "I have not differentiated myself among brothers, under Your Holy Name, I have treated them as my equal." When you present your case before Me I shall then say to your face "away with you, you have not treated your brothers as your equal, you have massacred daily My Body. Where is your triumph? While I was building, you were tearing down, while I was reassembling you were scattering, while I was uniting you were dividing!" Yet, even today, if you come to Me as you are, I can

---

[1] Apparently the Greek and Russian Orthodox priests have the right to ask the person who wants to receive Holy Communion whether they 'belong' to them. They refuse the Roman Catholics from receiving Holy Communion although the sacraments are the same.
[2] Apocalypse 3.

heal you, I can transfigure you and you will glorify Me. "Alas for those with child, or with babies at the breast, when My Day comes!" Write:[1] alas for those I find with sin coiled in them as with child and with adepts formed by them and of their own kind. ♥ *But it has been said that from your own ranks there will be men coming forward with a travesty of the Truth on their lips to induce the disciples to follow them. (Acts 20:30) I am shouting and I am trying to break through your deafness to save you, and if I reproach you it is because of the*

Greatness of the Love
I have for you.

But I tell you truly, I shall assemble one day <u>all</u> the separated parts of My Body together into One assembly. Do not weep My friend,[2] you who love Me. Endure what I endure, however, console Me and have faith in Me. You will achieve great works in My Name. Be tolerant as I am tolerant. I had been hungry, thirsty and often starving and you came to My help. Carry on your good works and I shall reward you. I tell you truly, you are not alone, I am with you. Be united in Me and live in peace. You are the posterity of My Blood and the heir of My Kingdom. Tell them that the Heart of the Lord is Love and that the Heart of the Law is based on Love. Tell My people that I do not want administrators in My House, they will not be justified in My Day because it is these very ones who have industrialized My House. ♥ *I have sent you My Spirit to live in your hearts, this is why the Spirit that lives in you will show you that My Church will be rebuilt inside your hearts and you will acknowledge each other as your brother in your heart.*

[3]*<u>Will I, brother, one more season</u>*
<u>go through the pain I have been</u>
<u>going through year after year?</u>
<u>or will you give Me rest</u>
<u>this time?</u>
<u>Am I going to drink one more</u>
<u>season the Cup of your division?</u>
<u>or will you rest My Body</u>
<u>and unify, for My sake,</u>
<u>the Feast of Easter?</u>

In unifying the date of Easter, you will alleviate My pain brother and you will

---

[1] Jesus means the explanation of this verse of Luke 21:23.
[2] Jesus speaks to those who truly love Him and are truly and sincerely working to unite the Churches. His friends.
[3] My Jesus, in saying all this, had taken the voice of a victim. Weary, begging, as though He depended on us. Like a prisoner in a cell going to the door of his cell and asking the guard, from the little window, how much longer yet was his sentence before the day of his liberation.

380

rejoice in Me and I in you ♥ and I will have the sight of many restored. "My Beloved! My Creator! He who is my Husband has revealed to us things that no human hand could have performed!", this is what you will cry out once your sight is restored, in My Name, ♥

- and I will come to you -[1]

I solemnly tell you: summon, assemble all of you and listen this time to your Shepherd. I will lead you in the way that you must go.

Send My Message to the ends of the earth. ♥ Courage daughter, smile when I smile. I am with you to guide your steps to heaven. IXθΥΣ ⟩⟨⟩

IN TIME OF FAMINE, I CAME

October 17th, 1991

Message given to the "reapers" God selected in the United States to print this book.

I give you all My Peace and bless you. I am with you to uphold your work in My Name and which I have blessed for this is the work assigned to you all to glorify Me.

- In time of famine, I came -

to fill your mouths with My Celestial Manna so that you will not perish. I will never desert you, Love will return as Love. IXθΥΣ ⟩⟨⟩

And Our Blessed Mother also gives them a message:

Ecclesia will revive. Glory be to God. I am the Queen of Heaven, your Mother and I bless you. Pray for peace, pray for faith, love and unity. Pray for the conversion of all My children. I want everybody to be saved. God's Works of Light cannot be hidden forever[2], this is why I have chosen you to be God's reapers. ♥ I love you all with a great love and I thank you for dedicating the

---

[1] Jesus said this as a King, majestically.
[2] That is because of the many obstacles Satan had put to stop the Messages of the Sacred Heart from spreading.

Lord's Books to Me.[1] Have faith little ones, the Lord is with you. ♥ Follow Him. Be confident for I am with you. Come.

I ASK LOVE, TO BREAK THE BARRIERS
OF YOUR DIVISION

October 20th, 1991

Message from the Sacred Heart to Belgium. Read out in Bruxelles at St Michael's Hall of the Jesuits' College, on 20th October 1991.

My Lord, be with me.

Feel confident because I Am is with you. My Vassula tell them this: if many have forgotten My Sacred Heart, I have never forgotten them. ♥ I have called them, assembling them here today to pray together. I desire My children united. I desire My entire Church to be united. Those that persist in remaining separated have already separated My Heart from theirs. Realize the gravity of your division, the urgency of My call and the importance of My request. I need your heart to unite you and rebuild My Church united into one inside your heart. All I ask is love, to break the barriers of your division. Pray, you who have offered Me your heart and unite your heart with My Sacred Heart for the unity of My Churches. I, the Lord, bless each one of you leaving the Sigh of My Love on your forehead. I Jesus love you. ΙΧθΥΣ ⋉⊃

NO POWER FROM BENEATH CAN OR WILL EVER
SEPARATE YOU FROM ME

October 21st, 1991

Your Mercy, O Lord, has breathed in me, and inspired a living Spirit within me, in the very core of where He dwells. It was Your Word, Lord, who heals all things that healed me. And the invisible God became suddenly visible to me. And the

---

[1]The group who printed the English books, dedicated one of them to our Blessed Mother.

dimness of my eyes saw a Light, a pillar of Blazing Fire, to guide my steps to Heaven. And the Darkness that imprisoned me and terrified my soul was overpowered by The Morning Star, and gave my soul Hope, Love and Peace and a great consolation, because I knew that Love and Compassion Himself was my Holy Companion for the journey of my life.

My child, Love is with you and no power from beneath can or will ever separate you from Me; walk in My Light and remain united to Me. ♥

COME TO ME LIKE THE PUBLICAN

October 22nd, 1991

Jesus dress me in humility, purity and observation to Your Law, for this will please the Father.

Peace be with you, for this I tell you: be like the publican ♥ *for many of you condemn your neighbour, forgetting how only yesterday, you too, were locked in the same sleep. Do not say "I have made my house tidy and ready for the Lord, He may come now to me anytime, I am ready to receive Him. I am not like my neighbour, who does not fast, does not pray but goes on living a wicked life." Receive your sight I tell you, your lips have already condemned you. Cure yourself first and do not condemn the others who do not know their left hand from their right hand. Come to Me like the publican and ask Me to be merciful to you, the sinner,[1] for you are all subjects to sin. Temple! Rise and serve Me your God, by helping the widow[2] you will be serving Me. Go now in Peace, I am with you.* ♥

Glory be to God.

---

[1] Greek rosary.
[2] That is, my mother. God made a point not to call her "mother" since the only Mother we have is our Blessed Mother. I'm supposed to leave and go shopping food with her.

I ALLOW MYSELF TO BE TOUCHED
THE TWO LAMPS

October 24th, 1991

Lord, allow me to serve You. This is my due to You now. You are known for Your Mercy and I know that if I cling to You, You will not just shake me off. I know You will rescue me.

> 'I have only to open my mouth for You to fill it.'
> (Psalm 81:11)

Please feed me with Your Manna.[1]

Remain in My favour. I am not a God who cannot be moved. ♥ My Heart is filled with Compassion and I allow Myself to be touched. Come, I am your Shield in these times of battle.

Lord, I am numbered among those who are violently attacked by Satan. How can Your people hear of Your marvels in the dark? The devil wants to paralyse all Your Plan! For how long yet Your Righteousness will lie in a land of oblivion? Show now, Lord of Mercy and of Justice, that You are our help and consolation.

You need not fear, in the end Our Hearts will prevail. ♥ I will show everyone how I can save. Scriptures have to be accomplished. You see it is written[2] that the beast that comes out of the Abyss is going to make war on the Two Lamps that stand before the Lord of the world, those Two Witnesses who represent My Body and are My Body; those that have proven they are My servants, by their great fortitude in times of suffering, trials and persecution; those who carry My Word and are My mouthpieces and those who have been given the Truth to be as angels and an Echo of the Word, since they have allowed My Spirit to be their Guide giving each one of them an Elijah ministry. ♥ The appeal that they make in My Name is in fact My appeal through them, they raise their voices to remind you of My Law, like Moses on the mountain at Horeb, but it is I, through them, that speak. And although for the people of the world these Two Prophets[3] will appear as overcome by the Enemy, I shall breathe life into them and they will stand up. "For as the earth makes fresh things grow, as a garden makes seeds spring up, so will I, the Lord, make both Integrity and Praise spring up in the sight of the

---

[1] The Holy Spirit.
[2] Apocalypse 11:7.
[3] The spirit of Elijah and Moses : the spirit of prophecies.

384

nations." (Isaiah 61:11) I will transfigure your wretched bodies into copies of My glorious Body, ♥ then you will see a new heaven and a new earth sprout up. The first earth and the first heaven shall disappear, that is: the old City known by the symbolic names Sodom and Egypt, for My Word was crucified again within her[1] because the people of the world did not recognize Me again. Although I came to My own Domain, My own people <u>again</u> did not accept Me but treated My Holy Spirit as they pleased, allowing the Beast to make war on those I have sent. These two cities in one. Sodom and Egypt, rejection they had of My Messengers and the total deafness similar to the stubbornness of Pharaoh, these cities will be replaced by the New Jerusalem. From Sodom and Egypt you shall be called:

- New Jerusalem -

City of Integrity, City of Holiness; and when this will happen, the survivors overcome with fear would only praise Me.[2] The earth now is pregnant and in labour, My child, crying aloud in the pangs of childbirth, but the time of waiting is very soon over. I am already breathing on you creation, reviving you one after the other, purifying you all. So if anyone has objected, he has not been objecting to you, but to Me, I who have given you My Holy Spirit of Truth, and if they re-crucified anyone between the two cities by the symbolic names Sodom and Egypt, they re-crucified My Word. But after three-and-a-half days[3] My Two Lamps will give out a brighter Light, because it will come from the brightness that surrounds the Spirit. ♥ So have hope My child, the pledge of My Spirit is for your times. ♥ You are part of My Household. Ecclesia shall revive.

α ☧ Ω

COME, DO NOT BE TEMPTED BY VIOLENCE ANY MORE

October 24th, 1991

- Message for the Philippines -

Peace be with you. Tell My people to reflect upon My Law. Write:

- I am reconciling the world -

---

[1] That is, the old City. Ap. 11:8.
[2] Apocalypse 11:13.
[3] Apocalypse 11:11 - symbolic number.

Tell them that it is I, Jesus. Should they ask what is My Message for them, tell them:

- I am coming to reconcile you to My Sacred Heart -

and in reconciling you to Myself, I will ask you for the sake of My great Love to reconcile with one another. I intend to reconcile the world to My Sacred Heart and thus make a new creation out of you all.[1]

<u>*This is the pledge of My Spirit.*</u>

I tell you solemnly, he who sows the seeds of self-indulgence will reap a harvest of corruption and when he faces Me in the Day of Judgement I will tell him:

"Go! Away from Me! Go to the Corrupt one who corrupted you!"

<u>*Unless I hear a cry of repentance*</u>

the smell of death that leads to death will continue to rise all the way to Heaven. I want no more of this. What I desire from you is:

<u>*- incense -*</u>

I desire you to be like an incense bowl filled with incense, on an altar. Beloved children, let your country be transformed into a huge Altar offering Me the fragrance of incense. ♥ I want you to live holy since I am Holy. ♥ Each day I stretch out My Hands towards you to lift you to Me. I have shown My Love for you through ages and today again, like a shepherd rescuing his sheep from the lion's mouth, I come to rescue you from the Viper. ♥ I shall in spite of your appalling wretchedness not overthrow you as I overthrew Sodom and Gomorrah. I know how oppressed your needy are and how the poor are crushed daily. I know too how miserable you are and oh! I know your crimes... and they are many. Due to the violence done to your sons the innocent blood shed in your country is great! Your misfortunes acquired from sin have challenged My Mercy and for the sake of the greatness of My Love I call your people today together. Summon everyone under My Holy Name and tell them that I do not put anyone on trial, neither do I come to menace you. Tell your people that I shall outpour My Spirit of Love upon them. Like a veil from above I shall spread over your country and like mist My Spirit of Love shall envelop you, and penetrate even from the hinges of your doors and windows. Your people will not be disappointed of My Visit. ♥ I shall with My Purifying Fire devour corruption and like a reaper I shall put in My Sickle

---

[1]Apocalypse 21:1.

and cut this harvest of evil, tie it together into a bundle and thrust it into the fire to be burnt and in its place I shall sow seeds from Heaven: seeds of Love. ♥ *This is your Lord speaking, this is the One who loves you more than any man can understand.*

It is I, Jesus, your Saviour,

at your doors now and I tell you again: Come! Come to Me, you who are oppressed, I shall comfort you and console you. Come! Come and have all the Treasures of My Sacred Heart. The Kingdom of God[1] is among you, you only have to step inside it. My House is your house. I have opened the door to My Kingdom for <u>everyone</u>. ♥ *Come, do not be tempted by violence any more, repay evil with love.*

<u>Forgive!</u>

How else will the Father forgive <u>you</u> if you are not willing to forgive? Eat from My fruit and not from the fruit of My enemy, for the children of darkness are wicked in dealing even with their own kind because Evil is their master who teaches them to be like him. And the man who is dishonest in little things will be dishonest in greater things too. ♥ *Call together your friends and pray, I shall hear you prayer.*

<u>Every repentant sinner will be heard in Heaven</u>

I Jesus bless you all leaving the Sigh of My Love on your forehead. ♥
ΙΧθΥΣ ⋈⊃

---

[1]That is the Church.

UNITY MESSAGE
IS THERE ANY GENEROUS MAN AMONG YOU?
SOLEMNITIES AND DISCOURSES DO NOT INTEREST ME

October 25th, 1991

Lord?

I Am. ♥

Lord, bind me to You even more now and keep me away from insults of men because I love ecumenically. Bind me to Your Heart and when I walk let Your Light be my Guide. When I lie down let Your Spirit watch over me and when I wake up make my spirit talk to Your Spirit. Let me act like You and court You. Make my heart eager to seek You so that I pay everything I vowed to You.

Remind us all, Lord, what You had given us. You had given us One sturdy Holy Church filled with Your Holy Spirit, not an empty rubble. You had given us One solid Staff, not two or three or a heap of splinters, where has all this gone?

Vassula, let Me tell you first. The insults of those who insult you fall on Me - so do not give up. Carry My Cross of Unity from nation to nation and be My Echo.
♥ To refresh the memories of My people I am sending My Holy Spirit to remind them to adopt a mutual love that leads to peace and mutual understanding. In My preliminary Messages about Unity I had asked you all to bend, but have I today anyone who is ready to listen to what My Spirit says?

- Is there among you any good man left?
- Is there anyone who really looks for Me?
- Has anyone yet lowered his voice to hear Mine?
- Who is the first righteous man among you who will decline and fade away so that My Presence be seen?
- Who among you is ready to lower his head and allow My Head to be revealed?
- Is there any generous man among you who will lower his voice and hear My supplicating prayer to the Father?

> *Am I, Father*
> *to drink one more season of the Cup of their division*
> *or will they at least unify the Feast of Easter*
> *alleviating part of My pain and sorrow?*
> *Will this reign of Darkness last much longer?*
> *They have severed My Body*

and have forgotten that it is My Head
which strengthens and holds the whole Body together.
O Father!
Reconcile them and remind them
that by My death on the Cross
I have given them My Peace.
Give them the Spirit of Truth
in its fullness into their hearts
and when they see their nakedness
they will understand.
Forgive them Father
for they know not what they are doing.

The Citadel of the proud shall fall into a heap of dust My child.[1]

Their pride and glory will fall when My Spirit besieges them, just wait and You shall see. ♥ *Write: are you really listening? Are you really listening to what I am saying? What I am saying to you means Peace for My own and for My friends. They would understand if they, from today, renounce their folly. For you who love Me without reserve, and who fear Me, My saving help is at hand's reach and the glory will then live in each one of you. Love and Loyalty can meet, Righteousness and Peace can embrace. Loyalty can reach up from earth, for Righteousness always leaned from Heaven. I have been bestowing you happiness, what has your soil given as harvest? Righteousness always preceded Me and Peace followed My Footsteps, am I to say the same for you? Who will make up for the years of your division? Solemnities and discourses do not interest Me. Pretence and lip-service do not deceive Me either.*

Oh daughter, what I wish them to understand, especially those who live in My Wounds is, the greatness of My sorrow. And the reason why I have put some things rather strongly is to enable them to preach something of the Spirit and not of the letter. I want to fill their spirit with My Transcendent Light so that they see things with My Eyes and not with theirs, to see things with My Divine Light and not theirs. I am known to be Faithful and Righteous and it does not mean because they lack fidelity and righteousness, that I too will show them less Fidelity, Righteousness and Peace and not come to rescue them. Even if all of them turn away from Me and from My Ways, I will remain Faithful and True.[2] *My Spirit will be at work restoring Peace among brothers and through My Cross and My Wounds I will unite you all in one single Body and have you glorify Me around One Single Tabernacle and the barrier which keeps you apart will be broken. The*

---

[1] Here I had the impression the Father was answering.
[2] Apocalypse 19:11.

ban will be lifted¹ and My Sacrificial Throne will be in its place. ♥ Come to Me as little children, that I may open the eyes of your soul, that you may <u>see</u> what Hope My Call holds for you. ♥

Bless me daughter. ♥ Come. ΙΧθΥΣ ><D

I bless You Lord. "Bring forward the people that is blind, yet has eyes, that is deaf and yet has ears. Let all the nations muster and assemble with every race. Let men hear You so that they may say, 'it is true.'" (Isaiah 43:8-9)

NO ONE CAN STOP THIS HOUR OF MY HOLY SPIRIT

October 29th, 1991

My God!

I Am. Alone you are not; I am present and with you; Vassula, allow Me to speak to you, have faith in Me, I am near you, come, concentrate and meditate on Me; work for My Glory. ♥ Daughter, tell them² in this way: blessed are the poor in spirit for theirs is the kingdom of heaven; you are <u>all</u> very precious to Me; pray more than ever before and I will supply the wretched, I will heal the blind and teach each one of you My Law from the stranger to your own; Love loves you. ΙΧθΥΣ ><D

This is a preliminary message, as an introduction for my whole trip in England

Later on:

Vassula, be constant in your prayers; I love you My child and oh! do I know your weaknesses. Daughter, <u>bring My children to the real faith bring everyone to Me</u>, this is part of your mission too. ♥ Ah My child, be fervent for Me your Lord.

My Lord, not everyone listens to these messages when I proclaim them. Is it possible that they have not understood? I am not only talking for myself I am also talking about the present apparitions and about others You have used as Your instruments in a supernatural way. I will put it to You directly: how many in the

---

¹Apocalypse 22:3.
²The people I would be meeting in England.

high hierarchy today lend an ear and are positive? How many?

And how many of the high priests and scribes lent an ear to Me and were positive, only yesterday? Vassula, there is a remnant chosen by grace to believe. ♥ *Scriptures say: I revealed Myself to those who did not consult Me (Romans 10:20) yet from the very beginning I have invited <u>everyone</u> to My School;*

<u>My Holy Spirit is your Guide, your Husband[1] and your Master</u>

I tell you truly that soon I will gather all nations in a circle of Love and My Spirit will dwell in you giving sight to the blind, since the Light that will be given you is: My Transcendent Light; but how hard it is for those who have accumulated riches in their spirit to penetrate into My Light! How hard it is for the wise to penetrate into the Spirit and perceive Its depths! How hard it is for them to enter into My Kingdom! I tell you solemnly, the rejects of your society and those you call unworthy are making it before these; yes! Those who could not tell good from evil, those who could not tell their left hand from their right! I have been and am still inviting <u>everyone</u> to sit at table with Me, but many have not responded to My invitation, they laughed and scorned at My Gracious Call and caused others who wanted to come, stumble by their teaching. ♥ *Compare all this with My parable of the wedding feast (Matthew 22:1-14)*

I will come back[2]

and they will tremble; they will tremble when they will realize Whom they were <u>rejecting</u> all this time. They renounced My Spirit and allowed themselves to be guided by their own spirit, they renounced My Light for their own, they renounced My Heavenly Knowledge given by Wisdom for a second-rate philosophy and their own rational knowledge;

<u>- they have apostatised -</u>

Since they have rejected My Spirit, My Light and My Knowledge, I shall take away My Kingdom from them and give it to a people who can produce its fruit; I shall then welcome these people as My own and ask them to come with Me and keep house with Me; in fact this hour is here already; I have decided to draw near Me the disreputable, those that hang around on every street corner, the unworthy, the nothing of the nothings, the wretched and those who never knew My Name; I will turn to a wretched lot who never loved Me and make a nation of Love out of them,

---

[1]Allusion to Isaiah 54:5.
[2]Second Pentecost: The outpour of the Spirit: Joel 3.

a holy nation, and they will glorify Me. ♥ They will be called priests of the Living God, priests of the Amen, and in this priesthood I shall rebuild My Church, in these hearts I shall unite you all, and My Body will rest. ♥ The hour is here, and no one can stop this hour of My Holy Spirit. When you will see the world disintegrating under your feet, when you will look to your left and see tottering kingdoms and cities reduced into a heap of dust and to your right mountains tumbling, know that these signs are the beginning of the outpouring of My Holy Spirit; when you see My pupils whom I Myself have formed, preach fearlessly in My Name, do not disrupt them, resist your temptation and discern the sound of their footsteps, I will keep sending you these saints to gather on their way all the severed members of My Body, and no one, not even the unclean spirits would be able to stop them, these will instead fall down before them because they will know that the Amen is their Master ♥

> *the Amen is soon with you My child*
> *He who is your Consoler*
> *and whose Home is in inaccessible Light*
> *will eventually plunge you into His Light and absorb you;*
> *- I am Love ♥ -*

Blessed be Your glorious and Holy Name, praised and extolled for ever.

November 5th, 1991

England, Manchester

Just before going to the meeting in St Augustine's Church the devil attacked me with the aim to spoil the meeting. (I prayed to St Michael twice and I prayed two decades of the Rosary, to Rosa Mystica, the devil's grip released.) Our blessed Mother then gives me this message.

I am with you My child; do not fear, I will not leave you an inch from My sight; work in peace, Vassula; I love you, pray now and go in peace and remember, I am with you. ♥

November 6th, 1991

England

- Before going to Strangeways Prison to read to them their message -

My child all the strength you will receive will come from Me; show, My child, what the Lord says to the world; show them how My Eyelids run with weeping; let My people pray for those who do not invoke My Name and I shall cure them; the impossible will become possible; the desert will turn into a garden and the rubble into an altar for Me your God; tell My children to pray, pray with their heart and I shall listen. ♥ *I call all those who are crushed with pain to offer Me their pain and rest in My Heart; I shall help them carry their cross; so My Vassula feel My Presence; see Me with they eyes of your soul; speak to Me and allow Me to use you to glorify Me.* ♥

YOU ARE ALL SO VERY PRECIOUS TO ME

November 8th, 1991

England - Manchester

Peace be with you; My purpose for descending in this way is for your salvation; what I have commenced and blessed I shall finish; tell My children that when I speak to them, using you as a means, I mean Salvation, I mean Peace, I do not mean destruction, but the devil means destruction, for what he means kills; Faithful love leans all the way down from Heaven to reach you and offer you His Heart ♥ *you are all so very precious to Me; the Holy One is revealing His Face: I call each one of you without any distinctions; you are all Mine and you all belong to Me and your life is in My Hands perpetually. Do not be like those who seem to talk about Unity but yet draw a sword for the ones who practise it; come to Me as one family and we shall all sup together, I and you, you and I; I am allowing everyone to hear My Voice; I bless you all. Adorn Me with prayers from your heart.* IXθΥΣ ⋉◁

I SHALL INCREASE IN YOU AND NOT DECREASE

November 9th, 1991

Manchester

Lord?

I Am. Little one be blessed; there still are a few more things I wish to write through you; so allow Me to use you. ♥ *Think, daughter, what you have earned as Knowledge from Me; I will reinforce My temple[1] so that its structure becomes solidly strong and will remain unscathed from any blow that may come upon it; I shall increase in you and not decrease; let My Spirit rest in you, the Holy One gives you His Peace.* ♥

THE DRIFTWOOD

November 13th, 1991

Yahweh, I love You. I adore You. Yahweh, my celestial Love I know you are with me. Yahweh my Father and Abba, tell Your so-Beloved Son that my heart lives for Him only. Tell Him that He is the Air I breathe, My Life. Tell Him that my voice for His Sake will be carried as far as I can to proclaim His Desires and His Fervent Love for us. Tell Him, Father, that no one and nothing will ever come between this love I have for Him. Tell Him that He is my Smile, my Joy and my Hope. Tell my Redeemer how I long for Him and how I pine away with love for Him day and night.

Daughter, beloved of My Soul, did you not know? Did you not know how My Spirit reposes on Nothingness? Have you not heard how I delight revealing My entire Face to children? Have you not read: "I have been found by those who did not seek Me and have revealed Myself to those who did not consult Me." (Romans 10:20)

- *your Joy is your Maker,*
- *your Love is your Anointed One,*
- *your Torch is My Holy Spirit,*

---

[1]Jesus means me.

Benefit, My child, from all the gifts I have given you and restore My House.

I happened to be taking a walk nearby a river when I saw a driftwood[1] drifting away with the worldly current; I leaned over and picked it out of the stream; I brought it Home with Me and planted it in My Garden of Delights; <u>from a dry piece of wood I made out of you a Tree</u>; I said: "grow! grow and take root in My Garden, in My own Property; and from your blossoms exhale a perfume to appease My Justice." I said: "crops of fruit shall sprout each month and your leaves will be the cure to many." Now and then I amuse Myself in pruning you; My delight is to see flowers in blossom and a constant growth in your fruit. ♥ Alone, the Water[2] from My Sanctuary[3] can give you growth and Life; I, Yahweh, will see to it that you prosper; I take pleasure in picking now and then on My way pieces of driftwood[4]. I can give life to anything I pick on My way.

FROM THE TIME IN FATIMA TO THIS EPOCH, NONE OF MY WARNINGS HAVE BEEN RESPECTED

November 13th, 1991

Vassula, peace be with you. If the earth will shake and wither under their very eyes it will be because they have transgressed My Law which is based on <u>Love</u>; they have violated all My Commandments. In spite of the multiple intercessions of your Holy Mother and in spite of My Warnings, from the time in Fatima to this epoch, none of My Warnings have been respected. The hours are fleeing and a mighty host such as the world has never seen, nor will ever see again is at hand! Few men will be left; how I shout to break through your deafness! A nation roaring like the roar of many waters will flood the world again, with fire and brimstone, I am rich in forgiving, but I hardly hear any cry of repentance. Oh men of little faith! Men of arguments only!

Write: all I hear except from only a remnant is: "why should we have to believe in messages? Why should we fast since these are not from Him? Why do penance

---

[1] God means me.
[2] That is the Holy Spirit.
[3] That is the Heart of the Lord.
[4] God was hinting to me of another privileged soul He allowed me to meet.

since we are righteous? Why should we believe this frenzied lot? Do not listen for they retail visions and prophecies of their own." I tell you truly, when that Day comes it would have been preferable you were never born! It takes only one man to blow a fire to produce any heat; today again a man is among you living under the same skies who is ready to blow a Fire that can burn and melt all elements within a matter of seconds! The earth, like a garment will wear out; I had warned you, but you payed no heed. My suffering is great but how else am I to expel the merchants from within My Church? How am I to throw out the vipers from their nests inside My Sanctuary, if I am not to come with Flame and a Blazing Fire? Traders, merchants, the lot will be extirpated and this could be done only by Fire! The sages will boast no more of their wisdom nor of their authority; the rich in spirit will be laid barren and naked and they will mourn; they will look for Me but where they look they will not find Me. They will invoke My Name again and again but I shall not hear them; I shall overthrow the lot. ♥ Be one with Me My child, have My Peace, I love you very much. Justice is at hand. ☧

Later on:

Lean on Me; I am with you My child. Ah My little child, carry for My sake your burden upon your shoulders, love Me My child and you shall live. Evangelize with love for Love; accept all that comes from Me. Come, I and you, you and I united in love. I love you so much, My Vassula, so much little one... Ecclesia will revive.
IXθΥΣ ⊃<⊃

MESSAGE FOR IRELAND

November 14th, 1991

Listen, Ireland, disperse no more, assemble, assemble all in one. Come to Me in peace and pray together for peace. Empty your hearts of all your evil inclinations and learn where peace is, where love is, where sanctity is. ♥ Pray for those whose hands are dripping with blood, they know not what they are doing.

I have come to take aside the best of the flock to ask them if they are willing to make a general renunciation of nine days. The demons in this country will be panic-stricken. I know that your crimes are many and that only a remnant have My Seal on their forehead. I have passed through you, Ireland, and I have staggered in your lawlessness, but look! the Hour is at Hand, your land is parcelled by a measuring line but so is your heart Ireland My daughter, right down to your entrails[1]. Re-erect My tottering House by assembling in peace and without differentiating yourselves under My Name. Even though you are a remnant faithful to Me, be not discouraged, I shall bring you new wine with a blessing to moisten your lips, be not discouraged, your Saviour is on His way of Return. You are the bricks of My Sanctuary and at the same time the builders of My House. By uniting and re-assembling, there will be a structure, but if you remain divided and scattered how am I to re-construct what is in ruin now? I need you all together to make one unity and re-construct My House. ♥ *I need all the bricks.*

My Kingdom on earth is My Church and the Eucharist is the Life of My Church, this Church I Myself have given you. I had left you with one Church, but hardly had I left, just barely had I turned My back to go to the Father, than you reduced My House to a desolation! You levelled it to the ground! and My flock is straying left and right... for how long am I to drink of the Cup of your division? Cup of affliction and devastation? You have offered the Holy One, the One you say you love, a cup so wide and so deep, filled with bitterness and sorrow, that My palate is drier than parchment, My Lips covered with blisters; the flavour of this cup this generation is offering Me is as bitter as venom. I am not alone to swallow My Tears, your Holy Mother is sharing My grief since Her Immaculate Heart is united in love to My Sacred Heart. ♥ *But soon, I shall renew you all with My Fire.*

Pray without ceasing, for the Hour is at hand. I bless you all sealing your foreheads with the Sigh of My Love. ΙΧθΥΣ ⋉⟜▷

PRAY WITH ME

November 15th, 1991

My Lord?

I Am. Come to Me at all times; pray with Me, say:

> *You are my only God*
> *my only Hope*
> *my only Love,*
> *You are my God unrivalled,*

---

[1] God is talking of the different denominations of His Church.

ever so Tender and Delicate
with the weak and the wretched,
let not the Chalice of Your Justice
brim over us;
allow the captives to be set free
before Your Day my Lord,
our faults in Your Eyes have been many
and our rebellion and apathy even greater
in number,
but Your Heart is throbbing
with Love and Compassion,
give us O Father, most Gracious
a powerful Breath of Your Spirit
to revive us all
for Your Glory. ♥ *Amen.*

I bless you, My child. ♥

I AM NOT A COMPLICATED GOD

November 18th, 1991

Jesus? Holy One?

I Am. Little one, daughter of Mine peace be with you, I the Lord bless you and bless you. Evangelize with love for Love. Tell them that I love each one of them in a special way. Tell them also that I am not a complicated God, I am not far, I am present at this very moment. Tell them how I long for their love, show them what the Lord's Heart is. Tell them that the Lord's Heart is nothing else but Love and Mercy and if Justice is brought down upon you it is because of the graveness of your sins and crimes. How many times I overlook all that you do not do in My favour and how many times I kept away the Father's Hand from falling upon you! Jesus is My Name and Jesus means Saviour; I am the Saviour of all mankind. ♥
IXθYΣ ⌁

CORK, IRELAND

November 22nd, 1991

*Beloved children, I give you My Peace. The world is falling into decay, but I have
not forgotten you. I am visiting you in your distress to help each one of you reach
your Room in Heaven. You are Mine and you are all very precious to Me;*
I am the Light of the world
*so do not fear, I ask you to pray for those who have hardened their heart and do
not believe in the Truth. Never cease your prayers.*

*I, the Lord, have passed through your cities, Ireland, and although at the moment
you do not know the Plans I have designed for you; remain in My Divine Love and
you shall feel strong,*

- *remain in My Sacred Heart and you shall prosper,*
- *remain in My favour by your constancy and faith,*
- *remain in Me and you shall live.*

*I, the Lord, bless each one of you leaving the Sigh of My Love on your forehead;
remember, Love loves you.* IXθYΣ ⊂▷

GOD WILL BE COMING TO YOU, BUT YOU DO NOT
KNOW IN WHICH WAY

November 24th, 1991

**My child, I am the only Mother of all mankind, every single one of you is My
child.**

Holy Mother will every one, one day accept this Truth?

**In the end every soul will accept this truth. Those who sincerely love God now,
will accept it. Never cease praying My child for the conversion of the world;
understand the more prayers I obtain the less evil will be promulgated. Prayers
are never wasted; I offer them to the Father whose Justice is at hand. Pray to
obtain God's Mercy. You do not know what God has reserved for this evil
generation, but have in mind how in rebellious times His Hand fell on sinful**

men, and that was then, a fraction of what He has now in store for you. His Justice will respond from His Holy Abode in accordance to the sins of this generation. He will come with Fire, thunder, hurricane and flame of devouring Fire to burn up the crimes of the world. No, you do not know what the Almighty has reserved for you to purge mankind. <u>The signs are there all around you</u>, but few see or notice them. Innocent blood is shed of My sons and daughters for Satan; this innocent blood is offered like a holocaust to the Evil one. Satan's plan is to strip this world from its creation, annihilate you all and engulf you all in flames. He wants one big holocaust out of all of you; I shout, I cry out, I shed Tears of Blood, but few pay attention; God will be coming to you but you do not know in which way.

Holy Mother, we are praying but as You say, we are very few. What to Do?!

Your prayers can change the world. Your prayers can obtain God's Graces for the conversion of sinners and the more conversion the more prayers will be made and heard for other conversions, do you understand? Prayers are powerful; this is why I insist of you not to abandon your prayers and your sacrifices, the faithful are needed now more than ever. God will remember all your sacrifices, My dearest children, love Him and glorify Him. ♥ Ecclesia shall revive in all Her glory. ♥

Later on:

Lord?

I Am. Delight Me and do not keep silent in proclaiming the Truth. I have blessed your mission. I am your Rock and Shelter. If you lie low My Presence shall be seen in all its splendour; you will pray, I am listening.

> Lord, forgive us our guilt
> our wickedness, our failures, our intolerance,
> our lack of love,
> forgive us the lack of our love
> and sensitivity.
> Convert
> the wicked, the impenetrable, the lethargic,
> the atheists,
> and transfigure them into vessels of light
> to glorify You.
> Humble the proud, lower the high,
> bend the rigid;
> Transfigure us all as in Your Transfiguration.
> Amen.

Once My Holy Spirit besieges you, <u>you will all be transfigured</u>; I am always ready to forgive you; I love you little one, we, us?

Yes Lord.

I SHALL USE THIS WEAKNESS TO DRAW MY PEOPLE TO UNITY
MANY OF THEM TALK OF UNITY AND BROTHERHOOD, BUT THEIR WORDS ARE FALLACIOUS, VOID

November 25th, 1991

Lord, have I failed You in any way? You have called me but have I <u>really</u> responded You? Have I really listened to Your Voice, or have I been ignoring It? Have I maybe been insensitive to the appeals of Your Sacred Heart? Have You taken Your Loving Eyes off me O Holy of Holies?

In the anguish of my spirit, I pray and ask You:

Where are those Eyes so
loving upon me?

Where is my Abode
Your Sacred Heart?

How is it I cannot hear
Your Voice
or feel Your Presence?

Have I lost Your Friendship
because of my insensitivity?

Have I lost Your Companionship
O Holy of Holies?

My priest! The corpse will be tossed inside a hole, buried and forgotten. Daughter from Egypt, have My Peace. I have placed you in the land of the living. Look at Me and be confident of My Love and Friendship I have for you, do not make Me weep out of pain, how would I desert you? but the evil one is desperately trying to loot all the riches I Myself have offered you; out of the pit I have taken you and

*back in the pit he wants you buried. Daughter, trust Me, orphaned I shall not
leave you, take My guarantee, daughter, I shall never abandon you!*

*Hear Me, be reassured, you have not wasted your breath;[1] you are so, so weak
and powerless and ah! how My Spirit can breathe freely in you! Whispering in
echoes I flutter at your ear My Words that are to be uttered in My Assemblies;
why, soul, you are unlearned and utterly powerless for all that are Knowledge and
Wisdom. So how could your spirit comprehend all of this unless the Spirit who
speaks through you is My Own? Vassula[2]... you are so very precious to Me...
listen My child, there is an Angel by your side to take pity on you, console you and
pray for you; wait, I have more to say. I recognize your stupendous weakness, this
is why I shall use this weakness to draw My people to Unity and show them how
I, the Lord, feel in their negligence. I will show them what is most desired by Me,
I shall, in your weakness, show them how I feel about those distinctions they have
created among them. Tell Me, are you not all alike, made by My Own Hands?*

Yes Lord.

Who has not been made according to the likeness of My Image?

No one Lord! How does their way of thinking affect You my Lord?

*Because of man's base pride, My Father's Cup is filled with His Justice, because
of their rigidity they are left uninhabited! Many of them talk of unity and
brotherhood, but their words are fallacious, void. Prove yourselves in your
Maker's Eyes by bending; prove yourselves in your Maker's Eyes by unifying the
date of Easter. Prove yourselves to Me by breaking bread together; robe yourselves
in majesty and splendour with humility and not with an outward appearance of
religion and piety, repent! once you lived in humility, simplicity and unbounded
love with rich food covering your table. Yes, the greatness of My Church exceeded
everything and every living creature because the Eucharist made the life of My
Church. If My Church today lacks brightness it is because many of My churches
have abolished My Perpetual Sacrifice.[3] Can one peer through this shadowed
darkness and still claim they can see? Can one boast of having escaped ambushes
in this darkness? But so long as you say: 'we see' your guilt remains! I have said
that there are other sheep I have that are not of the one fold and that I have to
lead as well; but no sooner do I bring a wandering lamb back to the fold to lead*

---

[1] The Tempter came to me saying that I was not doing enough for the Lord and that
all my meetings in England and Ireland were a total 'fiasco' and that all my words
said to them were wasted. I panicked and thought the Lord had turned His back to
me.
[2] Jesus uttered my name almost in a whisper.
[3] Predicted by the prophet Daniel 11:31.

a True Life in Me, no sooner do I restore back his sight than you charge on him to take away the Kingdom of Heaven from him. Could a devil open the eyes of the blind? Could he make him cry out 'Abba!' so, unless you repent, My Father's Hand will fall upon you. I can no longer sustain His Hand from falling; unless you forgive each one of you your brother, <u>from your heart</u>, My Father's Hand will fall more rapidly than you think. ΙΧθΥΣ ⋉⬭

REFLECT ON MY PASSION

December 3rd, 1991

Another message for the Philippines:

Tell My people that they are like bricks and I can use them for the restoration of My House; I can, if they allow Me, use each one of them. Allow Me to guide you all, abandon yourselves to Me without inquiring why, just trust Me your Lord. Offer Me your will but do not object at Me when I use it. Pray with your heart, and confess your sins. ♥ *Reflect on My Passion and all I have offered you.* ♥

I WILL HAVE YOU FASTENED TO ME TO STAND FIRM BY MY SIDE

December 4th, 1991

Before one of the meetings in the Philippines:

Lord?

I Am. Fear not, I have not abandoned you. I love you. Beloved daughter, your apostolate is to spread My Glorious Light in every nation; spread all that you received from Me, this, My child, is what you will have to do, the rest, I will do. ♥ *By doing the work I have given you I shall protect you. You have nothing to fear. I Jesus so much love you. Now, do not try to understand but by testing you I make your spirit grow in holiness. Be at My service child, by doing the work I have given you. I shall always encourage you to witness with zeal for Me and My House, and I will always discourage you from looking to your left and to your right. I shall not be harsh with you because of your appalling misery, since you will be serving Righteousness Himself, I will have you fastened to Me to stand firm by My Side, otherwise, alone, you will waver. Now, My Spirit, your Holy Companion will lead you with enthusiasm to My children. By grace you will speak for Me. I am with you and I shall never fail you. Come.* ♥ IXθYΣ ⤢⬭◗

YOUR TABLE IS FULL AND WITHOUT ME YOUR TABLE WILL BE EMPTY

December 5th, 1991

For the Philippine prayer group:

I bless all of them; tell My children that My Heart is ablaze and on fire ready to consume them. They have only to step inside My Sacred Heart and I will leave them ravished for Me their God.

Then to a particular one.

I am today offering you My Heart; take It; Jesus is My Name and Jesus means

- Saviour -

Love loves you: and you[1] My offspring, continue to weave all that I have given you. Empty you shall not be. Look, your table is full and without Me your table will be empty: it is I who provide your soul; so cling to Me and you shall live; My Holy Kiss is on your forehead, I love you, love Me. IXθYΣ ⤢⬭◗

MESSAGE FOR THE PRISONERS ON MUNTIN LUPA IN MANILA, PHILIPPINES

December 5th, 1991

Vassula, peace My child; say to the prisoners, did you not know? Have you not heard how Mercy leans all the way to all mankind? Here is your God leaning all

---

[1] Jesus then turned to me.

the way from His Throne to reach you;
- I have come to you -
to tell you of the Great Love I have for each one of you. I am your God speaking
through My instrument to give you My Message. I have come to speak to you in
your heart and console you, My friends. I tell you, the world is nothing before
me, so do not fear the world, come to Me and lean on Me and I shall shepherd you
to My everlasting Waters. I shall heal your wounds and dress them. My Eyes
never leave you and I tell you, with Me, your table shall always be full; with Me,
you will sup, My friends. And when the heavy scourge comes upon you, do not
let this confuse you, beloved ones; every time it comes upon you, look at My
Wounds that healed you and saved you from Death, look at Me, your Saviour. Do
not look to you left nor to your right, follow My Footprints; you will recognize
them by the trace of Blood in them; follow them, beloved ones, and they will lead
you where I Am. ♥ *I bless each one of you leaving the Sigh of My Love on your*
foreheads. Love loves you. IXθΥΣ ⤳⫰

For sister Theresa who takes care of the prisoners, and who transformed the
prisoners into devout beings to God:

I have given them a Rock and ah!... how I love this Rock. I the Lord bless her
and bless her for she has made out of a desert where the vipers nestle,

> *a productive ground*
> *a garden, where I the Lord*
> *can have My rest.* ♥

THE TWO HEARTS DEVOTION

December 8th, 1991

Lord?

I Am. Pray before you rest in Me, say with Me:

> *Jesus rest in me*
> *and I in You,*
> *united, linked together. Amen.*

I repeated it.

Be firm about the Two Hearts, united in love; I have spoken in many hearts already about this truth, a truth that many will reject but in the end Our Two Hearts will prevail. Such is the world; today they reject, but tomorrow they will honour this truth; I Jesus love you all. Have no other but Me in your heart. Have Me as first. Have My Peace. IXθYΣ ⤡⬭▷

IT IS A RUBBLE

December 12th, 1991

Philippines

My thoughts went back to Switzerland.

Lord, how is the church in Switzerland?

It is a rubble...

OUR HEARTS LIKE TWO LAMPS ARE SHINING NEAR EACH OTHER
ZECHARIAH 4:1-14 AND APOCALYPSE 11:3-13

December 24th, 1991

Christmas Eve

My Lord?

I Am. Lean on Me, child.

I saw with the eyes of my soul Jesus' Holy Face. He looked like a child with big innocent eyes.

Tremendous reparations have to be done to cicatrize the wounds of this earth; wounds and cuts made by wickedness and sin; delight the Eyes of your Saviour and expand;

<u>*let it be*</u>

that My Message becomes so ample, so vast, testifying itself, that Wickedness, Apathy and Atheism will be seized and will repent. ♥ *Child! Cling to the hem of My clothes and stretch[1] even more now, from one corner of the earth to the other.* ♥ *Enter into My Sanctuaries if they welcome you into My Sanctuaries; if men forbid you, do not let this afflict you nor bring you sorrow, do not despair; your oppressors will look back in those scenes in the day of the Purification and will weep* ♥ *remembering their rejection; they will realize how they were, rejecting Our Divine Hearts, not you; Our Two Hearts that prophesied.*

Daughter, follow My blood-stained Footprints and pronounce My Holy Name in any gathering. <u>*The time has come that you should not hesitate any more.*</u> *Plant Vineyards everywhere and anywhere you can, make gardens out of deserts. I have blessed My Messages to prosper and take root, so, courage, daughter.*

Suddenly I felt a 'sword of fire' pierce me, and I cried out: Lord! I miss You!

You miss Me because you saw My Glory... write: Citadel after citadel is being besieged by the Rebel. I come today and offer all mankind My Peace but very few listen. Today I come with peace-terms and a Message of Love, but the peace I am offering is blasphemed by the earth and the Love I am giving them is mocked and jeered in this Eve of My Birth. Mankind are celebrating these days without My Holy Name. My Holy Name has been abolished and they take the day of My Birth as a great holiday of leisure, worshipping idols. Satan has entered into the hearts of My children, finding them weak and asleep. I have warned the world. Fatima's Message speaks: that in My Day I shall make the sun go down at noon and darken the earth in broad daylight; I will allow the Dragon to bite this sinful generation and hurl a Fire the world has never seen before or will ever come to see again to burn her innumerable crimes. You will ask: "will all the inhabitants perish, the good with the bad?" I tell you: the living will envy the dead; out of two men one will be taken; some will ask: "where are Elijah and Moses who are to come?" I tell you, you evil generation: We[2] have not been speaking in parables all these years; Elijah and Moses have come already and you have not recognized them but treated them as you pleased. You have not listened to Our Two Hearts, the Immaculate Heart of My Mother and My Sacred Heart, you faithless generation... Our Two Hearts have not been speaking to you in parables nor in riddles. All Our Words were Light and Our Hearts like Two Lamps are shining near each other, so bright, that everyone may see, ♥ ♥ *but, you have not understood. Our Hearts, like Two Olive Trees[3] one to the right and one to the left were for so many years*

---

[1] Jesus means to widen the scope, in spreading His urgent message.
[2] Christ means the Two Hearts who are the two witnesses in Apocalypse 11:1-13 and in Zechariah 4:1-14.
[3] Apocalypse 11:4 and Zechariah 4:3.

trying to revive you. Like Two Olive Branches pouring oil[1] to heal your sick generation and cicatrize your wounds, but your generation treated Our Two Hearts as they pleased; Our Two Hearts are anointed[2] and are living. They are like a sharp sword, double-edged[3] prophesying, but the rebellious spirit in this generation is re-crucifying My Word[4] the double-edged sword, and are rejecting Our Two Hearts who speak to you today; just like Sodom's and Egypt's rejection of My messengers. This era's stubbornness has surpassed Pharaoh's because their claims to their knowledge have become a battlefield to My Knowledge[5] indeed Our Two Hearts have become a plague to the people of the world[6] but soon, very soon now, My Voice shall be heard again. I shall visit you by thunder and fire. Justice is at hand and Our Two Hearts you have combated shall prevail in the end[7] and the kingdom of the world will become My Kingdom[8]. This is all very close now.

Open your eyes and look around you; I am giving you all the signs of the Times, and you, you who are labouring to bring to the surface the devotion of the Alliance of the Two Hearts, do not lose courage; the Book of Apocalypse speaks as well as the Book of Zechariah of this Truth. Do not fear, spread this devotion with trust and with courage.

A PRAYER: YAHWEH VISITED ME

January 16th, 1992

O Lord, I cannot find words to praise You, yet I want to talk to You...

I shall help you. Write:

> *Yahweh visited me*
> *like a gust of wind.*
> *His Spirit lifted me*

---

[1]Zechariah 4:12.
[2]Zechariah 4:14.
[3]Apocalypse 1:16.
[4]Allusion to Apocalypse 11:8-10.
[5]Allusion to Apocalypse 11:7.
[6]Apocalypse 11:10.
[7]Allusion to Apocalypse 11:11.
[8]Apocalypse 11:15.

and showed me
His Countenance,
He revealed to me:
Tenderness, Love and
Infinite Goodness.
He then showered me with Blessings
and offered me Manna in abundance,
to share It with my brothers.
He walked with me in the land of oblivion,
from down among the dead,
He took me,
among those who have forgotten Him,
He raised me,
restoring the memory of my soul.
O Lord, Yahweh, how grateful I am!
May Your Sweetness O Lord
be on us all.
Blessed be Yahweh
for ever and ever. Amen.

and now daughter, the terrors of the night are behind you and before you I Am.
♥ *I shall bring you safely Home, back where you belong;*

α ☩ ω

LET YOUR PRAYERS BE LIKE AN ADVOCATE TO DEFEND YOUR GENERATION

January 17th, 1992

Lord of Mercy, your people need to be consoled.
Your Body, divided, is sinking
and there are very few who can comfort You.
Your people are in despair.
Listen therefore, Lord of Mercy, and see our sorrow.
Amen.

Soaked in My Blood I am from all that My Eyes are witnessing and from what My Ears are hearing. Daughter, I mean to make you the sword of My Word. Through you I shall pierce hearts of men to allow My Word to penetrate profoundly in them. My Voice shall echo in them and though their heart has not a breath of life inside it, My Word, the giver of Life, will revive their heart and from it will issue a fragrance, appeasing My Wounds. Daughter of Mine, courage. Many will continue to live an unholy life and many will continue sinning and offending My Holiness, heedless of My warnings, heedless of the signs I am giving the world today and wickedness will go on increasing My Cup of Justice. ♥ *Wickedness and atheism, thirst of power and rationalism are worn like a signet ring on these men.*

Ah, My Vassula... there will be a loss such as never seen! The sinner lurks for his chance and like a prowler, he shall come by night! Multiple will be the wails from rulers, magistrates and influential men, all will wail! My daughter, hear My sighs, listen to My Heart.

O beloved of My Soul, come and console My Heart, hunger for Me. I am the Resurrection, love Me. Let your prayers be an advocate to defend your generation from My Father's wrath, let your cries and your prayers be like a plea to the Father. I, the Lord, bless you child. Come...

A ☧ Ω

FIRST DAY OF THE WEEK OF UNITY

January 18th, 1992

Give us Lord Your discerning
Spirit
To gain knowledge and Wisdom.
Give us Yahweh the ear
of the humble and the lowly
to search for Your Knowledge
and Wisdom.

Give Your Church her triumph
by uniting us all in
one Body. Amen.

Evangelize with love for Love. Live for Me, breathe for Me. All that I have said to you shall soon take place, you shall see more wonders through Me. The panoply is not yet worn by My Church. ♥ *The crown of triumph soon will be worn, adorning Her victory. I love you for giving Me your time and offering it so generously to Me. We love you.[1] It makes Me happy to know that you want to share My Work with Me. Have My Peace.* ΙΧθΥΣ ⊂▷

THEIR CITIES ARE EMPTY WITH EMPTINESS

January 20th, 1992

For the Swiss group:

This prolonged silence from My part[2] would not have lasted had I been approached with love. How can they claim they love Me when they have no peace nor any love among them? Like a wasting sickness, sin devours them. My Magnificence has not penetrated them nor has My Splendour. I came to water their aridity with My Tears; I came to console them, yet have I received any in return? Their cities[3] are empty with emptiness and rubble today, like drought in a dry land they became. My Word has come to their ear, yet they did not hear it. My Throne of Grace approached them and offered them My Peace and sound Teaching from Wisdom Herself to set them free and yet, they did not share it with faith nor love. Anyone who claims to be in the light but hates his brother, hates Me. ♥ *The original request which was given to them in My Message was:*

Love, peace, unity
and reconciliation among brothers.

Now all I have to say is:

examine yourselves before Judgement comes, you have very little time left now. Pray and avoid all evil. Never condemn or judge one another. Set your hearts for Me, set your minds on Me. Stay awake for the cleansing time is soon upon you. ♥ *Be filled then with My Spirit of Love so that your sins will not suffocate you.* ΙΧθΥΣ ⊂▷

---

[1] The Holy Trinity spoke.
[2] Jesus had eclipsed Himself for some time in Switzerland.
[3] Souls.

BEWARE OF FALSE PROPHETS

January 20th, 1992

Vassula, be on your guard. Many claim they hear Me and are carrying projects but they are not Mine. They make plans not inspired by Me. Remember, you will be approached by those who do not consult Me, they rave with prophecies that are not pronounced by Me. You have already heard and seen it all. They announce month by month what will happen to you next. Let them come forward, do not be afraid. I shall cover you My child. ♥

WHAT COULD I HAVE DONE FOR ALL OF YOU THAT
I HAVE NOT DONE?
OUR PERFECT UNION

Later on:

<u>Jesus, let Your Holy Face smile on us</u> and we shall revive. Our division devoured us like fire. Since You alone perform marvels, bring us together and let men renounce their folly. Your Plan is to unite us by unifying the date of Easter thus bringing us reconciliation. I am calling for Your Divine Help.

My child, bear joyfully My Cross. Praise the Father for His generosity. Hear Me: the wicked may hope to destroy My Plan of Unity but they will be heading for their downfall. When I proposed Peace, universal Peace, nearly all were for war, how can I take up their cause to defend them when My Father's Hand raises upon them? The net they have spread now will catch them inside. ♥ *What could I have done for all of you that I have not done? I have taken your faults on Myself, I have reconciled you to the Father and My Life I laid down for you. So what could I have done more that I have not done?*

Vassula, of My Sacred Heart, rejoice Me and <u>allow My Spirit in the inner room of your soul</u>. Allow My Spirit to breathe and dwell in the depths of your soul; leave Me free to shatter all impurities and imperfections that confront Me. My Vassula, although your soul will leap like on fire every time I will lift My Hand to shatter all that still keeps you captive, do not fear, do not run away in horror, allow Me to uproot in your soul all these infirmities. I shall come like a tempest inside you and carry out the decision of My Heart and that is your preparation for our perfect union. ♥ *I had said in the beginning that you will be My Net and My Target but then you had not understood the latter, you had not understood that in* *order to prepare you for this perfect union, I need to purify you and adorn your soul. I would have to bend My bow and set you as a target for My arrow. Oh what will I not do for you! No, it will not be without wounds and torments but then do not fight away the Holy One. Allow My Spirit to augment in you and My Divine Fire roar in your soul, you will be molten under the action of My Divine Fire. Do not lament then when I come to you like a hammer shattering your imperfections, do not ask your Holy One what is He doing? I am on My way to the inner room, My dwelling place and persistent blocks will not stop Me from proceeding, I shall burst them all with a tempest. I shall devour these rivals.*

O Lord go in moderation!

I want to bring to completion your purification, therefore do not restrain Me from proceeding. You are so dear to Me so let My Tenderness envelop you, refuse Me nothing soul. I want to make out of you a docile instrument since My Presence will be felt inside you like a fire and like an arrow. Do not fear, I shall not break you, I shall only break My rivals, I shall only be combating inside you. I shall also be mindful of your frailty. I have formed you and ordained you for this mission to be My Echo, so allow your King to rule over you, allow your Sovereign to reign over you. Nothing will escape My Eyes. Every little impurity will be seiged by My Purity and annihilated and My Light shall continue to glow inside you and My Spirit shall flow in your spirit like a river. ♥ So seek My Holy Face untiringly and you will understand that I Am is smiling on you. ♥

A ☧ Ω

THE ISLANDS WILL TREMBLE ON MY DAY

January 20th, 1992

Peace be with you. Hear Me daughter: have you looked around you? What have you seen?

I have seen upheavels and even greater divisions to come among us before UNITY. I cannot see the end of our struggle to unite, nor the end of atheism.

My Soul, arbitrator of your generation, has witnessed much more than upheavels, divisions and atheism. I tell you, many are plotting against Me in My Own House. This very minute I hear them conspiring, but soon the islands will tremble on My Day and although this generation will wail, I shall not listen. Heaven's door will be shut in that Day and the earth naked will groan like a widow, bereft in her sorrow. My Heart turns over inside Me and is sick already from the pitiful sound that will ring out from you, generation. Indeed, I shall not be gloating over you, since I take no pleasure in abasing and afflicting the human race. Once more there will be poured on you, but as never before My Holy Spirit, from a faint flickering Flame, My Fire shall roar and renew you all. Then, like a man entering a conquered city, I the Lord, shall invade you with My Glory and ecclesia shall revive. ♥ Justice will prevail in the end and you, daughter, do not fear to cry out for Me, do not be afraid of men, especially those who oppose you. Be happy, daughter, I can read the innermost parts of these men and My jealous Ear overhears everything. They think they know everything but they know nothing.

Daughter, I prayed for you to the Father, to consider your frailty. Vassula, try and understand the Father. Frail you are, but I have rooted you well inside Me so that you may not swerve or sway when violent tempests come from time to time upon you. You are His offspring and this is why out of His Jealous Love and His Generosity He allows such oppositions. Have you not heard how He renders through suffering, souls, to perfection and that suffering is part of your training? So be patient daughter, be generous too and do not shudder and complain for nothing. ♥ Do not weary labouring, follow the marks of My Blood I have left behind for Eternity. Those who follow these marks will enter into My Kingdom. Learn that the Father is not ruthless but ever so gentle with you. Wisdom loves you, therefore daughter, observe the Commandments, live according to the Gospel. Have Me as your Holy Companion and pray for My priests who represent Me. ♥

YOU WILL SEE GREATER THINGS THAN THIS

January 24th, 1992

During Holy Mass Jesus told me:

This is only the beginning. You will see greater things than this.

This was said after I was praising Him for His Wonders and His Works, since with His Power He opened the hearts of many in the World Council of Churches. The Lord had been preparing since summer, messages about unity, directives of His Desires. Then He allowed certain hearts in the WCC to open and receive His Word thus allowing me to go over to them in the week of unity to offer them Jesus' messages and read them out to them.

CONSECRATION TO THE SACRED HEART

January 26th, 1992

Vassula of My Sacred Heart, do you want to consecrate yourself entirely to Me?

Yes, my Lord, I want.

Then say these words:

> ### Sacred Heart of Jesus
> *come and invade me completely so that my motives will be Your Motives, my desires Your Desires, my words Your Words, my thoughts Your Thoughts. Then allow me to creep in the deepest place of Your Sacred Heart.* ♥ *Annihilate me altogether. I, Vassula, shall worship Your Sacred Heart from the core of mine. I promise to serve Your Sacred Heart with a fire inside me. I shall, with zeal, serve You more fervently than before. I am weak but I know that your Strength shall sustain me. Do not allow me to lose sight of You, nor allow my heart to flutter elsewhere. I, Vassula, will look for Your Sacred Heart alone and desire You alone.*
>
> ### Sacred Heart of Jesus
> *make me dislike all that is contrary to Your Holiness and to Your Will. Sift me through and through and make sure that not one rival remains within me. From today, tighten the bonds of Love with which you have enlaced me and make my soul thirst for You and my heart sick with love for You.*
>
> ### Sacred Heart of Jesus
> *do not wait, come and consume my whole being with the Flames of Your ardent Love. Whatever I will do from now on, will be done merely for Your Interests and Your Glory and nothing for me. I, Vassula, consecrate my life for you and from today am willing to be the slave of Your Love, the victim of Your Burning Desires and of Your Passion, the benefit of Your Church, and the toy of Your Soul. Make my traits resemble those of Your Crucifixion through the bitterness I will encounter in the deafness of souls and to see them fall. Give my soul its fill.*
>
> ### Sacred Heart of Jesus
> *do not spare me from Your Cross, like the Father had not spared You. Arrest my eyes, my thoughts and my desires to be captives of Your Sacred Heart. Unworthy I am and I deserve nothing, but*

help me to live my act of consecration by being loyal, invoking Your Holy Name untiringly. Make my spirit repulse all that is not You.

Sacred Heart of Jesus

make my soul bear more than ever before, the Marks of Your Body for the conversion of souls. I, Vassula, voluntarily submit my will to Your Will, now and forever. Amen.

and now My Spirit will rest in you. ♥ Vassula, it pleases Me to see you spend your time for Me. All your sacrifices done in My Name do not go in vain.
ΙΧθΥΣ ⤸⬤▷

UNITY

January 27th, 1992

Peace be with you little child. This grace has been given to you so that I, through you, will open the eyes of the blind and the ears of the deaf. ♥ I will continue to manifest Myself through you in this way. You are a most imperfect instrument but My Compasssion sees your efforts in your imperfection and My Wrath gets disqualified by My Tenderness. ♥ Never doubt of My Love. I want weakness so that I may do everything.

It is I, Jesus
who shall give you[1] the directives
to Unity.

The hour has come for My Body to be glorified. Men shall soon learn in which way I wish them to unite, My Way will not be their way... Now I have revealed My desires to them, I have revealed My Heart to them, with My Power I shall unify the dates of Easter, it will not be forced upon you. I shall find a means with Peace. Yes, with immense power I shall surprise you. Today I have told them which course to take, and tomorrow I will lead them where I chose. ♥
ΙΧθΥΣ ⤸⬤▷

---

[1]To humanity.

I HAVE SEEN RUSSIA

January 30th, 1992

Italy - Gera-Lario

Lord?

I Am.

Am I to write what I have seen at dawn?

Write. ♥

I have seen Russia.

Do not weep, she will recover. Weep bitterly rather for those who have gone away from Me. I will rebuild her. ♥ *Weep for the man who is dead. I will embellish her, Vassula.*

O God, I have seen her misery! What I have seen is this: A woman approached me, young, not very beautiful but neither ugly. Her name: Russia. She came over to me and I noticed from her clothing that she was poor. She opened her mouth to talk to me and I saw then that half of her teeth were missing and that made her very ugly, but I knew that a woman, so young, would do something if half of her teeth were gone, unless extreme poverty covered her. Russia, in spite of her poverty and misery was courageous and on her feet. She showed me her bread-giver, an old-fashioned instrument. Russia was telling me that she will work on it, to be able to earn whatever and keep alive. I was torn inside me with sadness. Then, another woman came, she was also Russia, she too, most of her teeth were missing. Then two more women came all of who their teeth were missing and showing extreme poverty.[1] Then, suddenly, a young man enters, he was the Husband of Russia. I noticed that He was well-built, healthy, tall and very good-looking.

I thought: how could he stand someone like Russia, with no beauty in her and repulsive for lack of teeth... While I was thinking all these things, Russia's Husband approached her tenderly and put His Arm around her shoulders and I saw in His Eye, Infinite Tenderness, Love and Fidelity for ever and ever. I saw that He would never abandon her in spite of her unattractiveness. I recognized You, my Lord.

---

[1] Four women poverty-stricken, does that mean four years of famine in Russia?

No, I shall not abandon her, nor does she repulse me. I am her Father and her Spouse and My Name is Faithful and True. I shall dress her up again, giving her fine clothes, and her heart will be the ornament of a sweet and gentle disposition. I have never ceased to rain a downpour of blessings on her, I shall never deprive her of My Love. Ah Vassula, be patient as I am patient. ♥ Lean now on Me.

IXθYΣ ✗◯▷

THEY ARE NOT LISTENING TO OUR TWO HEARTS

January 31st, 1992

No less than the height of heaven over earth is the greatness of Your love for those who fear You. (Psalm 103:11)

Come and absorb all that is Me, absorb Love. I am Love, yet I suffer loneliness because of the rejection of My Own. My children have forsaken the paths of Righteousness, the Fountain of Wisdom, they are not listening to Our Two Hearts but it had been said that the Rebel, that is the spirit of Rebellion, who "speaks words against the Most High and harasses the Saints of the Most High"[1] will challenge My Power. This spirit of Rebellion "considers changing seasons and My Law."[2] Look around you, only and you will understand, Rationalism and Modernism are the prime enemy of My Church because both of these lead to atheism. Both of them want to devour the whole earth, but My daughter, I will breathe My Fire upon these renegades so that the scales from their eyes once fallen, they may see what great disorder they have produced and what oppression they had put upon Our Two Hearts. ♥ I am going to pass through all of you.

Repent!
for the Kingdom of Heaven is close at
hand.
Come, write My next Message for all those
who will assemble to hear My Word in Nice.

---

[1]Daniel 7:25.
[2]Daniel 7:25.

LOVE HAS NO LIMITS

France

Peace be with you. My Return is imminent and My Face will be revealed from Heaven against all the impiety of the world, so be prepared. Everyone who proved to be false will see what fatal wounds they have given to their soul. I will come among you in Splendour and in Glory. The Spirit of Truth will be revealed in you to cleanse your soul, you shall see Me face to face[1] and you shall see yourselves fully as you are known. So come to Me as you are now, do not wait to be saints. Come and understand what I seek most from you, I love you with an everlasting Love. I have offered you My Life taking your faults on Myself. I have reconciled you to the Father and I allowed the hands that I Myself formed

- to crucify Me -

So what could I have done more that I have not done? If you say you love Me, take My Cross and follow Me and do not look with consternation upon the other small crosses I place on your path. Love has no limits, love endures with patience whatever comes. Love is not resentful but delights in the Truth and whatever the Truth offers. Love is forgetful to calumnies said about you. So seek love, bless your enemies. I want you holy but My beloved ones you are still so very far from perfection because the love of money is rooted deep inside this generation. Dear children, do you really want to follow Me? Then decide to follow My Footprints imbued still with My Blood. Do not fear, My Footprints will lead you to Me in your Abba's Arms, they will lead you to Him who held you first. ♥ Have confidence and rely on Our saving Love. I tell you:

in the end Our Two Hearts
will prevail. ♥ ♥

Take My Hand, daughter, do not fear. I shall take care of you. I Am is with you.
ΙΧθΥΣ ⳇ

---

[1] That is: spirit with Spirit.

THE SECOND EVE

January 31st, 1992

O Abba, if Scriptures say: "Much hardship has been made for man, a heavy yoke lies on the sons of Adam from the day they come out of their mother's womb, till the day they return to <u>the mother of them all</u>." (Sirach 40:1) Then my Lord You have said also to me in one of Your Messages for Our Heavenly Mother that She is the Second Eve, thus taking the place of Eve and what I discover again in Scriptures is that It confirms once more that Our Blessed Mother, Mary, is the Mother of all humanity.

Daughter, you have given ear to Wisdom and My Own Heart is glad and My Soul rejoices when from your lips comes the Knowledge I have given you. ♥ *Remain a nothing and allow Wisdom to instruct you; remain in My favour and do not fear the fiery wolves, do not fear them My child.[1]* ♥

O Abba, You are shaken by terrible sights coming from us, Your children; godlessness, hatred, Satanism, abortions, greed for power even in the Church, injustice etc... and yet You came to me, who portrayed the godless, to save me from destruction; Your Graciousness which is a torrent of blessings came upon me. You offered me Your Friendship and became my Holy Companion and my Friend. Before the

Truth and Your
Covenant

you made me stand. O how bitter it is to feel Your Heart so sad, breathing in me Your Passion, uttering sighs of sorrows.

WEEP FOR YOUR BROTHERS AND YOUR SISTERS

I am profoundly sad, daughter; but do not weep for Me, weep for your brothers and your sisters, because sin devours them like cancer; reserve your tears, daughter, for them; Vassula, your wounds are nothing compared to My Wounds; pray for them before My Finger touches the earth and melts it; I know you are delicate and faint but have I ever abandoned you? Prophesy and reveal My Heart to all races and all nations. ♥

α ☧ ω

---

[1] Something between me and God.

COMPASSION AND LOVE IS REVEALING HIMSELF TO MANKIND

February 6th, 1992

Daughter, I give you My Peace. ♥ *If anyone will ask you: "what is this all about?"[1] answer: Compassion and Love is revealing Himself to mankind; Salvation leans all the way from Heaven to reach the Wretched, supplicating them to renounce their folly; what God is saying to us today means, Peace, Reconciliation and Love;*

- Infinite Love -

IXθYΣ ⤳

THE NIGHT IS ALMOST OVER THE WORLD OF TODAY WILL ROLL LIKE A SCROLL

February 11th, 1992

Message for New York, USA:

Vassula, allow Me to use your hand, write:

Peace be with you all; children I tell you solemnly that the Real Light is already on His way of Return; I am telling you this, My Own children, that you may all be ready to receive Me; the night of your era is soon over; understand how sins obscure the light in you; the love of this passing world is vile and could bring in you nothing but darkness; but I tell you,

the night is almost over

and your tripping or falling is soon coming to an end because the Power of My Holy Spirit will be in full union with you all, to guide you to live:

a True Life in Me, your God.

---

[1]God means the Messages.

Happy those who admit the Truth and live in accordance to the Truth, his room in heaven will not remain void for eternity but will be filled with his presence. I, Jesus, ask you to offer Me your heart and I shall place it into My Own Sacred Heart and revive it. I shall fragrance your heart and purify it. I shall fill your heart with My Light and My Warmth. I shall imbue your heart with My Love and I shall restore it entirely bringing it back to holiness, and with My Divinity adorn it; if you only realized what I am offering you, you would not hesitate or waver, to give Me all your heart, but you would listen to Me this time:

seek good and not evil
pray with love
and do not judge.

Soon My Light, like a Fire will pass through you to cleanse your soul from impurities; I shall enter My cities[1] and shine in them; it will mean light not darkness; it will be an overflow of Light; your cities then will be renewed and holy with My transcendent Light, then... the New Heavens and the New Earth will come upon you and the world of today will roll away like a scroll and like flowers that draw their life from light, you too, My beloved ones, will be inundated in My Light to revive. Can flowers survive without any water? Then why do so many of you today refuse the flow of My Holy Spirit and doubt that this Water rising from My Throne[2] is coming from Me? Have you not read:

The Throne of God and of the Lamb will be in its place in the city; his servants will worship Him, they will see Him face, to face and His Name will be written on their foreheads. It will never be night again and they will not need lamplight or sunlight, because the Lord God will be shining on them.[3]

Have you not yet understood? My Spirit is like a River and wherever this River flows, <u>everyone</u> teeming in it,[4] sick, lame, blind,[5] all will be healed and will become witnesses of the Most High. Like fruit trees with leaves that never wither and fruit that never fails,[6] you shall all be. You will bear fruit every month because this Water (My Holy Spirit) comes from My Sanctuary[7] in which your spirit will make its Abode. I mean to deliver you from the clutches of the Evil one and restore the memory of your soul. I mean to open the hearts of stone, making them utter from henceforth noble praises for Me your God. Generation, do not

---

[1]That is our souls.
[2]Apocalypse 22:1.
[3]Apocalypse 22:3-5.
[4]Ezekiel 47:9.
[5]Spiritually.
[6]Ezekiel 47:12.
[7]Ezekiel 47:12.

say: *"my wounds are incurable"* and refuse beforehand to be healed. *Do not say:* *"my Redeemer never listens to me."* Today, your Redeemer says to you: the Tears of Blood I shed over you year after year, generation, testify My grief. I deprive no one of My Mercy, so come to Me, fall into My Arms and you will be healed. Do not fear Me, I am an Inexhaustible Source of Love and Forgiveness, and <u>you</u>, you who say: *"my Redeemer never listens to me"*, I tell you: I am with you all the time and like a thirsty traveller I thirst for your words of love, I thirst for your prayers. Invoke Me with your heart and I will reply. Do not say: *"He is hiding His Face from me"*, then look on the other side; I am watching every single one of your steps and I never leave you from My Sight. I am with you all the time, but in your obscurity you fail to see Me, in your aridity you do not hear Me; turn your eyes upwards towards Heaven and search for Heavenly things, generation, and you will see My Glory.

It is for you to decide.

My Heart is open for everyone to come and live inside It. Be rooted in Me and you shall live. I bless you all, leaving the Sigh of My Love on your foreheads.
IXOYE ⤛⬤⟩

YOUR PRIESTS NEED PRAYERS!

February 13th, 1992

Lord, is it fair to reduce the newly converted Greek prayer group into naught? Is it fair that they are chased away by one priest and dispersed to return into the desert they were once in?

Vassula, your priests need prayers!!

Lord, will you allow him to dry up a whole vineyard? You have turned deserts into Rivers and arid ground into Springs of Water!

Vassula, your priests need prayers!

> You have filled the starved with Your Fruits, Lord,
> You satisfied the hungry,
> You lifted the weary and
> exalted the poor and the wretched,
> You brought happiness to the suffering,

and the sick were healed with Your Love,
and those who were desperately
thirsty, You gave them Water,
Do not abandon them...

I shall not abandon them. My Vassula, your priests need prayers... look, have faith in Me; ecclesia shall revive, My healing balm is:

LOVE

But there is no love among many of us!

I shall pour out My Spirit on all mankind, and make the heart of the inflexible melt and their iniquities will be purged in My Fire.

Lord, I will dare say one more thing: That little prayer group now is terrified by this priest as You know. I am not worthy myself, I am lost without You and the light inside me flickers almost to extinction without Your Light.

Your heart is set to tell Me more, finish your sentence My daughter. ♥

...unity could not be built without the Greek Orthodox priests. The sort of unity You desire does not please them.

Yet, My Vassula, I have a list of generous men, they will be an example for the conversion of this generation. But have in mind this priest. Honour My priests and offer Me sacrifices of reparation and I will solicit you with My favours. ♥ *Resign yourself to Me and allow Me to test you now and then; I will heal all the disloyalty My Eyes witness.*

A ☧ Ω

UNITY MESSAGE
BUT WHAT AM I TO DO WITH ALL THEIR INCENSE

February 14th, 1992

Vassula, peace be with you; let Me feel your love, resign yourself to Me, enter into My Heart and put into practice all that I have given you. ♥

Lord, You showered me with blessings without the slightest merit. I am, as You see, in Your Hands, so do whatever You please with me.

Live then for Me and console Me; be the sign of unity this generation rejects, yes, be the sign of unity coming from Me, and scorned and rejected from within your own House, from your people[1]. Through you I display My Love for <u>all</u> nations, and through you I will continue to speak and point out how they reduced My Church to a desert. I offered your people[2] a pact of Peace which can lead you all to brotherly unity. I have chosen <u>you</u> as a signpost for what unity will be like, but they do not listen; they do not bend either, instead they run to offer Me incense, but what am I to do with all their incense? I want incense from their heart, I want peace from their heart, I want praises from their heart, I want love, mercy and compassion from their heart.

*I want reconciliation from
their heart.*

Ah, daughter, do not weary crossing this desert, your Redeemer is near you and we are bonded together; I have posted you for this mission to flash like lightening My Words to all nations; tell them that if they say to be witnesses of the Most High, let them then show Me their peace through integrity and honour through devotedness. Tell them to examine their path and return to Me, and I shall give them the Spirit of understanding. ♥ *Today I am offering them Mercy in a time of trouble. I am offering them Compassion in their appalling misery. I am giving them the Gift of My Love. Repeatedly I have been stretching out My Hand to lift them to Me and yet how often have they responded? I have been showing them My pity and My Compassion; how long am I to allow them to rock Me with sorrow by rejecting to do My Will? Must I still hold back the Father's Hand? The Father's Justice is flaring up already to light up the crimes of this world... I poured out from babe's mouths My bitter supplications, for*

peace and reconciliation among brothers

but look, how My supplications were received... ah, My daughter, be the defender of the Truth.

Lay your head on My Heart and when you will hear the sound of My Heart-beats your courage will return to you; do not give in to the promptings of your weaknesses, trust Me, trust Me;... look[3], courage daughter, I am by your side and so long as I am by your side, you will be kept on your feet; ... daughter? I shall never abandon you.. ♥ *listen, hear Me Vassula, I am sharing My Cross with you, look, My Vasssula, My Love is before your eyes and My Loyalty surrounds you. Whenever I see from far off an anger from a legion of demons heading towards*

---

[1] The Greek Orthodox priests.
[2] The Greek Orthodox priests.
[3] I felt Jesus was trying to uplift My spirit.

you to strike you and hurl themselves on you to tear you to pieces, I come between you and them, leaving them trembling. Console then your heart in My Heart and do not fear, courage! No demons will be allowed to strike you nor will I allow them in their fierce rage to leap on you and burn you. I am standing near you to give you signals when to open your mouth to speak in My Name. ♥ Come, the Light is your Companion. ΙΧθΥΣ ⫷⊃⫸

MESSAGE FOR THE GREEK PRIESTS

February 18th, 1992

Lord, I will not let my eyes off You, lest I fall again in apostasy.

Allow me to worship You at Your Footstool. O Lord, display now Your Power on us all. Bring upon us all Your Tempest that will whirl away our sins. Let Your Fire (the Holy Spirit) come upon us to enliven us and purify us. It is hard to cross this treacherous desert in the dark.

Maranatha! Come!

Peace My beloved, do not be in terror, My decision has been taken; I shall ravage the earth with My Purifying Fire and I shall carry out My Plan sooner than foreseen, the time of waiting is soon over. ♥ As for you, My child, do not be intimidated by Folly; turn your eyes towards Me and lean on Me, I am your Strength.

Look! Pray for your priests[1], pray that they may turn to Me and draw from Me: resourcefulness, Peace and Love; many are decaying and very fast too; pray for those[2] who play havoc with My blossoming flowers[3]; tell your priests[4] that if among them there are a few who are still alive, it is due to My Tears; I water their faith with My tears, so I weep in agony to keep this remnant alive; <u>My Church is crumbling like rotten wood</u> and all I hear from them is:

'Is there a drought?'

---

[1] The Greek Orthodox priests.
[2] The Greek Orthodox priests.
[3] The newly converted Greek youth. Converted through our Lord's messages.
[4] The Greek Orthodox priests.

426

They flout piety, they list bitter accusations against the Works of My Holy Spirit and allow their mouth to condemn them! The hour of darkness brought the Hour of Adoration to nil; worse still, they have established a monopoly of ostentation and presumption; I, their Lord, stand before them and ask them: "Why do you scorn the consolation that I give to My children today through the smallest part of My Church?" The Heavens will wear away soon and you are still unaware and in deep sleep; I shall come to you like a thief without telling you at what hour to expect Me[1], I am asking you now with Tears in My Eyes, tell Me: What happened to My flock? Where are My perennial pastures? Why are My sons and daughters in captivity? Where is the youth of today? Why has the fragrance I had given you turned into a stench?, I weep over you, I weep over your excessive pride. Your excessive pride made My Church resemble a gaping grave; but you too will be subdued. My Fire is close now; I will bring you down from your glory... and when you will ask 'what happened?' I will tell you then: "My Kingdom has been taken from you and given to a people who will now produce its fruit"[2] It is the Spirit who gives life, surely you have enough respect for My Holy Spirit? Then why do you offend My Holy Spirit by persecuting Him? Judge for yourselves what I am saying, why are your young people separating from Mother Church to follow a second-rate philosophy? You have done well in remembering My Holy Spirit so constantly and in maintaining the traditions just as I passed them on to you, however, you speak without love and you are <u>blinded</u> by your zeal! You have lost the insights of My Mysteries because of your zeal! Have you not read: 'there is a remnant, chosen by grace; by grace, you notice, <u>nothing therefore to do with good deeds,</u> or grace would not be grace at all! (Romans 11:5-6) I love you all but it is not without suffering, because you are objecting to My Holy Spirit's gifts; you are not objecting to a human authority, <u>but to Me your God.</u> ♥ I am reminding you of one last thing: one day you will see Me face to face and I will ask you to give Me an account of the way you looked after the souls I had entrusted you with; today still you are making Me out to be a liar because you do not believe any more the testimony I had given you all about the Reminder of My Word!

My Holy Spirit

Wash your hearts clean and the heavens will shine on you. From above, I have been watching you, City of Tradition, you have practised the exact observances of the Law of My Primitive Church, but today you are blinded by ostentation and pay little attention or none at all to the weightier matters of My Law, Mercy! Love! Humility!

<u>and a spirit of Forgiveness.</u>

---

[1] Apocalypse 3:3.
[2] Matthew 21:34.

My sorrow is great and I groan inwardly as I wait for you to seek for the greater gifts of My Spirit; I am weary of seeing you preach spiritual things unspiritually. Had they understood the depths and the weightier matters of My Spirit today they would have accepted the gifts too of My Spirit, but the pride that you take in yourselves is incessantly lacerating Me. ♥ *I have entrusted you with thousands of souls to teach and help them <u>gently</u>, drawing them into My Heart, reminding them of <u>My Tenderness</u>, <u>My Love</u> and My great thirst for them, but you pass premature judgement on them and load them with burdens that are unendurable, burdens that you yourselves do not move a finger to lift! In My days I was the stumbling block and today My Holy Spirit is again, the stumbling block, for many of My sacerdotal souls.* ♥ *The Eyes of the Lord, I am telling you are not only turned towards the righteous and the virtuous, My Eyes also turn towards the wretched and the ones you call unworthy. The stars from the sky will soon drop to the earth and the powers of heaven will shake and you will <u>still</u> be unaware. This earth will soon disappear and the new heavens and the new earth will be upon you and you will <u>still</u> be running away from My Spirit.* ♥ *Yet, if even today you humble yourselves and <u>sincerely</u> admit you are sinners and unworthy, I shall take away the spirit of lethargy that is hovering over your nation!*

You say yourselves rich, show Me your riches then; 'Famine' is the only word I hear from your country. 'Famine' is written all over you. If you say yourselves rich, then where are your glorious pastures? Why do I stumble on decaying corpses? How is it I hear no sound from you? My Holy Spirit in His Infinite Mercy descends now to feed you all and fill your spirit with My Celestial Manna. As a Shepherd I shall look for My strayed sheep, I shall tend their wounds with everlasting Love, I will support the weak and the weary and those you pasture no more; I will console My children; so do not hinder Me or become an obstacle in these days of Mercy; <u>do not contradict what you teach on My Spirit</u>. I have told you all this now before My Day comes. Will I hear: 'God, here I am! I am coming to repent! I will stop insulting Your Spirit of Grace because I know that if I do, I would be severely punished.' It is for your salvation that I speak and if I reproach you it is because of the

<u>*greatness of the Love I have for you.*</u>

ΙΧθΥΣ ⤳ *Vassula, pray for your priests to learn real humility from Me.* ♥

I HAVE GIVEN YOU THE GIFT OF MY LOVE

March 1992

Satan could have easily killed me this morning. While I was dusting a glass shelf with icons and religious objects on it, it fell breaking the lower shelf too. I saw big pointed blades falling all around me and all the way out of that room in the entrance hall. When it stopped I waited in silence to see where the blood will trickle. I had nothing, not even a scratch. Normally I should have been sliced from my stomach all the way to my feet.

Later on:

My Vassula, let Me lead you step by step. Stay small My flower and lean on your Saviour. I love you, child. Satan desperately tries to lay a hand on you and lame you[1]. Not only does he use people to gather false accusations against you, but in his anger, he will use even the law of nature to turn against you; but I am your Devout Keeper and your Shelter, so do not fear. My Eyes are upon you incessantly. Hide always in My Sacred Heart. ♥ Come, we shall continue to pursue souls for their salvation. I shall lead you, My beloved, everywhere on earth and wherever I pass through I will leave a trace of the subtlest odours behind Me, I will spread My fragrance of myrrh from soul to soul to ravish their hearts. Delight your Saviour, flower, and allow Me to use you progressively. I shall not break you nor will I wrench from you your liberty. Let your heart remain captive of My Love, though without tiring of Me. I am your Beloved Companion who have given you a Treasure:

> *I have given you the*
> *Gift of My Love.*

I shall give you My Strength and My Patience. Flower, My Spirit rests on you to guide you and remind you of My Teachings so be generous and offer your time to germinate this earth. Have reverence always for Me. Am I not your sole Love? Am I not the King of Kings? Work hard with Me and contrary to what you think, most of your efforts are not futile, My Power gives them a Divinity that reach their aim. If the Tempter whispers in your ear telling you that your words are ineffectual, I tell you, My child, do not listen to him. I shall continue to pour out My Heart on you all and descend untiringly from Heaven to nourish the hungry, satisfying every taste. I shall continue to expose My Sacred Heart and demonstrate

---

[1] I understood it spiritually.

My Tenderness towards everyone. ♥ *Whosoever will eat Me and drink Me will be transfrmed to live a*

A True Life in Me, your God.

Whosoever will turn towards Me will be saved. By just one look at Me and I will transfigure you. Daughter, remain unnoticed and nothing, remain hidden by your helplessness, by your frailty so that My Bounty and My Power may spread even more now; the sowing is not finished and the whole world will soon echo with My Voice. Daughter, you are very precious to Me and I love you to tears, I love you all to tears, and from Heaven My Lips moistened with Grace bring to all of you My Message of Peace. From all Eternity I have loved you and blessed you, and from your crib I had watched over you and defended you. I know how misery enwrapped you all to total blindness. Seek Me and I shall give you Light. I will give you Life again and make your soul long for all that is Holy. Therefore, daughter, continue to seek My Holiness and My Perfection. Bless Me and praise Me. Sow when I sow, sow abundantly and wherever I take you to sow. Soon you shall pass this era's threshold to enter into an Eternal Peace. ♥ Endure in the meantime all that I endure, alone you are not. Persevere, My child, and remember Who is near you blessing you. Love loves you. ΙΧθΥΣ ⊂⊃

IN MY TIMES OF PERSECUTIONS
JESUS EXPLAINS AP. 6:12-17

March 3rd, 1992

Lord, I have not spoken in secret, all I say is in prayer and in Your Assembly praising You. I am trying to obey Your Sacred Heart and the Instructions I received from You. I do my best to display them as they were given me. Although I am poor and can hardly give You anything, I have given You the only thing I have and You had told me is mine. I have offered Your Majesty, my will, that You may use it if it pleases You for Your Merciful Designs.

I know, My child, but have they not also hated Me for no reason? Anyone who issues from Me to witness for the Truth will be hated, persecuted and hunted like game. A servant is not greater than His Master... These persecutors would be blameless in the Father's Eyes if they had not known My Law, but as it is they have seen My Law, yet only in darkness. They call themselves doctors of the Law and believe they know everything but in reality they know nothing. They think that by judging you and condemning you in public they are doing a very holy duty for

430

Me, your God. Had they followed My Commandments and kept them they would not have judged. Had they any love in them they would have kept My Words and My Law. But in reality they are not judging you, they are judging My Good Works on you all. I have only commissioned you to go out and be My Echo. In being My Echo I expect you to bear fruit, fruit that will last... but they have not understood. My child, continue to do the work I have commissioned you for. Bring souls to Me that I may consume them in My Sacred Heart. I am thirsty for souls.

Listen, the evidence of My Holy Works are shining on you all to take away this darkness. The evidence of My Holy Works are their good fruit, fruit that lasts. The evidence of My Holy Works is the gift of Peace I am giving you and the Love I am infusing you with. The evidence of My Holy Works is My salvation calls to the

Eucharistic Life

The Father and I want true worshippers, worshippers who will worship in spirit and truth. ♥ My Spirit of Truth descends all the way to your doorstep to remind you that in the end

- Our Two Hearts will prevail -

This is to fulfil the words written in Scriptures: 'after the three and a half days, God breathed life into them and they stood up.' (Apocalypse 11:11) Yes, in all Glory, for, 'these are the Two Anointed Ones' (Zc 4:14) who stand side by side. Our Two Hearts are like 'Two Olive Trees, one to the right and one to the left.' (Zc 4:3) My Sacred Heart has fathomless Riches and many things to say to you all.

My little children,

I am the Resurrection and the Life

I come to resurrect your devotion to My Sacred Heart and the Immaculate Heart of your Mother, so do not fear, stay on your guard, for many will come using My Name manipulated by the Evil One, to deceive you and blow away the little flame left in you and leave you in total darkness. Many will fall away because their roots were not in Me. Pray that you may not be tempted by the Evil one. Alas for you who continue to persecute My mouthpieces saying: 'we would never have joined in shedding the blood of the prophets, had we lived in our fathers' day.' I tell you, all of this will recoil on your heads unless you repent! My beloved children, the burglar comes by night[1] so stay awake and do not allow him to break in your house. Be in constant prayer to Me, to pray without ceasing is to be aware of My Presence before you. To be aware of My Presence is to be awake, to be awake is to be sound and with light. Your house is your soul. See to it then that the light inside you is not darkness. Do not let the Tempter find you asleep. ♥

You are My friends, remember? Love one another as I love you, anything you will ask in My Name I shall give you. Some of you today are sad because the world is passing premature judgement on My Sacred Heart and the Immaculate Heart of your Mother, but soon Our Two Hearts will show the world how wrong it was, about judging when I will reveal My Holy Face[2] in them.

Daughter, write: 'when I will break the sixth seal, there will be a violent earthquake and the sun will go as black as coarse sackcloth. The moon will turn red as blood all over, and the stars of the sky will fall on to the earth like figs dropping from a fig-tree when a high wind shakes it. The sky will disappear like a scroll rolling up and all the mountains and islands will shake from their places. Then all the earthly rulers, the governors and the commanders, the rich people and the men of influence, the whole population, slaves and citizens, will take to the mountains to hide in caves and among the rocks. They will say to the mountains and the rocks, 'fall on us and hide us away from the One who sits on the Throne and from the anger of the

Lamb[3]

For the Great Day of My Purification is soon upon you and who will be able to survive it? Everyone on this earth will have to be purified, everyone will hear My Voice and recognize Me as the Lamb. All races and all religions will see Me in their interior darkness. This will be given to everyone like a secret revelation to reveal the obscurity of your soul. When you will see your insides in this state of grace you will indeed ask the mountains and the rocks to fall on you. The darkness of your soul will appear as such that you would think the sun lost its light and that the moon too turned into blood. This is how your soul will appear to you, but in the end, you will only praise Me. If a stranger comes your way and tells you that the food[4] I have been giving you is vile, do not listen to him, listen to the language of My Sacred Heart, the language of My Cross. Let your fidelity to My Sacred Heart bloom once more, consecrate yourselves all to My Sacred Heart and

---

[1] That means Satan comes in a dark soul much easier.
[2] That is in the Purification Day, when we will see our sins with God's Eyes.
[3] Apocalypse 6:12-17. Here Jesus indicates plainly that in the day of purification, everyone in the world will experience his state of his soul and again everyone will recognize the Lamb, meaning Jesus.
[4] These messages.

the Immaculate Heart of your Mother. ♥ *I will be visiting you again, My little children. So courage My friends, you are hounded but it is only by the world. You are insulted for My sake? Rejoice! For I was too. You are treated as the offal of the world because you love Me? I bless you and join you in your sufferings. You are the jest of your people? But so was I, your King. You are not more than Me your Master. My secret intentions are revealed <u>now</u>, in your dormant times. The revelation of My Sacred Heart is revealed in these end of Times again to awaken your hearts and bring you all back fervently to this Devotion. So among you there must be no premature judgement. Love Me and bless Me. I am always with you and I will continue to reveal the riches of My Sacred Heart in each one of you.* ♥

Vassula, My child, I shall strengthen your stem and replace the petals your accusers ripped from you to give you this joy I feel whenever you offer Me your will. Love loves you. IXθYΣ ⊰⊙⊱

ASK THE FATHER TO RELENT
CANADA IS MINE

March 4th, 1992

I am listening Lord now.

My child, listen and write: I am Boundless Tenderness and Compassion but My people heap in My Church one betrayal on another. Am I to keep silent? My Body, from the sole of My Foot to My Head hurts and is in great agony. I have got impressive Wounds and I am taunted by My Own. A great and innumerable multitude is on its way to perdition. Many of My sacerdotal souls flout piety. I pronounced warnings since the Time of Fatima to this day. I have emptied My Heart on you, generation, but many of you have forgotten the ransom that was paid to free you...[1] Vassula, you are not listening as I want you to listen...[2] for the sake of My Love, child, speak to Me! Do not lack courage, I love you!

Lord, my persecutors are now putting in print something against me.

They are <u>My</u> persecutors too, not yours only, but I tell you they will quite certainly destroy themselves by their own work of destruction if you do not pray for them

---

[1] Jesus suddenly stopped.
[2] Jesus changed tone, like He was pleading.

and their reward will be evil for the evil they are doing. My Heart is a vast ocean of Love and Forgiveness.

I know Lord, but they tempt back the ones who have only just escaped from the evil one.

Daughter, Wisdom has given you a gift, to hear, write and understand Love's Desires. These points, daughter, are not easy to understand by unspiritual people; they will never accept anything of My Spirit; they see it all as nonsense; they will go on teaching with the current of the world, like philosophy is taught. Then have you not read that the spiritual gifts from My Holy Spirit will be hard to understand so long as they think and come to Me like philosophers? Have you not read that these are the points that these people distort as long as they are not in the Spirit the same way as they distort the rest of Scripture? Scripture has warned you all about these people; believe and grow in the grace I have given you, soon My Purifying Fire will come upon you all to dissolve in flames the crimes of this world. ♥ Your Holy Mother and I have emptied Our Hearts to you all since the day of Fatima, but My observances that I desire from you are not carried out and only a remnant are listening; this generation is deceiving itself, they have broken all My Commandments, how can I not come to you by Fire and thunder you as I thundered Sodom and Gomorrah?

Because maybe we are more than ten Lord? (There was some silence)

...You stupefy Me! You stupefy Me because I had started to believe your lips would never dare utter Abraham's bargain. ♥ I have been provoking you to utter cries of mercy before the deadly hour comes, I have been provoking you to offer Me prayers, but they are not sufficient...

What must I do Lord? I am all day with You, working for You and serving Your Interests. You are my Life, my Breath in this exile. I know I am a wretch and sinning as much as I breathe, yet You came to me and lifted my soul to You to taste Your Sweet Knowledge as Your disciples tasted it. You have revived my heart and turned my ear towards Your Sacred Heart. Your Mighty Hand caressed my head and made my heart, since then, sing praises to You. I suffer loneliness and excruciating agonies to rip one's heart when from time to time You turn away Your Holy Face from me, leaving my soul alone in the dark night, but I am dragging on because I love You to madness.

Vassula of My Sacred Heart, I have raised you

<u>to drive My Church into Unity</u>

(Jesus said this very calmly)

434

I have raised you to appease the Father's Justice.

I have raised you to embellish My Church. I have allowed you to step into My Hall to glorify Me. I have courted you to love Me. I have taken you out of the land of Egypt to thrust you out as one thrusts a net to catch souls for Me. You are to relent the Father's Justice by adoring Me, by praying, by penance, sacrifice, fasting <u>and</u> by reducing your size. ♥ You have no merits but your humble plea can reach the Father. Will you drink now from the same Cup that the Father has given Me? Do not fear, there is not much left in it now. I have been letting you sip from it now and then, daughter, I have been drawing your head towards My Cup, delicately, so do not move back now with disdain. Love what I love. ♥ Do not be afraid and do not <u>ever</u> imagine that I am going to lead you to Me without My Cross. Be concerned on what I am concerned. Ask Me to cure the rest of you. Ask My graces. Ask My blessings... ask the Father to relent.

Ask the Father to relent... we are at the verge of a destructive fire...

shsh... ask the Father to relent[1], that is why I am continually welcoming you to pray; and about the wicked accusations that are being circulated against you, do not fear. Be at peace and do not give way to sadness. I have called you for the revival of My Church and I will not fail you. Pray constantly. Be patient till the end. ♥ My Day is very near and I will come like a thief in the night. This is why My child Satan together with the beast[2] are incessantly attacking all those who come from Me and making war against My mouthpieces, but in the end they[3] will be defeated. ♥ The devil has gone down to you in a rage together with the beast, but Love will conquer evil. <u>Canada is Mine</u>. The beast[4] could make virulent sounds to cover My Voice in this country because it knows that they are the people My Sacred Heart loves, but I, the Lord, <u>will stay there</u>, and I tell you that all evil spirits roaming in that nation are already fearing at the sound of My Footsteps and at the sound of My Sacred Heart. My Holy Spirit will not shun from the beast nor from those who have been convinced by it. I will expand even more now My graces, 'for no angel, no prince, nothing that exists, nothing still to come, not any power, or height or depth, nor any created thing, can ever come between you and My Love'[5] No one will be able to stop the outpouring of My Holy Spirit. ♥ I am sending you to them[6] to remind them all of the greatness of My Love. I will give you enough resources to hold your ground. ♥ Love is with you. ♥

ΙΧθΥΣ ⟨═⟩

---

[1] Jesus said these words very softly, giving me so much to hope for.
[2] That is freemasonry (see Apocalypse 13)
[3] Satan and the beast.
[4] Freemasonry.
[5] Romans 8:35-39.
[6] That is the Canadians.

MESSAGE - CALL TO UNITY

March 27th, 1992

My Vassula, write: dear friends, dear companions, dear brothers, there is not such love as Mine; what have you done with My Love? My brothers, be united by following the rules of My Heart which are Love and Humility. The things you think to unite are earthly things and they will not bring you to unity, they can do nothing and offer nothing; but many of you have become slaves of your minds. So long as you do not reconcile in humility with each other and love one another as I love you, your separation will remain. My children, must I go through the pain again this Easter season?[1] Many of you have seen the dumb speaking, the lame walking and the blind with their sight, but yet you continue to praise Me only with your lips. I tell you truly as I once said: 'anyone who blasphemes against My Holy Spirit will not be forgiven[2] By persecuting My Holy Spirit you are hardening your hearts, and if your hearts are hardened by the lure of sin, all that is wicked will not be seen by you[3] thus you will bring condemnation upon you and judgement without mercy, as you have not been merciful. ♥ I watch from above all of you, each one of you. I tell you, whoever continues to work for his own interests and his own glorification has already lost My Heart. Their[4] convictions are not My convictions for in their minds they are the same as Satan. Rivalry and competition for earthly power devours their minds, egoism and pride have already condemned them. All these earthly things will make them perish by their very use! Seldom do I hear their prayers. Today you are surrounded by false teachers[5] who openly and without fear stand before Me and proclaim Satan's knowledge that is based on a lie. They disown My Divinity by disowning My Resurrection.[6] Pray for these false teachers that they may escape damnation! and I tell each one of you now:

> *anyone who claims to
> be in the light but hates
> his brother is still in
> the dark[7]*

Whoever believes in his state of darkness that he is glorifying Me, believes in he

---

[1] By having the Feast of Easter separated.
[2] Luke 12:10.
[3] One cannot, in this state recognize their evil and so cannot REPENT to be forgiven.
[4] Jesus talks about these people to me.
[5] The modernists and sects.
[6] This is also why the Holy Shroud disturbs them so much!
[7] 1 John 2:9.

who first tempted your parents.[1] I have been giving you signs, but you do not believe in My signs because your voices are drowning My Voice that speaks through My mouthpieces. The night will soon be with you and many will taste death because you were never grounded in the truth but were based on lies. I come to you through these signs to open your eyes and heal you, yet when I tell you the truth and tell you that it is I, the One whom you say, 'He is your Lord' that speaks to you, you turn away giving your ear to Satan so that he may use you. No, you do not understand My Language not more than you understand My wonders because you have preferred the devil. Whatever I say or ask does not penetrate in you since you have lost the sense of the language of My Spirit. I am thirsty for your salvation, I am thirsty to share My Kingdom with you, I am thirsty for you to reconcile with each other so that you may truly say: I am reconciled with God. ♥ Your division is a sin and no one can claim to be righteous when from his lips he discredits not only his brothers <u>but the leader of them all</u>.[2] Justice, mercy, good faith! These you should have practised without neglecting the other parts of My Law; and you, you who delight in your division and swear by My Throne and by Me, I, who sit on it, I tell you as I have said once:

> You are like whitewashed tombs that look handsome on the outside, but inside are full of dead men's bones and every kind of corruption.

How can you <u>believe</u> you can escape damnation? You fail to please Me and your corpses litter this desert you are living in. By sinning in your division against each other, it is <u>I</u>,

the Lamb

against whom you sin. This sin of your division which massacres daily My Body. It is I, the Lamb, whom you lead by force and by your own law to be re-crucified. It is My Body you are mutilating and bruising.

<u>I Am the Victim</u>.

Can you not see? Can you not see that you are in communion with demons? Can you not see with whom you are sharing at your table? How can I rejoice when all I see are demons at table with you? So long as you rejoice in your division you are under Satan's power who without ceasing is anointing with a lie those who rejoice in their division. Each one of you is looking to one another for approval of these messages of unity and are not concerned that this Easter My Body again will go

---

[1] Adam and Eve.
[2] The Pope.

through excruciating pains <u>because</u> of your division.[1] Believe that I am He, do not be the slaves of your mind, come to Me as long as the day lasts, soon the night will envelop this world. I have asked to see you[2] and talk to you, and so I did, for it is on account of uniting you that I have prompted you with My Messages of Unity ♥ but how hard it is for those who are slaves of their mind to enter into the Mysteries of Wisdom! How hard it is for the rich in spirit to enter into My Kingdom! I tell you:

> *many who are first will be last,*
> *and the last first.*

My child, be My Heaven by devoting yourself to Me. I am with you.
ΙΧθΥΣ ⊃

WHO IS WILLING TO GIVE UP HIS INTERESTS FOR MINE?

March 30th, 1992

All day long I desire you my God, all day long I pine away with love for You, because of Your Tenderness and Your Infinite Mercy, my God. Your Love that You showed me makes my soul cry out more than ever to You to rescue me. I long for the House You live. I long for Your Sacred Court. So tell me my Lord and God, what can I expect? Will You reconsider my frailty? Ah, free me from all my sins and reconsider me. All my hopes are in You my God. Amen.

Ah My Vassula, be My consoling instrument. I, Jesus, bless you. Fear not My child, I am the All Faithful and by your side. My child, for the sake of My Love I have tested your faith and I found My glorification. I am no stranger for you so allow Me to draw you one more time inside My Wounds, do not fear, I will show My glory through you and men will learn how I suffered. Come, approach Me, My Fire of Love is flaming out of My Sacred Heart and if you allow Me, I will visit you in this way and make a vivid torch out of you. You are destined to honour Me and lead souls to Me so that I may consume them. I will make vessels of Light out of them, brilliant flames that never cease, that never dim and that can never be snuffed. Ah My little one, every fibre of My Heart cries out for Love! Peace! Unity! I am your Holy Companion, creation, your most Faithful Friend

---

[1]Christ suffers mystically.
[2]All those who invited me to give the messages of unity and talk to them in the World Council of Churches in Geneva.

who invites you night and day at My table. I appeal for your friendship without ceasing, to save you... My Father has reserved a Fire for the sins of this generation and like a gale it will come suddenly upon you. People say: 'we will have peace; even when their heart is for war against Me and the powers of Heaven. Like a gust of wind I shall come to pronounce sentence on this godless generation, like a hurricane I shall blow on you and scatter you like chaff.

Lord, what about those who love You? What about Your victim souls? Surely there must be a few men who love You? There are a few, my King, who have not abandoned you to serve false gods or the beast.

Put them on a scale... and see which of the two is the weightier part. To this day many do not feel neither contrition nor fear. I am willing to give you all My Mercy before My Justice and I am willing to give everyone a single heart with a spirit of Love in them, but I need more victim souls. I need sacrificial love. How many are ready to sacrifice? How many are ready to offer themselves to Me to turn them into crucifixes? Will the ear of anyone yield to My supplications? How many are willing to become peacemakers and sow seeds which will bear fruit in purity? Who can remain uncontaminated by the world until My return? Who will be quick to listen? I am kind and ever so compassionate but very few want to be in union with Me. Who will give away his motives for My Motives? Who is willing to give up his interests for Mine? Who will seek what is least sought in this world and bear It with Love?

- My Cross -

and who is ready to seek what is least sought among you, who will seek: Love? Come, pray for the conversion of the world. ♥ IXθΥΣ ⤜⟩

THE FOLLOWING ARE THREE PRAYERS JESUS RECOMMENDS US TO PRAY DAILY.

Jesus: May. 4th, 1988

NOVENA OF CONFIDENCE TO THE SACRED HEART OF JESUS:

O Lord Jesus Christ
To Your Most Sacred Heart
I confide this intention...
(Here mention your request)

Only look upon me,
Then do what Your Heart inspires...
Let Your Sacred Heart decide...
I count on it...I trust in it...
I throw myself on It's mercy...
Lord Jesus You will not fail me.
Sacred Heart of Jesus, I trust in Thee.
Sacred Heart of Jesus, I believe in Thy love for me.
Sacred Heart of Jesus, Thy Kingdom Come.
O Sacred Heart of Jesus, I have asked for many favours, but I earnestly implore this one. Take it, place it in Thy Sacred Heart. When the Eternal Father sees it covered with Thy Precious Blood, He will not refuse it. It will be no longer my prayer but Thine. O Jesus, O Sacred Heart of Jesus I place my trust in Thee. Let me never be confounded. Amen.

PRAYER TO ST. MICHAEL

St. Michael the Archangel, defend us in the day of battle, be our safeguard against the wickedness and snares of the devil. May God rebuke him, we humbly pray, and do thou O Prince of the Heavenly Host, by the Power of God, cast into Hell, Satan and all the other evil spirits, who prowl through the world seeking the ruin of souls. Amen.

MARY, QUEEN OF HOLY ANGELS - PRAY FOR US!

THE MEMORARE OF ST. BERNARD

Remember, O most gracious Virgin Mary that never was it known that any one who fled to thy protection, implored thy help and sought thy intercession, was left unaided. Inspired with this confidence, I fly unto thee. O Virgin of Virgins, My Mother! to Thee do I come, before Thee I stand sinful and sorrowful. O Mother of the Word Incarnate! despise not my petitions, but in thy mercy, hear and answer me. Amen.

EDITORS AND NATIONAL DISTRIBUTORS

COPIES OF "True Life In God" available from:

ENGLISH

United Kingdom

J.M.J. Publications (Chris Lynch)
"Vassula"
P.O. Box 385, Belfast 9, Northern Ireland
Fax: (0232) 331433

United States

Signs Of The Times (Maureen Flynn)
6 Pidgeon Hill Drive, Suite 260
Sterling, Virginia
U.S.A. 20165
Tel: (703) 450-7766
Fax: (703) 450-7796

Friends of Medjugorje (Diana Berger)
Oak Medical Centre
407 West Oak
West, Texas
U.S.A. 76691
Tel: (817) 826-4546
Fax: (817) 826-5054

101 Foundation (Rosalie Turton)
P.O. Box 151
Asbury, New Jersey
U.S.A. 08802
Tel: (908) 689-8792
Fax: (908) 689-1957

Canada

Trinitas Canada (Gilles Larose)
P.O. Box 266, Mount Royal Station
Mount Royal, Quebec, Canada
(H3P 3C5)
Tel: (514) 738-2779
Fax: (514) 738-2779

Australia

Carley LeGrand
91 Auburn Road
Auburn. Victoria 3123
Western Australia
Fax: 8829675

Switzerland

Tom Austin
Ave G Coindet 7
1800 Vevey
Switzerland

FRENCH

FRANCE
La Vraie Vie en Dieu
F.X. de Guilbert (O.E.I.L.)
27 Rue de L'Abbé Grégoire
Paris, 6e, France

CANADA
L'Informateur Catholique
C.P. 330, Chertsey
Québec, Canada J0K 3K0
Tél.: (514) 882-9838

GERMAN

Das wahre Leben in Gott
Miriam-Verlog
D-7893, Jestetten
Germany
Tel: 07745-7267

ITALIAN

La Vera Vita in Dio
Edizioni Dehoniane
Via Casale San Pio V, 20
00165, Roma

SPANISH

La Vera Vida en Dios
Padre Giorgio Masi
Apartado Postal 39
76800 San Juan Del Rio
Queretaro, Mexico

Translations in progress: Greek, Danish, Russian, Polish, Korean, Portu

VIDEO AND AUDIO CASSETTES

UNITED KINGDOM AND IRELAND

Available from: **J.M.J. Publications,** P.O. Box 385, Belfast, N. Ireland

Video and Audio cassettes
(90 min.) Vassula and Fr. Gerard McGinnity-Belfast, N. Ireland (March, 1991)
(120 min.) Vassula's personal experience in suffering the Passion of Christ, Switzerland

CANADA AND UNITED STATES

In Canada, write **Trinitas Canada,** P.O. Box 266, Mount Royal Station,
Mount Royal, Quebec (H3P 3C5)
In U.S.A., write **Signs of the Times,** 6 Pidgeon Hill Drive, Suite 260,
Sterling, Virginia 20165

VIDEO CASSETTES
(120 min.) Vassula and Fr. Michael O'Carroll in Ottawa, Canada (June 1992)
(120 min.) Vassula's personal experience in suffering the Passion of Christ , Switzerland.
(3:5 hours) Vassula: Weekend Presentation in Independence, Mo (January, 1992)
            Two cassettes: 90 and 120 minutes respectively
(40 min.) Vassula praying the Rosary in five languages, with meditations upon each
           mystery extracted from the messages of Jesus.
(60 min.) Vassula in Palm Beach, Florida (March, 1992)
           English with simultaneous translation in Spanish.

AUDIO CASSETTES
Vassula interviewed by Fr. Gerard McGinnity in Belfast, N. Ireland
Vassula interviewed by Fr. Michael O'Carroll in London, U.K.
Vassula's presentation in Ottawa, Canada, prefaced by Fr. M. O'Carroll
Vassula's address to the World Council of Churches in Geneva
Vassula's weekend presentation (two tapes) in Missouri, U.S.A.
Vassula praying and meditating the Rosary in five languages

Example of the dual handwriting of Vassula in receiving the Messages from Jesus (January 20th, 1992: Notebook 57)

+ 20.1.92

peace be with you; hear Me, daughter:

have you looked around you? what have you seen?

I have seen upheavels and even greater divisions to come among us, before UNITY; I cannot see the end of our struggle to unite, nor the end of atheism.

My Soul, arbitrator of your generation, has witnessed much more than upheavels, divisions and atheism; I tell you, many are plotting against Me, in My Own House this very minute I hear them conspiring,

but soon, the islands will tremble on My Day,
and although this generation will wail, I
shall not listen, Heaven's door will be shut in
that Day; and the earth naked, will groan
like a widow, bereft in her sorrow; My
Heart turns over inside Me and is sick already
from the pitiful sound that will ring out
from you, generation; indeed, I shall not be
gloating over you, since I take no pleasure in
abasing and afflicting the human race;
once more there will be poured on you, but as
never before My Holy Spirit, from a faint

flickering Flame, My Fire shall roar and renew
you all; then, like a man entering a conquered
city, I, the Lord, shall invade you with My
Glory and ecclesia shall revive ♡ justice
will prevail in the end; and you, daughter,
do not fear to cry out for Me; do not be
afraid of men, especially those who oppose
you, be happy, daughter, I can read the innermost parts of these men and My jealous
Ear overhears everything; they think they know
everything, but they know nothing; daughter,
I prayed for you to the Father, to consider

your frailty, Vassula, try and understand the
Father; frail you are, but I have rooted you
well inside Me, so that you may not swerve
or sway when violent tempests come from time
to time upon you; you are His offspring, and
this is why out of His Jealous Love and His
Generosity He allows such oppositions; have you
not heard how He renders through suffering,
souls, to perfection and that suffering is part of
your training? so be patient, daughter, be
generous too and do not shudder and complain
for nothing ♡ do not weary labouring, follow

the marks of My Blood ∧ I have left behind for Eternity, those who follow these marks will enter into My Kingdom; learn that the Father is not ruthless but ever so gentle with you; Wisdom loves you; therefore, daughter, observe the Commandments, live according to the Gospel, have Me as your Holy Companion and pray for My priests who represent Me ♡

24.1.92

During Holy Mass Jesus told me:

" This is only the beginning. You will see greater things than this."

This was said after I was praising Him for

His Wonders and His Works, since with His Power He opened the hearts of many in the World Council of Churches. The Lord had been preparing since summer messages about unity. Directives of His Desires. Then He allowed certain hearts in the W.C.C. to open and receive His Word, thus allowing me to go over to them in the week of unity to offer them Jesus' messages.

26.1.92

Vassula of My Sacred Heart, do you want to consecrate yourself entirely to Me?

yes, my Lord, I want.

then say these words:

Sacred Heart of Jesus, come and invade me completely so that my motives will be Your Motives, my desires Your

NOTES AND COMMENTS